SCULPTING IDOLATRY IN FLAVIAN ROME

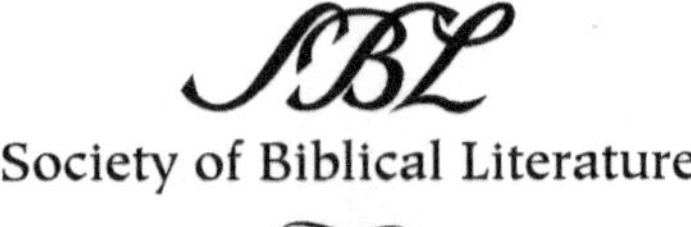
Society of Biblical Literature
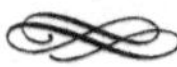

Early Judaism and Its Literature

Number 33

SCULPTING IDOLATRY IN FLAVIAN ROME
(AN)ICONIC RHETORIC IN THE WRITINGS OF FLAVIUS JOSEPHUS

SCULPTING IDOLATRY IN FLAVIAN ROME

(An)Iconic Rhetoric in the Writings of Flavius Josephus

Jason von Ehrenkrook

Society of Biblical Literature
Atlanta

SCULPTING IDOLATRY IN FLAVIAN ROME

(AN)ICONIC RHETORIC IN THE WRITINGS OF FLAVIUS JOSEPHUS

Library of Congress Cataloging-in-Publication Data

Ehrenkrook, Jason von.

Sculpting idolatry in Flavian Rome : (an)iconic rhetoric in the writings of Flavius Josephus / by Jason von Ehrenkrook.

p. cm. — (Society of Biblical Literature early Judaism and its literature ; no. 33)

Includes bibliographical references and index.

ISBN 978-1-58983-622-8 (paper binding : alk. paper) — ISBN 978-1-58983-623-5 (electronic format)

1. Josephus, Flavius—Criticism and interpretation. 2. Idolatry. 3. Idols and images—Worship. 4. Idols and images—Rome. 5. Sculpture, Hellenistic. 6. Jews—History—168 B.C.–135 A.D. 7. Judaism—History—Post-exilic period, 586 B.C.–210 A.D. I. Title.

PA4224.E37 2011b

296.4′6—dc23 2011041858

Printed on acid-free, recycled paper
conforming to ANSI/NISO Z39.48-1992 (R1997) and ISO 9706:1994
standards for paper permanence.

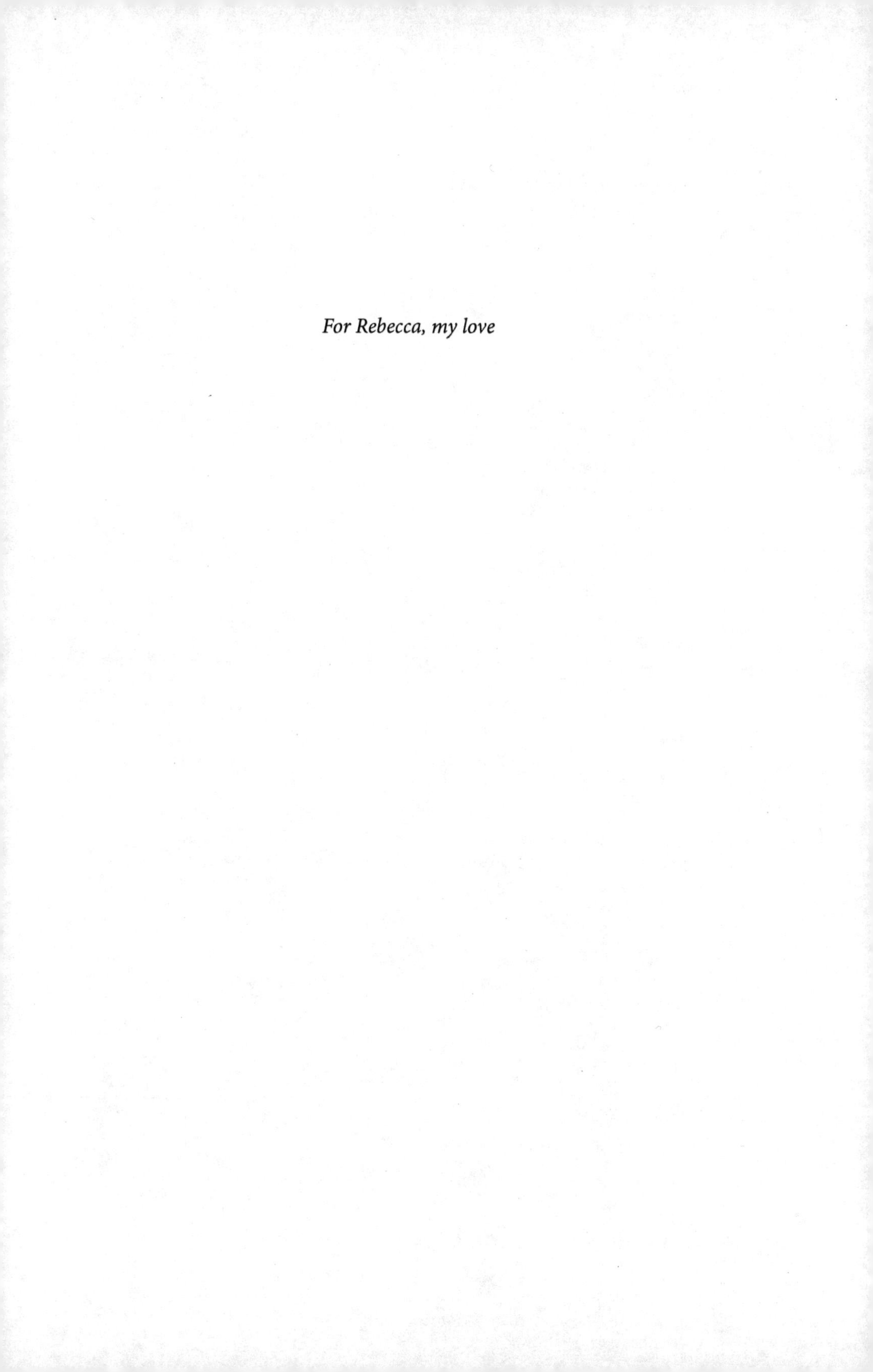

For Rebecca, my love

Contents

Abbreviations

Ancient Sources

Ab urb.	Livy, *Ab urbe condita*
Abr.	Philo, *De Abrahamo*
Abst.	Porphyry, *De abstinentia*
Adv. nat.	Arnobius, *Adversus nationes*
A.J.	Josephus, *Antiquitates Judaicae*
Alex.	Lucian, *Alexander*
Ann.	Quintus Ennius, *Annales*
Ant. rom.	Dionysius, *Antiquitates romanae*
Apol.	Tertullian, *Apologeticus*
Avod. Zar.	*Avodah Zarah*
Bibl. hist.	Diodorus Siculus, *Bibliotheca historica*
Bell. Cat.	Sallust, *Bellum catalinae*
Bell. civ.	Lucan, *Bellum civile*
B.J.	Josephus, *Bellum Judaicum*
C. Ap.	Josephus, *Contra Apionem*
Cat. Maj.	Plutarch, *Cato Major*
Cels.	Origen, *Contra Celsum*
Cher.	Philo, *De cherubim*
Civ.	Augustine, *De civitate Dei*
Cohort. ad gent.	Pseudo-Justin Martyr, *Cohortatio ad gentiles*
Contempl.	Philo, *De vita contemplativa*
Cor.	Plutarch, *Marcius Coriolanus*
De Anim.	Galen, *De animi cuiuslibet peccatorum dignotione et curatione*
Decal.	Philo, *De decalogo*
Deipn.	Athenaeus, *Deipnosophistae*
Descr.	Pausanias, *Graeciae descriptio*
Det.	Philo, *Quod deterius potiori insidari soleat*
Deus.	Philo, *Quod Deus sit immutabilis*
Dial.	Justin Martyr, *Dialogus cum Tryphone*
Div.	Cicero, *De divinatione*
Ebr.	Philo, *De ebrietate*
En.	*Enoch*
Ep Jer	Epistle of Jeremiah
Evag.	Isocrates, *Evagoras* (*Or.* 9)
Fort. Rom.	Plutarch, *De fortuna Romanorum*
Gall.	Lucian, *Gallus*

Geogr.	Strabo, *Geographica*
Hist.	*Historiae* (of Herodotus, Tacitus or Thucydides)
Hist. rom.	Cassius Dio, *Historia romana*
Idol.	Tertullian, *De idolatria*
Inst.	Gaius, *Institutiones*
Is. Os.	Plutarch, *De Iside et Osiride*
Jub.	*Jubilees*
Jupp. trag.	Lucian, *Juppiter tragoedus*
L.A.B.	*Liber antiquitatum biblicarum*
Leg.	Cicero, *De legibus*
Legat.	Philo, *Legatio ad Gaium*
Lev. Rab.	*Leviticus Rabbah*
LXX	Septuagint
Mar.	Plutarch, *Marius*
Men.	Lucian, *Menippus*
Mek. R. Yish.	*Mekilta de R. Yishmael*
Mos.	Philo, *De vita Mosis*
Nat.	Pliny the Elder, *Naturalis historia*
Noct. att.	Aulus Gellius, *Noctes atticae*
Opif.	Philo, *De opificio mundi*
Philops.	Lucian, *Philopseudes*
Praep. ev.	Eusebius, *Praeparatio evangelica*
Praescr.	Tertullian, *De praescriptione haereticorum*
Princ. Iner.	Plutarch, *Ad principem ineruditum*
Protr.	Clement of Alexandria, *Protrepticus*
Prov.	Philo, *De providentia*
Ps.-Phoc.	Pseudo-Phocylides
Rosh Hash.	*Rosh HaShanah*
Sacr.	Philo, *De sacrificiis Abelis et Caini*
Sat.	Satirae (of Juvenal or Horace)
Sib. Or.	*Sibylline Oracles*
Spec.	Philo, *De specialibus legibus*
Strom.	Clement of Alexandria, *Stromata*
T. Reu.	*Testament of Reuben*
Tanḥ.	*Midrash Tanḥuma*
Tg. Neof.	*Targum Neofiti*
Tg. Ps.-J.	*Targum Pseudo-Jonathan*
Vesp.	Suetonius, *Vespasian*
Virt.	Philo, *De virtutibus*
Vit. soph.	Philostratus, *Vitae sophistarum*
Wis	Wisdom of Solomon

Modern Sources

AJA	*American Journal of Archaeology*
AJP	*American Journal of Philology*
ANRW	*Aufsteig und Niedergang der römischen Welt*
BJRL	*Bulletin of the John Rylands University Library of Manchester*

CBQ	*Catholic Biblical Quarterly*
CIJ	*Corpus inscriptionum judaicarum*
CIL	*Corpus inscriptionum latinarum*
CQ	*Classical Quarterly*
GR	*Greece and Rome*
HSCP	*Harvard Studies in Classical Philology*
HTR	*Harvard Theological Review*
HUCA	*Hebrew Union College Annual*
IEJ	*Israel Exploration Journal*
JANER	*Journal of Ancient Near Eastern Religions*
JAOS	*Journal of the American Oriental Society*
JBL	*Journal of Biblical Literature*
JCP	*Jahrbücher für classische Philologie*
JHS	*Journal of Hellenic Studies*
JJS	*Journal of Jewish Studies*
JQR	*Jewish Quarterly Review*
JR	*Journal of Religion*
JRS	*Journal of Roman Studies*
JSJ	*Journal for the Study of Judaism in the Persian, Hellenistic and Roman Period*
JSP	*Journal for the Study of the Pseudepigrapha*
JTS	*Journal of Theological Studies*
LCL	Loeb Classical Library
LIMC	*Lexicon iconographicum mythologiae classicae*. Edited by H. C. Ackerman and J.-R. Gisler. 8 vols. Zurich, 1981–97
NEA	*Near Eastern Archaeology*
NovT	*Novum Testamentum*
NRSV	New Revised Standard Version
NTS	*New Testament Studies*
OTP	*Old Testament Pseudepigrapha*. Edited by J. H. Charlesworth. 2 vols. New York, 1983
PAAJR	Proceedings of the American Academy of Jewish Research
PEQ	Palestine Exploration Quarterly
PG	Patrologia graeca
PP	Past and Present
PSAS	*Proceedings of the Seminar for Arabian Studies*
PT	*Poetics Today*
RB	*Revue biblique*
REG	*Revue des études grecques*
SCI	*Scripta Classica Israelica*
SEG	Supplementum epigraphicum graecum
SJ	*Studia Judaica*
SPhilo	*The Studia Philonica Annual*
TA	*Tel Aviv*
TZ	*Theologische Zeitschrift*
YJC	*Yale Journal of Criticism*
ZNW	*Zeitschrift für die neutestamentliche Wissenschaft und die Kunde der älteren Kirche*

Acknowledgments

This book is a revision of my doctoral dissertation, submitted to the Department of Near Eastern Studies at the University of Michigan, Ann Arbor. Since good scholarship does not emerge in a vacuum, and original ideas are never created *ex nihilo*, I am acutely aware of my debt, not only to the hundreds of scholars in print—including many not listed in the bibliography—who have helped stimulate my thinking, but also to the numerous faculty members, colleagues, and students with whom I have had the privilege to interact over the past several years.

I wish especially to thank Professor Gabriele Boccaccini of the University of Michigan. It was in my inaugural semester of graduate school, during a seminar on methodology in the study of Second Temple Judaism, that Gabriele first whet my appetite for this fascinating realm of scholarly research. A second Boccaccini seminar, one focused on the central protagonist of the present study, Flavius Josephus, was even more formative, opening my eyes to numerous possible lines of inquiry that have ultimately blossomed into this project. The breadth and depth of his own scholarly interests have been a particularly useful resource, and his critical reading of the ensuing pages has certainly helped to broaden my thinking and sharpen my arguments.

Professor Yaron Eliav, also at the University of Michigan, deserves special thanks for his role in shaping the present study. Yaron first introduced me to the possibility of exploring material culture (statues) in literary texts, offering me for two consecutive summers a position as research assistant for the Interdisciplinary Statuary Project. My responsibility in this project was to begin collecting data for a sourcebook on statues in Greek literature, a task that happily exposed me to a broad range of comparative material relevant for the present study. Yaron also helped guide me through the various phases of research, reading carefully and commenting thoroughly on preliminary drafts of each chapter. Without question, the success of this project is deeply indebted to his critical eye.

Several other members of my dissertation committee likewise played a crucial role in the formation of this book. Professor Raymond Van Dam first exposed me to the labyrinth of Roman history, and his attention to detail both in the present project and in various seminar papers has played a vital role in my intellectual development. Professor Brian Schmidt's knowledge of the Hebrew Bible and the iconography of Israelite culture were particularly crucial for the present study, and his incisive questions and comments brought into clearer focus several important methodological issues. Professor Gary Beckman's careful reading of the manuscript thankfully rescued me from several potentially embarrassing mistakes.

I am also indebted to the Frankel Institute for Advanced Judaic Studies, whose generous postdoctoral research fellowship afforded me the time and space to work on revising this project. I presented portions of this work at the institute's workshop and colloquium series, and I am particularly appreciative of my colleagues at the institute, especially for their many valuable comments, questions, and insights. I should also mention my new colleagues in the Department of Religious Studies at the University of Pittsburgh, who have warmly welcomed me into the real world of academia, helping me adjust to the rigors of full-time teaching. My anonymous reviewers also deserve thanks for their many useful comments, criticisms, questions, and corrections. The SBL editorial staff , and especially the diligent eye of John Turnbull, deserve credit for their excellent work in preparing a clean and attractive finished product. It perhaps goes without saying, but I'll say it anyway—I wish to exonerate all of the aforementioned people who have unquestionably contributed to all that is positive in this book by taking full responsibility for any mistakes, dubious argumentation, or other shortcomings that may still remain in the ensuing pages, whether due to my own ignorance or stubborn refusal to accept constructive criticisms.

Finally, my family—Rebecca, Brooke, Kaitlyn, Mikayla, and Tyler—deserves special recognition. As much as I enjoy the smell of the library, the pleasure of reading and thinking about ancient Jewish literature, and the thrill of engaging students in the classroom, it is the love, joy, and laughter of home that fills my life with the deepest and most profound sense of satisfaction.

Department of Religious Studies
University of Pittsburgh
Pittsburgh, PA
May 24, 2011

1

Reading Idolatry in(to) Josephus

Iconoclasm in Josephus: Rhetoric and Reality

The relationship between Jews in antiquity and figurative images was at best strained and, at worst, downright volatile. Or at least this is the impression one gets from reading the Jewish historian Flavius Josephus. A golden statue of an eagle that Herod the Great erected over the gate of the temple in Jerusalem fell victim to an axe in the hands of an angry mob (*B.J.* 1.648–655; *A.J.* 17.148–164). The trophies Herod installed in the theater in Jerusalem met a similar fate, having been dismantled by the king in order to pacify a crowd of offended Jews (*A.J.* 15.267–279). The figurative images adorning Herod the Tetrarch's palace were spared destruction at the hands of an iconoclastic commission (one that included Josephus), but only because a band of restless Galileans had already set the palace aflame (*Vita* 65–66). Gaius Caligula's short-lived attempt to erect a statue of himself in the Jerusalem temple likewise stirred the masses into a frenzy, almost resulting in the martyrdom—or suicide, depending upon one's perspective—of thousands (*B.J.* 2.184–203; *A.J.* 18.261–309). Even the seemingly innocuous images of the emperor affixed to Pontius Pilate's military standards incited the indignation of many in Jerusalem (*B.J.* 2.169–174; *A.J.* 18.55–59).

In the light of such narratives in Josephus, it is no surprise that many scholars identify the period before 70 C.E. as an age of strict aniconism—or perhaps better, an *anti-iconic* age, a period in history when Jews would not tolerate any kind of figural representation, regardless of context or function.[1] In the words of Cecil

1. The term *aniconic* can encompass a broad semantic field ranging from an outright rejection of images, regardless of form or subject matter, to the use of nonfigural cult objects, such as conical or pillared representations of a deity or symbols of "sacred emptiness," whether empty divine thrones or chariots (e.g., Arnobius, *Adv. nat.* 1.39); see especially the discussion of this term in the following studies: David Freedberg, *The Power of Images: Studies in the History and Theory of Response* (Chicago: University of Chicago Press, 1989), 33–35; Tryggve Mettinger, *No Graven Image? Israelite Aniconism in Its Ancient Near Eastern Context* (Stockholm: Almqvist & Wiksell, 1995), 19; Peter Stewart, *Statues in Roman Society: Representation and Response* (Oxford: Oxford University Press, 2003), 64–72; Milette Gaifman, "Beyond Mimesis in Greek Religious Art: Aniconism in the Archaic and Classical Periods" (Ph.D. diss., Princeton University, 2005). W. Barnes Tatum, followed by Steven Fine, employs the terms *anti-iconic* and *anti-idolic* to distinguish between the resistance

Roth: "There is overwhelming evidence that human images, whether in the flat or in the round, were not tolerated by the Jews in the period before the destruction of Jerusalem."[2] This period of strict and inflexible aniconism is, moreover, typically contrasted with the centuries following the destruction of the temple, when the obvious flourishing of figurative art in synagogues is viewed as evidence for Judaism's softening stance toward such images.

But there is reason to suspect that the situation during the Second Temple period was more complicated than is typically allowed. In the first place, this near ubiquitous claim that Jews during the early Roman period were strictly aniconic is partly the remnant of a persistent idea in Western intellectual history, often rooted in the faulty assumption of a binary opposition between Jews and pagans/Judaism and Hellenism, that Jews by and large "don't do art."[3] Second, this "overwhelming evidence" of strict and inflexible aniconism, to borrow Roth's words, is derived primarily from two historical sources—a scarcity of figurative remains in the archaeological record of Second Temple Jerusalem read through the lens of Josephus, especially his so-called iconoclastic narratives.[4] Yet, as I will argue in chapter 2, it is notoriously difficult to move from the archaeological record (or lack thereof) of one specific region to a sweeping characterization of the beliefs of an entire people scattered throughout the Mediterranean basin. Archaeology is thus quite limited for the topic at hand, at best suggestive but hardly conclusive.

Moreover, and herein lies the primary focus of this book, very few have considered the extent to which the portrait of aniconism that emerges from Josephus' narratives is even a reliable indicator of the actual situation. Josephus' reports of iconoclastic activity are simply taken at face value, so much so that many even suppose that the author, who likely composed much of his oeuvre while seated in

---

to images *in toto* (anti-iconic) and the resistance to cult images (anti-idolic) (W. Barnes Tatum, "The LXX Version of the Second Commandment [Ex 20:3–6 = Deut 5:7–10]: A Polemic against Idols, Not Images," *JSJ* 17 [1986]: 177–95; Steven Fine, *Art and Judaism in the Greco-Roman World: Toward a New Jewish Archaeology* [Cambridge: Cambridge University Press, 2005], 70). For this book, my use of "aniconic" corresponds with Tatum's "anti-iconic," that is, as a religiously derived opposition to all forms of theriomorphic and anthropomorphic images, and not just representations of the divine and other such artistic objects of "pagan" worship.

2. Cecil Roth, "An Ordinance against Images in Jerusalem, A.D. 66," *HTR* 49 (1956): 169. According to Roth, Jerusalem authorities instituted an official proscription of figurative images on the eve of the Jewish revolt in 66 C.E.

3. Fine, *Art and Judaism*, 2. See my critique of this approach below in chapter 2, as well as the discussion in Kalman P. Bland, *The Artless Jew: Medieval and Modern Affirmations and Denials of the Visual* (Princeton: Princeton University Press, 2000), and Margaret Olin, *The Nation without Art: Examining Modern Discourses on Jewish Art* (Lincoln: University of Nebraska Press, 2001).

4. I am using "iconoclastic" loosely to refer to the Josephan narratives mentioned in the opening paragraph, that is, the stories of Jews resisting Roman images. At least one of these episodes, the case of Herod's eagle, does in fact fit a strict definition of iconoclasm.

the shadow of Venus herself,[5] embraces a more strict interpretation of the biblical prohibition against images (i.e., the so-called second commandment) than even the rabbis of the Tannaitic and Amoraic periods.[6]

This propensity to read the scarcity of figurative remains in the light of a straightforward interpretation of Josephus is particularly evident in Steven Fine's recent analysis of the problem of Jews and art before the destruction of the temple. After a survey of the archaeological record and the relevant material in Josephus, which according to Fine is fairly uniform,[7] he draws the conclusion that there emerged in the late Second Temple period a growing "receptivity among Jews of a more radical anti-iconic tendency."[8] This "visual conservatism,"[9] according to Fine, bespeaks an "increasingly strident" application of the second commandment.[10] From this perspective, the iconoclastic stories in Josephus represent a fairly precise barometer of how Jews, including Josephus, viewed images in antiquity. That is to say, Josephus' literary portrait of a religiously derived strict aniconism is thought to represent accurately the situation on the ground.

One notable exception to this straightforward reading of Josephus is the art historian Joseph Gutmann. In an important article published in the *Hebrew Union College Annual* in 1961, Gutmann argued in part that Josephus' supposedly strict interpretation of the second commandment should not be taken at face value but was instead indicative of the author's apologetic concerns before his Roman audience.[11] More specifically, according to Gutmann, Josephus attempted to circumvent the implication that Jewish resistance to Roman images was the manifestation of a "Jewish hatred of Rome's oppressive rule" by linking—inaccurately, in Gutmann's estimation—this resistance to a strict observance of Jewish law.[12] In other words, the image of strict aniconism rooted in religious concerns is a Josephan *rhetorical construct*, an attempt to mask the truth, namely that Jewish icono-

5. Presumably Vespasian's villa—Josephus' residential quarters while in Rome (*Vita* 423)—was replete with divine and honorific statues.

6. For example, Roth's study of Josephus concludes that the author "shows himself more rigid than the Rabbis of the Talmudic period (Roth, "Ordinance against Images," 176). Louis H. Feldman likewise contrasts Josephus' overwhelmingly negative perspective with the more accommodating Rabbinic tradition (*Josephus and Modern Scholarship [1937–1980]* [Berlin and New York: De Gruyter, 1984], 512).

7. On several occasions, Fine speaks of the "consistency of Josephus's approach" (*Art and Judaism*, 80). As will be argued below in chapters 3–5, Fine's supposition of uniformity or consistency in the Josephan corpus does not withstand a close scrutiny of this material.

8. Ibid., 75.

9. Ibid., 78.

10. Ibid., 81. Edwyn Bevan likewise points to Josephus as evidence that Jews in the first century understood the scope of the second commandment to include all figurative images, that is, images of living creatures (*Holy Images: An Inquiry into Idolatry and Image-Worship in Ancient Paganism and in Christianity* [London: George Allen & Unwin, 1940], 48). See especially the discussion below in chapter 3.

11. Joseph Gutmann, "The 'Second Commandment' and the Image in Judaism," *HUCA* 32 (1961): 161–74.

12. Ibid., 170.

clasm was in fact an act of political subversion, an expression of a deep-seated anti-Roman sentiment. For Gutmann, encapsulated in Josephus' assertion in *Contra Apionem* (hereafter *C. Ap.*) that Moses forbade images "not as a prophecy that Roman authority ought not be honored" is a potentially revealing glimpse into the true motive of Jewish iconoclasm: a refusal to submit to Roman hegemony, and not a religious commitment to strict aniconism (*C. Ap.* 2.75).[13]

More recently, John Barclay has taken up the subject of images and idolatry in Josephus, focusing specifically on the treatment of this issue in *C. Ap.* and, like Gutmann, drawing attention to the rhetorical dimension of this material.[14] Barclay summarizes his argument as follows: "I hope here to trace how Josephus places Jewish aniconic peculiarity on the map of Greek and Roman culture, and in so doing will highlight his rhetorical subtlety, as he skilfully conveys his disdain of non-Jewish religious practices without offending his Roman (or Romanized) audience."[15]

Commenting on *C. Ap.* 2.73–78, which seemingly prohibits any kind of figurative image, religious or otherwise, Barclay identifies this passage as "a masterpiece of rhetorical deflection" and its author as a "spin-doctor" of the highest order.[16] Specifically, in Barclay's interpretation of this text, Josephus is careful to *Romanize* the Jewish resistance to images, to frame his discussion of images in a way that would be entirely palatable to a Roman ear. This, however, is not to deny any subversive quality in Josephus' discourse. Indeed, "[t]here is venom in that term [*despiciens* used in *C. Ap.* 2.75], a cultural snarl: but so sweet is the smile on this Jewish face turned towards Rome that the sneer can pass almost unnoticed."[17]

My book builds on the provocative suggestions of both Gutmann and Barclay, with a particular (though not exclusive) focus on the iconoclastic narratives in *Bellum Judaicum* and *Antiquitates Judaicae* (hereafter *B.J.* and *A.J.* respectively). A closer examination of this material demonstrates that there is more here than initially meets the eye, that Josephus is not simply describing what happened, but is instead *sculpting* events, as it were, shaping unique portraits of aniconism that contribute to larger rhetorical themes within each of his main compositions. Moreover, the resulting images of aniconism and iconoclasm that emerge in Josephus' corpus, which on the surface certainly seem to depict a fundamental antithesis between εἰκών and Ἰουδαῖος, and by extension between Hellenism and Judaism, are actually patterned after certain modes of thought and perceptions that were prevalent throughout the Greco-Roman world. Thus, embedded in this discourse on cultural *conflict* is, ironically enough, evidence for *confluence*, further support-

13. Unless otherwise noted, translations of primary sources are my own.

14. John M. G. Barclay, "Snarling Sweetly: Josephus on Images and Idolatry," in *Idolatry: False Worship in the Bible, Early Judaism, and Christianity* (ed. Stephen C. Barton; London: T&T Clark, 2007), 73–87.

15. Ibid., 74.

16. Ibid., 79.

17. Ibid., 81.

ing the notion that Jews in antiquity were part and parcel of their Mediterranean milieu.[18]

The data examined in the ensuing chapters, however, actually encompass a broader range of textual material. The book takes as its starting point the "iconic" lexicon employed throughout the Josephan corpus, most notably the author's use of εἰκών, ἀνδριάς, and ἄγαλμα, as well as other key Greek terms that comprise Josephus' discourse on images (see appendix 1). This "iconic" material still remains relatively unexplored to date, and I thus attempt to investigate Josephus' "iconology,"[19] paying special attention to the rhetorical function of this discourse on images within each respective literary context. Additionally, I aim in the following chapters to situate Josephus' "iconic" material within a wider comparative context, including relevant data drawn from a broad selection of Jewish and Greco-Roman sources, both textual and archaeological.

Chapter 2 functions mainly to locate my investigation of Josephus within the broader conversation on Jews and images in antiquity, considering both scholarly constructs of the ancient aniconic Jew and primary source material *outside* Josephus—both literary and archaeological—that may attest to a contentious relationship between Jews and sculpture (and more broadly figurative art), especially during the Second Temple period. I argue in chapter 2, however, that this data is much more complex than is typically allowed. While the archaeological record for Second Temple Jerusalem and a broad range of literary sources describing Jerusalem may suggest an uneasy relationship with figurative images, this should not be taken as indicative of a monolithic viewpoint characteristic of all Jews throughout the Mediterranean basin. Rather, it is much more likely that there existed during the period in question a variety of ideological perspectives, as well as a diverse range of local or regional practices with regard to the use of figurative images. Moreover, even those Jewish texts most saturated with animosity toward images—Jewish idol polemics—restrict their focus to *cult* images and further betray a profound awareness of perceptions attested in a wide range of "pagan" sources. Thus, the typical polarization of "Jew" and "Image" does not in fact tell the whole story.

I continue to situate Josephus within his Jewish context in chapter 3, focusing on a much more narrow body of comparative material—specifically on Jewish interpretations of the biblical prohibition of images. Scholars have by and large argued, based primarily on evidence drawn from Josephus, that Jews during the Second Temple period took a more restrictive stance in their interpretation of this proscription, expanding the scope of prohibited items to include *all forms of figurative art*, regardless of context or function. I argue instead that the vast majority

---

18. On this perspective, see, for example, Erich Gruen, *Heritage and Hellenism: The Reinvention of Jewish Tradition* (Berkeley: University of California Press, 1998); Lee I. Levine, *Judaism and Hellenism in Antiquity: Conflict or Confluence?* (Peabody, Mass.: Hendrickson, 1999).

19. For the theoretical underpinnings for the study of the discursive dimension of images, see especially W. J. T. Mitchell, *Iconology: Image, Text, Ideology* (Chicago: University of Chicago Press, 1986); idem, *Picture Theory: Essays on Verbal and Visual Interpretation* (Chicago: University of Chicago Press, 1994).

of, although not all, Jewish sources from both before and after the destruction of the temple demonstrate precisely the opposite, namely that Jews by and large understood the biblical prohibition of images to encompass *only* images with some kind of cultic association. This is not to deny that *some* Jews during the period in question may have taken a more restrictive exegetical stance. However, the extant literary evidence demonstrates that the more restrictive approach to the second commandment was the exception rather than the rule. Moreover, with respect to Josephus' interpretation of the second commandment, there emerges in his corpus an interesting tension between his formulation of the proscription within an exegetical context, wherein he explicitly restricts the scope to *cult* images, and within a narrative context, wherein Josephus seemingly broadens the scope to include images *in toto*. I argue that this tension is significant, suggesting that the portrayal of strict aniconism, which plays a prominent role in Josephus' various iconoclastic narratives, has less to do with the author's actual exegetical opinions and more to do with his rhetorical concerns, namely, his interest in linking the Jewish resistance to images with broader narrative *topoi*.

The next two chapters focus on the rhetorical function of Josephus' discourse on images in *B.J.* and *A.J.*, respectively. I argue in chapter 4 that Josephus in *B.J.* forges an explicit link between sculpture and sacred space, deploying the former as a boundary marker for the latter. While the notion that sculpture can function to demarcate the sacred appears in numerous Greco-Roman sources, Josephus exploits and inverts this perception in order to map Judea and Jerusalem as sacred territories *without* sculpture, setting up a stark contrast with Greek landscapes. Furthermore, this rhetorical maneuver functions in the wider narrative context of *B.J.* both to negotiate Jewish identity and to articulate the legitimate boundaries of imperial authority at a moment in history saturated with tyranno-phobia—shortly after the demise of the Julio-Claudian regime and the accession of a new imperial family.

Chapter 5 continues to investigate the poetics of images and idolatry in Josephus, focusing on his twenty-volume magnum opus, *Antiquitates Judaicae*. Specifically, I argue that Josephus in *A.J.* crafts a view of the mythic past that emphasizes the pious aniconic origins of the Jewish constitution. Moreover, this formulation of the Jewish πολιτεία and its vision of an imageless people, which functions to articulate an ideal exemplar of virtue (ἀρετή) and piety (εὐσέβεια), serving as a critical index for present behavior, is drawn from the well of Roman cultural discourse, especially the tendency in Roman sources to idealize the deep past and to envision a pristine age of *Roman* aniconism. In so doing, Josephus *Romanizes* Jewish iconoclastic behavior, framing the Jewish resistance to images in the present (first century C.E.) as an attempt to preserve an aniconic piety that the Romans had failed to maintain.

JOSEPHUS PAST AND PRESENT

Given the focus of this book, it is necessary to consider briefly Josephus' curriculum vitae as well as his reception in modern scholarship. In particular, this select survey of research on Josephus situates the book within a wider scholarly context, underscoring especially its contribution to the study of this Jewish author and his literary corpus.

Josephus' Vita: From Joseph ben Matthias to T. Flavius Josephus

The central protagonist of this investigation affords a fascinating glimpse into the social and cultural complexities of the Greco-Roman Mediterranean.[20] Joseph ben Matthias was born into a priestly family from Jerusalem in 37/38 C.E., the first year of Gaius Caligula's tenure as emperor in Rome (37–41 C.E.).[21] By this point in history, Rome's presence in Judea had long been established. The initial "friendship and alliance" (φιλίαν καὶ συμμαχίαν) with Rome (1 Macc 8:17), solicited shortly after the Hasmonean-led revolt against the Seleucid monarch Antiochus IV Epiphanes (175–164 B.C.E.), soon gave way to Judean subjugation under Roman hegemony in the wake of Pompey's invasion of Jerusalem (63 B.C.E.), first under the rule of the client king Herod the Great, and then, following the death of Herod in 4 B.C.E. and a decade of political instability, under the direct jurisdiction of Roman governors in 6 C.E. This latter arrangement continued, with a brief interlude during Agrippa I's tenure as client king (41–44 C.E.), up to the Judean revolt in 66 C.E.

Unfortunately, apart from the brief and somewhat tendentious opening to *Vita*, very little is known of Josephus' life prior to the revolt. Presumably, as a member of an aristocratic priestly family, Josephus was given a fitting education in Jerusalem, including, one would assume, at least some training in the Jewish scriptures,

---

20. Important scholarly accounts of the life of Josephus include Richard Laqueur, *Der jüdische Historiker Flavius Josephus: Ein biographischer Versuch auf neuer quellenkritischer Grundlage* (Gießen, Germany: Münchow, 1920), 245–78; Henry S. J. Thackeray, *Josephus: The Man and the Historian* (New York: Ktav, 1929), 1–22; Shaye Cohen, *Josephus in Galilee and Rome: His Vita and Development as a Historian* (1979; repr., Leiden: Brill, 2002), 181–231; Louis H. Feldman, "Flavius Josephus Revisited: The Man, His Writings, and His Significance," *Aufsteig und Niedergang der römischen Welt: Geschichte und Kultur Roms im Spiegel der neueren Forschung* II.21.2 (1984): 779–87; Tessa Rajak, *Josephus: The Historian and His Society* (Philadelphia: Fortress Press, 1984), 11–45, 144–229. See also Steve Mason's commentary on Josephus' *Vita*: Steve Mason, *Life of Josephus* (Flavius Josephus: Translation and Commentary 9; ed. Steve Mason; Leiden: Brill, 2001).

21. In addition to the account in *B.J.* of his own role in the Judean revolt, Josephus recounts his personal biography in *Vita*, a one-volume appendix to *A.J.*, with an obvious emphasis on his role as general in the defense of Galilee. It should be noted that the title *Vita* is not original to the composition and does not actually reflect the nature of this work. Josephus is not writing an autobiography as such, but instead a personal apology, an attempt to refute certain accusations against his own character and role in the revolt. Moreover, given the apologetic purpose of the work, we should approach the details of his biography with a healthy measure of skepticism, particularly in light of the obvious discrepancies between *B.J.* and *Vita* (on which see especially Cohen, *Josephus in Galilee and Rome*). Besides his own works, fragments of data on Josephus—mostly pertaining to his prediction of Vespasian's accession to the imperial throne—can be found in a few classical sources (Suetonius, *Vesp.* 5.6; Appian, *Frag.* 17; Cassius Dio, *Hist. rom.* 66.1).

though we should perhaps be wary of Josephus' own exaggerated claims of intellectual prowess.[22] A few years prior to the revolutionary outbreak, Josephus traveled to Rome at the age of twenty-six as part of an official delegation sent to petition for the release of Judean priests who had been imprisoned by the procurator Marcus Antonius Felix (ca. 63/64 C.E.). It was during this trip that Josephus first gained exposure to Roman aristocratic circles, most notably Nero's wife Poppaea Sabina (*Vita* 16).[23] Shortly after returning to Judea, Josephus found himself embroiled in the early stages of the Judean revolt and was eventually appointed general of the Galilean forces in the fall of 66 C.E.[24]

It is precisely Josephus' first encounter with the rising Flavian star that reversed his fortunes and in the process irreparably tarnished his reputation for centuries to come. In the summer of 67 C.E., Vespasian laid siege to the Galilean city of Jotapata, wherein Josephus and his troops were stationed.[25] After forty-seven days, the city was captured and its inhabitants slaughtered, although Josephus and forty others successfully avoided the massacre by hiding in a nearby cave. The Romans, however, soon discovered their hiding place, and when faced with the prospect of surrender, the majority of survivors argued, in opposition to Josephus, that suicide was the preferable choice.[26] And so the group cast lots to determine the order of suicide, and when Josephus conveniently—or in his words, "whether by chance or by the providence of God" (εἴτε ὑπὸ τύχης εἴτε ὑπὸ θεοῦ προνοίας)—found himself one of two remaining survivors, he successfully persuaded his companion

22. Josephus' self-representation in *Vita* 8–12 accords well with standard Greco-Roman ideals of *paideia*, particularly his claim to have initiated at the age of sixteen a rigorous examination of the three main Judean philosophical sects. The pursuit of an eclectic exposure to various schools of philosophy was a common trope in Greco-Roman literature; see, for example, the second-century C.E. Galen, who claims to have studied under a Stoic, a Platonist, a Peripatetic, and an Epicurean before deciding against forging a philosophical allegiance (Galen, *De Anim.* 5.102; see also Lucian, *Men.* 4–5 and Justin Martyr, *Dial.* 2). On this passage in general, see the discussion in Mason, *Life of Josephus*, 12–21. For a less skeptical treatment of Josephus' claims in *Vita* 10–11, see Rajak, *Josephus*, 34–38. On the three philosophical schools as a rhetorical device, see most recently Gunnar Haaland, "What Difference Does Philosophy Make? The Three Schools as a Rhetorical Device in Josephus," in *Making History: Josephus and Historical Method* (ed. Zuleika Rodgers; Leiden: Brill, 2007), 262–88.

23. Elsewhere Josephus identifies Poppaea as a devout, god-fearing woman (θεοσεβής), perhaps suggesting she was at least sympathetic to Jewish customs (*A.J.* 20.195).

24. Josephus gives two not entirely compatible accounts of his appointment in *B.J.* 2.562–568 and *Vita* 17–29.

25. Josephus recounts these events, with a stunningly herculean view of himself, in *B.J.* 3.141–408.

26. On Josephus and suicide, see Raymond Newell, "The Forms and Historical Value of Josephus' Suicide Accounts," in *Josephus, the Bible, and History* (ed. Louis H. Feldman and Gohei Hata; Detroit: Wayne State University Press, 1989), 278–94; Steven Weitzman, "Unbinding Isaac: Martyrdom and Its Exegetical Alternatives," in *Contesting Texts: Jews and Christians in Conversation about the Bible* (ed. Melody D. Knowles et al.; Minneapolis: Fortress Press, 2007), 79–89.

to choose life in the hands of Rome (*B.J.* 3.391). Josephus was then brought before Vespasian, where he delivered the famed prophecy of the general's imperial destiny, a proclamation that ultimately launched this rebel general into a comfortable literary career in the heart of the empire, with the benefit of Roman citizenship, a generous stipend, and residency in one of Vespasian's villas (*Vita* 423).

Josephus spent his remaining days, some thirty or so years, living in Rome, where he composed at least three major literary works in Greek. His first, a seven-volume account of the Judean revolt against Rome (*B.J.*), was likely composed somewhere between 75 and 81 C.E.,[27] though some have argued that the flattery of Domitian in book 7 indicates that this last volume was composed during the reign of the last Flavian emperor.[28] His second major work, a twenty-volume account of the antiquities of the Jewish people (*A.J.*), was published in 93/94 C.E.,[29] perhaps with the one-volume appendix (*Vita*) following shortly thereafter.[30] The precise date for his final work, the two-volume defense of the Jews in the response to hostile slanders (*C. Ap.*), is more difficult to determine, except that it follows the publication of *A.J./Vita*, given the references Josephus occasionally makes to this composition.[31]

Josephus' Nachleben: From Devious Quisling to Respected Roman Author

In the light of the aforementioned Jotapata episode, it is not entirely surprising that scholarship on Josephus during the late nineteenth and early twentieth centuries was largely concerned with Josephus' character flaws and deficiencies

27. For the *terminus a quo*, Josephus mentions in *B.J.* 7.158–161 the dedication of Vespasian's *Templum Pacis*, which occurred in 75 C.E. (Cassius Dio, *Hist. rom.* 66.15.1). For the *terminus ante quem*, Josephus mentions in *Vita* 363 that Titus gave his official imperial signature to *B.J.*, thus locating the completion of the work sometime before Titus' death but during his brief reign (79–81 C.E.).

28. Cohen, *Josephus in Galilee and Rome*, 84–90; Seth Schwartz, "The Composition and Publication of Josephus' *Bellum Judaicum* Book 7," *HTR* 79 (1986): 373–86. Thackeray first proposed, on literary grounds, that book 7 was a later appendix. Specifically, Thackeray argued that the final book reflected a different style, indicating that Josephus no longer had his literary assistants at his disposal (Thackeray, *Josephus*, 34–35, 105). For a critique of this view, see the discussion and literature cited in Mark Brighton, *The Sicarii in Josephus's Judean War: Rhetorical Analysis and Historical Observations* (Atlanta: Society of Biblical Literature, 2009), 33–41.

29. Josephus explicitly dates *A.J.* to the thirteenth year of Domitian's reign, that is, between September 93 and September 94 C.E.

30. D. A. Barish, "The 'Autobiography' of Josephus and the Hypothesis of a Second Edition of His 'Antiquities'," *HTR* 71 (1978): 61–75; Cohen, *Josephus in Galilee and Rome*, 170; Rajak, *Josephus*, 237–38; Per Bilde, *Flavius Josephus between Jerusalem and Rome* (Sheffield, England: Sheffield Academic Press, 1988), 104–13; Mason, *Life of Josephus*, xiv–xix. Seth Schwartz argues instead that *Vita* was appended to a second edition of *A.J.* in 97/98 C.E.; Seth Schwartz, *Josephus and Judaean Politics* (Leiden: Brill, 1990), 20.

31. John M. G. Barclay, *Against Apion* (Flavius Josephus: Translation and Commentary 10; ed. Steve Mason; Leiden: Brill, 2007), xxvi–xxviii . For references to *A.J.*, see *C. Ap.* 1.1–2, 54, 127; 2.136, 287.

as a historian.[32] According to Feldman's assessment of the earlier stages of modern research, "scholars were virtually unanimous in condemning [Josephus]."[33] This, however, was not always the case. In fact, Josephus' works were well-known and quite popular in Christian circles up through the Renaissance, particularly through the Latin translation of Hegesippus. The author's popularity in Christianity is perhaps understandable, given the scattered references to important figures in the early Christian story, including Jesus, as well as the widespread belief that Josephus' account of the destruction of the temple represented an important testimony of divine judgment against the Jews for their rejection of Jesus.[34] But there is even indication that Josephus was known in Jewish circles. While the silence on Josephus in the rabbinic corpus may be significant, that his works were translated/adapted in the Hebrew *Josippon* suggests that at least some Jews found Josephus' writings to be a valuable resource.[35]

However, while Josephus' works were considered important up to the modern era, Josephus the person received very little attention until the early twentieth century, at which time his supposed character flaws became the center of attention. Norman Bentwich, Jewish-British author and one-time president of the Jewish Historical Society, published in 1914 an influential study of Josephus that summarily dismissed the author as one who "hardly merits a place on his own account in a series of Jewish Worthies, since neither as a man of action nor as a man of letters did he deserve particularly well of his nation."[36] In part because of Josephus' reputation as a Jewish "renegade and turn-coat,"[37] Bentwich's negative assessment dominated Jewish scholarship on Josephus in this early period, perhaps best ex-

---

32. My analysis of scholarly trends in the study of Josephus is indebted to the useful bibliographies compiled by Heinz Schreckenberg, and even more so, Louis Feldman. See Heinz Schreckenberg, *Bibliographie zu Flavius Josephus* (Leiden: Brill, 1968); idem, *Bibliographie zu Flavius Josephus: Supplementband mit Gesamtregister* (Leiden: Brill, 1979); Louis Feldman, *Josephus and Modern Scholarship*; idem, *Josephus: A Supplementary Bibliography* (New York: Garland, 1986). In addition to these resources, Per Bilde's synthesis of Josephan scholarship, although published over two decades ago, is still useful (Bilde, *Flavius Josephus*, 123–71).

33. Feldman, "Flavius Josephus Revisited," 779.

34. Jesus: *A.J.* 18.63–64; John the Baptist: *A.J.* 18.116–119; Jesus' brother James: *A.J.* 20.200–203. As Gabriele Boccaccini notes, because both of his main works end with the destruction of Jerusalem, "Josephus was turned by Christians into the witness *par excellence* of the theological 'end' of Judaism. The destruction of Jerusalem meant the punishment of a blind and even 'deicidal' people, whose existence and role as precursor had been rendered useless by the advent of the Messiah" (Gabriele Boccaccini, *Portraits of Middle Judaism in Scholarship and Arts: A Multimedia Catalog from Flavius Josephus to 1991* [Turin, Italy: S. Zamorani, 1992], xi–xii).

35. On Josephus before the modern period, see especially Heinz Schreckenberg, *Die Flavius-Josephus-Tradition in Antike und Mittelalter* (Leiden: Brill, 1972). See also the brief discussion in Boccaccini, *Portraits of Middle Judaism*, x–xii.

36. Norman Bentwich, *Josephus* (Philadelphia: Jewish Publication Society of America, 1914), 5.

37. Thackeray, *Josephus*, 2. See also Mary Beard, "The Triumph of Flavius Josephus,"

emplified in the Jewish historian Abraham Schalit, whose own biography was in many respects an inversion of the life of Josephus. Schalit was brought up in a Diaspora setting, rejected this "exile" by moving to Palestine in 1929, and supported the cause of Jewish sovereignty in Zion.[38] Not surprisingly then, Schalit was, at least in his early work, less than friendly toward this Jew who moved *to* the Diaspora in support of *foreign* hegemony, referring to Josephus as "a contemptible individual."[39] Jews, however, were not alone in damning Josephus to the fate of despicable traitor. Cambridge theologian and church historian F. J. Foakes Jackson similarly judged Josephus "conspicuously deficient in patriotism."[40]

This obsession with Josephus' perceived character flaws was matched with equal fervor in many early scholarly assessments of Josephus as historian. Source-critical approaches dominated in the late nineteenth and early twentieth centuries, fostering an image of Josephus as a "mindless copyist,"[41] an "unimaginative pen-pusher who had merely plagiarized the works of others and pieced together the stolen goods without adding much thought to the matter."[42] Richard Laqueur's *Der jüdische Historiker Josephus* marks an important attempt to move beyond the notion of a mindless or passive copyist, instead approaching the Josephan corpus as the product of a creative author. Laqueur's proposal, however, which has become a widely influential theory of Josephus' development as a person and then author, is still steeped in an assumption that Josephus was a deeply flawed character. The devout priest became a traitorous tyrant in Galilee, then a Flavian lackey whose *B.J.* was commissioned by the emperor as an official statement of imperial propaganda.[43] After losing his imperial sponsorship, Josephus set out in his later works to repent for his earlier betrayals, with *A.J.* representing a nationalistic attempt at rapprochement with his Jewish heritage.[44] Thus Laqueur rejects the claim that

---

in *Flavian Rome: Culture, Image, Text* (ed. A. J. Boyle and W. J. Dominik; Leiden: Brill, 2003), 544.

38. Daniel R. Schwartz, "On Abraham Schalit, Herod, Josephus, the Holocaust, Horst R. Moehring, and the Study of Ancient Jewish History," *Jewish History* 2 (1987): 10.

39. Abraham Schalit, "Josephus und Justus: Studien zur Vita des Josephus," *Klio* 26 (1933): 95. Schwartz also cites a personal letter, written in Hebrew, which captures the extent of Schalit's animus toward Josephus: "I believe that we may in complete tranquility admit Josephus' baseness, without our having to be embarrassed. There are such base people throughout the world—among every people and tongue—and there is no necessity to declare this reptile pure" (Schwartz, "On Abraham Schalit," 22 n. 12). Schwartz, however, goes on to argue that later in his life Schalit softened his stance somewhat, even to the extent of moderately rehabilitating the image of this "reptile." See also Solomon Zeitlin, "Josephus—Patriot or Traitor?" *Jewish Chronicle* 94 (1934): 26–30.

40. F. J. Foakes Jackson, *Josephus and the Jews: The Religion and History of the Jews as Explained by Flavius Josephus* (London: SPCK, 1930), xii.

41. Laqueur, *Der jüdische Historiker Flavius Josephus*, viii. This remark does not reflect Laqueur's view of Josephus, but his assessment of contemporary scholarship.

42. Bilde, *Flavius Josephus*, 126.

43. Laqueur, *Der jüdische Historiker Flavius Josephus*, 247–58.

44. Ibid., 258–61.

Josephus contributed *nothing* original to his works, but Josephus' originality to Laqueur still reflects the motives of a devious quisling.

The main outline of Laqueur's hypothesis reappears, with some modification, in a number of subsequent studies. Most notably, Shaye Cohen's examination of the relationship between *B.J.* and *Vita* maintains Laqueur's view that *B.J.* represents the work of Flavian propaganda: "If any historian was a Flavian lackey, it was Josephus."[45] With the accession of Domitian, Cohen argues that Josephus underwent a radical change, becoming "more 'nationalistic,' more conscious of religious considerations, less concerned about flattering Rome. . . . With this religious outlook comes a pro-Pharisaic bias."[46] In other words, Josephus in his later years attempted to distance himself from his pro-Roman youth while aligning with the now emerging Pharisaic-Rabbinic movement. More recently, Seth Schwartz has continued this interpretive approach, seeing in an earlier Aramaic version of *B.J.* a Flavian-commissioned "propagandistic tract" for the war against the Jews,[47] in the Greek edition of *B.J.* a piece of High Priestly propaganda,[48] and finally in *A.J.* a piece of "Pharisaic propaganda."[49]

What is common in the Laqueur trajectory of scholarship is the notion of *discontinuity* and *inconsistency* across Josephus' literary oeuvre, based upon the hypothesis that Josephus experienced a radical change in his attitude between *B.J.* (pro-*Roman*) and *A.J.* (pro-*Jewish*). The resulting image of Josephus is thus something of "an unscrupulous manipulator of his circumstances."[50] When in the good graces of the emperor, Josephus dutifully fulfills his role as Flavian mouthpiece; however, when circumstances turn sour under Domitian, Josephus scrambles to reclaim his place among those he had formerly betrayed. One can thus easily see in this interpretive approach the dark shadow of the Jotapata episode, which has continued to haunt Josephus' legacy well into the modern context.

Nevertheless, several scholars have recently attempted a more positive assessment of Josephus' career and literary motives. In 1984 Horst Moehring argued that Josephus was "a Roman Jew. He was not a Jewish renegade, and he was not a man

---

45. Cohen, *Josephus in Galilee and Rome*, 86.

46. Ibid., 236–37.

47. Schwartz, *Josephus and Judaean Politics*, 10. Cohen and Schwartz are prominent recent representatives of this approach, but Laqueur's influence was felt almost immediately after the publication of his volume, as seen, for example, in Hans Rasp, "Flavius Josephus und die jüdischen Religionsparteien," *Zeitschrift für die neutestamentliche Wissenschaft und die Kunde der älteren Kirche* 23 (1924): 27–47. One notable exception was Thackeray, who rejected the idea that Josephus changed his attitude between *B.J.* and *A.J.*: "But this severance of Roman ties and adoption of another and more patriotic theme do not, to my mind, indicate any abrupt change of attitude" (*Josephus*, 52). Thackeray nevertheless maintained that *B.J.* was a piece of Roman political propaganda and that *A.J.* was composed at a time when Josephus was released from such imperial constraints.

48. Schwartz, *Josephus and Judaean Politics*, 82–88.

49. Ibid., 170–208.

50. David McClister, "Ethnicity and Jewish Identity in Josephus" (Ph.D. diss., University of Florida, 2008), 32.

with split loyalties. In him, the Jew and the Roman had become one man."[51] In the same year Gabriele Boccaccini published an article in Italian, which was later republished in English in his volume *Middle Judaism*, claiming that "Josephus's work is not that of a base quisling but that of an apologist who proclaims his faithfulness to the fathers and tries to give his culture and his people a consideration denied by many."[52] Per Bilde rejects both the notion of Josephus as a Flavian lackey and *A.J.* as an extended treatise of repentance and has instead drawn attention to Josephus' skill as a creative author and historian.[53] Perhaps no scholar has devoted more attention to the rehabilitation of Josephus as literary artist than Steve Mason, whose numerous publications have stressed the rhetorical dimensions of Josephus' works.[54] In particular, Mason's work emphasizes what he calls the "rhetorical-thematic study of Josephus," the careful examination of literary *topoi* within each of Josephus' main compositions.[55]

One important facet in Mason's scholarship, as indeed in other recent contributions to the study of Josephus, is the heightened emphasis on the author's *compositional* context, that is, Josephus' place in the cultural and literary world of Flavian Rome.[56] This focus naturally includes a careful consideration of the question of intended audience. A consequence of Laqueur's hypothesis was that Josephus' shift

51. Horst R. Moehring, "Joseph ben Matthia and Flavius Josephus: The Jewish Prophet and Roman Historian," *Aufsteig und Niedergang der römischen Welt: Geschichte und Kultur Roms im Spiegel der neueren Forschung* II.21.2 (1984): 869.

52. Gabriele Boccaccini, "Il Tema della Memoria in Giuseppe Flavio," *Henoch* 6 (1984): 147–63; idem, *Middle Judaism: Jewish Thought, 300 B.C.E. to 200 C.E.* (Minneapolis: Fortress Press, 1991), 242.

53. Bilde, *Flavius Josephus*, 173–206.

54. See especially Steve Mason, "Josephus, Daniel, and the Flavian House," in *Josephus and the History of the Greco-Roman Period* (ed. Fausto Parente and Joseph Sievers; Leiden: Brill, 1994), 161–91; idem, "The *Contra Apionem* in Social and Literary Context: An Invitation to Judean Philosophy," in *Josephus' "Contra Apionem": Studies in Its Character and Context with a Latin Concordance to the Portion Missing in Greek* (ed. Louis H. Feldman and John R. Levison; Leiden: Brill, 1996), 187–228; idem, *Flavius Josephus on the Pharisees: A Compositional-Critical Study* (Leiden: Brill, 2001); idem, "Flavius Josephus in Flavian Rome: Reading on and between the Lines," in *Flavian Rome: Culture, Image, Text* (ed. A. J. Boyle and W. J. Dominik; Leiden: Brill, 2003), 559–89; idem, "Figured Speech and Irony in T. Flavius Josephus," in *Flavius Josephus and Flavian Rome* (ed. Jonathan Edmondson, Steve Mason, and James Rives; Oxford: Oxford University Press, 2005), 243–88; idem, "The Greeks and the Distant Past in Josephus's *Judaean War*," in *Antiquity in Antiquity: Jewish and Christian Pasts in the Greco-Roman World* (ed. Gregg Gardner and Kevin L. Osterloh; Tübingen: Mohr Siebeck, 2008), 93–130.

55. Steve Mason, "Introduction to the *Judean Antiquities*," in *Judean Antiquities 1–4* (Flavius Josephus: Translation and Commentary 3; ed. Steve Mason; Leiden: Brill, 2000), xxii.

56. This emphasis on Josephus' Flavian context is especially apparent in several recent collections of essays, most notably A. J. Boyle and W. J. Dominik, eds., *Flavian Rome: Culture, Image, Text* (Leiden: Brill, 2003); Jonathan Edmondson, Steve Mason, and James Rives, eds., *Flavius Josephus and Flavian Rome* (Oxford: Oxford University Press, 2005); Joseph Sievers and Gaia Lembi, eds., *Josephus and Jewish History in Flavian Rome and Beyond* (Leiden: Brill, 2005).

in attitude was thought to reflect a similar shift in audience, that while *B.J.* was aimed at a Roman (imperial) audience—or, more precisely, that it was a treatise of official Flavian propaganda targeting Jewish readers—*A.J.* was directed toward a Jewish audience.[57] Mason in particular has been a vocal critic of this interpretation, arguing instead for a broad continuity of readership for all of his works, namely that Josephus was writing consistently—though not necessarily exclusively—for a gentile and, more specifically, a *Roman* audience.[58]

His study of the audience for *B.J.* is particularly interesting in this regard. Building on the work of Raymond Starr,[59] Mason argues that the publication of materials in antiquity, including that of *B.J.*, was primarily a local and social event. A work in progress was usually disseminated (via oral presentations) in stages through concentric circles of acquaintances, from an inner circle of close friends to a wider group of associates among the literary elite. According to Mason, Josephus' circle of acquaintances, and hence the target audience in mind when he composed *B.J.*, were primarily members of the Roman intelligentsia.[60] His discussion of the audience of *A.J./Vita* adds even more specificity, arguing that this work was addressed to Roman sympathizers—Mason suggests people like the ex-consuls T. Flavius Clemens and M. Acilius Glabrio—who were "keenly interested in Jewish matters."[61] This is apparent in particular in Josephus' repeated attempts to explain basic details about Jewish culture, explanations that would have been unnecessary if composed primarily for Jewish readers.

Not everyone has been persuaded by Mason's arguments. Hannah Cotton and Werner Eck argue that Josephus was likely a "lonely and extremely isolated" figure with very limited contacts among Roman elites.[62] Jonathan Price offers perhaps the most pointed rebuttal of this notion of a Roman audience. Whereas Mason sug-

57. A variation of this approach is evident in Etienne Nodet's recent discussion of *A.J.*, which argues that this text was written as a teaching manual for Jews living in the Roman empire ("Josephus' Attempt to Reorganize Judaism from Rome," in *Making History: Josephus and Historical Method* [ed. Zuleika Rodgers; Leiden: Brill, 2007], 110–13). Tessa Rajak goes even further, claiming that "the content and approach [of all of Josephus' writings] suggest that the audience was always expected to consist as much of Jews who knew Greek, that is to say Jewish residents of the cities of the Roman empire" ("The *Against Apion* and the Continuities in Josephus' Political Thought," in *The Jewish Dialogue with Greece and Rome: Studies in Cultural and Social Interaction* [ed. Tessa Rajak; Leiden: Brill, 2001], 197).

58. Steve Mason, "'Should Any Wish to Enquire Further' (Ant. 1.25): The Aim and Audience of Josephus's *Judean Antiquities/Life*," in *Understanding Josephus: Seven Perspectives* (ed. Steve Mason; Sheffield: Sheffield Academic Press, 1998), 64–103; idem, "Of Audience and Meaning: Reading Josephus' *Bellum Judaicum* in the Context of a Flavian Audience," in *Josephus and Jewish History in Flavian Rome and Beyond* (ed. Joseph Sievers and Gaia Lembi; Leiden: Brill, 2005), 71–100.

59. Raymond J. Starr, "The Circulation of Literary Texts in the Roman World," *CQ* 37 (1987): 213–23.

60. Mason, "Of Audience and Meaning," 71–100. Mason also rejects the idea that *B.J.* was written under imperial sponsorship (77).

61. Mason, "Aim and Audience," 101.

62. Hannah M. Cotton and Werner Eck, "Josephus' Roman Audience: Josephus and

gests an oral reading to a widening circle of Roman literary elites, Price considers it "likely that Josephus refrained from public performance entirely."[63] Moreover, Price argues that the extant evidence suggests that "all or most of Josephus' known readership was in or from the East," calling into question Mason's argument that Josephus targets gentile readers living in Rome.[64] More to the point, Price concludes: "His most ardent and consistent interests remained not those which preoccupied and fascinated the writers in Rome, but those which continued to agitate in the East. His persistent *persona* and literary project were Jewish."[65]

Price may or may not be correct when he claims that Josephus' works *only* gained circulation in the East, and, in any case, it is extremely difficult to demonstrate conclusively Mason's hypothesis that Josephus disseminated his works orally to a gentile audience in Flavian Rome. The full extent of Josephus' readership is in fact likely beyond our reach. Nevertheless, even granting our general ignorance of Josephus' *actual* readers, this does not preclude the possibility that Josephus at the very least *imagined* that his work would be read by contemporary literary elites in Rome. While Price correctly highlights aspects of Josephus' narratives that reflect a non-Roman ("Eastern") perspective, he wrongly assumes an either/or scenario—that is, that Josephus *either* wrote for Jews and emphasized Jewishness *or* he wrote for Romans and emphasized *Romanitas*. Such a binary opposition, however, is unnecessary. As a Roman citizen living in the capital city during the Flavian period, Josephus could not help but breath in this cultural air, so to speak. But as a Jew and priest from Judea, Josephus likewise could not help but maintain, and hence reflect, this ethnic and religious identity as well as the cultural heritage of his past, that is, an "Eastern" perspective. Both worlds were inextricably linked in the mind of Josephus, and they emerge at various points to greater or lesser degrees in his literary corpus.[66] In this light, a focus on the extent to which Josephus' writings reflect distinctly *Roman* concerns is entirely warranted.

In sum, two important methodological considerations emerge from this brief and selective survey of scholarship. First, Josephus' corpus should not simply be

---

the Roman Elites," in *Flavius Josephus and Flavian Rome* (ed. Jonathan Edmondson, Steve Mason, and James Rives; Oxford: Oxford University Press, 2005), 52.

63. Jonathan J. Price, "The Provincial Historian in Rome," in *Josephus and Jewish History in Flavian Rome and Beyond* (ed. Joseph Sievers and Gaia Lembi; Leiden: Brill, 2005), 105.

64. Ibid., 107.

65. Ibid., 118.

66. On the tensions between Price and Mason, John Barclay seems to reflect the mediating position suggested above, based in part on postcolonial theories and, in particular, on Mary Louise Pratt's study of travel narratives. Specifically, Barclay identifies "the efforts of Josephus and his oriental predecessors as exercises in 'autohistory'—the attempt to tell their own histories in an idiom comprehensible to the majority culture(s), but with primary reference to their own traditions and *on their own terms*" ("Judean Historiography in Rome: Josephus and History in *Contra Apionem* Book 1," in *Josephus and Jewish History in Flavian Rome and Beyond* [ed. Joseph Sievers and Gaia Lembi; Leiden: Brill, 2005], 35). See also Barclay's discussion in "The Empire Writes Back: Josephan Rhetoric in Flavian Rome," in *Flavius Josephus and Flavian Rome* (ed. Jonathan Edmondson, Steve Mason, and James Rives; Oxford: Oxford University Press, 2005), 315–32.

read for its referential value, that is, as a reservoir of historical nuggets culled from his sources, but as the work of a creative author in his own right. Emerging from this first point is a second important methodological premise: Josephus' compositional context matters, and we should therefore pay careful attention to his *Roman* context and more specifically to his setting in *Flavian* Rome. This observation thus requires a comparative approach to the material at hand, exploring Josephus' literary corpus within the context of other roughly coeval Greek and Latin texts, particularly those closest in proximity to Josephus' own social location (i.e., Flavian Rome).

CONTRIBUTIONS OF THE PRESENT STUDY

Before defining in positive terms the contribution of this book, it is perhaps worth detailing at the outset the limits of this analysis, that is, precisely what this book *does not* set out to accomplish. Although in my effort to situate the material in Josephus within a broader context I consider a wider selection of Jewish sources that likewise deal with the issue of images, and in particular the second commandment (chapter 3), it is not my intention in the ensuing discussion to provide a *comprehensive* account of Jewish discourses on and responses to images in antiquity. While I do think such an investigation would be worth pursuing, it would require substantial interaction with a much broader range of literature than was possible in the present context.

In a similar vein, this book does not attempt to explain fully the causes of the increased iconoclastic activity in Judea during the first centuries B.C.E./C.E. Notwithstanding my emphasis on the rhetorical nature of Josephus' iconoclastic narratives, the fact remains that some Jews during this period likely destroyed Herod's statue of an eagle in the temple, complained about the trophies he erected in the theater, commissioned the destruction of the images in Herod the Tetrarch's palace, resisted the intrusion of Pilate's military standards, and vehemently objected to the proposed statue of Caligula. While Gutmann argues that this iconoclastic activity had little to do with a religious opposition to images, but was instead indicative of a latent resistance to Roman hegemony,[67] I suspect that the situation was likely more complex than *either* a religious (i.e., strict exegetical stance on the second commandment) *or* a political explanation. In the first place, each episode ought to be examined in its own right, without assuming that all were similarly motivated. Moreover, such distinctions between political or religious motives are somewhat anachronistic, particularly with the ever increasing presence of the imperial cult in the East, which undoubtedly played a prominent role in this iconoclastic activity. But in any case, such questions, though interesting in their own right, are not within the purview of the present analysis.

With this in mind, the present investigation makes the following contributions to scholarship on Josephus and, more broadly, to the study of Jews in the ancient Mediterranean world. First, by examining the *Nachleben* of the biblical

67. Gutmann, "The 'Second Commandment' and the Image," 170.

prohibition against images (chapter 3), and by emphasizing the *rhetorical* function of Josephus' iconoclastic narratives (chapters 4–5), this book problematizes the widespread claim that Jews during the Second Temple period, including Josephus, were uniformly against figurative images *in toto*, regardless of the question of cultic function. Rather, a closer reading of a broad range of Jewish sources from the period in question belies such a monolithic interpretation, demonstrating instead that Jews by and large (both before and after the destruction of the temple) restricted the scope of prohibited images to those with some kind of cultic association. Moreover, the fact that Josephus clearly *crafts* distinct portraits of iconoclasm that function differently within their respective literary contexts ought to caution against reading this material in a straightforward fashion. That is, rhetoric has very likely masked something of the underlying reality, rendering problematic any attempt to see in Josephus an exact account of events (and people's motives) on the ground. This is not to suggest, of course, that Josephus' rhetoric had nothing to do with reality, that Jews had absolutely no qualms about figurative art during the Second Temple period.[68] Rather, my investigation of Josephus mainly establishes that, with regard to the question of Jews and images during the Second Temple period, this highly tendentious author cannot bear the interpretive weight typically placed upon him.

Second, by focusing on the discursive dimension of visual and material culture—what we may call the "semiotics" of images, the language used to describe and recount daily encounters with these artifacts, and the way in which this "iconology" preserves perceptions of images that were common throughout the Greco-Roman Mediterranean—this book provides an important glimpse into the social context of Greco-Roman art and especially the extent to which Jews in antiquity were full participants in this ubiquitous facet of their visual landscape. W. J. T. Mitchell's work in art history provides an important stimulus here, in particular his shift in focus away from formal features of an artistic object—its style, aesthetics, and the degree of naturalism in representation—to the *visual experience* surrounding an image, that is, the interplay between object and viewer.[69] An important consequence of Mitchell's work is a more pronounced emphasis on the role of people's perceptions, especially the extent to which viewers *see into* images a whole host of assumptions, beliefs, associations, and experiences, be they political, religious, or otherwise, which collectively comprise what may be identified as a world of iconic perceptions.[70]

I argue (especially in chapters 2, 4, and 5) that Jews, including Josephus, do not stand outside of but are instead fully embedded within this world of iconic perceptions. Although Josephus' literary corpus displays a healthy measure of animosity toward images, as indeed does a broader range of ancient Jewish literature, a closer

---

68. As noted briefly above, and as will be developed much more extensively in chapter 2.

69. Mitchell, *Iconology*; idem, *Picture Theory*.

70. See also Richard Leppert's study of "visual culture," which focuses in part on how people relate to images in a variety of ways corresponding to differing "cultures of perception" (*Art and the Committed Eye: The Cultural Functions of Imagery* [Boulder, CO: Westview Press, 1996], 11).

reading of this anti-iconic language within a comparative context demonstrates the extent to which Jews were participants in what may be described as an iconic *lingua franca* in the Greco-Roman Mediterranean, a common language used to describe, assess, and recount daily encounters with these artifacts. This dynamic should thus caution against interpreting the anti-iconic language in Josephus and other ancient Jewish texts merely as evidence for the Jewish struggle *against* the forces of "paganism" or "Hellenism."

Third, by focusing on the compositional strategies in the Josephan corpus, paying special attention to the development and function of key literary themes, this study contributes to our understanding of Josephus' literary creativity and his place as a provincial author writing in Greek from the capital city. In short, far from being a "mindless copyist" with little originality, Josephus' corpus betrays the skills of a creative literary artist. In highlighting this dimension of Josephus, I thus add my voice to those scholars who advocate viewing Josephus' writings as something more than a repository of "factual nuggets" to be mined for various historical reconstructions or background details for the study of the New Testament and Christian origins. Josephus ought to be examined as an author in his own right, and his corpus is just as valuable for an understanding of the social and cultural dynamics of Flavian Rome as it is for Second Temple Judea.

Finally, and perhaps most important, insofar as I underscore (especially in chapters 4–6) the extent to which Josephus engages in the cultural politics of Flavian Rome, this book sheds light on the processes by which some Jews in antiquity negotiated identity within a Greco-Roman milieu, particularly amid the devastating consequences of the revolt against Rome. As noted briefly above, and as will be developed more fully, Josephus Romanizes the Jewish resistance to images, and in so doing he articulates a notion of Jewish identity that reflects in part the values of *Romanitas*.[71] But we should not interpret this Romanization of Jewishness as the compromise of an assimilating traitor who has abandoned his culture and people. Rather, Josephus is here exploiting the "complex Roman tradition *in the interests of his own cultural tradition*,"[72] formulating a notion of Jewish identity that could enable Jews living in Rome, who had only recently witnessed the triumphal display of their own subjugation and felt the humiliating sting of the punitive *fiscus Iudaicus*, to perhaps thrive under otherwise difficult circumstances.

71. For a similar approach to the question of identity in Josephus, see for example Martin Goodman, "Josephus as Roman Citizen," in *Josephus and the History of the Greco-Roman Period: Essays in Memory of Morton Smith* (ed. Fausto Parente and Joseph Sievers; Leiden: Brill, 1994), 329–38; idem, "The Roman Identity of Roman Jews," in *The Jews in the Hellenistic-Roman World: Studies in Memory of Menahem Stern* (ed. Isaiah M. Gafni, Aharon Oppenheimer, and Daniel R. Schwartz; Jerusalem: The Zalman Shazar Center for Jewish History, 1996), 85–99; Paul Spilsbury, *The Image of the Jew in Flavius Josephus' Paraphrase of the Bible* (Tübingen: Mohr Siebeck, 1998); idem, "Reading the Bible in Rome: Josephus and the Constraints of Empire," in *Josephus and Jewish History in Flavian Rome and Beyond* (ed. Joseph Sievers and Gaia Lembi; Leiden: Brill, 2005), 209–27.

72. Barclay, "The Empire Writes Back," 14 (emphasis mine).

2

Jewish Responses to Images in Cultural Context

This investigation flows from an important premise: Josephus' writings, and in particular his discourse on the Jewish resistance to images, bear the unmistakable imprint of his Roman context. In other words, although Josephus writes primarily about Judea and Jews, and although his corpus may provide an invaluable witness to Judean politics both before and after the destruction of the temple,[1] Josephus was during the decades of his literary career breathing the socio-politico-cultural air of Flavian Rome, and this experience profoundly shaped his various narratives. As a result, the relationship between Josephus' literary portrayals of Jewish aniconism/iconoclasm and the underlying events that actually took place is far from straightforward. Undoubtedly, rhetoric has in some sense masked reality.

Nevertheless, we must not suppose a vast and impassable chasm between rhetoric and reality, as if Josephus' descriptions of strict aniconism have nothing to do with the reality that stands behind his prose. Josephus the Flavian author was (and remained) a provincial transplant in the capital city, and the modern historian should not so easily dismiss this home away from Rome. Josephus is at once a product of Jerusalem *and* Rome, and his experiences in *both* geographical locales have left their marks on his narratives. Although his rhetoric may have masked reality, Josephus, as a product of and participant in the social, political, and religious experiences of first-century Judea, preserves in some measure the reality of this world.[2]

This qualification is particularly important at the outset, given the inherent risk of unintentional misrepresentation or distortion in a study predominantly focused on the rhetorical dimension of Jewish aniconism in Josephus. To argue that Josephus' portrayal of aniconism caters to a Roman audience in order to address Roman concerns, and to further suggest that this rhetorical agenda perhaps masks or distorts the underlying reality, can give the impression that Jews in actuality had no qualms about sculpture and figurative art during the Second Temple period. Indeed, Gutmann's study of the second commandment in Greco-Roman antiquity illustrates the potential for such misunderstanding.[3] As noted in chapter 1, Gut-

1. For example, Seth Schwartz argues that we can recover in Josephus' writings a significant amount of information on Judean politics during the thirty years *after* the destruction of the temple (*Josephus and Judaean Politics*).

2. P. J. Rhodes makes a similar point in his study of Greek historians such as Thucydides ("In Defense of the Greek Historians," *GR* 41 [1994]: 157–58).

3. Gutmann, "The 'Second Commandment' and the Image," 161–74.

mann argues that the rhetorical interests of the available sources, mainly Philo and Josephus for the Second Temple period, *creates an impression* of strict aniconism that ultimately belies the fact that Jews throughout Greco-Roman antiquity shared a broad acceptance of figurative art. Gutmann is fundamentally correct to underscore the rhetorical dimension of this material, and indeed this book is an attempt to flesh out in more detail his provocative thesis. Nevertheless, to suggest *on this basis alone* a broad and consistent continuity between the Jews living in first-century Jerusalem and, for example, third-century Dura Europos, whose synagogue remains attest to rich and vibrant artistic traditions, is questionable. The suggestion is questionable not only because it places on the rhetorical contrivances of Philo and Josephus more interpretive weight than they can bear, but also because it ignores important data outside of these authors, most notably the archaeological record, but also other literary texts that may shed light on how different Jews viewed the prohibition against images.[4]

With this in mind, I will attempt in the present chapter to redress this potential imbalance, considering both the cultural and material context of first-century Jerusalem/Judea as well as a wider selection of literary data—from both Judea and the Diaspora—attesting to a broad and complex range of Jewish responses to images. Josephus does indeed depict a city and people fiercely resistant to images, and especially sculpture, and while we should be wary of any straightforward reading of this narrative material, there is a fairly significant body of evidence outside Josephus, both literary and archaeological, that at the very least suggests an uneasy attitude toward sculptural representation for some Jews living in Jerusalem during this period. Nevertheless, a critical examination of this corroborating evidence does not fully support the *communis opinio* in scholarship that Second Temple Jews uniformly resisted sculpture in response to a religious ban on all forms of figurative art, enacted to protect the Jews from idolatry. The situation was likely much more complex, and even this tendency to resist Roman sculpture should not be viewed simply as a *struggle against* religio-cultural alterity, but as an *expression of* the wider Mediterranean milieu. This chapter will thus attempt to probe (though certainly not exhaust) the complex array of factors that shaped Jewish responses to statues, and more broadly figurative art, throughout the Roman Mediterranean.

Quid Roma et Hierosolymis? The Sculptural Void of Early Roman Jerusalem

Tertullian's now famous quip—*Quid Athenis et Hierosolymis*? ("What has Athens to do with Jerusalem?")—is here reformulated to reflect the two main urban experiences of Flavius Josephus (Tertullian, *Praescr.* 7.9). The early Christian apologist originally proffered this rhetorical question to underscore a fundamental antithesis between what the two urban centers represented in his mind (and indeed,

4. Lee Levine rightly criticizes Gutmann for overlooking the archaeological record in his analysis of the second commandment ("Figural Art in Ancient Judaism," *Ars Judaica* 1 [2005]: 11 n. 10).

what he had hoped to shape in the mind of his readers), Athens for the Academy and, by extension, Tertullian's primary opponent, those irascible "heretics," and Jerusalem for the Church. For Tertullian, Athens ought not have anything to do with Jerusalem, and vice versa.

Although Tertullian's formulation has in subsequent centuries conveniently encapsulated the notion of an interminable antithesis between Judaism/Hebraism and Hellenism, we should not so quickly assume such a radical polarization with respect to the topic at hand, the cultural and physical landscapes of Rome and Jerusalem. Jerusalem, as a provincial city on the eastern frontier of the Roman Empire, was in the first century C.E. a complex blend of "East" and "West."[5]

In the wake of the monumental renovations initiated by Herod the Great, which to some extent mimicked, albeit on a much smaller scale, Augustus' own coeval renovations of Rome (*Res Gestae Divi Augusti* 19–21),[6] Jerusalem's urban landscape was in many respects not unlike that of Rome, or for that matter any other major urban center throughout the Roman Mediterranean. Although Herod's legacy, thanks in large part to Josephus and the Gospels, has been less than favorable,[7] his urban expansion nevertheless brought about a tremendous boon to Jerusalem's reputation, as well as its economic coffers, so much so that the elder Pliny, writing a few years after the destruction of Jerusalem, could claim that formerly the city was "by far the most famous city in the East" (*longe clarissima urbium Orientis*; Pliny the Elder, *Nat.* 5.70).[8] The Jerusalem of Josephus' day could thus boast most

5. Lee Levine's essay on Second Temple Jerusalem underscores the city's cultural diversity, although Levine tends to mute the inherent complexity by speaking of the "Jewish component" and the "Hellenistic dimension" of Jerusalem, as if we could ferret out the cultural components of two hermetically sealed entities (see "Second Temple Jerusalem: A Jewish City in the Greco-Roman Orbit," in *Jerusalem: Its Sanctity and Centrality to Judaism, Christianity, and Islam* [ed. Lee I. Levine; New York: Continuum, 1999], 56).

6. For a discussion of the ideological underpinnings of Augustus' renovations, see Paul Zanker, *The Power of Images in the Age of Augustus* (Ann Arbor: University of Michigan Press, 1988), esp. 101–66.

7. Indeed, he is remembered mainly as a brutal tyrant, bloody murderer of his own kin, and ruthless oppressor of his Judean subjects, a reputation that even Augustus is said to have humorously acknowledged, at least according to the fifth-century C.E. Macrobius, who places in Augustus' mouth the following remark: "I would rather be Herod's pig (ὗς) than his son (υἱός) (*Saturnalia* 2.4.11, cited in Menahem Stern, ed., *Greek and Latin Authors on Jews and Judaism* [2 vols.; Jerusalem: Israel Academy of Sciences and Humanities, 1974], 2:665–66). This negative assessment of Herod is central to Emil Schürer's analysis of the Judean king (*The History of the Jewish People in the Age of Jesus Christ* [175 B.C.–A.D. 135] [ed. Fergus Millar, Geza Vermes, and Matthew Black; 3 vols.; Edinburgh: T&T Clark, 1973–1987], 1:287–329). Though Herod's flaws are not masked in Abraham Schalit's analysis, his portrayal of Herod is in many respects more palatable (see *König Herodes: Der Mann und Sein Work* [Berlin: De Gruyter, 2001]; Schwartz, "On Abraham Schalit," 11).

8. On Herod's building program more generally, see the recent discussions by Duane W. Roller, *The Building Program of Herod the Great* (Berkeley: University of California Press, 1998); Achim Lichtenberger, *Die Baupolitik des Herodes des Großen* (Wiesbaden, Germany: Harrassowitz Verlag, 1999); Sarah Japp, *Die Baupolitik Herodes' des Großen: Die Bedeutung

of the major architectonic structures found elsewhere in the Greco-Roman world: monumental tombs on the outskirts of the city patterned after Greek and Roman architectural trends,[9] several elaborate palaces and elite residential homes,[10] an agora (*B.J.* 5.137), the enigmatic xystus, which perhaps should be identified as a gymnasium (*B.J.* 5.144; 6.325, 377),[11] a Bouleuterion (*B.J.* 5.144; 6.354), a large theater and amphitheater (*A.J.* 15.268),[12] a hippodrome (*B.J.* 2.44; *A.J.* 17.255), and of course, most notably, Herod's massive temple devoted to the Jewish God, which in Josephus' partisan judgment was a structure "more noteworthy (ἀξιαφηγητότατον) than any under the sun" (*A.J.* 15.391–419; quote at 15.412).

Moreover, the centrality of the Herodian temple to the Judean cult, as well as the commercial vitality this magnificent structure and its operation created, invariably produced a centripetal force that brought into the city a massive influx of people spanning the entire Mediterranean basin and the western Mesopotamian region, both pilgrims and permanent residents who found employment in this newly stimulated economy.[13] This expanded population very likely transformed

der Architektur für die Herrschaftslegitimation eines römischen Klientelkönigs (Leidorf, Germany: Rahden/Westf., 2000); Peter Richardson, *Building Jewish in the Roman East* (Waco Tex.: Baylor University Press, 2004), esp. 253–307. See also the brief summary in John Strange, "Herod and Jerusalem: The Hellenization of an Oriental City," in *Jerusalem in Ancient History and Tradition* (ed. Thomas L. Thompson; London and New York: T&T Clark International, 2003), 97–113.

9. For a general discussion of these tombs, see Gideon Foerster, "Art and Architecture in Palestine," in *The Jewish People in the First Century: Historical Geography, Political History, Social, Cultural, and Religious Life and Institutions* (ed. Shmuel Safrai et al.; Philadelphia: Fortress Press, 1987), 999–1002; Lee I. Levine, *Jerusalem: Portrait of the City in the Second Temple Period (538 B.C.E.–70 C.E.)* (Philadelphia: Jewish Publication Society, 2002), 206–13; Fine, *Art and Judaism*, 60–65.

10. See especially Nahman Avigad, *The Herodian Quarter in Jerusalem: Wohl Archaeological Museum* (Jerusalem: Keter, 1989); Hillel Geva, ed., *Jewish Quarter Excavations in the Old City of Jerusalem: The Finds from Areas A, W, and X-2 Final Report* (3 vols.; Jerusalem: Israel Exploration Society, Institute of Archaeology, Hebrew University of Jerusalem, 2003).

11. Levine, *Jerusalem*, 324–25.

12. Though see Joseph Patrich's recent discussion of the theater, which posits that it was only a temporary wooden structure that was dismantled after Herod's reign, and thus would have been missing from the urban landscape during Josephus' lifetime ("Herod's Theatre in Jerusalem: A New Proposal," *IEJ* 52 [2002]: 231–39).

13. On the population of Jerusalem in antiquity, see especially Magen Broshi, "Estimating the Population of Ancient Jerusalem," *BAR* 4, no. 2 (1978): 10–15. It is difficult to determine with any certainty the number of residents in Jerusalem, and the sources are largely silent on the matter. Tacitus claims that at the time of the siege of Titus there were six hundred thousand residents, but this only after "streams of rabble" from surrounding villages took refuge within the city limits (*Hist.* 5.12.2; 5.13.3 [trans. Moore, LCL]). On pilgrimage to Jerusalem and its impact on the economy, see Martin Goodman, "The Pilgrimage Economy of Jerusalem in the Second Temple Period," in *Jerusalem: Its Sanctity and Centrality to Judaism, Christianity, and Islam* (ed. Lee I. Levine; New York: Continuum, 1999), 69–76. Goodman argues that the mass pilgrimage spoken of in numerous sources began only during

Jerusalem into a cosmopolitan melting pot of cultures,[14] so much so that a visitor to this city "would undoubtedly have been struck by the many similarities between Jerusalem and other Greco-Roman urban centers."[15]

Thus, although often described as "a quintessentially Jewish city,"[16] the portrait of Herodian and early Roman Jerusalem—the Jerusalem of Josephus' upbringing—is hardly that of an isolated enclave of devotees to the Judean cult, a Jewish haven from the "corrupting" forces of Hellenism. Rather, not unlike Rome (though again on a much smaller scale), we have here a culturally diverse urban center, marked by many of the typical Roman urban accoutrements, and bustling with people from all parts of the Mediterranean basin and beyond, even extending far into Parthian territory. As Martin Goodman aptly states in his recent assessment of Augustan Rome and Herodian Jerusalem, "A casual visitor to Rome and Jerusalem in the last decades of the first century B.C.E. might have been more struck by similarities, since it was during these years that both cities metamorphosed from ramshackle agglomerations into shining testimonies to massive state expenditure."[17]

Notwithstanding these similarities, however, Goodman's hypothetical visitor to Rome and Jerusalem would have found equally striking at least one conspicuous difference in their respective urban landscapes: the almost complete absence of the public or private display of sculpture or other types of figurative iconography. As is well-known, figurative art in a wide range of formats—for example, three-dimensional freestanding statues, both life-sized and colossal, sculpture in relief, wall paintings, mosaics, and so on—and with a diverse array of subject matter—for example, gods and other mythological figures, heroes from the distant past, kings and emperors, other local dignitaries, family portraits, and so on—were ubiquitous in Rome, as indeed throughout the Greco-Roman Mediterranean. Peter Stewart's description of a typical journey up the Via Appia toward Rome, though based on evidence dating to the second century C.E., could equally apply to Josephus' visual horizon as he first entered the city in the previous century: "Yet the road from this point [the Villa of the Quintilii] entered a world of sculpture, in every part of which statues assailed the viewer."[18]

---

the reign of Herod the Great; furthermore, Goodman suggests that the potential economic impact of pilgrimage was a major motivating factor in Herod's sizable personal investment in the expansion of the temple complex (see especially pp. 71–75).

14. This multicultural dynamic is expressed in the Acts of the Apostles' description of the population in Jerusalem during the feast of Pentecost (Shavuot): "Parthians, Medes, Elamites, and those who live in Mesopotamia, Judea and Cappadocia, those from Pontus, Asia, Phrygia and Pamphylia, Egypt and those from parts of Libya around Cyrene, and visitors from Rome, both Judeans and proselytes, Cretans and Arabs" (Acts 2:9–11).

15. Levine, *Jerusalem*, 62.

16. Levine, "Second Temple Jerusalem," 53.

17. Martin Goodman, *Rome and Jerusalem: The Clash of Ancient Civilizations* (New York: Alfred A. Knopf, 2007), 33.

18. Stewart, *Statues in Roman Society*, 2. Stewart notes elsewhere that many ancient sources show an awareness of a "population problem," that is, of a particular city becoming

The emptiness of Jerusalem, however, was surely quite striking when compared with this world full of images. To be sure, Roman Palestine during the second and third centuries C.E. was not entirely bereft of statues, and the same was undoubtedly true in the first century.[19] For example, the portrait of Caesarea Maritima that emerges in Josephus is that it is replete with statuary (*B.J.* 1.408–415), an impression confirmed by the archaeological evidence,[20] and there is no reason to suppose that other major urban centers in first-century Palestine—for example, Ascalon, Scythopolis, Samaria-Sebaste, Caesarea Philippi—were any different. Jerusalem, however, was apparently a notable exception to this rule. The archaeological remains of Second Temple Jerusalem to date, in contrast with almost every other major urban center in the Mediterranean basin, have yielded no three-dimensional freestanding sculpture of any type, divine or otherwise.

The absence of statues from the archaeological record of first-century Jerusalem does not necessarily mean that statues did not exist anywhere in the city; neither does it require the conclusion that *all* Jewish residents were antagonistic to this and other forms of figural art.[21] Indeed, we know for a fact that at least one statue stood within the city's walls, the large golden eagle that Herod erected over the "great gate" of the temple, likely a reference to the entry point into the main sanc-

too congested with statues (pp. 128–36). Indeed, Pliny the Elder's excursus on statuary in Rome in book 34 of his *Naturalis historia* certainly gives the impression of a vast sculptural population. Cassius Dio likewise poignantly captures the proliferation of statuary in Rome when he likens the statues to a "large crowd in the city" (πολὺν δὲ καὶ ὄχλον τῇ πόλει) (*Hist. rom.* 60.5.5). Dio's account subsequently describes how Claudius addresses this population problem: "And since the city was being filled with many images (ἐπειδή τε ἡ πόλις πολλῶν εἰκόνων ἐπληροῦτο) . . . he [Claudius] placed most of them in another location" (*Hist. rom.* 60.25.2–3).

19. Yaron Z. Eliav, "Viewing the Sculptural Environment: Shaping the Second Commandment," in *Talmud Yerushalmi and Graeco-Roman Culture* (ed. Peter Schäfer; Tübingen: Mohr Siebeck, 2003), 413–15. See also Cornelius Vermeule and Kristin Anderson, "Greek and Roman Sculpture in the Holy Land," *The Burlington Magazine* 123 (1981): 7–8, 10–19; Moshe L. Fischer, *Marble Studies: Roman Palestine and Marble Trade* (Konstanz, Germany: UVK, 1998); Moshe L. Fischer, "Sculpture in Roman Palestine and Its Architectural and Social Milieu: Adaptability, Imitation, Originality? The Ascalon Basilica as an Example," in *The Sculptural Environment of the Roman Near East: Reflections on Culture, Ideology, and Power* (ed. Yaron Z. Eliav, Elise Friedland, and Sharon Herbert; Louvain: Peeters, 2008), 483–508.

20. On sculptural remains in Caesarea Maritima, see especially the following studies: Shmuel Yeivin, "Excavations at Caesarea Maritima," *Archaeology* 8 (1955): 122–29; Michael Avi-Yonah, "The Caesarea Porphyry Statue," *IEJ* 20 (1970): 203–8; Robert Wenning, "Die Stadtgöttin von Caesarea Maritima," *Boreas* 9 (1986): 113–29; Rivka Gersht, "The Sculpture of Caesarea Maritima" (Ph.D., diss., Tel Aviv University, 1987) (in Hebrew); Rivka Gersht, "Caesarean Sculpture in Context," in *The Sculptural Environment of the Roman Near East: Reflections on Culture, Ideology, and Power* (ed. Yaron Z. Eliav, Elise Friedland, and Sharon Herbert; Louvain: Peeters, 2008), 509–38.

21. See especially the scholarship discussed below, particularly the sweeping assertions of Rachel Hachlili, who sees in the lacuna of figurative remains a uniform Jewish resistance to figurative art.

tuary building from the court of the Israelites (*B.J.* 1.649–655; *A.J.* 17.150–164).[22] Moreover, that the iconoclasts—Judas and Matthias and their youthful band of pupils—who destroyed this image just prior to Herod's death were deeply offended by the statue should not be taken to mean that *all* Jews, priests or otherwise, passing before the statue during worship were equally disturbed. Although we do not know precisely when this statue was erected, Josephus' reference to the eagle as an ἀνάθημα might suggest that it was set up at the completion and dedication of the temple building in 18 B.C.E. (*A.J.* 17.151, 158).[23] If this is the case, then the statue stood in a prominent position—clearly visible to the thousands of Jews who worshiped at the temple annually—for approximately fourteen years, *perhaps* without controversy. It is thus not unreasonable to suppose that at least for some Jews the statue was seen as relatively harmless, not necessarily a violation of the second commandment,[24] but perhaps simply an ornament of Herod's beneficent rule on behalf of the Jews or a symbol of loyalty to the Roman Empire.[25]

Although outside of Jerusalem and Judea proper, Josephus likewise mentions portrait statues of Agrippa I's daughters erected in the monarch's house in Tiberias (*A.J.* 19.357). While we cannot be certain if Agrippa, or for that matter any of the other Herodian monarchs, similarly erected portrait statues in the various Herodian residential quarters scattered throughout Judea,[26] such as Jerusalem or

---

22. On the location of the gate, see Jan Willem van Henten, "Ruler or God? The Demolition of Herod's Eagle," in *The New Testament and Early Christian Literature in Greco-Roman Context: Studies in Honor of David E. Aune* (ed. John Fotopoulos; Leiden: Brill, 2006), 278.

23. Michael Grant suggests 18 B.C.E. as the likely date for its erection (*Herod the Great* [New York: American Heritage Press, 1971], 207). In contrast, A. H. M. Jones assumes that the eagle was installed toward the end of Herod's life, and thus the iconoclastic response was immediate (*The Herods of Judaea* [Oxford: Clarendon Press, 1967], 147–48).

24. This, of course, remains only a supposition (though a plausible one, I think), since the largely silent historical record—excepting the episode involving Judas and Matthias—makes it nearly impossible to determine precisely what most Jews actually thought of this statue. Erwin Ramsdell Goodenough claims that the eagle was generally accepted as a legitimate Jewish symbol and that the iconoclastic reaction had more to do with a hatred of Herod than of the statue itself (*Jewish Symbols in the Greco-Roman Period* [13 vols.; New York: Pantheon Books, 1953–1968], 8:925). Similarly A. H. M. Jones suggests that only a small minority opposed the statue (*The Herods of Judaea*, 148). So also Gideon Fuks, "Josephus on Herod's Attitude towards Jewish Religion: The Darker Side," *JJS* 53 (2002): 242. On the use of the eagle as a Jewish symbol in late antiquity, see Rachel Hachlili, *Ancient Jewish Art and Archaeology in the Land of Israel* (Leiden: Brill, 1988), 332–34.

25. On the eagle imagery as a symbol of benefactions, see van Henten, "Ruler or God," 275. For the view that Herod's eagle erected in the temple was a tribute to Rome, see Schalit, *König Herodes*, 734. See also the discussion in Pawel Szkolut, "The Eagle as a Symbol of Divine Presence and Protection in Ancient Jewish Art," *SJ* 5 (2002): 1–11.

26. According to Josephus, Herod the Great resented that his subjects did not honor him with portrait statues (*A.J.* 16.157–158). See the discussion of Herodian portraiture in Roller, *The Building Program of Herod the Great*, 270–77.

Jericho, it is certainly possible that they did, even if archaeology has yet to yield concrete proof.[27]

If we broaden our scope to include not just freestanding three-dimensional statues but other types of figurative representations, several other exceptions are extant in the archaeological record. Excavations in the residential district of the Upper City of Jerusalem (present-day Jewish Quarter) have uncovered fragments of a fresco with images of birds, a bronze animal paw that functioned as a table-leg fitting, a tabletop with a fish carved in relief, and a bone gaming disk embossed with a human hand.[28] Three Roman period gemstones with figurative engravings were also found in the vicinity: a banded agate gemstone depicting the god Hermes/Mercury; a glass paste gemstone depicting a goddess; and a brown carnelian gemstone depicting a scorpion.[29] These are comparable to several other figurative gemstones found elsewhere in Jerusalem.[30]

Another example of figurative art from a slightly earlier (Hasmonean) period can be found in Jason's tomb in western Jerusalem, which includes graffiti representations of a stag and multiple human figures aboard a ship.[31] Similarly, the fresco on the plastered walls of the main chamber in the Goliath tomb in Jericho, although adorned mostly with floral motifs—vines, grapes, and leaves—also in-

---

27. A water basin with figurative sculpture was recently found in the lower bath complex of the Herodium, which may suggest that other sculpted items, perhaps even three-dimensional freestanding statues, might have been erected in similar locations.

28. Avigad, *The Herodian Quarter*, 45–46, 65; Fine, *Art and Judaism*, 77. In this vein, Mark Chancey also notes a few locations in Galilee that included figural representations, such as a mosaic from a house in Magdala depicting a boat and a fish (*Greco-Roman Culture and the Galilee of Jesus* [Cambridge: Cambridge University Press, 2005], 197).

29. Malka Hershkovitz, "Gemstones," in *Jewish Quarter Excavations in the Old City of Jerusalem: The Finds from Areas A, W, and X-2 Final Report* (ed. Hillel Geva; 3 vols.; Jerusalem: Israel Exploration Society, Institute of Archaeology, Hebrew University of Jerusalem, 2003), 2:296–301. In Hershkovitz's estimation, these stones, which likely came from individual rings of Jews living in the Upper City, suggest that some Jews were not properly observing the second commandment. More specifically, she claims that "at the end of the Second Temple period, the Jewish prohibition of graven images was maintained in the public sphere, while private individuals utilized seals with figurative imagery" (300). Meir Ben-Dov similarly appeals to a public/private distinction to explain such exceptions: "The stringent observance of the [second] commandment . . . , so conspicuous in the monumental buildings on the Temple Mount, evidently did not extend to private homes; Jerusalemites permitted themselves the vice of adorning their dwellings with scenes from the animal kingdom" (*In the Shadow of the Temple: The Discovery of Ancient Jerusalem* [trans. Ina Friedman; Jerusalem: Keter, 1985], 150).

30. For example, a translucent dark red glass gemstone with a Tyche bust and cornucopia set into an iron finger ring was found in a first-century C.E. tomb on Mount Scopus. Another, including a representation of the bust of a youth (perhaps Apollo), was found in a burial cave nearby; see Hershkovitz, "Gemstones," 2:297.

31. L. Y. Rahmani, "Jason's Tomb," *IEJ* 17 (1967): 70–72; Andrea M. Berlin, "Power and Its Afterlife: Tombs in Hellenistic Palestine," *NEA* 65 (2002): 142–43.

cludes the representation of birds perched on branches.[32] Several finds from the Cave of Letters in the Judean desert may likewise attest to the presence of figurative art in Second Temple Judea, especially the patera with a mythological scene (Thetis riding a sea centaur) in relief and a seal impression of Heracles killing a lion.[33]

Numismatic evidence likewise attests to the existence of figurative representation in Jerusalem.[34] Occasionally Herodian period coins included figurative images. For example, Herod the Great minted coins featuring an eagle on the reverse and a cornucopia and inscription (ΒΑΣΙΛ ΗΡΩΔ) on the obverse.[35] Both Philip and Agrippa I used anthropomorphic and theriomorphic iconography on their coins, though Agrippa's third series minted within Jerusalem in 41/42 C.E. is a noteworthy exception that may suggest a more cautious approach in the Judean capital.[36] Nevertheless, the ubiquitous Tyrian shekel, which included the head of Heracles-Melqart on the obverse and an eagle on the reverse, demonstrates that figurative coins were not uncommon in Jerusalem during the first century. This coin, because of the annual half-shekel tax that was required of all adult Jewish males,[37] became the main currency for the temple's banking operations. According to Ya'akov Meshorer, the Tyrian shekel was apparently minted in Tyre only up to 19/18 B.C.E., after which the shekels were struck in Jerusalem until the onset of the revolt against Rome in 66 C.E.[38] Although the symbols on these later Jerusalemite shekels are noticeably more crude,[39] it is nevertheless striking that there was no apparent attempt to purge the iconography of its figurative and even pagan elements, at least until the Judean rebels began minting the "shekel of Israel" during the revolt.[40]

32. Rachel Hachlili, *Jewish Ornamented Ossuaries of the Late Second Temple Period* (Haifa, Israel: Reuben and Edith Hecht Museum, University of Haifa, 1988), 12–13.

33. Yigael Yadin, *The Finds from the Bar Kokhba Period in the Cave of Letters* (2 vols.; Jerusalem: Israel Exploration Society, 1963), 1: pl. 17 (patera); fig. 44 (seal).

34. In general, see Martin Goodman, "Coinage and Identity: The Jewish Evidence," in *Coinage and Identity in the Roman Provinces* (ed. Christopher Howgego, Volker Heuchert, and Andrew Burnett; Oxford: Oxford University Press, 2005), 163–66.

35. Ya'akov Meshorer, *A Treasury of Jewish Coins from the Persian Period to Bar Kokhba* (Jerusalem: Yad Ben-Zvi Press, 2001), 67–68.

36. Ibid., 96–98.

37. See Exod 3:13–15; Josephus, *A.J.* 3.194; 7.318; 9.161; 18.312.

38. Meshorer, *Treasury of Jewish Coins*, 73–78.

39. There is no basis, however, for Meshorer's claim that this "demonstrative crudity" from the Jerusalem mint was "an expression of contempt for the Tyrian designs" (Ibid., 77).

40. Paul Corby Finney's study of the Tiberian silver denarius in Mark includes the unwarranted claim that *all* Jews, based on a putative strict "halakic demand for aniconism," would have found it offensive to even look at a coin with a figurative image: "the fact still stands that gazing at a Roman denarius would have raised certain problems for all Jews, but especially for those who lived on ancestral Palestinian lands that had been annexed by Gentile outsiders" ("The Rabbi and the Coin Portrait [Mark 12:15b, 16]: Rigorism Manqué," *JBL* 112 [1993]: 634). According to Finney's argument, the Marcan episode, which ignores the question of idolatrous images, indicates that aniconism was "a quintessentially Jew-

We should be cautious, however, not to read too much into the exceptions detailed above, as if the few remaining fragments of figurative remains were the tip of a much larger iceberg, a glimpse of what might still lie beneath the sands of time. In the first place, the precise provenance—whether Jewish or non-Jewish—of many of these finds is ambiguous at best. For example, if Yigael Yadin is correct that the patera from the Cave of Letters bears traces of iconoclasm, specifically that the faces were intentionally rubbed out, then it is possible that Jewish rebels stole these artifacts from a Roman military encampment and subsequently rendered them usable through defacement.[41] Likewise, given the diverse ethnic population inhabiting first-century Jerusalem, the few scattered gemstones found within the city limits could plausibly have belonged to non-Jews. Moreover, even granting a Jewish provenance for the exceptions detailed above, their scarcity is nevertheless a striking feature that may actually support the claim that Jews in Judea by and large avoided figurative art, and especially statues, during this period. At best, these exceptions can only modestly qualify some of the sweeping claims one finds in scholarship that Jews during this period uniformly rejected all forms of figurative art. As such, even taking into account the limited scope of excavations to date, the accidents of survival inherent in the archaeological record, and the few exceptions noted above, the lack of sculptural finds in Second Temple Jerusalem still stands in stark contrast with other urban landscapes in the Greco-Roman Mediterranean.

Moreover, this deficiency in material remains comports with the testimony from a broad range of literary sources. Josephus is of course important in this regard and will be explored in more detail in subsequent chapters. Nevertheless we may briefly note here that statuary is conspicuously absent in his numerous descriptions of Jerusalem's urban landscape, with the exception of the Herod's golden eagle in the temple complex. Josephus also mentions Roman trophies in the Jerusalem theater that were wrongly thought to be statues, the temporary "invasion" of Pilate's military standards, which included some kind of sculpted bust of the emperor, and the near erection of a statue of the emperor Gaius Caligula.[42] As with the eagle episode, Josephus reports that each of these incidents elicited a negative reaction on the part of some residents in the city. The summary in *B.J.* of Petronius' attempt to erect a statue of Caligula in Jerusalem, although playing an integral role in Josephus' use of sacred space as a literary strategy (see chapter 4), captures the uniqueness of Jerusalem (and Judea) vis-à-vis the rest of the Roman world: apart

---

ish subject" and not of particular concern for early Christianity (644). This interpretation, however, wrongly assumes a fundamental distinction between an aniconic Judaism on the one hand and a more openly iconic Christianity on the other, a dubious assumption for any period in history, but particularly for the last half of the first century C.E., when the so-called parting of the ways was at best only in its infancy.

41. This is indeed the interpretation of Yadin, who sees in the traces of iconoclasm an indication that Roman military cult objects were desecrated according to the halakhic guidelines later laid down in the Mishnah (Yadin, *Cave of Letters*, 1:44–45).

42. Theater trophies: *A.J.* 15.267–282; Pilate's standards: *B.J.* 2.169–174; *A.J.* 18.55–59 (see also the account of Vitellius and his two legions, who intentionally avoided Judea because of their standards; *A.J.* 18.120–122); Caligula's statue: *B.J.* 2.184–203; *A.J.* 18.256–309.

from the Jews, "all the subjected nations (πάντων γὰρ τῶν ὑποτεταγμένων ἐθνῶν) had erected the images of Caesar in their cities along with the other gods" (*B.J.* 2.194).

Philo of Alexandria similarly underscores the uniqueness of Jerusalem as a city without statues.[43] Embedded in his account of the Caligula crisis is Agrippa's letter to the emperor, which attempts—apparently with some success—to dissuade Caligula from erecting his statue in the temple. Agrippa's description of the temple and city as presented in Philo is worth quoting in full:

> γεγέννημαι μέν ὡς οἶδας Ἰουδαῖος· ἔστι δέ μοι Ἱεροσόλυμα πατρίς ἐν ᾗ ὁ τοῦ ὑψίστου θεοῦ νεὼς ἅγιος ἵδρυται πάππων δὲ καὶ προγόνων βασιλέων ἔλαχον ὧν οἱ πλείους ἐλέγοντο ἀρχιερεῖς, τὴν βασιλείαν τῆς ἱερωσύνης ἐν δευτέρᾳ τάξει τιθέμενοι καὶ νομίζοντες ὅσῳ θεὸς ἀνθρώπων διαφέρει κατὰ τὸ κρεῖττον τοσούτῳ καὶ βασιλείας ἀρχιερωσύνην.... ἔθνει δὴ τοιούτῳ προσκεκληρωμένος καὶ πατρίδι καὶ ἱερῷ δέομαι ὑπὲρ ἁπάντων.... τοῦτο Γάιε δέσποτα, τὸ ἱερὸν χειρόκμητον οὐδεμίαν ἐξ ἀρχῆς μορφὴν παρεδέξατο διὰ τὸ ἕδος τοῦ ἀληθοῦς εἶναι θεοῦ γραφέων μὲν γὰρ καὶ πλαστῶν ἔργα μιμήματα τῶν αἰσθητῶν θεῶν εἰσιν τὸν δὲ ἀόρατον εἰκονογραφεῖν ἢ διαπλάττειν οὐχ ὅσιον ἐνομίσθη τοῖς ἡμετέροις προγόνοις.
>
> I [Agrippa] am, as you know, a Jew, and Jerusalem is my ancestral city, in which the holy temple of the Most High God is situated. Now it also happens that I have kings for my grandparents and ancestors, most of whom were called high priests. They considered their kingship to be second in importance to that of the priestly office, supposing that, just as God is superior to men, so also the high priesthood is superior to kingship.... Therefore, being joined with such a nation, homeland, and temple, I implore you on behalf of all of them [i.e., the Jews].... Oh Lord Gaius, from the beginning this temple has never admitted any form made by human hands, because it is the dwelling place of the true God. For the works of painters and sculptors are imitations of gods perceived by the senses; but to paint or sculpt the invisible was not considered pious by our ancestors. (*Legat.* 278–279, 290)

Leaving aside questions related to the authenticity of the letter—overall Philo does seem to embellish Agrippa's role as savior of the Jews—and the accuracy of the claim that no μορφή "made by human hands" has ever been erected in the temple complex,[44] Philo's testimony supports the general impression drawn from Josephus and archaeology, namely that statues were by and large not to be found in the urban landscape of first-century Jerusalem.

A similar image of Jerusalem likewise emerges from non-Jewish sources. Speaking of the temple in Jerusalem, Livy remarks in the 102nd book of his *Ab urbe condita*: "They do not state to which deity pertains the temple at Jerusalem, nor is any image found there, since they do not think the God partakes of any

---

43. As far as we know, Philo visited Jerusalem at least once in his lifetime, when he went to offer sacrifices and pray in the temple (Philo, *Prov.* 2.64).

44. Obviously Herod's eagle belies this claim.

figure."[45] In even more explicit terms, Tacitus broadens the scope to include by implication the entire city of Jerusalem: "They set up no statues (*simulacra*) in their cities, still less in their temples; this flattery is not paid their kings, nor this honour given to the Caesars" (*Hist.* 5.5.4 [Moore, LCL]). Admittedly we have no evidence that Tacitus ever visited Jerusalem, and in another context the author seemingly contradicts himself on the question of images in Jerusalem, claiming the Jews had erected a statue of an ass in the temple (*Hist.* 5.4.1–2).[46] Moreover, his propensity to cast the "superstition" of the Jews in the worst possible light should give pause to any straightforward reading of his portrayal of the Jews and Judea.[47] Nevertheless, given the multiple sources that attest to this phenomenon, there is no reason to doubt Tacitus' remarks in this instance. Similarly, although limiting his remarks to divine statuary, Cassius Dio comments that no statue of the Jewish God had ever been erected in Jerusalem (*Hist. rom.* 37.17.2).

In sum, although our hypothetical visitor to Jerusalem might otherwise feel at home with his or her surroundings, the almost complete lack of public or private sculpture unequivocally marked this urban landscape as a peculiarity in the Greco-Roman Mediterranean. The Jerusalem that Josephus experienced prior to his relocation to Rome was by and large a statueless Jerusalem. Even if Josephus exaggerates Jewish animosity toward figurative images in his major compositions, this curious "silence" in the archaeological record, confirmed by a broad range of literary sources, cannot and should not be ignored. Why then the absence of sculpture in first-century Jerusalem?

---

45. Preserved in the *Scholia in Lucanum* 2.593; citation from Stern, *Greek and Latin Authors*, 1:330.

46. This occurs in his discussion of the origins of the Jews, wherein Tacitus laments their (from his perspective) despicable cultic practices, the *novos ritus* introduced by Moses which are said to be "opposed to those of all other religions" (Moore, LCL). As evidence, Tacitus marshals the well-known Greco-Roman caricature of the Jews as abominable ass-worshipers, asserting quite explicitly that they kept in their temple "a statue of that creature" (*effigiem animalis*). Tertullian uses this apparent contradiction to demonstrate that Tacitus the historian is nothing but a liar (*Apol.* 16.1–4). In fairness to Tacitus, Menahem Stern does mention several factors that may lessen what might otherwise appear to be a careless contradiction. In the first place, Tacitus' reference to the ass-statue may not reflect his own opinion but the opinion of the many authors (*plurimi auctores*) who proposed a particular theory of Jewish origins (see Tacitus, *Hist.* 5.3.1). Second, the ass-statue, designated in Latin as the *effigies animalis*, could refer in Tacitus' mind not to a formal cult statue but to a votive offering to the aniconic God; see Stern, *Greek and Latin Authors*, 2:37. On Tacitus' use of sources, the basic work remains Edmund Groag, "Zur Kritik von Tacitus' Quellen in den Historien," *Jahrbücher für classische Philologie* Suppl. XXIII (1897): 709–99.

47. Indeed, René Bloch has recently suggested that Tacitus' reference to an empty temple in *Hist.* 5.9.1 is a subtle insult insofar as it mirrors his earlier depiction of the Dead Sea as a "dead realm": "The realm of the dead (*Totenreich*) and the Jewish cult correspond. The 'geography' of the Temple is thus described in the same fashion as that of the parched lands in the vicinity of the Dead Sea" (*Antike Vorstellungen vom Judentum: Der Judenexkurs des Tacitus im Rahmen der griechisch-römischen Ethnographie* [Stuttgart: Franz Steiner Verlag, 2002], 104–5).

Exegetical Stridency as Religio-Cultural Opposition

For the most part, scholars appeal to a rigid interpretive approach to the prohibition against images in the Jewish Bible, the so-called second commandment, to explain the absence of sculpture in Second Temple Jerusalem (Exod 20:2–6; Deut 5:6–10).[48] More often than not, this strict enforcement of the biblical prohibition is viewed as a kind of cultural or religious fortification for Jerusalem, not unlike Nikos Kazantzakis' evocative image of Jerusalem as a city "moated on every side by the commandments of Jehovah."[49] Rachel Hachlili's summary of Jewish art during the Second Temple period is in this sense representative of a wide swath of scholarship:

> Jewish art of the Second Temple period (second century B.C.E.–first century C.E.) is aniconic and non-symbolic. Most of the motifs used are taken from the environment. They consist of plant and geometric motifs expressing growth and productivity and are similar to patterns used in Graeco-Roman pagan art. *In the struggle against paganism*, Judaism at that time offered staunch resistance, especially by insisting on obedience to the "no graven image" commandment and by guarding against its violators. Hence the strict adherence to a non-figurative art form.[50]

According to Hachlili, the preponderance of nonfigurative (floral and geometric) material remains, coupled with the almost complete lack of any figurative art in the archaeological record—not just statues, but wall paintings, coins, furniture, and so on—is directly linked to a particularly "strict" interpretation of the Mosaic prohibition against images, whereby the proscription is taken to encompass *all* forms of figurative art. Moreover, this stridency against figurative art is seen as part of a larger war against "paganism," with the second commandment functioning as the primary weapon of "staunch resistance" on the battlefront. This framework of antithesis/struggle is clearly articulated in Hachlili's historical sketch of "indisputable" facts on the following page:

> During the Second Temple period the Jews rejected the representation of figurative images in their art and used only aniconic, non-figurative motifs and patterns, which reflected their *struggle against both paganism and Christianity*. However, from the third century until the seventh century, Jews employed figurative art, images and symbols. They did so with rabbinical tolerance or even approval.[51]

In other words, for Hachlili the absence of figural remains during the Second Temple period bespeaks an ongoing *religious* warfare between "Judaism" on the one

---

48. See chapter 3 for a discussion of this text and its interpretation during the Greco-Roman period.

49. Nikos Kazantzakis, *The Last Temptation of Christ* (trans. P. A. Bien; New York: Simon & Schuster Inc., 1960), 7.

50. Hachlili, *Ancient Jewish Art and Archaeology in the Land of Israel*, 1 (emphasis mine).

51. Ibid., 2 (emphasis mine).

side of the equation and "Christianity" and "paganism" on the other side. Presumably, though this is not stated explicitly, this religious conflict subsided in subsequent centuries, since Hachlili allows for a measure of "rabbinical tolerance" from the third though seventh centuries.

In his assessment of the archaeological record from the late Hellenistic and early Roman periods, Nahman Avigad similarly views a strident application of the second commandment as evidence of Judaism's struggle against an "other," although in this instance the battle is both cultural and religious. According to Avigad:

> The situation in the Hasmonean and Herodian periods was entirely different. Then, triumphant Hellenism began its assault on Judaism by *attempting to force its culture and religion* on the Jews. The Jews, in turn, felt the deepest obligation *to defend themselves against Hellenism*. Naturally, at a time when foreign rulers were bent on introducing statues of gods or themselves into the Temple and forcing Jews into idolatry, the use of any image whatsoever was stringently prohibited. Thus, during this period, the enforcement of the Torah injunctions was *infinitely stricter* than at any other time in Jewish history.[52]

Whereas the opponent in Hachlili's interpretation is strictly religious, Avigad appeals to the category of Hellenism—here construed as a clearly defined religio-cultural force threatening "Judaism" during the Hellenistic and early Roman periods—against which Jews struggle armed with an "infinitely stricter" interpretation of the second commandment. This battle against Hellenism, which according to Avigad was rooted in an "uncompromising orthodoxy," is exemplified in the iconoclastic destruction of Herod's eagle in the temple and Herod the Tetrarch's palace, which was adorned "with figures prohibited by the Torah."[53]

The framework of aniconism as religio-cultural opposition evident in both Hachlili and Avigad, though applied to a narrowly defined chronological moment (Second Temple period), emerges in part from a regnant assumption of an interminable struggle between Jews and art, that is, the supposition that Jews are fundamentally iconophobic. The polarization of "image" and "Jew" has long dominated the intellectual landscape, particularly in the last three centuries.[54] Georg Hegel's (1770–1831) claim that Jews despise (*verachten*) the image was based in part on the belief that Judaism throughout its history had seemingly "stepped out of nature itself," that is, that Jews embodied a fundamental antithesis to the spirit of the Greeks (and Jesus). [55] If the Greek nation, as evidenced by its penchant for producing beautiful works of art, represented a colossal step forward in the

52. Nahman Avigad, *Beth She'arim* (3 vols.; New Brunswick, N.J.: Rutgers University Press, 1976), 3:277–78 (emphasis mine).

53. Ibid., 3:278.

54. Several recent publications have documented this phenomenon, most notably Bland, *The Artless Jew*; Olin, *The Nation without Art*; Fine, *Art and Judaism*, 5–21.

55. Georg W. F. Hegel, "Der Geist des Christentums und sein Schicksal," in *Hegels theologische jugendschriften nach den handschriften der Kgl. Bibliothek in Berlin* (ed. Herman Nohl; Tübingen: Mohr Siebeck, 1907), 250–60. According to Hegel, Judaism's "otherness,"

development of the human spirit, an evolutionary process that would reach its apogee in German national art,[56] then an artless Judaism must be in some sense "frozen in time," in the words of Mark Lilla, "an anachronistic relic of the infancy of the human race."[57] In a similar vein, Solomon Formstecher (1808–89), in his *Die Religion des Geistes*, published only a decade after Hegel's death, asserted that the long-standing conflict (*Kampf*) between Judaism and Paganism, which he viewed as "hostile opponents,"[58] required Judaism to consider "the plastic arts as its fierce enemy."[59] And again, a few pages later, Formstecher unequivocally remarks: "Judaism is an enemy of the creative arts."[60]

If Jewish animosity toward visual representation was symptomatic of a much deeper Hebraic-Hellenic hostility, as is frequently thought,[61] then it stands to reason that the presence or absence of figurative remains in antiquity serves in some sense as a barometer for this wider struggle against an external enemy (however defined). As this hostility ostensibly increased during the Second Temple period, particularly after the crisis of Antiochus IV Epiphanes in 167 b.c.e., Jews became more aggressively defensive, resulting in a border patrol that included a more rigorous interpretation of the second commandment. In other words, a heightened "pagan" threat demanded higher and stronger halakhic walls, so to speak, and to meet this demand the second commandment was transformed from a prohibition against idol worship into a prohibition against any type of figurative art.

Conversely, the flourishing of figurative remains after the destruction of the temple perhaps suggested a weakening of the "pagan" threat. Indeed, this is precisely what Ephraim Urbach argues in his discussion of the postdestruction era when he claims that within Judaism during the so-called rabbinic period "the idolatrous impulse was virtually dead, while even in the surrounding gentile world its influence had been greatly weakened."[62] Stated differently, the threat of the "other" was rapidly waning, the potential for its influence on Judaism weakening, and as

---

its lack of this Greek spirit, is particularly manifested in a supposed intrinsic inability to recognize, appreciate, and enjoy beauty (250).

56. According to Olin, art historian Josef Strzygowski (1862–1941) followed Hegel by contrasting "two races"—the Greeks/Romans and the Semites—and identifying German nationalist art as the ultimate flowering of the race of the Greeks (see Olin, *The Nation without Art*, 18–23).

57. Mark Lilla, *The Stillborn God: Religion, Politics, and the Modern West* (New York: Alfred A. Knopf, 2007), 190. This quote is taken from Lilla's assessment of Hegel's view of the Jews.

58. Solomon Formstecher, *Die Religion des Geistes: Eine wissenschaftliche Darstellung des Judenthums nach seinem Charakter, Entwicklungsgange und Berufe in der Menschheit* (Frankfurt am Main: J. C. Hermann, 1841), 69.

59. Ibid., 68.

60. Ibid., 71.

61. Bland's discussion of scholarship on Jewish art underscores the role of this Hellenism-Hebraism dichotomy (*The Artless Jew*, 21–26).

62. E. E. Urbach, "The Rabbinical Laws on Idolatry in the Second and Third Centuries in the Light of Archaeological and Historical Facts," *IEJ* 9 (1959): 236. The idea that the Jewish inclination toward idolatry was dead by this period was first expressed in 1888 by Solomon

a result there was a greater inclination on the part of the rabbis toward halakhic leniency with regard to the second commandment, which then explains the proliferation of figurative art in late antique synagogue remains.

In sum, in the interpretive approach of Hachlili, Avigad, and Urbach, the archaeological record more or less mirrors Jewish exegetical practice as part of a larger cultural and religious struggle. On the one hand, the scarcity of figurative art prior to the destruction of the temple is directly linked to a rather *strict* interpretive stance—the second commandment prohibits figurative art in toto. On the other hand, the emergence of a rich and extensive body of figurative remains in the centuries that followed suggests a trend toward exegetical *leniency*, that is, toward a less restrictive stance toward the Mosaic proscription. Lee I. Levine has recently, and succinctly, articulated a nuanced form of this diachronic model, identifying

> three major shifts in Jewish attitudes toward figural art throughout antiquity: (1) the transition from the relative openness to such art in the biblical and post-biblical periods to the extreme and sharply restrictive policy under the Hasmoneans; (2) the return to figural images in the post-70 era that engendered a wide range of practices; and (3) a swing of the pendulum toward aniconism some time in the late sixth or during the seventh century C.E.[63]

Moreover, with respect to this supposed strict aniconism of the Second Temple period, a rigid exegetical approach is thought to have characterized *all* Jews, or at least the vast majority of Jews. That is to say, the prohibition against all figurative art is construed to be in some sense an official dogma of "normative" or "mainstream Judaism" during the period in question. This is evident particularly in Hachlili's sweeping assertions: "*Judaism* at the time offered staunch resistance . . ." and "During the Second Temple period *the Jews* rejected the representation of figurative images. . . ."[64] Indeed, she continues this unqualified assessment in her study of Jewish art in the Diaspora, where Judaism *both* in the Diaspora *and* Palestine is viewed as a "purely aniconic" religion.[65]

Schechter, when he claimed that this inclination had been "suppressed by the sufferings of the captivity in Babylon" ("The Dogmas of Judaism," *JQR* 1 [1888]: 54).

63. Levine, "Figural Art," 9.

64. Hachlili, *Ancient Jewish Art and Archaeology in the Land of Israel*, 1–2 (emphasis mine).

65. Rachel Hachlili, *Ancient Jewish Art and Archaeology in the Diaspora* (Leiden: Brill, 1998), 237. Such an unqualified claim is not surprising, given Hachlili's methodological assumptions spelled out in the opening chapter of this volume, specifically her notion that Judaism and Hellenism were antithetical and that there existed a strong halakhic link between Diaspora Judaism and Palestinian Judaism. She contends that although Jews living in the Diaspora were in some sense "part of Hellenistic society," they nevertheless "remained loyal to the Torah and practiced Jewish law. No literary sources, inscriptions or archaeological data have ever indicated tendencies of assimilation or adoption of the Greek culture" (11). In other words, loyalty to Torah translates into the absence of Greek culture. According to Hachlili, Diaspora Jews were able to maintain this cultural and religious purity only because they maintained a strong connection with Judea, which functioned as a clear authoritative center for halakah. She notes that the *apostoli* (envoys sent by the *nasi*) were "a fixed institu-

Complicating the Notion of a Purely Aniconic Religion

It is probably undeniable that the second commandment, or more broadly religious ideology, played some kind of role in shaping Jewish responses to Greco-Roman images and may even explain in part the absence of figural remains in Second Temple Jerusalem. Nevertheless, the image of a "purely aniconic" religion that emerges in the aforementioned studies, based on the predominantly unqualified link between extant material culture and exegetical/religious practice, is fundamentally flawed both in its tendency to overstate the role of exegetical stridency—a topic I will explore more fully in the next chapter—and, more important for the present discussion, in its underlying model of cultural interaction. Specifically, the idea of Jewish aniconism as an expression of hostility toward a cultural or religious Other—whether conceived as Hellenism, Paganism, or even Christianity—fails to account for the polychromatic palette of ancient Mediterranean cultures, what Goodman felicitously terms the "kaleidoscope of customs" within the Roman world,[66] and overlooks the integral and participatory place of Jews within this milieu.

Beyond the Judaism/Hellenism Divide

The polarization of Judaism and Hellenism, or Hebraism and Hellenism, has had a long and vibrant life in Western thought.[67] Indeed, the typical story of Jews in antiquity is one of dichotomies, of opposition and antagonism. This should not surprise us. Every good story needs conflict, a protagonist struggling against an irrepressible enemy, and it is certainly not difficult to find such moments of contention in the record of ancient Jews: the Seleucid king Antiochus IV Epiphanes attempting to annihilate the way of the Judeans, only to meet resistance at the hands of the heroic Hasmonean family, especially guided by the valiant leadership of Judas Maccabeus (the "Hammer"—if ever a nickname embodies conflict, this is it!); Pompey Magnus likewise striking at the heart of the Jews in 63 B.C.E. by desecrating their sacred center, the temple in Jerusalem; and, of course, the apex of the Jewish struggle against the Other, the revolt against Rome and subsequent destruction of the temple, whose smoldering ashes coupled with the tragic mass suicide atop the fortress of Masada have become enduring symbols of the Jewish struggle for freedom from oppression. In fact, this narrative of struggle and opposition would become the very lifeblood of the Zionist movement that emerged in

---

tion" during the Second Temple period and functioned "to supervise the communities, to control administration, to inspect the implementation of the *halacha*, and to levy the taxes due to the *Nasi* office" (12).

66. Goodman, *Rome and Jerusalem*, 147.

67. The Hebraism-Hellenism dichotomy from antiquity to modernity is the central focus of a fascinating collection of essays in volume 19 (1998) of the journal *Poetics Today*. In the introductory essay, David Stern succinctly remarks: "*Hellenism* and *Hebraism*—Athens and Jerusalem, the Greek and the Jew—are surely the most famous terms commonly invoked to summon up the distinct, often seemingly irreconcilable strands that make up the Western tradition" ("Introduction," *PT* 19 [1998]: 1 [emphasis in original]).

the late nineteenth and early twentieth centuries, so much so that a young Martin Buber had hoped to awaken within his generation "a Masada of the spirit" that would ultimately energize a people in its pursuit of land and independence.[68]

Recent scholarship, however, has called into question this model of conflict as well as the underlying notion of culture that feeds it.[69] In the first place, the literary sources tend to exaggerate opposition in part because of its crucial role in narrative discourse; stories thrive on conflict and hostility, clearly delineated protagonists and antagonists, so a measure of skepticism is warranted when encountering the static polarities that invariably emerge from such literary portrayals.[70] Of course, this is not to deny the existence of cultural conflict in antiquity. A superficial reading of Menahem Stern's *Greek and Latin Authors on Jews and Judaism* underscores the cultural friction that often arose over perceived Jewish peculiarities, that is, over practices that many Greeks and Romans considered odd or barbaric. Many Jews were likewise more than willing to dish out their share of cultural scorn, prominently displayed in the numerous idol polemics composed during the period in question.[71] Nevertheless, as will be argued below, even the seemingly lethal rhetorical barbs launched from within such idol polemics of the Jews should *not*

---

68. Gilga G. Schmidt, ed., *The First Buber: Youthful Zionist Writings of Martin Buber* (Syracuse, N.Y.: Syracuse University Press, 1999), 185. This notion of opposition, an us-against-the-world mentality, has even left its mark on Jewish comedy, as is evident in Mel Brooks' quip that for Jews "humor is just another defense against the universe" (Sally Ann Berk and Maria Carluccio, *The Big Little Book of Jewish Wit and Wisdom* [New York: Black Dog & Leventhal, 2000], 189).

69. Martin Hengel's influential *Judentum und Hellenismus*, followed by several subsequent publications that collectively called into question the *communis opinio* of a distinction between "Palestinian Judaism" (unmarked by the influence of Hellenism) and "Hellenistic Judaism," were pivotal in moving the discussion beyond the prevailing hermetically sealed polarities (*Judentum und Hellenismus* [Tübingen: Max Niemeyer Verlag, 1969]); idem, *Jews, Greeks, and Barbarians* (Philadelphia: Fortress Press, 1980); idem, *The "Hellenization" of Judaea in the First Century after Christ* (Eugene, Oreg.: Wipf and Stock, 1989). See also the recently published collection of essays building on Hengel's provocative work, which includes an essay by Hengel revisiting the topic (John J. Collins and Gregory E. Sterling, eds., *Hellenism in the Land of Israel* [Notre Dame, Ind.: University of Notre Dame Press, 2001]). More recently, several have argued that even Hengel's work, while correctly moving the discussion beyond the model of conflict rooted in a putative Jewish *resistance* to Hellenism, is nevertheless flawed in its insistence that Judaism and Hellenism are somehow definable as distinct entities, insofar as Judaism in Hengel's model is viewed as a kind of receptacle for the influence of Hellenism. On the critique of the influence model, see especially the discussion and literature cited in Michael L. Satlow, "Beyond Influence: Explaining Similarity and Difference among Jews in Antiquity," in *Jewish Literatures and Cultures: Context and Intertext* (ed. Anita Norich and Yaron Z. Eliav; Providence, R.I.: Brown Judaic Studies, 2008), 37–53.

70. Eliav, "Viewing the Sculptural Environment," 412.

71. For example, such notable texts as the Epistle of Jeremiah, Wisdom of Solomon, additions to Daniel, portions of *Jubilees*, the *Sibylline Oracles*, and the *Apocalypse of Abraham*, *inter alia*.

be viewed as indications of their cultural "Otherness," characteristics that mark Jews as outsiders to Greco-Roman culture.

In one sense, then, Jews were not different from any other *ethnos* living in the Roman Mediterranean basin—Egyptians, Greeks, Celts, Idumeans, Nabateans, Syrians, and so on[72]—insofar as they, like all Mediterranean *ethnē*, embodied a rich and complex convergence of customs that were "not strictly bounded and differentiated from each other but instead shade one into the other."[73] The Greco-Roman milieu can thus aptly be described, in the words of Lee Levine, as a "veritable potpourri of cultural forces, a marketplace of ideas and fashions from which one could choose. In this light, therefore, Hellenization is not merely the impact of Greek culture on a non-Greek world, but rather the interplay of a wide range of cultural forces on an *oikumene*."[74] Building on this perspective, though going a step further than Levine, Michael Satlow has recently called for an end to the language of "conflict" and "influence" or "borrowing" as a means of describing cultural interaction insofar as this terminology reifies "abstract, second-order" categories such as Hellenism and Judaism.[75] Hellenism was not a clearly defined, tangible, monolithic culture that Judaism could either *accept* or *reject*, as if Judaism were a "cultural vacuum" that could potentially be filled;[76] rather, there were many Hellenisms, so to speak, numerous and variegated *regional* expressions of hybrid

72. So Martin Goodman: "[T]he oddities of the Jews in the Graeco-Roman world were no greater than that of the many other distinctive ethnic groups" ("Jews, Greeks, and Romans," in *Jews in a Graeco-Roman World* [ed. Martin Goodman; Oxford: Clarendon Press, 1998], 4).

73. Daniel Boyarin, *Border Lines: The Partition of Judaeo-Christianity* (Philadelphia: University of Pennsylvania, 2004), 18. Moreover, even ethnic identity itself was inherently fluid in antiquity; see especially Jonathan M. Hall, *Ethnic Identity in Greek Antiquity* (Cambridge: Cambridge University Press, 1997); Shaye Cohen, *The Beginnings of Jewishness: Boundaries, Varieties, Uncertainties* (Berkeley: University of California Press, 1999); Irad Malkin, ed., *Ancient Perceptions of Greek Ethnicity* (Cambridge: Harvard University Press, 2001); Jonathan M. Hall, *Hellenicity: Between Ethnicity and Culture* (Chicago: University of Chicago Press, 2002); McClister, "Ethnicity and Jewish Identity in Josephus."

74. Levine, *Judaism and Hellenism*, 19.

75. Satlow, "Beyond Influence," 43. See also the discussion in Steve Mason, "Jews, Judaeans, Judaizing, Judaism: Problems of Categorization in Ancient History," *JSJ* 38 (2007): 457–512. Carol Dougherty and Leslie Kurke put forward a similar critique of models of cultural interaction in classical studies, arguing that the language of influence or borrowing obscures the inherent "complexity and messiness" of cultural contact ("Introduction: The Cultures within Greek Culture," in *The Cultures within Ancient Greek Culture: Contact, Conflict, Collaboration* [ed. Carol Dougherty and Leslie Kurke; Cambridge: Cambridge University Press, 2003], 4).

76. Contra the assumption of many scholars, as for example in Jonathan Goldstein, "Jewish Acceptance and Rejection of Hellenism," in *Aspects of Judaism in the Graeco-Roman Period* (vol. 2 of *Jewish and Christian Self-Definition*; ed. E. P. Sanders, A. L. Baumgarten, and Alan Mendelson; Philadelphia: SCM Press, 1981), 64–87, 318–26. Dougherty and Kurke use the phrase "cultural vacuum" to critique influence models in classical studies ("The Cultures within Greek Culture," 3).

cultures.[77] Similarly, the notion of Judaism as a bounded ideological movement obscures "the on-going messy negotiations that constitute culture."[78] Although the language of Judaism and Hellenism may still be useful as heuristic constructs in certain situations,[79] this should not obscure the fact that Jews were part and parcel of their Mediterranean milieu, that is, "that 'Judaism' is itself a species of Hellenism."[80]

Aesthetic Preference and Regional Variation

The inherent fluidity and complexity of ethnic identity and cultural interaction in the Mediterranean world has important methodological implications for the topic at hand.[81] Specifically, the attempt to move beyond intangible abstractions such as Judaism and Hellenism requires an approach that focuses more on local or regional expressions of culture.[82] From this perspective, the task is not so much to decipher *Judaism's* stance toward images, or the stridency or leniency of *Judaism's* interpretation of the second commandment, but how *Jews* in various geographical settings negotiated their sculptural and artistic milieu. Admittedly, such an approach may not necessarily yield radically different results, and in any case it is still not likely that we will find Jews in a particular locale erecting cult statues to

77. In his recently published essay on Syrian Hellenism, Maurice Sartre aptly remarks: "[T]here were many ways of being Greek, and each region where the Greek language and culture spread developed its own 'hybrid' culture" ("The Nature of Syrian Hellenism in the Late Roman and Early Byzantine Periods," in *The Sculptural Environment of the Roman Near East: Reflections on Culture, Ideology, and Power* [ed. Yaron Z. Eliav, Elise Friedland, and Sharon Herbert; Louvain: Peeters, 2008], 28). In a similar vein, Yaacov Shavit critiques J. G. Droysen's notion of *Verschmelzung*, noting specifically that "Droysen ignored the heterogeneous character of Hellenism in various Eastern lands, and the difference in character and content of the Hellenistic component from one syncretistic culture to another" (*Athens in Jerusalem: Classical Antiquity and Hellenism in the Making of the Modern Secular Jew* [London: Vallentine Mitchell, 1997], 283).

78. Satlow, "Beyond Influence," 43. Several have recently argued that Judaism as an ideological system emerged only in response to the establishment of Christianity as a distinct religion, that is, sometime in the fourth century C.E. For example, Daniel Boyarin remarks: "[W]hen Christianity separated religious belief and practice from *Romanitas*, cult from culture, Judaism as a religion came into the world as well" ("Semantic Differences; or, 'Judaism'/'Christianity'," in *The Ways That Never Parted: Jews and Christians in Late Antiquity and the Early Middle Ages* [ed. Adam H. Becker and Annette Yoshiko Reed; Minneapolis: Fortress Press, 2007], 72). See also the discussion in Mason, "Jews, Judaeans, Judaizing, Judaism," 460–80.

79. See for example the recent discussion in Gabriele Boccaccini, "Hellenistic Judaism: Myth or Reality?" in *Jewish Literatures and Cultures: Context and Intertext* (ed. Anita Norich and Yaron Z. Eliav; Providence, R.I.: Brown Judaic Studies, 2008), 55–76.

80. Boyarin, *Border Lines*, 247.

81. See also the useful methodological discussion in Jaś Elsner, "Archaeologies and Agendas: Reflections on Late Ancient Jewish Art and Early Christian Art," *JRS* 93 (2003): 114–28.

82. This is noted by Satlow, "Beyond Influence," 51–53.

yhwh. Nevertheless, a regional approach to the data—including both Jewish and non-Jewish *comparanda*—can potentially nuance our understanding of the complex relationship between Jews and Greco-Roman art.

For example, returning to the scant remains of figurative art in Second Temple Jerusalem, I noted above the prevailing tendency to see in this archaeological lacuna evidence for exegetical stridency, an indication that Jews embraced a more restrictive interpretation of the second commandment. Moreover, when juxtaposed with the preponderance of figurative art adorning the synagogue in Dura Europos from the third century c.e., scholars by and large appeal to an exegetical transmutation to explain this difference: after the destruction of the temple in 70 c.e. Judaism became more lenient toward Greco-Roman figurative art. But this is not the only possibility. It could be that the figurative remains of third-century Dura Europos are not the result of a diachronic exegetical change in Judaism but simply reflect a unique expression of local Jewish culture. Clearly the Jewish community of third-century Dura did not consider figurative art to be prohibited by the second commandment. Why could this not be true of first-century Jews living in Dura?

Admittedly we do not possess evidence for this particular Diaspora community from an earlier period to test this possibility, so it remains only a speculation. There is perhaps some indication, however, from other predestruction Diaspora settings that may suggest that the absence of figurative remains in Second Temple Jerusalem was a *Judean* phenomenon. The remains of an early synagogue (ca. second/first century b.c.e.) on the island of Delos, for example, include a number of lamps decorated with figurative motifs, which, according to Levine's assessment, may "reflect a different cultural and artistic norm from that of late Second Temple Judaea."[83]

An honorary inscription on a stele of Parian marble from Berenice (Cyrene), dating either to the late first century b.c.e. or sometime in the first century c.e.,[84] is perhaps even more enticing. The inscription includes a resolution on behalf of the Jewish πολίτευμα to honor Decimus Valerius Dionysius for his benefactions, which included plastering the floor and painting the walls of the ἀμφιθέατρον:[85]

22 Δέκμος Οὐαλέριος Γαΐου Διονύσιος
23 ἔ̣[δ]α̣[φ]ος ἐκονίασεν καὶ τὸ ἀμφι-
24 θέατρον καὶ ἐζωγράφησεν τοῖς

83. Lee I. Levine, *The Ancient Synagogue: The First Thousand Years* (New Haven: Yale University Press, 2000), 103. There is debate over the identification of this building as a synagogue, some of it revolving around the presence of this imagery, which includes pagan motifs. For a more detailed discussion of the various arguments for and against the synagogue identification, see L. Michael White, "The Delos Synagogue Revisited: Recent Fieldwork in the Graeco-Roman Diaspora," *HTR* 80 (1987): 133–60.

84. The inscription includes damaged-date letters that might specify 8–6 b.c.e., but G. Roux and J. Roux have proposed more broadly a date between 30 b.c.e. and 100 c.e. ("Un décret des Juifs de Bérénike," *REG* 62 [1949]: 289).

85. Gert Lüderitz, ed. *Corpus jüdischer Zeugnisse aus der Cyrenaika* (Wiesbaden, Germany: Ludwig Reichert, 1983), no. 70 (p. 149).

25 ἰδίοις δαπανήμασιν ἐπίδομα
26 τῶι πολίτευματι

22 Decimus Valerius Dionysios son of Gaius
23 plastered the floor and the amphi-
24 theater he also painted from
25 his own expenses, a contribution
26 to the *politeuma*.

The compound verb used for painting in line 24, ζωγραφέω, as is apparent from its constituent parts, normally signifies the painted representation of living beings, such as are found in abundance on the walls of the Dura synagogue, though it can also denote painting in general, without regard to specific subject matter.[86] Whether or not ἀμφιθέατρον refers to a general public building—a Roman amphitheater—used by all citizens of Berenice, or the communal building of the Jewish πολίτευμα has been much discussed.[87] Given that this is a communal inscription honoring benefactions bestowed upon the πολίτευμα (line 26), and that a second inscription likewise associates this πολίτευμα with an ἀμφιθέατρον,[88] it seems likely that the structure in question was a Jewish communal building, a synagogue. If indeed this was the case, then the Berenice inscription possibly indicates the use of figurative art within a Jewish context *during the Second Temple period*, calling into question the supposition that Judaism transmuted from an aniconic to an iconic religion across the 70 C.E. divide. Instead, it is much more likely that the presence or absence of figurative art was locally or regionally, and not necessarily chronologically, determined.

While the inscription from Berenice attests to the possible presence of flat figurative representation in a Jewish context during the Second Temple period, is there any evidence for a more amicable relationship with three-dimensional freestanding sculpture in certain Diaspora locations? There is some material and literary evidence associating third-century C.E. Diaspora Jewish communities with sculpture. A stele inscription from Aphrodisias commemorates donors to a memorial building erected for the relief of suffering within the community.[89] The

86. Two other epigraphical uses of the ζωγραφ- word group appear in a Jewish context—one on a Sardis inscription and the other on a catacomb (Vigna Randanini) inscription from Rome—though neither sheds light on the interpretation of the Berenice inscription (see Louis Robert, ed., *Nouvelles inscriptions de Sardes* [Paris: Librairie d'Amérique et d'Orient, 1964], 49; David Noy, ed., *Jewish Inscriptions of Western Europe: The City of Rome* [Cambridge: Cambridge University Press, 2005], no. 277).

87. See the discussion and secondary literature cited in Levine, *The Ancient Synagogue*, 91–92. Levine favors the identification of ἀμφιθέατρον as a Jewish communal building.

88. Lüderitz, *Corpus jüdischer Zeugnisse aus der Cyrenaika*, no. 71. This inscription, likewise recorded on a stele of Parian marble, dates to 24/25 C.E., during the festival of Sukkot.

89. The inscription is published in J. Reynolds and R. Tannenbaum, *Jews and Godfearers at Aphrodisias* (Cambridge: Cambridge Philological Society, 1987), 5–7. Reynolds and Tannenbaum identify the building as a kind of soup kitchen (22). See also the discussion in Paul R. Trebilco, *Jewish Communities in Asia Minor* (Cambridge: Cambridge University Press, 1991), 153–54.

two faces of the stele include three categories of people: Jews, Proselytes, and God-Fearers. The last group of names on face *b*, categorized under the heading καὶ ὅσοι θεοσεβῖς ("and as many as are God-fearers"), includes two interesting names listed with occupations: Ὀρτάσιος λατύ(πος?) and Παράμονος ἰκονο(γράφος?), or possibly ἰκονο(ποιός?). According to Reynolds and Tannenbaum, λατύπος likely refers to someone who cuts stones, perhaps carving relief portraits into stone, and ἰκονογράφος or ἰκονοποιός would designate either a painter or sculptor, depending on which reading is preferred.[90] The precise identity of the God-fearers, whether pious Jews or non-Jews associated with the synagogue, is difficult to determine with certainty. The editors of the inscription prefer pious non-Jews precisely because involvement in the sculpture industry is assumed to be incompatible with Jewish identity—in their words, "*something* is not quite kosher about them."[91] But for the present discussion, this only begs the question. In either case, however, it is at the very least apparent that several persons closely associated with the Jewish community in Aphrodisias were involved in the commercial production of figurative sculpture and/or painting.[92] Even more explicitly, the Bavli mentions a third-century C.E. synagogue in Nehardea that actually housed an anthropomorphic statue (*b. Rosh Hash.* 24b; *b. Avod. Zar.* 43b).[93]

However, both the Aphrodisias inscription and the Bavli reference postdate the destruction of the temple and could thus be taken as evidence for the notion that 70 C.E. marked a "turning-point" toward leniency, inaugurating a period when the Jewish authorities officially loosened their grip on the interpretation of the second commandment.[94] Is there any evidence for the use of three-dimensional sculpture *prior to* the destruction of the temple? Two inscribed statue bases possibly connected to two Egyptian synagogues, one located in Alexandria and the other in Naucratis, may be of relevance here.

The inscription from Naucratis, which dates somewhere between 30 B.C.E. and 14 C.E. and appears on what looks to be a base for a statuette, reads as follows:

[- - Ἀ]μμωνίου συναγωγὸς
[- - σ]υνόδῳ Σαμβαθικῇ
[(ἔτους) .. Καί]σαρος, Φαμενθὼ ζ΄.[95]

---

90. Reynolds and Tannenbaum, *Jews and Godfearers at Aphrodisias*, 120.

91. Ibid., 55.

92. This is not surprising, given Aphrodisias' fame as a center for the production of sculpture. On the question of Jewish artisans working with sculpture, see *b. Avod. Zar.* 51b–52a (cf. *m. Avod. Zar.* 4:4) and the discussion in Urbach, "Rabbinical Laws on Idolatry," 161–65.

93. The term used is אנדרטא, an Aramaic transliteration of the Greek term ἀνδριάς. See the discussion in Richard Kalmin, "Idolatry in Late Antique Babylonia: The Evidence of the Babylonian Talmud," in *The Sculptural Environment of the Roman Near East: Reflections on Culture, Ideology, and Power* (ed. Yaron Z. Eliav, Elise Friedland, and Sharon Herbert; Louvain: Peeters, 2008), 637–38.

94. Urbach, "Rabbinical Laws on Idolatry," 154–56.

95. William Horbury and David Noy, eds. *Jewish Inscriptions of Greco-Roman Egypt* (Cambridge: Cambridge University Press, 1992), no. 26.

Apparently this statue, if indeed we have a statue base here,[96] was erected to honor a son of Ammonius, a "synagogue" leader whose name is now missing, for his benefactions bestowed upon the Sambathic association. Admittedly, there are more questions than answers in this fragmentary inscription. In the first place, the titular use of συναγωγός is not unique to Greek-speaking Jews but could be used for a wide range of Greco-Roman associations. Neither does the reference to a Σαμβαθικος, a name possibly derived from the Hebrew for Sabbath, resolve the ambiguous identification of this σύνοδος. Victor Tcherikover discusses at length the twenty-nine Egyptian papyri that contain the name *Sambathion* and related variants, concluding that while in some cases the identification of the individuals in question may be Jewish, in other cases they are likely Egyptians who respect the Jewish Sabbath.[97] The editors of the inscription in question think the association in Naucratis consists of non-Jewish members who observe the Sabbath, but Levine rightly cautions against excluding a priori a Jewish identification.[98]

Similar ambiguities are present in the Alexandrian dedicatory inscription (ca. Ptolemaic to the early Roman period), which reads as follows:

> Ἀρτέμων
> Νίκωνος πρ(οστάτης)
> τὸ ια´ (ἔτος) τῇ
> συναγωγῇ
> [..]ντηκηι.[99]

This statue dedication offered to the συναγωγή again raises the notoriously slippery question of identity, and, according to the editors, "it is hard to envisage the 'synagogue' here as Jewish" precisely because of the accompanying statue.[100] But given the diversity of artistic remains evident in other Jewish sites throughout the Greco-Roman Mediterranean, it seems at the very least unwise to reject *on this basis alone* a possible Jewish identification; it is plausible that some Jewish communities living in certain regions were not entirely adverse to the use of sculpture

96. Two holes in the upper and lower sides of the stone suggest this identification, though the editors of the inscription leave the question somewhat open (ibid., 45).

97. Victor A. Tcherikover and Alexander Fuks, eds., *Corpus Papyrorum Judaicarum* (3 vols.; Cambridge: Harvard University Press, 1957–1964), 3:43–56. John Barclay leaves the question of identity open, but Louis Feldman and Meyer Reinhold are much more certain that "[t]hese people cannot be Jews" (see John M. G. Barclay, *Jews in the Mediterranean Diaspora: From Alexander to Trajan [323 BCE–117 CE]* [Berkeley: University of California Press, 1996], 123–24; Louis H. Feldman and Meyer Reinhold, eds., *Jewish Life and Thought among Greeks and Romans: Primary Readings* [Minneapolis: Fortress Press, 1996], 144).

98. Horbury and Noy, *Jewish Inscriptions of Greco-Roman Egypt*, 45; Levine, *The Ancient Synagogue*, 81.

99. Horbury and Noy, *Jewish Inscriptions of Greco-Roman Egypt*, no. 20.

100. Ibid., 33. See also Tessa Rajak, "Benefactors in the Greco-Jewish Diaspora," in *The Jewish Dialogue with Greece and Rome: Studies in Cultural and Social Interaction* (ed. Tessa Rajak; Leiden: Brill, 2001), 381–82.

and perhaps even participated in the widespread practice of erecting honorary statues on behalf of a benefactor.[101]

My point in bringing this material into the discussion is not necessarily to demonstrate conclusively that some Jews during the Second Temple period did in fact make use of figurative painting or erect honorary statues in their synagogues. The remains from certifiably Jewish sites in Second Temple Diaspora are too sparse and the few surviving bits of data too ambiguous to draw any firm conclusions. Rather I wish only to sound a methodological warning, namely that the very real potential for regional variation in Jewish society should temper any impulse to immediately discount this as a possibility. As such, especially in light of the inscription from Berenice, the different approaches toward figurative art seemingly evidenced in the archaeological record of Jerusalem and Dura Europos need not be based on diachronic exegetical changes, a shift from stridency to leniency, but is perhaps more plausibly explained by synchronic regional variation. In other words, that the archaeological record in one location—Judea—seems to indicate that Jews *in this particular region* generally avoided the various types of figurative art used throughout the Greco-Roman world does not necessarily preclude the possibility that coeval Jews in other locations were more receptive to such artistic forms, including perhaps even three-dimensional, freestanding sculpture.

A regional approach to the question of Jewish aniconism can also potentially shed more light on the absence of figurative finds in Second Temple Judea. Without discounting any possible role the second commandment may have played in this process, a glance at one of Judea's immediate neighbors, the Nabateans, may allow for a fuller and more nuanced explanation for the apparent resistance to figurative art.[102] Although many Nabatean sites include a significant array of figurative images (e.g., Petra), several exceptional locations exhibit a marked preference for nonfigurative art, especially geometric and floral motifs.[103] For example, the tombs of Mada'in Ṣaleḥ, dating between 1 B.C.E. and 75 C.E., are mostly devoid of figurative art, and there are no statues, reliefs, or portrait busts representing the deceased, in contrast with what can be seen in the tombs of Palmyra and elsewhere. Instead the residents at this particular site apparently used conical-shaped memorial stones to commemorate the dead.[104] Likewise, no architectural reliefs

---

101. Levine considers these inscriptions "evidence of communities whose conception of Judaism did not preclude such images" (Levine, *The Ancient Synagogue*, 81–82).

102. For a general discussion of the region of Nabatea in the context of Roman rule, including the annexation of the Nabatean kingdom into *Provincia Arabia* in 106 C.E., see Fergus Millar, *The Roman Near East: 31 BC–AD 337* (Cambridge: Harvard University Press, 1993), 387–436.

103. On Nabatean art, see especially Joseph Patrich, *The Formation of Nabatean Art: Prohibition of a Graven Image among the Nabateans* (Jerusalem: Magnes Press, 1990), 79–101; Joseph Patrich, "Nabataean Art between East and West: A Methodological Assessment," in *The World of the Nabataeans Held at the British Museum, 17–19 April 2001* (ed. Konstantinos D. Politis; vol. 2 of *The International Conference The World of the Herods and the Nabataeans*; Stuttgart: Franz Steiner Verlag, 2007), 79–101.

104. Patrich, *Nabatean Art*, 119–23.

have been found in er-Ramm, and the temple in this village includes no figurative decoration on the extant wall frescoes.[105] Nabatean painted pottery is "almost exclusively floral,"[106] and the jewelry, oil lamps, and coin finds similarly show a preference for nonfigurative images.[107] This phenomenon evident in material culture is more or less confirmed in the ethnography of Strabo, who, based on the testimony of a philosopher friend who lived for a time in Nabatean territory in the second half of the first century B.C.E., remarks: τόρευμα γραφή πλάσμα οὐκ ἐπιχώρια ("relief sculptures, painting, and molded images are not customary in the country").[108]

How do we explain this phenomenon? Did some Nabateans resist the wave of Greco-Roman figurative art because of a religious prohibition similar to that found in the Hebrew Bible? Actually, this is not entirely implausible, and indeed the avoidance of figurative sculpture is particularly conspicuous in Nabatean cultic contexts, where the Nabateans prefer to represent their gods with non-anthropomorphic stones (*maṣṣebot*).[109] Moreover, although technically outside of the geographical borders of Nabatea proper, several Arabic inscriptions from the south Arabian ancient Raybūn, dating between the second and first century B.C.E., may indicate that a similar prohibition existed outside of a Judean (and monotheistic) context. The inscriptions speak of votive offerings to a deity intended to absolve a sacrilege, and, according to the reading proposed by Serguei Frantsouzoff, the sacrilege spoken of here is the production of anthropomorphic images of the god or goddess.[110] Frantsouzoff thus concludes: "It follows from the three texts interpreted above that in ancient Raybūn the creation of images of deities was considered as a wrong, sinful action which required repentance."[111] If such

105. Ibid., 151–52.

106. Ibid., 127, Ill. 42. One exception was a painted bowl found on the ruins of Masada, on which a combination of floral motifs was used by the artist to create three human figures with an "Orans" gesture of prayer (ibid., 128, Ill. 43).

107. Ibid., 132–38.

108. Strabo, *Geogr.* 16.4.26.

109. On non-anthropomorphic representations of the gods, see especially Patrich, *Nabatean Art*, 50–113; Mettinger, *No Graven Image*; Peter Stewart, "Baetyls as Statues? Cult Images in the Roman Near East," in *The Sculptural Environment of the Roman Near East: Reflections on Culture, Ideology, and Power* (ed. Yaron Z. Eliav, Elise Friedland, and Sharon Herbert; Louvain: Peeters, 2008), 297–314.

110. Serguei A. Frantsouzoff, "A Parallel to the Second Commandment in the Inscriptions of Raybūn," *PSAS* 28 (1998): 61–67.

111. Ibid., 65. Frantsouzoff further supports his hypothesis with reference to "the complete lack of any statue or picture of a god or a goddess of the local pantheon among the numerous artifacts of the South Arabian civilization" (65). On the relationship between the inscriptions and the Jewish second commandment, he remarks: "To my mind, it would be reasonable to assume that some specific beliefs of a group of early Semitic tribes, a sort of taboo imposed on the creation of images of deities, was the origin of both a prescription of the South Arabian polytheistic religion and a statement of the Mosaic law" (66). On the idea of a early Semitic antecedent to the biblical command, see also Tallay Ornan, "Idols and

a prohibition did exist in south Arabia, then it is certainly possible that a similar prohibition was in circulation in Nabatea.

Nevertheless, the absence of any Nabatean literary or epigraphical evidence addressing the issue makes it especially difficult to determine the precise reasons for this artistic preference, and Patrich rightly cautions against a purely "religious" explanation.[112] Specifically, according to Patrich's assessment, this tendency toward nonfigurative art is not solely because of a "religious obligation" but also "the continuing validity of *a unique aesthetic approach* and the desire to maintain it, to a conservatism and national consciousness that did not permit the abrogation of the extant, the ancient, and the rooted, by the accidental and the fashionable."[113] In various contexts Patrich speaks of the nonfigurative preference as a reflection of "the spirit of the Nabateans,"[114] "the spirit of the descendants of the desert,"[115] and "the spirit of the nation."[116] Whether or not one agrees with Patrich's interpretation of this data—and I would suggest that it is a bit too Hegelian in "spirit"—this comparative material underscores the difficulty of moving from surviving stones to ancient religious beliefs. More important for purposes of this analysis, however, it suggests that the penchant for floral and geometric motifs over against figurative images in Judea may be *in part* because of regional aesthetic preferences, artistic tendencies specific to this particular geographic locale.[117]

Idol Polemics in the Sculptural Environment of the Ancient Mediterranean

In addition to the possibility for regional variation and distinct artistic preferences and practices, the fact that Jews were integral members of and participants in this multicultural milieu suggests that the conventional model of Jewish responses to sculpture, which reduces the issue of response to either "acceptance" or "rejection," fails to adequately account for the complex interplay between viewer and image in antiquity.[118] This is especially apparent when considering the most

---

Symbols: Divine Representation in First Millennium Mesopotamian Art and Its Bearing on the Second Commandment," *TA* 31 (2004): 90–121.

112. Although ironically, the subtitle of Patrich's book, "The Prohibition of a Graven Image among the Nabateans," betrays this reflexive tendency to interpret the lack of artistic remains strictly through the lens of religious categories.

113. Patrich, *Nabatean Art*, 152 (emphasis mine).

114. Ibid., 49.

115. Ibid., 114.

116. Ibid., 166.

117. Indeed, rather than seeing the preponderance of floral and geometric motifs in Herod the Great's domestic space as an attempt to conform to Jewish religious strictures, as it is often presented in scholarship on Herodian architecture, regional aesthetic preference perhaps more plausibly explains his almost exclusive use of nonfigurative art.

118. An important theoretical stimulus for the ensuing discussion is David Freedberg's study of responses to images. In contrast with Freedberg, however, who purports to uncover responses that "precede context" and are in some sense universal or ahistorical, I

prominent form of figurative representation in antiquity—statues. Beyond simply adorning the physical landscape, statues were inextricably woven into the fabric of daily life, serving a variety of social, religious, and political functions. In other words, far from being *objets d'art* eventually destined for a dusty shelf or museum, statues were "objects working in society."[119]

An awareness of this socio-cultural function of statues shifts the focus away from the formal features of the object itself—for example, its style, degree of naturalism, and the aesthetic beauty of the work—to the *visual experience* elicited by the image, underscoring the fundamental role of perception in the dynamic relationship between object and beholder.[120] Viewers in antiquity did not simply *see* statues as works of art, objects with a particular form or style, freestanding matter shaped into a variety of geometric configurations. Rather, they *saw into* statues a host of assumptions, beliefs, associations, and experiences that collectively comprise what I identified in chapter 1 as a world of iconic perceptions. Not surprisingly, then, responses to statues in Greco-Roman antiquity were complex and variegated: statues were admired, feared, manipulated, destroyed, animated, worshipped, invoked, and embraced; speaking statues were thought to convey oracles from the gods; weeping or sweating statues were viewed as portents of impending doom; naked statues aroused sexual yearnings.[121] Statues in antiquity could thus be seen as in some sense *living* artifacts, both in terms of their capacity to elicit interpersonal encounters and their potential, at least from the perspective of many living in antiquity, to embody powerful forces and to display manifestations of the divine realm.

---

would suggest that all response is in some sense historically and contextually bound (Freedberg, *The Power of Images*, quote at xx).

119. Stewart, *Statues in Roman Society*, 10.

120. W. J. T. Mitchell has noted this shift from object to viewer, what he labels a new "pictorial turn," in art-historical studies (*Picture Theory*, 11–34). This shift in art history is likewise apparent in several studies of Roman art; see especially Cyril Mango, "Antique Statuary and the Byzantine Beholder," *DOP* 17 (1963): 55–75; Jaś Elsner, *Art and the Roman Viewer: The Transformation of Art from the Pagan World to Christianity* (Cambridge: Cambridge University Press, 1995); John R. Clarke, *Art in the Lives of Ordinary Romans: Visual Representation and Non-elite Viewers in Italy, 100 B.C.–A.D. 315* (Berkeley: University of California Press, 2003); Stewart, *Statues in Roman Society*.

121. See the following representative examples of the diverse perceptions of and responses to statues in antiquity. Destruction and disfiguration of statue: Juvenal, *Sat.* 11.19–31 (destroyed for profit); Tacitus, *Ann.* 3.14 (statue that is dismembered); Plutarch, *Alcibiades* 19.1.2 (a mutilated statue); Pausanias, *Descr.* 1.25.7.11 (Athena stripped). Statue animation: Lucian, *Philops.* 3.343–53 (statues that move about, take baths, cure, curse, and punish people—Lucian, however, mocks those who believe in animated statues); Eunapius, *Vit. Soph.* 475 (Maximus animates a goddess); Augustine, *Civ.* 4.19 (Fortuna speaks); see also the discussion of the Epistle of Jeremiah and the cited literature below. Statues as portents: Plutarch, *Camillus* 6.4.2–4; Cassius Dio, *Hist. Rom.* 40.17.1.4 (sweating statue as portent), 46.33.3.4 (rotating and bleeding statue as portent), 51.17.5.5 (frowning statue as portent); Augustine, *Civ.* 3.11 (weeping Apollo as portent). On statues and erotic desire, see the discussion of the Wisdom of Solomon below.

A fundamental premise of the argument in this chapter is that Jews in Greco-Roman antiquity did not stand *outside* of this "sculptural environment,"[122] as the model of conflict would seem to suggest, but were instead *insiders*, integral participants in this complex cultural sphere, being both shaped by and simultaneously contributing to this world of iconic perceptions. Not surprisingly, given the ubiquity of statues in the Roman world, this physical reality left an indelible mark on Jewish sources from the Second Temple period.

For example, the *Ladder of Jacob*, a pseudepigraphical text that possibly originates in Palestine from the first century C.E.,[123] recasts the dream of the biblical patriarch Jacob at Bethel (Gen 28:11–22) to include on the twelve steps of Jacob's famed heavenly staircase twenty-four portrait busts of kings, "including their chests" (*Lad. Jac.* 1:5; 5:1–4).[124] This reference at the very least shows an intimate awareness of a particularly popular form of Roman statuary—as a perusal of any sculpture display in modern archaeological museums will confirm—and the widespread practice of displaying in private and public contexts such portrait busts to represent not only ancestors, local elites, and other dignitaries, but especially emperors.[125]

In a similar vein, the pseudepigraphical Wisdom of Solomon (first-century B.C.E. Egypt) includes a familiar etiology of anthropomorphic portraiture and the custom of commissioning private familial statues, locating the origins of this practice in the distant past when a grieving father sculpted an image to memorialize the premature death of his child (Wis 14:15).[126] This account is not unlike Pliny

122. Yaron Eliav coined this term to capture this colorful and multifaceted process of interacting with statues in antiquity. To quote in full: "By characterizing this phenomenon as a 'sculptural environment,' I mean to embrace not only the outward appearance (subject matter and style) and physical reality (materials and display context) of statues, but also the political, religious, and social implications, interactions and tensions associated with them in the diversified milieu of the Roman East" ("Viewing the Sculptural Environment," 413). See also the introduction to a recently published collection of essays: Yaron Z. Eliav, Elise A. Friedland, and Sharon Herbert, eds., *The Sculptural Environment of the Roman Near East: Reflections on Culture, Ideology, and Power* (Louvain: Peeters, 2008), 1–11.

123. Admittedly, given that only fragments of this text have survived in Slavonic manuscripts from a much later period, it is difficult to be precise on the date and provenance. See the discussion in H. G. Lunt, "Ladder of Jacob: A New Translation and Introduction," in *The Old Testament Pseudepigrapha* (ed. James H. Charlesworth; 2 vols.; New York: Doubleday, 1985), 2:404–05.

124. Trans. Lunt, *OTP* 2:407.

125. On portrait busts and their function in Roman society, see the discussion in Stewart, *Statues in Roman Society*, 79–117. The rabbis of the Mishnah and Talmudim similarly betray a close familiarity with the customs of familial portraiture and other private or domestic sculpture displays; see Yaron Z. Eliav, "Roman Statues, Rabbis, and Greco-Roman Culture," in *Jewish Literatures and Cultures: Context and Intertext* (ed. Anita Norich and Yaron Z. Eliav; Providence, R.I.: Brown Judaic Studies, 2008), 102.

126. For the author of this text, this seemingly innocuous practice functions as the catalyst for the impious (ἀσεβής) worship of statues as gods (Wis 14:16). See further Jason von Ehrenkrook, "Image and Desire in the Wisdom of Solomon," *Zutot* 7 (2011): 44–46. The

the Elder's etiology of portrait statues, only in Pliny's version a father sculpts an image of his daughter's absent lover and so invents the practice of anthropomorphic sculpture (*Nat.* 35.151). What both etiologies share, however, is the widespread perception that portraiture functioned to forge a permanent connection between the grieving and the one grieved, whether a deceased child or departed lover. Anthropomorphic representation collapsed the distance between separated individuals, rendering present that which was otherwise absent.

Other Jewish texts from the Second Temple period similarly display an awareness of a whole range of details associated with Greek and Roman sculpture. For example, several Jewish authors bear witness to the fact that, in contrast with the impression given by the rather drab appearance of statues in modern museums, statues in antiquity were vibrant and polychromatic, having been painted "with various colors" (σπιλωθὲν χρώμασιν διηλλαγμένοις; Wis 15:4),[127] and very often adorned (even excessively so) with colorful garments and jewelry (Ep Jer 6:8–16). Similarly, several Jewish texts demonstrate a familiarity with the practice of sculptural maintenance, especially the various processes employed to wash and treat statues for protection (Ep Jer 6:13, 24).[128]

Beyond an awareness of their physical surroundings, however, a careful reading of the literary sources, even those saturated with decidedly anti-iconic language, demonstrates the extent to which Jews were full participants in a rather lively discourse on statues. For purposes of this analysis, I will focus primarily on the Jewish idol polemic, a *locus classicus* of iconic antagonism. Given that the number of Greco-Roman Jewish texts from within this tradition is quite vast and well beyond the scope of the present book, I will restrict my analysis to two exemplary texts, the Epistle of Jeremiah and the Wisdom of Solomon. While it is true that these texts recycle the standard biblical-prophetic *topos* of the lifeless image, they nevertheless attest to what may be described as an iconic lingua franca in the Greco-Roman Mediterranean, a common language used to describe, assess, and recount daily encounters with these artifacts.

Mek. R. Yish., tractate Pisha 13, likewise mentions the practice of creating images of deceased ancestors (*imagines maiorum*) and children (Eliav, "Roman Statues," 102).

127. See also Wis 13:14 and *Sib. Or.* 3.589 for other Jewish references to the practice of painting statues.

128. In a similar vein, a midrash to Leviticus includes the following remark attributed to R. Hillel, in response to a question about whether or not bathing in a bath house was a religious duty: "'Yes,' he replied, 'if the statues of kings, which are erected in theaters and circuses, are scoured and washed by the man who is appointed to look after them, and who thereby obtains a salary—nay more, he is exalted in the company of the great of the kingdom—how much more I, who have been created in the image and likeness, as it is written: For in his own image God made mankind'" (*Lev. Rab.* 34.3); trans. Judah Jacob Slotki in H. Freedman and Maurice Simon, eds., *Midrash Rabbah* (London: Soncino Press, 1939), 428.

Dissecting a Statue in the Epistle of Jeremiah

The overarching aim of the pseudepigraphical Epistle of Jeremiah, likely composed sometime during the Hellenistic period, is to ridicule the idolatrous worship of non-Jews, to render absurd the practice of cultic devotion to sculpted representations of the gods.[129] In many respects then, this text represents a very explicit and seemingly mundane continuation of the standard biblical-prophetic idol polemic, an expansive "replay of the structure and motifs of the [biblical] genre."[130] According to Carey Moore's assessment, "most of the material in the Epistle depends for its ideas, imagery, and phraseology upon a few classic descriptions of idolatry" in the biblical corpus, namely passages from Jeremiah, Deutero-Isaiah, and the Psalms.[131] Indeed, even a cursory glance at the Epistle confirms this impression. The repeated reference to the lifeless nature of the statue, its inability to see, speak, or hear, its material origins and craftsmanship, recall familiar *topoi* drawn deeply from the well of the biblical-prophetic corpus.

Nevertheless, as has long been noted, Jews did not hold a monopoly on the materiality critique of images,[132] and the Epistle of Jeremiah should thus be seen as something more than a simple recycling of an "inherited genre."[133] This critical approach to cult statues, whether in the form of sophisticated philosophical critiques or satirical parodies, was quite common in intellectual circles in Greco-Roman antiquity,[134] which may explain in part why such idol parodies gained widespread

---

129. The date, provenance, and even original language of this text are uncertain. Most commentators argue for a Hebrew original that dates to the late fourth or early third centuries B.C.E., either in Babylonia or Palestine; see the discussion and bibliography in Carey A. Moore, *Daniel, Esther, and Jeremiah: The Additions* (Garden City, N.Y.: Doubleday, 1977), 326–32. For purposes of this analysis, it is enough to note that the *topoi* included in the Greek Epistle of Jeremiah could plausibly fit anywhere in a Hellenistic or Roman Mediterranean context.

130. Wolfgang M. W. Roth, "For Life, He Appeals to Death (Wis 13:18): A Study of Old Testament Idol Parodies," *CBQ* 37 (1975): 39. See also P. C. Beentjes' study of this text, which focuses almost exclusively on its use of the prophetic polemic ("Satirical Polemics against Idols and Idolatry in the Letter of Jeremiah [Baruch ch. 6]," in *Aspects of Religious Contact and Conflict in the Ancient World* [ed. Pieter Willem van der Horst; Utrecht: Faculteit der Godgeleerdheid, Universiteit Utrecht, 1995], 121–33).

131. Moore, *Daniel, Esther, and Jeremiah*, 319. Not surprisingly, the author is particularly fond of the idol parody in Jer 10:1–6, and the very raison d'être of this pseudepigraphical composition is the reference to a letter written to the exiles in Babylon in Jer 29:1.

132. Charly Clerc, *Les théories relatives au culte des images chez les auteurs grecs du IIme siècle aprés J.-C.* (Paris: Fontemoing, 1915), 90–123; Bevan, *Holy Images*, 17–23.

133. Roth, "For Life, He Appeals to Death," 41.

134. Moshe Barasch, *Icon: Studies in the History of an Idea* (New York: New York University Press, 1992), 49–62; Alain Besançon, *The Forbidden Image: An Intellectual History of Iconoclasm* (trans. Jane Marie Todd; Chicago: University of Chicago Press, 2000), 30–37. However, Millette Gaifman rightly cautions against reading many of these critical sentiments through the lenses of the Christian apologists who excerpt them for polemical purposes (Gaifman, "Beyond Mimesis," 93–96).

currency in Jewish literature during the Second Temple period.[135] For example, the Greek philosopher Heraclitus (late sixth century B.C.E.) criticized people for praying to divine statues "that cannot hear" (οὐκ ἀκούουσιν; Heraclitus of Ephesus, frg. 128), and several centuries later the Roman satirist Juvenal similarly mocks a statue of Jupiter for its inability to speak (Juvenal, *Sat.* 13.114–115).[136] Horace's satire of an apotropaic Priapus in Rome, opening with language strikingly similar to that found in Deutero-Isaiah and the Wisdom of Solomon (esp. Isa 44:9–17 and Wis 13:11–19), is perhaps most famous in this regard: "Once I was a fig-wood stem, a worthless log (*inutile lignum*), when the carpenter, doubtful whether to make a stool or a Priapus, chose that I be a god" (*Sat.* 1.8.1–3 [Fairclough, LCL]).[137]

It is tempting to view the *topos* of lifelessness inherent to this materiality critique as an attack on the naïve identification of the statue with the god. And in certain contexts this may in fact be the case, as for example when Plutarch seems to ridicule some Greeks for failing to make such a distinction explicit in their language: "There are some among the Greeks who have not learned nor habituated themselves to speak of the bronze, the painted, and the stone effigies as statues of the gods and dedications in their honour, but they call them gods" (*Is. Os.* 379C8 [Babbitt, LCL]). But it is not altogether clear that many people in antiquity really fused so completely the god and image or failed to see the many statues of Zeus and others for what they really were, material representations of heavenly realities. On the other hand, the repeated drumbeat of the impotent statue in a wide swath of Greco-Roman literary sources was not empty rhetoric, but very likely indicates that for many people statues were anything but impotent. More specifically, although cult statues of stone, wood, or precious metals were not the gods themselves, they could potentially become conduits of the divine realm.

The notion of the cult statue as a divine receptacle is widely attested in Greek and Latin literature.[138] Arnobius' *Adversus nationes* (late third century C.E.), although a vitriolic diatribe intended to refute paganism (and, not incidentally, to prove genuine the author's own conversion to Christianity), very likely preserves

135. Johannes Tromp, "The Critique of Idolatry in the Context of Jewish Monotheism," in *Aspects of Religious Contact and Conflict in the Ancient World* (ed. Pieter Willem van der Horst; Utrecht: Faculteit der Godgeleerdheid, Universiteit Utrecht, 1995), 111–12. On the idol polemic in Jewish literature, see especially the following texts: Epistle of Jeremiah; Bel and the Dragon; *Jubilees* 12:2–5; 20:8–9; the *Sibylline Oracles*; and the *Apocalypse of Abraham*. On the idol polemic in the *Apocalypse of Abraham* see especially Daniel C. Harlow, "Idolatry and Alterity: Israel and the Nations in the *Apocalypse of Abraham*," in *The "Other" in Second Temple Judaism* (ed. Daniel C. Harlow et al.; Grand Rapids: Eerdmans, 2011), 302–30.

136. For other similar critiques, see also Heraclitus B frg. 5; Ps-Heraclitus, Epistula 4; Plutarch, *Is. Os.* 71; *Fragmenta* (*Sandbach*) 157.107 (where Plutarch describes a wooden statue as ἄψυχον); Epictetus 2.8.13–14.

137. See the discussion of this and other similar Priapus traditions in Stewart, *Statues in Roman Society*, 72–77.

138. See the discussion and literature cited in Deborah Tarn Steiner, *Images in Mind: Statues in Archaic and Classical Greek Literature and Thought* (Princeton, N.J.: Princeton University Press, 2001), 114–20.

how many people in antiquity viewed the relationship between the deity and its image:

> Sed erras, inquit, et laberis, nam neque nos aera, neque auri argentique materias, neque alias, quibus signa confiunt, eas esse per se deos, et religiosa decernimus numina; sed eos in his colimus, eosque veneramur, quos dedicatio infert sacra, et fabrilibus efficit inhabitare simulacris.
>
> "But you err," says he [Arnobius' pagan interlocutor], "and you are mistaken, for we do not hold the conviction that bronzes or gold or silver, or any other stuff out of which statues are made, are of themselves gods and sacred deities, but in them we worship and reverence those whom the act of sacred dedication introduces and causes to dwell in the fabricated images."[139] (*Adv. nat.* 6.17)

The reference to *dedicatio* as an invitation to fill the statue with numinous powers underscores the extent to which "cultural performances"—concrete acts of ritual associated with cult statues—can encode beliefs about the cosmos, especially the place of the divine within the human realm.[140] In Greco-Roman antiquity there seems to have been a range of acts associated with the formal consecration of a statue, for example the bathing, anointing, dressing, and crowning of the god's image.[141] This formal process of *consecratio* and the various rites associated with it were thought to imbue a statue with the deity's πνεῦμα or *numen*, as is apparent in Tertullian's claim that Romans "draw to themselves the demons and every impure spirit by means of the bond brought about by consecration (*consecratio*)" (*Idol.* 15.5).[142]

---

139. Trans. George E. McCracken, *Arnobius of Sicca: The Case against the Pagans* (2 vols.; Westminster, Md.: Newman Press, 1949), 2:470. Note also the remarks by the Neoplatonic philosopher Plotinus (third century C.E.): "And I think that the wise men of old, who made temples and statues in the wish that the gods should be present to them, looking to the nature of the All, had in mind that the nature of the soul is everywhere easy to attract, but that if someone were to construct something sympathetic to it and able to receive a part of it, it would of all things receive soul most easily" (*Enneads* 4.3.11 [Armstrong, LCL]).

140. On ritual as a cultural performance, see especially the discussion in Clifford Geertz, "Religion as a Cultural System," in *The Interpretation of Cultures: Selected Essays* (ed. Clifford Geertz; London: Fontana Press, 1993), 112–13. See also the application of Geertz's theory to the study of images in Barasch, *Icon*, 33–34.

141. In general, see the discussion in B. Frischer, *The Sculpted Word: Epicureanism and Philosophical Recruitment in Ancient Greece* (Berkeley: University of California Press, 1982), 113–14; Freedberg, *The Power of Images*, 83; Barasch, *Icon*, 34–36; Steiner, *Images in Mind*, 109–13. Steiner views the bathing of a statue as "an attempt to give renewed power to an image whose numinous quality has suffered depletion or impairment" (110); and again, it is "a gesture aimed at the renewal and revivification of the power of the image" (111).

142. Trans. J. H. Waszink and J. C. M. Van Winden, *Tertullianus De Idolatria: Critical Text, Translation, and Commentary* (Leiden: Brill, 1987). Elsewhere Tertullian identifies the cult statue as a demonic body, *daemoniis corpora* (*Idol.* 7.1). See also the second-century C.E. apologist Minucius Felix, who likewise attests specifically to the link between rites of *consecratio* and a statue's formal cultic status: "[A statue] is wrought, it is sculptured—it is not yet a god; lo, it is soldered, it is built together—it is set up, and even yet it is not a god;

Beyond these formal rites, however, were the numerous daily life rituals—human encounters with cult statues, ranging from touching or kissing the deity's image to adorning the statue with garlands, wreaths, and even coins affixed to the statue with wax—that similarly attest to the perception that various acts could potentially invite a deity, or even the *genius* of an emperor, to inhabit and empower its image. Lucian's *Philopseudes*, for example, mentions the adornment of an Athenian statue (not a cult statue but an image of an Athenian general), including wreaths, crowns, and coins, that seems to be associated with the statue's power of animation, its ability to move about, take baths, and perform healing miracles (*Philops.* 18–20).[143]

That the god or goddess could inhabit a cult statue through *consecratio* and other ritual practices explains in part the widespread belief in the efficacy of images: if a god could be said to dwell in a statue, then it stands to reason that some statues could potentially possess powers that other statues might not possess. Plutarch mentions a statue of Fortune (ἄγαλμα τῆς Τύχης) that purportedly spoke immediately after it was consecrated (καθιερόω; *Fort. Rom.* 319A1), and similar types of phenomena—statues that could sweat and bleed, move about, perform healings, and so on—are widely reported in Greek and Latin texts.[144] While it is tempting to pursue rational explanations for such phenomena, for example looking to climate conditions or the possibility of fraud,[145] Nigel Spivey cautions against immediately

lo, it is adorned, it is consecrated, it is prayed to—then at length it is a god, when man has chosen it to be so, and for the purpose has dedicated it" (*Oct.* 23.13) (trans. R. E. Wallis in Alexander Roberts and James Donaldson, eds., *Ante-Nicene Fathers: The Writings of the Fathers Down to A.D. 325* [24 vols.; Edinburgh: T&T Clark, 1867–1872], 4:187). For Minucius, however, as for Tertullian, it is not actually the gods who accept the invitation to inhabit the statue but demons (*Oct.* 27.1). See the discussion in Steiner, *Images in Mind*, 114–16.

143. See also the discussion and literature cited in Stewart, *Statues in Roman Society*, 192, 263.

144. On the animation of statues, see especially Clerc, *Les théories relatives au culte des images*, 45–49; Bevan, *Holy Images*, 23–43; F. Poulsen, "Talking, Weeping, and Bleeding Statues," *Acta Archaeologica* 16 (1945): 178-95; Mango, "Antique Statuary and the Byzantine Beholder," 59–64; Barasch, *Icon*, 36–39; Nigel J. Spivey, "Bionic Statues," in *The Greek World* (ed. Anton Powell; London and New York: Routledge, 1995), 442–59. For a look at the attribution of animation beyond the confines of Greco-Roman antiquity, see Freedberg, *The Power of Images*, 283–316.

145. Accusations of fraud and other attempts at rationalizing the animated image are indeed found in numerous ancient texts as well. For example, Plutarch explains sweating, crying, bleeding, and speaking statues as follows: "For that statues have appeared to sweat, and shed tears, and exude something like drops of blood, is not impossible; since wood and stone often contract a mould which is productive of moisture, and cover themselves with many colours, and receive tints from the atmosphere.... It is possible also that statues may emit a noise like a moan or a groan, by reason of a fracture or a rupture, which is more violent if it takes place in the interior. But that articulate speech, and language so clear and abundant and precise, should proceed from a lifeless thing, is altogether impossible" (Plutarch, *Cor.* 38.1–2 [Perrin, LCL]). On the accusation of fraud, Lucian mentions a statue that was uniquely designed to speak oracles, with windpipes having been installed

dismissing anecdotes of animation with "scientific disdain."[146] Whatever the explanation, that such anecdotes abound in the ancient sources bespeaks the widespread *perception* that statues possessed powers of vivification.

And Jewish sources were no exception. The frequent link between demons and idols in Jewish literature may attest, as in the case of the early Christian apologists (cited above), to the belief that spirits—albeit "evil" ones—did indeed inhabit and animate statues.[147] The author of Revelation attests, albeit couched in the highly symbolic language characteristic of apocalyptic literature, to the possibility of vivifying imperial statues in language that evokes the process of *consecratio*:

> Καὶ ἐδόθη αὐτῷ δοῦναι πνεῦμα τῇ εἰκόνι τοῦ θηρίου, ἵνα καὶ λαλήσῃ ἡ εἰκὼν τοῦ θηρίου καὶ ποιήσῃ [ἵνα] ὅσοι ἐὰν μὴ προσκυνήσωσιν τῇ εἰκόνι τοῦ θηρίου ἀποκτανθῶσιν.
>
> And [the second beast] was enabled to give life to the image of the [first] beast, in order that the image of the beast would speak and would cause to be killed those who do not worship the image of the beast. (Rev 13:15)

The pseudepigraphical *Vita Adae et Evae* similarly deploys the language of *consecratio* in its retelling of the creation narrative: God infused Adam's *similitudo* with the spirit of life (*spiritus vitae*), transforming him into an *imago Dei* that was now worthy of *adoro*, worship (*Vita Adae et Evae* 13.3).[148]

I submit that this broader context—the perception of statues as conduits for the divine realm; the rituals inviting the god to inhabit his or her statue; and the numerous stories attesting to the resulting animation of images—is at the center of the idol polemic in the Epistle of Jeremiah. What is relevant in this text for the present discussion is not its broad agreement with the critique of a statue's material origins and craftsmanship, but the way this text exploits specific details associated with the animation of statues in order to subvert the notion that the statue was a vessel of divine agency. The author, with a healthy dose of derision, juxtaposes rituals of animation with assertions of impotence, lambasting those who crown and clothe cult statues that cannot speak (Ep Jer 6:8–12), who clean statues that cannot see (Ep Jer 6:13–19), and who polish statues that cannot feel, statues that have "no breath in them" (ἐν οἷς οὐκ ἔστιν πνεῦμα; Ep Jer 6:24–25).

---

into the statue's head (Lucian, *Alex* 26), not unlike the extant statue head, currently kept in Copenhagen, that has a channel cut through its head from the back of the neck to its mouth (Stewart, *Statues in Roman Society*, 193).

146. Spivey, "Bionic Statues," 453.

147. See for example *1 En.* 19:1; *Jub.* 1:11; *L.A.B.* 25:9; 1 Cor 10:19–20. Saul Lieberman, although focused on a slightly later period, argued that many Jews did in fact believe that demons resided in statues (*Hellenism in Jewish Palestine* [New York: Jewish Theological Seminary, 1950], 121). Ephraim Urbach, however, disputes this assertion ("Rabbinical Laws on Idolatry," 154).

148. See the discussion in Crispin H. T. Fletcher-Louis, "The Worship of Divine Humanity as God's Image and the Worship of Jesus," in *The Jewish Roots of Christological Monotheism* (ed. Carey C. Newman, James R. Davila, and Gladys S. Lewis; Leiden: Brill, 1999), 127–28.

The assertion that cult statues are devoid of πνεῦμα counters the widespread claim to the contrary, a line of attack that attempts to discredit the notion of vivified statues "by turning the idol inside out."[149] This explains the rather curious attempt to inspect the "heart" (καρδία) of the statue in order to expose that which *does* inhabit the sculpted object:[150]

> ἔστι μὲν ὥσπερ δοκὸς τῶν ἐκ τῆς οἰκίας, τὰς δὲ καρδίας αὐτῶν φασιν ἐκλείχεσθαι τῶν ἀπὸ τῆς γῆς ἑρπετῶν, κατεσθόντων αὐτούς τε καὶ τὸν ἱματισμὸν αὐτῶν.
>
> They [cult statues] are like a beam of wood from a house, but their hearts, so they say, are licked up when creeping creatures from the earth devour them and their clothes. (Ep Jer 6:20)

As is apparent in the use of the verb φημί to introduce hearsay, the author is drawing in rather explicit terms on a well-known *topos* in Greco-Roman antiquity: to dissect the inside of a statue is to discover a place literally teeming with vile creatures.

This facet of a statue's realia, moreover, became a popular detail to exploit for ridicule. For example, Lucian's repeated attempts to ridicule the notion of animated images include occasional recourse to creeping critters, especially mice and rats, inhabiting statues, perhaps most famously expressed in his colorful description of the insides of several renowned colossi: "[I]f you stoop down and look inside, you will see bars and props and nails driven clear through, and beams and wedges and pitch and clay and a quantity of such ugly stuff housing within, not to mention numbers of mice and rats that keep their court in them sometimes" (Lucian, *Gall.* 24 [Harmon, LCL]).[151] This rhetoric of internal corruption was picked up with polemical fervor by several early Christian apologists, most notably Arnobius, who seemingly revels in the gory details exposed in his dissection of a statue: gods imbued not with numinous powers but with newts, shrews, mice, cockroaches, and spiders, among other detestable elements that invade both the internal and external parts of statues (*Adv. nat.* 6.14–16).[152]

In this light, when the author of the Epistle of Jeremiah speaks of critters devouring the καρδία of a cult statue, he is not simply asserting evidence for its essential materiality, but is also seeking to subvert the belief that gods could inhabit and animate the image by pointing to what really lies beneath: vile and disgusting corruption. The repeated refrain "do not fear them" (φοβηθῆτε αὐτούς) is thus not an empty structural device but in fact presupposes a latent fear of the potential

149. Steiner, *Images in Mind*, 120.

150. On the καρδία of a statue, see also the fifth-century B.C.E. Democritus, who refers to a statue as "conspicuous in their dress and adornment for viewing (*theorien*), but empty (*kenea*) of heart" (B195DK), as cited in Steiner, *Images in Mind*, 122–23.

151. See also *Jupp. trag.* 8. In a similar vein, though with less specificity, Plutarch likens imperial hypocrisy—rulers who appear dignified on the surface but are actually corrupt within—to a statue's godlike external appearance that only conceals its internal corruption (*Princ. Iner.* 780A5).

152. See also Tertullian, *Apol.* 12.

vitality of statues:[153] the author seeks to deny the cult statue a divine power that apparently many people, including those for whom this text was primarily composed, perceived the statue to possess.[154] In this sense, one should read the polemic against lifeless idols in the Epistle of Jeremiah not so much as an attempt to bolster the Jewish faith against the "superstitious" beliefs of outsiders, that is, as an exercise in "elevating the Jewish religion intellectually above the pagan religions,"[155] but as a rhetorical exorcism of sorts, a form of (literary) "apotropaic mutilation" that functions to vacate the idol of its numinous powers on behalf of a Jewish community that feared such powers.[156] The larger point, for purposes of this discussion, is the extent to which this text betrays a profound awareness of prevailing perceptions of and rituals associated with cult statues. Far from a simple regurgitation of *topoi* from the biblical prophets, the Epistle of Jeremiah is fully immersed in the Greco-Roman sculptural environment.

Agalmatophilia and the Wisdom of Solomon

Whereas the Epistle of Jeremiah betrays a fear of the statue's capacity to channel numinous powers, the Wisdom of Solomon, a Jewish pseudepigraphon dated perhaps to the late first century B.C.E., addresses a different form of sculpted potency, the capacity of a statue to arouse sexual yearnings, to cast its erotic charms on the viewer.[157] Like the Epistle of Jeremiah, one finds in this text a strong and repeated emphasis on the materiality and consequent impotence of statues, again clearly inspired by, but not restricted to, the biblical corpus (in particular, Isa 44 looms rather large). But here also, there is more than initially meets the eye, as the author shows himself fully conversant with a wider perception of statues—in this case, the potential link between sculpture and erotic desire.

Indeed, it is precisely this perception of statuary that stands behind the Wisdom of Solomon's assertion that the invention of idols is the "origin of *porneia*" (ἀρχὴ γὰρ πορνείας; Wis 14:12).[158] The connection between sculpture and erotic

153. Ep Jer 6:16, and repeated with slight variations in 6:23, 29, 65, 69.

154. For a similar argument focused on Christian pronouncements of empty and impotent idols in late antique Egypt, see David Frankfurter, "The Vitality of Egyptian Images in Late Antiquity: Christian Memory and Response," in *The Sculptural Environment of the Roman Near East: Reflections on Culture, Ideology, and Power* (ed. Yaron Z. Eliav, Elise Friedland, and Sharon Herbert; Louvain: Peeters, 2008), 671–74.

155. Tromp, "The Critique of Idolatry," 108.

156. The phrase "apotropaic mutilation" comes from David Frankfurter's study of Christian responses to Egyptian statuary, in which the author argues that the traces of iconoclasm/mutilation in the archaeological record of late antique Egypt attest to a latent fear of the power residing in these images; Frankfurter, "Vitality of Egyptian Images," 676.

157. A version of this section was published in von Ehrenkrook, "Image and Desire," 41–50.

158. Cf. Wis 14:27, where the worship of idols is more broadly identified as "the beginning, cause, and end of every evil" (παντὸς ἀρχὴ κακοῦ καὶ αἰτία καὶ πέρας ἐστίν). The pseudepigraphical *Testament of Reuben* likewise links idolatry with *porneia*, but here it is *porneia* that leads to idolatry, a formulation that is perhaps influenced by the biblical story

desire is made even more explicit in the author's attempt to contrast the "virginity," as it were, of the Jews with those who had fallen prey to this crafted temptress:

> οὔτε γὰρ ἐπλάνησεν ἡμᾶς ἀνθρώπων κακότεχνος ἐπίνοια, οὐδὲ σκιαγράφων πόνος ἄκαρπος, εἶδος σπιλωθὲν χρώμασιν διηλλαγμένοις· ὧν ὄψις ἄφροσιν εἰς ὄρεξιν ἔρχεται, ποθεῖ τε νεκρᾶς εἰκόνος εἶδος ἄπνουν. κακῶν ἐρασταὶ ἄξιοί τε τοιούτων ἐλπίδων καὶ οἱ δρῶντες καὶ οἱ ποθοῦντες καὶ οἱ σεβόμενοι.
>
> For neither has the deceitful intent of humans led us astray, nor the useless labor of painters, a form that was stained with many different colors, whose external appearance stirs up desire in fools, and they long for the lifeless form of a dead image. Lovers of evil things and even worthy of such objects of hope are the ones who perform such deeds, and who desire and worship [images]. (Wis 15:4–6)

The constellation of key terms used in this text to describe human interactions with statues, namely ἐρασταί, ποθέω, and σέβομαι, underscores the capacity of a statue to arouse *both* cultic *and* sexual attention. This passage has thus been correctly linked with the various traditions in Greek and Latin sources that attest to the erotic power of statues.[159] For example, the famed legend of Pygmalion, as told in Ovid's *Metamorphoses*, moves the reader from the frustration of unrequited love—a sculptor who falls in love with the impenetrable coldness of an "ivory damsel"—to the warmth, softness, and receptivity of a Venus-induced vivified lover (Ovid, *Metam.* 10.243–289).[160] And to this we may add the numerous anecdotes (embedded in both narrative and poetry) about actual sexual acts performed with statues, conventionally categorized under the term agalmatophilia.[161]

Perhaps the most famous act of agalmatophilia involves Praxiteles' legendary Aphrodite of Cnidus, whose beauty, as Pliny the Elder informs us, was so remarkable as to create a veritable pilgrimage industry (*Nat.* 36.4.20). Although the sexual encounter that resulted in a semen-stained statue is preserved in a number of sources,[162] the fullest (and hence most interesting) version appears in Pseudo-Lucian's story of three friends whose quest to determine whether male or female love is superior brings them to the renowned sanctuary of Aphrodite at Cnidus. While the travelers inspect and marvel at Aphrodite's incomparable beauty, espe-

---

of Solomon: "For *porneia* is the destruction of life, separating a person from God and leading to idols (προσεγγίζουσα τοῖς εἰδώλοις)" (*T. Reu.* 4:6).

159. Friedo Ricken, "Gab es eine hellenistische Vorlage für Weish 13–15?" *Biblica* 49 (1968): 70–71; Maurice Gilbert, *La critique des dieux dans le Livre de la Sagesse* (Rome: Biblical Institute Press, 1973), 192–93.

160. Also in Clement of Alexandria, *Protr.* 4.57.3–5; Arnobius, *Adv. nat.* 6.22. See the discussion in Freedberg, *The Power of Images*, 340–44; and Jaś Elsner, "Visual Mimesis and the Myth of the Real: Ovid's Pygmalion as Viewer," *Ramus* 20 (1991): 154–68.

161. For a discussion of this facet of human-statue encounters, see Freedberg, *The Power of Images*, 317–44; Nigel J. Spivey, *Understanding Greek Sculpture: Ancient Meanings, Modern Readings* (London: Thames and Hudson, 1996), 173–86; Steiner, *Images in Mind*, 185–250; Stewart, *Statues in Roman Society*, 265–66.

162. E.g., Pliny the Elder, *Nat.* 36.4.20–22; Lucian, *Imagines* 4.263; Arnobius, *Adv. nat.* 6.22.

cially her backside—one "pilgrim" remarks with obvious delight that her buttocks smile ever so sweetly (ὑδὺς ὁ γέλως)—they do notice one slight flaw: a stain, on one of her thighs (Ps.-Lucian, *Erotes* 14–15). A female attendant then proceeds to explain the origins of this mark. A young man fell madly in love with the goddess and spent every waking hour gazing at her beauty. Seizing an opportunity to consummate his deepest desire (τῶν ἐν αὐτῷ πόθων), he unleashed his lusts (ἐπιθυμία) in a nocturnal rendezvous, resulting in the enduring "marks of these erotic embraces" (τῶν ἐρωτικῶν περιπλοκῶν ἴχνη; *Erotes* 16).

The legend of the Cnidian Aphrodite, which is but one of many similar stories,[163] thrives on the harsh juxtaposition of form and substance, the tension between realism and lifelessness: a statue's beautiful form (εἶδος), which arouses desire (πόθος), juxtaposed with its cold, hard, unresponsive, and impenetrable surface; a lover whose erotic charms tease to arousal only to shut down at the brink of consummation.[164] The third-century C.E. Flavius Philostratus, author of the *Vitae sophistarum*, quotes the opening line of a speech by the sophist Onomarchus of Andros—bearing the title "The one who loved a statue" (ἐπὶ τοῦ τῆς εἰκόνος ἐρῶντος)—that captures this underlying frustration of love for the lifeless statue: "O living beauty in a lifeless body (ἐν ἀψύχῳ σώματι)." This lament leads the speaker to then chastise the statue for unrequited love: "You unloving (ἀνέραστος) and malicious (βάσκανος) one, faithless to your faithful lover (ἐραστής)" (*Vit. soph.* 598–599). In this case, form approximates, but ultimately falls short of life.

It is precisely this tension between form and substance that the author of the Wisdom of Solomon exploits for polemical purposes, attempting to circumvent the beguiling charms of a statue by stressing the absurdity of the πόθος of lovers (ἐρασταί) who pursue a lifeless form (εἶδος ἄπνουν). For the author of this text, εἶδος is deceptively charming, and the more beautiful the εἶδος, that is, the more it approaches a *mimesis* of life, the greater its capacity to deceive the viewer. Indeed, in the preceding paragraphs pseudo-Solomon explicitly draws on the Platonic no-

---

163. In addition to the Cnidian Aphrodite, Pliny the Elder also mentions the statue of Eros at Parium, upon which a man from Rhodes left traces of his passion (*Nat.* 36.4.22). In his *Deipnosophistae*, Athenaeus discusses the capacity of a statue to arouse sexual desire and supports this claim with several similar anecdotes: a bull who was aroused by a bronze cow at Pirene; a youth from Samos who tried to consummate his love for a statue of Parian marble; and a man who had sex with a marble boy at Delphi (*Deipn.* 13.84). While most of the accounts of agalmatophilia in Greek and Latin sources focus on male arousal, a few sources perhaps raise the possibility of female arousal. In his misogynistic satire on Roman wives, Juvenal describes the women who frequent the temple of Pudicitia in the Forum Boarium as follows: "Here [at the temple] at night they set down their litters, here they piss on and fill up the image of the goddess with their long streams, and taking turns they ride (*equito*) her, and they romp about with only the moon as witness" (*Sat.* 6.309–311). When Pliny the Elder chastises the Emperor Augustus' daughter Julia for crowning the statue of Marsyas during her "nocturnal debauchery" (*luxuria noctibus*; *Nat.* 21.6), he may likewise be implicitly referring to a "nocturnal romp" with the statue itself, as indeed Peter Stewart suggests (Stewart, *Statues in Roman Society*, 266). Finally, the Babylonian Talmud briefly mentions a queen who used a phallic statue to pleasure herself (*b. Avod. Zar.* 44a).

164. Steiner, *Images in Mind*, 204–7.

tion of the deceptive nature of τέχνη to liken the realism of a statue's form—an artisan who "with skill forces a likeness into that which is more beautiful" (ἐξεβιάσατο τῇ τέχνῃ τὴν ὁμοιότητα ἐπὶ τὸ κάλλιον)—to a hidden trap (ἔνεδρον) that ensnares the masses (Wis 14:19–21).[165] It is true that pseudo-Solomon's stress on the lifeless and impotent essence of a statue, namely that divine statues are inanimate matter, nothing more than stone, wood, or metal in the hands of an artisan, is undoubtedly inspired by the biblical-prophetic critique of idolatry, especially Deutero-Isaiah's derisive parody of an artisan who fashions a block of wood into both a god and kindling for a fire (Isa 44:9–20).[166] Nevertheless, the nexus between the statue and a lover's πόθος, combined with juxtaposition of εἶδος with ἄπνοον to underscore a disjunction between sensual visuality and reality, demonstrates the extent to which the author of this text has absorbed the iconic language and perceptions of the Greco-Roman Mediterranean.

CONCLUSION

My intent in the present chapter was not to set out a full and comprehensive account of Jewish responses to images in Greco-Roman antiquity, though such an investigation would be potentially fruitful. Rather I wished only to stress the inherently complex process of negotiating the sculptural (and more broadly artistic) environment of the Greco-Roman Mediterranean, which in many respects mirrored the equally complex process of negotiating identity in the ancient world.

The image of the aniconic Jew that emerges in Josephus' narratives is not altogether unwarranted insofar as it bears the unmistakable imprint of the author's Judean upbringing. The scant archaeological remains attesting to figurative/sculpted art in Second Temple Judea, combined with the literary testimony from a broad range of sources—Jewish or otherwise—suggest at the very least an ambivalent, perhaps even uneasy attitude toward figurative art, especially three-dimensional freestanding statues, for many Judeans during the period in question. Nevertheless, the near ubiquitous claim in scholarship that Second Temple Judaism (Judean and Diaspora) adhered to a strict halakhic prohibition—based on an

165. See also the similar use of the agalmatophilia traditions in Clement of Alexandria's idol polemic (*Protr.* 4) and the discussion in Simon Goldhill, "The Erotic Eye: Visual Stimulation and Cultural Conflict," in *Being Greek under Rome: Cultural Identity, the Second Sophistic, and the Development of Empire* (ed. Simon Goldhill; Cambridge: Cambridge University Press, 2001), 172–80.

166. See also Jer 10:1–16; Hab 2:18–19; Hos 8:6; 13:2; Ps 115:3–8; Ps. 135:15–18; and the discussion in Roth, "For Life, He Appeals to Death," 21–47. The author of the Wisdom of Solomon is clearly drawing from the parody of Isa 44 when he derides the lifeless materiality of an idol: "But miserable, with their hopes set on dead things, are those who give the name 'gods' to the works of human hands (ἔργα χειρῶν ἀνθρώπων), gold and silver fashioned with skill, and likenesses of animals, or a useless stone, the work of an ancient hand," a remark that introduces a satirical parody of a carpenter who uses parts of a tree for various utensils and fuel for the fire, while the remaining "cast-off piece" is then fashioned into a god (Wis 13:10–19).

idiosyncratic reading of the second commandment—of all forms of figurative art does not adequately account for the multiple and variegated factors that invariably shaped Jewish responses to images.

Of course, this is not to suggest that the second commandment, or more precisely the interpretation of the second commandment, *did not play any role* in the process of negotiating images in antiquity—only that biblical exegesis was but one of many complex factors. Moreover, even granting that the biblical prohibition of images did in fact play a role in this process, perhaps even an important one, it is still necessary to define with more precision how this legal prohibition functioned during the Second Temple period. Is there any merit to the suggestion that Jews by and large interpreted the second commandment as a prohibition against all forms of figurative art, regardless of context or function? It is precisely this question that will occupy the focus in the next chapter.

3

The Second Commandment in Josephus and Greco-Roman Jewish Literature

In the previous chapter I argued that Jewish responses to images in antiquity cannot simply be reduced to a question of legal exegesis. That is to say, this issue was vastly more complex than a particular interpretive approach to the biblical prohibition against images. Nevertheless, the Mosaic proscription of images, especially the formulation in the Decalogue (the so-called second commandment), remains a significant factor. Indeed, the long and storied history of this interdiction demonstrates the extent to which the second commandment has left an indelible (though variegated) imprint on all three Abrahamic traditions, those religious communities that identify themselves as the rightful heirs to, and infallible exegetes of, Mosaic revelation.

Nowhere is this more evident than in the Byzantine iconoclastic controversies following Leo III the Isaurian's (emperor from 717–741 c.e.) destruction of the famed Christ of the Chalkitis, the iconic protector of Constantinople erected above the Golden Gate of the imperial palace.[1] Both Iconodules and Iconoclasts claimed Mosaic legislation as support for their position. For the Iconoclast, the matter was fairly straightforward: Moses prohibited the production of divine images and, hence, of the second person of the Trinity. Thus, to install icons of Christ was tantamount to pagan idolatry.[2] The Iconodules, by contrast, condemned this interpretive approach as a remnant of the excessive and obscuring literalism of Jewish exegetical practices, a reading of sacred scripture that misses entirely the "hidden, spiritual meaning," the truest sense of Moses' words.[3] The prohibition originally given to Moses was predicated upon the heretofore unseen, and unseeable, nature of God (Deut 4:15). But Christ's incarnation must of necessity alter the scope of this prohibition to allow the pictorial representation of the God who now could be seen. Consequently, to reject images of Christ was "the equivalent of the

1. Besançon, *The Forbidden Image*, 114–15. Besançon subsequently likens this incident to Luther's Ninety-five Theses posted on the door of the Wittenberg Church in that both were an explicit symbol of reformation (123).

2. Bevan, *Holy Images*, 132.

3. John of Damascus (*PG* 94, cols. 1236ff.), cited in Herbert L. Kessler, "'Thou Shalt Paint the Likeness of Christ Himself': The Mosaic Prohibition as Provocation for Christian Images," in *The Real and Ideal Jerusalem in Jewish, Christian, and Islamic Art* (ed. Bianca Kühnel; Jerusalem: Hebrew University, 1998), 137–38.

Jewish rejection of Christ's incarnation which made God visible to humans."[4] In the words of Alain Besançon, the "prohibition of Horeb became invalid from the moment God manifested himself in the flesh, sensible not only to hearing but to sight. Thereafter, God had a visible 'character,' an 'imprint carved' in matter, in his flesh."[5] It is thus only a short step from here to Alexios Aristenos' twelfth-century gloss on Canon 82 from the Quinisext Council of 692 C.E., in which the original prohibition against images is radically transformed into a command to make an image of Christ.[6]

By linking the Iconoclasts with the supposedly defective hermeneutics of the Jews, the implication was clear: Iconoclasts were heirs to Jewish iconophobia, and to oppose the Christian use of icons was nothing less than to judaize Christianity.[7] The nexus of iconoclasm and a judaizing impulse is explicitly articulated by the presbyter John of Jerusalem in his address to the Second Council of Nicea in 787 C.E. Specifically, John asserted that the "pseudo-bishop of Nacoleia and his followers," representatives of the iconoclastic party, "imitated the lawless Jews" by following the teachings of a "wicked sorcerer" from Tiberias, who had already persuaded the Caliph Umar II "to obliterate and overthrow absolutely every painting and image in different colours whether on canvas, in mosaics, on walls, or on sacred vessels and altar coverings."[8]

The aniconic Jew in John of Jerusalem, that is, the obsessive literalist whose approach to the second commandment precluded the possibility of art as such, is likely a fictitious construct, a literary foil that functions mainly to censure by association the author's opponents, the Christian Iconoclasts. Nevertheless, as documented in the previous chapter, John's "wicked sorcerer" is not dissimilar to the scholarly reconstruction of the Second Temple aniconic Jew, excepting of course the former's polemical vitriol. For the majority of scholars, the scarcity of figurative archaeological remains prior to the destruction of the Second Temple, coupled with the literary sources from the period in question (with a particular emphasis on Josephus), is indicative of a rather strict interpretation of the second commandment. Conversely, the emergence of a rich and extensive body of figurative art after the destruction of the temple suggests for many scholars a trend toward leniency, that is, that Jews were gradually accepting a less restrictive stance toward the Mosaic proscription.

Both the original and the revised editions of Emil Schürer's classic *Geschichte des jüdischen Volkes im Zeitalter Jesu Christi*, which link the supposedly strict exegetical stance of the Second Temple period to the "extreme scrupulousness" of

4. Kessler, "The Mosaic Prohibition," 139. See also Bevan, *Holy Images*, 134–35.

5. Besançon, *The Forbidden Image*, 126.

6. The full text, which in Herbert Kessler's view draws on the language of the second commandment, reads: "Thou shalt not paint a lamb as a type of Christ, but Christ himself" ("The Mosaic Prohibition," 128–30).

7. Ibid., 138–39.

8. Cited in Leslie W. Barnard, *The Graeco-Roman and Oriental Background of the Iconoclastic Controversy* (Leiden: Brill, 1974), 16–17. According to Barnard, the actual influence of Byzantine period Judaism on the Iconoclasts was at best minimal (34–50).

the Pharisees/Rabbis, have in some sense crystallized into a virtual orthodoxy the notion of a shift toward exegetical leniency across the 70 C.E. divide: "In order to avoid anything even seeming to approach idolatry, they [the Pharisees] stressed above all in the first century A.D., the Mosaic prohibition of images," which, according to Schürer, was taken to mean that Jews "should have nothing to do with any pictorial representations at all."[9] A parenthetical note addressing the "spread of Hellenism" reflects even more explicitly the chronological schematic summarized above (and discussed in detail in chapter 2):

> [R]epresentational art was nevertheless extremely restricted up to the end of the first century A.D. There was however *a substantial change in the second and third centuries*. In this period there is significant evidence, not least from tombs and synagogues, of the acceptance of representational forms, including those of the human figure. With this went *a more lenient attitude on the part of the rabbis*, who, in effect, drew the line only at the actual worship of images, especially those of the emperor.[10]

Thus, according to the *communis opinio* in scholarship, before 70 C.E. Jews by and large thought that Moses had proscribed images in toto. Only after the destruction of the temple did Jews begin to restrict the scope of the second commandment to cultic images, or images intended for worship.

I will attempt in the present chapter to test this scholarly paradigm by examining the *Nachleben* of the Jewish prohibition against images in Greco-Roman antiquity. After looking briefly at one of the primary source texts, Exod 20:2–6, I will consider Josephus' interpretation of this prohibition and then place the Josephan material within a wider midrashic context, that is, within Jewish exegetical traditions between the second century B.C.E. and second century C.E.[11] In so doing, I will argue two main theses. First, although scholars tend to see in Josephus a consistently rigid interpretation of Exod 20:2–6 (especially vv. 4–5), wherein the scope of the prohibition is thought to include all figurative art,[12] a closer analysis of this material brings a much more complicated picture to the surface. Specifically, there emerges an apparent tension between Josephus' reading of this commandment—those places where the author explicitly sets out to explain or exegete the prohibition against images—and how his Jewish characters seemingly practiced this legislation "on the ground," that is, his narrative portrayals of Jewish resistance to (or acceptance of) images. Whereas in the latter we may observe an apparent

9. Schürer, *History of the Jewish People*, 2:81.

10. Ibid., 2:59 (emphasis mine).

11. Along with Peter Enns, I am using the term "midrash" to refer to an "*interpretive* phenomenon" rather than a "*literary* phenomenon." That is to say, although there emerged in the centuries that followed the destruction of the Second Temple a literary genre known as "midrash," the term may also be used to describe any exegetical activity—specific attempts to interpret Jewish scripture—that occurs in a wide range of Jewish (and Christian) literary genres from antiquity (Peter Enns, *Exodus Retold: Ancient Exegesis of the Departure from Egypt in Wis 10:15–21 and 19:1–9* [Atlanta: Scholars Press, 1997], 16).

12. For example, Fine, *Art and Judaism*, 80.

exegetical rigidity that *seemingly* precludes all figurative images regardless of context or function, the former reflects a more nuanced understanding of the second commandment, one in which the scope of proscribed images was limited to *cultic* objects, namely images (whether of pagan deities or of the Jewish God) intended for worship. Second, although we can detect a similar spectrum of exegetical possibilities—ranging from proscribing all images to cultic images—within our comparative context, the predominant tendency in Greco-Roman Jewish literature, both before and after the destruction of the Second Temple, was to define the scope of the second commandment according to this criterion of worship. This at the very least problematizes the assumption that prior to 70 C.E. the Mosaic legislation was uniformly understood as a proscription of all figurative art.

THE SECOND COMMANDMENT IN THE HEBREW BIBLE

The prohibition against images in the Hebrew Bible is a complicated subject that encompasses a vast and diverse body of textual material—numerous legal proscriptions and prophetic pronouncements[13]—as well as a host of literary and historical problems, ranging from questions surrounding the origins and extent of Israelite aniconism to the very definition of aniconism.[14] Thus a full treatment

---

13. See, for example, the list of texts in Brian Schmidt, "The Aniconic Tradition: On Reading Images and Viewing Texts," in *The Triumph of Elohim: From Yahwisms to Judaisms* (ed. Diana Vikander-Edelman; Grand Rapids: Eerdmans, 1996), 78. See also the detailed study by Cristoph Dohmen, *Das Bilderverbot: Seine Entstehung und Entwicklung im Alten Testament* (Bonn: Hanstein, 1985). Specifically, Dohmen identifies five different types of texts in the Hebrew Bible that deal with the question of images: (1) narratives that mention cult images in passing; (2) Deuteronomic texts that address cult reform; (3) prophetic texts that ridicule cult images; (4) prophetic texts that mention foreign cult statues but whose larger concern is not the image per se but the religion/god that stands behind the image; and (5) legal texts prohibiting cult images, the so-called *Bilderverbot* (38). For Dohmen, the *Bilderverbot*, which itself develops out of an earlier *Fremdgötterverbot*, is the final phase of a complicated evolutionary process that only emerges during the exilic or postexilic periods in the now familiar legal formulation of the Decalogue (175–77).

14. For some of the more important discussions of this prohibition in Israelite religion, see R. H. Pfeiffer, "The Polemic against Idolatry in the Old Testament," *JBL* 43 (1924): 229–40; Jean Ouellette, "Le deuxième commandement et le role de l'image dans la symbolique religieuse de l'Ancien Testament: Essai d'interprétation," *RB* 74 (1967): 504–16; Carmel Konikoff, *The Second Commandment and Its Interpretation in the Art of Ancient Israel* (Geneva: Imprimerie du Journal de Genève, 1973); Robert P. Carroll, "The Aniconic God and the Cult of Images," *ST* 31 (1977): 51–64; José Faur, "The Biblical Idea of Idolatry," *JQR* 69 (1978): 1–15; Dohmen, *Das Bilderverbot*; Ronald S. Hendel, "The Social Origins of the Aniconic Tradition in Early Israel," *CBQ* 50 (1988): 365–82; Mettinger, *No Graven Image*; Schmidt, "The Aniconic Tradition," 75–105; T. J. Lewis, "Divine Image: Aniconism in Ancient Israel," *JAOS* 118 (1998): 36–52; Martin Prudký, "'You Shall Not Make Yourself an Image': The Intention and Implications of the Second Commandment," in *The Old Testament as Inspiration in Culture* (ed. Hana Hlaváčková; Třebenice: Mlýn, 2001), 37–51; Knut Holter, *Deuteronomy 4 and the Second Commandment* (New York: Peter Lang, 2003).

of this topic and all of the relevant data is well beyond the scope of the present study. Nevertheless, given that during the Greco-Roman period an important focal point was the legal prohibition expressed in the Decalogue, that is, the so-called second commandment appearing in Exod 20:2–6 and Deut 5:6–10,[15] I will restrict my focus to this particular formulation, and more specifically to the Exodus version.[16]

As the following comparison of Exod 20:2–6 demonstrates, the Septuagint translation follows carefully the structure of the Hebrew text:

MT	LXX
2 אנכי יהוה אלהיך אשר הוצאתיך מארץ מצרים מבית עבדים:	2 ἐγώ εἰμι κύριος ὁ θεός σου, ὅστις ἐξήγαγόν σε ἐκ γῆς Αἰγύπτου, ἐξ οἴκου δουλείας.
3 לא יהיה־לך אלהים אחרים על־פני:	3 οὐκ ἔσονταί σοι θεοὶ ἕτεροι πλὴν ἐμοῦ.
4 לא תעשׂה־לך פסל וכל־תמונה אשר בשמים ממעל ואשר בארץ מתחת ואשר במים מתחת לארץ:	4 οὐ ποιήσεις σεαυτῷ εἴδωλον, οὐδὲ παντὸς ὁμοίωμα, ὅσα ἐν τῷ οὐρανῷ ἄνω, καὶ ὅσα ἐν τῇ γῇ κάτω, καὶ ὅσα ἐν τοῖς ὕδασιν ὑποκάτω τῆς γῆς.
5 לא־תשתחוה להם ולא תעבדם כי אנכי יהוה אלהיך אל קנא פקד עון אבת על־בנים על־שלשים ועל־רבעים לשנאי:	5 οὐ προσκυνήσεις αὐτοῖς, οὐδὲ μὴ λατρεύσῃς αὐτοῖς· ἐγὼ γάρ εἰμι κύριος ὁ θεός σου θεὸς ζηλωτής, ἀποδιδοὺς ἁμαρτίας πατέρων ἐπὶ τέκνα ἕως τρίτης καὶ τετάρτης γενεᾶς τοῖς μισοῦσίν με,
6 ועשה חסד לאלפים לאהבי ולשמרי מצותי:	6 καὶ ποιῶν ἔλεος εἰς χιλιάδας τοῖς ἀγαπῶσίν με καὶ τοῖς φυλάσσουσιν τὰ προστάγματά μου.

My translation of the Hebrew text is as follows:

> 2 I am YHWH your God, who brought you out of the land of Egypt, out of the house of slavery. 3 You shall not have any other gods besides me. 4 You shall not make for yourself a statue (פסל), or any representation (תמונה) of that which is in the heavens above, or on the earth below, or in the waters beneath the earth. 5 You shall not bow down to them, nor worship them, because I am YHWH your God, a jealous God, bringing the sins of the parents on the children, on the third and on the fourth generations of those who hate me, 6 but demonstrating kindness to thousands, to those who love me and keep my commandments.

---

15. Eliav, "Viewing the Sculptural Environment," 418; Carl S. Ehrlich, "Du sollst dir kein Gottesbildnis machen: Das zweite Gebot im Judentum," in *Bibel und Judentum: Beiträge aus dem christlich-jüdischen Gespräch* (ed. Carl S. Ehrlich; Zürich: Pano, 2004), 71–86.

16. For purposes of this analysis, the differences between the Exodus and Deuteronomy versions are minimal. Nevertheless, one difference that some interpreters consider significant is the absence of the conjunction ו on כל תמונה in Deut 5:8. For a discussion of this (and related) grammatical issue, see Dohmen, *Das Bilderverbot*, 213–77; Cornelis Houtman, *Exodus* (3 vols.; Kampen, Germany: Kok, 1993), 3:21–22; Schmidt, "The Aniconic Tradition," 79–80.

There is much debate within both the Jewish and Christian traditions over the proper enumeration of this portion of the Decalogue, specifically whether the prohibition against making and worshiping images (20:4–6) is distinct from or integral to the prohibition against other gods (20:3; לא יהיה־לך אלהים אחרים על־פני).[17] Although later Jewish tradition, with the notable exception of Philo and Josephus (see below), will identify 20:2 as the "first commandment" and 20:3–6 as the "second commandment,"[18] the grammar of the Hebrew text indicates that this "second commandment" actually consists of four specific prohibitions—expressed with four volitional clauses (לא + the imperfect verb)—flowing directly from the opening affirmation "I am YHWH your God." This can be represented in the following structural layout:

אנכי יהוה אלהיך
לא יהיה־לך אלהים אחרים על־פני
לא תעשׂה־לך פסל וכל־תמונה
לא תשתחוה להם
ולא תעבדם

The first לא clause prohibits all other gods besides YHWH; the second prohibits making sculpted images and other representations; the third prohibits bowing down "to them"; and the fourth prohibits worshiping "them." Although grammatically there are four volitional clauses, the last two are conceptually parallel and

17. On the general problem of enumerating the Decalogue, see Tatum, "The LXX Version," 179–80; Houtman, *Exodus*, 3:3–5. This question is important in both Jewish and Christian circles, in part because it bears directly on how these prohibitions should be interpreted. In Christianity, the Catholic and Lutheran traditions identify all of Exod 20:2–6 as a single commandment (the first), following Augustine; hence, the prohibition against images is subsumed under the prohibition against other gods. In contrast, the Reformed tradition, exemplified in John Calvin, identifies 20:3 as the first and 20:4–6 as the second (following the tradition of Philo and Josephus outlined below), a distinction that was important for their rejection of the ecclesiastical use of images. The traditional Jewish division, exemplified in Rabbi Benno Jacob's commentary on Exodus, identifies the first commandment as Exod 20:2 and the second as Exod 20:3–6 (Benno Jacob, "The First and Second Commandments," *Judaism* 13 [1964]: 3–18). Indeed, Jacob elsewhere refers to this as the "only correct division. . . . Anything else never existed among genuine Jews," an assertion that unwittingly (or not?) banishes Philo and Josephus from the realm of Judaism (see Benno Jacob, "The Decalogue," *JQR* 14 [1923]: 148). Nisan Ararat innovatively suggests that 20:2–4 (the prohibition against other gods and their images) should be the first commandment, and 20:5–6 (the prohibition against bowing down to these gods) should be the second commandment, an interpretive maneuver that further illustrates the importance of "properly" dividing the Decalogue in these various faith traditions ("The Second Commandment: 'Thou Shalt Not Bow Down unto Them, Nor Serve Them, for I the Lord Thy God Am a Jealous God'," *Shofar* 13 (1995): 44–57.

18. For example, in *Tg. Neof.* Exod. 20:2–5, the "first saying" (דבורייא קדמיא) is the acclamation of YHWH's unique relationship with his people, and the "second saying" (תנינא דבירא) combines the prohibition against other gods and images (likewise in *Tg. Ps.-J.* Exod. 20:2–5).

joined with a conjunction and thus should probably be classified as a single prohibition against certain kinds of cultic devotion. Concerning the second volitional clause, we may further observe that the type of image forbidden in 20:4—פסל (εἴδωλον) or תמונה (ὁμοίωμα)—is qualified with three subordinate clauses (אשר) that serve to clarify the scope of the prohibited object. On the surface this qualification seems rather comprehensive, with the "triadic cosmological schema"—the heavens, the earth, and the waters—seemingly encompassing images of all observable phenomena, or at least of all "*faunal* forms inhabiting the sky, earth, and sea."[19] In sum, then, encapsulated in this text are three interrelated prohibitions addressing the problems of foreign deities, images, and certain types of cultic activity.

Several important questions or exegetical problems surface in this text that will shape subsequent interpretive traditions.[20] First, what is the relationship between the various prohibitions? I touched on this briefly from a grammatical point of view, but this issue emerges as a hermeneutical puzzle in many interpretations of the Decalogue. Is the prohibition against making and worshiping images (20:4–6) integral to or distinct from the prohibition against other gods (20:3)? Furthermore, this question is inextricably linked with the issue of referent: what do the forbidden images represent? Are images of foreign gods in view here, the אחרים אלהים of 20:3? Or, if the prohibition against images is viewed as in some sense independent of 20:3, is the prohibition restricted to only images of YHWH, or to images in toto?[21] Even more pertinent to the subject at hand, is the prohibition against *making* images distinct from the volitional clauses focused on cultic activities, whether the latter has in view the worship of images (פסל and תמונה) or

19. Schmidt, "The Aniconic Tradition," 81–83.

20. Several scholars have highlighted the role that perceived textual problems played in giving rise to various exegetical solutions. For example, Géza Vermès notes: "Before any other consideration, homiletical or doctrinal, the task of the [ancient] interpreter was to solve problems raised by the Bible itself" (*Scripture and Tradition in Judaism* [Leiden: Brill, 1973], 83). See also Enns, *Exodus Retold*, 13–15.

21. See, for example, J. J. Stamm, *The Ten Commandments in Recent Research* (trans. M. E. Andrew; Naperville, Ill.: Alec R. Allenson, 1967), 84; Schmidt, "The Aniconic Tradition," 80–81; John Barton, "'The Work of Human Hands' (Psalm 115:4): Idolatry in the Old Testament," in *The Ten Commandments: The Reciprocity of Faithfulness* (ed. William P. Brown; Louisville: Westminster John Knox Press, 2004), 196. Both Stamm and Barton see the second commandment as a requirement for the aniconic worship of YHWH. Schmidt, however, considering a wider swath of textual and archaeological material, argues that only certain types of YHWH images were prohibited, specifically theriomorphic or anthropomorphic images. However, since inanimate, floral, and composite (part human, part animal) representations were not prohibited, then it raises the possibility of a legitimate representation of YHWH from one of these three categories (96). For Schmidt, one possible example of an acceptable YHWH image is the drawing on pithos A from Kuntillet 'Ajrud, which perhaps depicts a composite representation of YHWH (96–103); see also Brian Schmidt, "The Iron Age Pithoi Drawings from Horvat Teman or Kuntillet 'Ajrud: Some New Proposals," *JANER* 2 (2002): 91–125. In contrast, Martin Prudký argues that the only legitimate representation of YHWH was textual, not visible ("The Intention and Implications of the Second Commandment," 49).

foreign gods (אלהים אחרים) or both?[22] If yes, then one could easily read this text as an interdiction against any kind of artistic representation, regardless of content or function.[23] Moreover, there are questions regarding the forbidden object itself. The Hebrew term פסל is typically used for sculpted or carved images, that is, images hewn from wood or stone.[24] Is the prohibition thus restricted to sculpted images, or does the ensuing term (תמונה) broaden the scope to include other forms of artistic representation?[25] More important, does the cosmological triad encompass all observable phenomena or only certain kinds of phenomena, such as animals and humans?

It is not my intention to answer these questions in this chapter. Rather, I only wish to underscore the inherent ambiguity in the legal formulation of this proscription, an ambiguity that later exegetes will in part attempt to clarify.[26] With this in mind, I will now consider a broad range of exegetical traditions surrounding the second commandment, focusing first on the writings of Josephus and then situating his material within a wider comparative context.

---

22. Walther Zimmerli argues that the antecedent of the plural "them" (20:5) is not the singular פסל or תמונה (20:4) but rather the plural אלהים אחרים (20:3). On this basis, he concludes that the prohibition against making an image was inserted later into legislation that originally dealt only with having and worshipping other gods ("Das Zweite Gebot," in *Festschrift für Alfred Bertholet zum 80* [ed. Walter Baumgartner et al.; Tübingen: Mohr Siebeck, 1950], 550–63). Henning Reventlow counters Zimmerli by arguing that the third-person plural suffix refers not to אלהים אחרים but to both פסל *and* תמונה (*Gebot und Predigt im Dekalog* [Gütersloh, Germany: G. Mohn, 1962], 31). As Holter observes, following F.-L. Hossfeld, Zimmerli's interpretation only works in Deuteronomy's version of the commandment, since the absence of the conjunction ו between פסל and כל תמונה creates a grammatically singular object, whereas in Exodus פסל וכל תמונה satisfies the grammatical requirements of the plural suffixes in 20:5 (see Holter, *Deuteronomy 4 and the Second Commandment*, 72–77). See also the discussion in Tatum, "The LXX Version," 180–81; Schmidt, "The Aniconic Tradition," 79–81.

23. Indeed, A. J. Wensinck argues that it was the "lawgiver's intention" that each prohibition stand alone. Thus, the prohibition against making images is not tied to idol worship per se but is rooted in the idea that such an act imitates the creative capacity of God and thus represents a "usurpation of the divine creative function" ("The Second Commandment," *Mededeelingen der Koninklijke Akademie van Wetenschappen* 59 [1925]: 159–65 [quotes on pp. 6–7]).

24. Two exceptions are Isa 40:19 and 44:10, where פסל is used of molten images.

25. Here the added conjunction in the Exodus version plays a significant role in the discussion. For example, according to Tatum the Exodus version prohibits any kind of image, sculpted or otherwise, but the Deuteronomy version, because it lacks the conjunction between the פסל and תמונה, prohibits only sculpted images, since from this perspective תמונה is subsumed under the broader category of פסל (Tatum, "The LXX Version," 180).

26. Bevan, *Holy Images*, 46.

Reading the Second Commandment in Josephus

Josephus refers to the second commandment at least nineteen times throughout his corpus of writings (see appendix 2). He explicitly explains the legislation of Exod 20 and Deut 5 on two occasions—*A.J.* 3.91; *C. Ap.* 2.190–192—and in numerous other instances makes reference to the commandment, either in accounts of fallen biblical heroes such as the legendary King Solomon (*A.J.* 8.195), or in the context of iconoclastic stories, that is, narratives detailing Jewish opposition to a variety of statues or other forms of figurative art.[27] *A.J.* 3.91 and *C. Ap.* 2.190–192 are clearly exegetical or midrashic in nature, since in both texts Josephus explicitly sets out to explain the Mosaic legislation, in *A.J.* the δέκα λόγοι ("ten sayings")[28] and in *C. Ap.* αἱ προρρήσεις καὶ ἀπαγορεύσεις ("the warnings and prohibitions").[29] The iconoclastic narratives, however, though often (but not always) including a brief summary of the prohibition, serve mainly to censure perceived violations and to explain the behavior of certain "iconoclasts" by appealing to ὁ πάτριος νόμος (or alternatively νόμος / νόμιμος [τῶν Ἰουδαϊκῶν], τὸ πάτριον ἔθος, among other such legal designations).[30] What is particularly relevant for the present discussion is the apparent tension between *exegesis* and *praxis*, that is, between Josephus' reading of the second commandment within an exegetical context and how this proscription is seemingly applied in various narrative contexts. Specifically, the retrospective glances at ὁ πάτριος νόμος in his historical narratives seem to conflict with Josephus' own reading of the second commandment in *A.J.* 3.91 and *C. Ap.* 2.190–192.

---

27. E.g., *B.J.* 1.650; *A.J.* 17.151; 18.55; 18.263–264.

28. Niese's *Editio maior* reads ὡς διαφυγεῖν μηδένα καὶ λόγων but in the notes suggests the emendation μηδένα τῶν δέκα λόγοι, which Thackeray follows in the Loeb edition (see Benedict Niese, ed., *Flavii Josephi Opera* [7 vols.; Berlin: Weidmann, 1885–1895], 1:176; Étienne Nodet, ed., *Flavius Josèphe, Les Antiquitiés Juives* [2 vols.; Paris: Les Éditions du Cerf, 1990–1995], 1:160–61). Although Louis Feldman generally follows Niese's Greek text in his recent translation of and commentary on *A.J.* 1–4, in this particular instance he translates the clause "so that none of the ten sayings escaped them," apparently accepting the proposed emendation (*Judean Antiquities* 1–4 [Flavius Josephus: Translation and Commentary 3; ed. Steve Mason; Leiden: Brill, 2000], 252). Whether or not this emendation is correct, Josephus does explicitly enumerate ten λόγοι in *A.J.* 3.91–92, and elsewhere he refers to the δέκα λόγοι written on two tablets (*A.J.* 4.304). Philo of Alexandria identifies the δέκα λόγοι as the foundational legislation from which all other "special laws" are derived (τὰ μὲν γένη τῶν ἐν εἴδει νόμων; *Spec.* 1.1; cf. *Decal.* 1.154).

29. On Josephus' summary of Mosaic legislation, see Géza Vermès, "A Summary of the Law by Flavius Josephus," *NovT* 24 (1982): 289–303.

30. On legal terminology in Josephus (esp. in *C. Ap.*), see Rajak, "The *Against Apion*," 206–8. On the concept of ancestral law in Josephus, see Bernd Schröder, *Die "väterlichen Gesetze": Flavius Josephus als Vermittler von Halachah an Griechen und Römer* (Tübingen: Mohr Siebeck, 1996), esp. 27–157.

Appearances in Exegetical Context

In his introduction to the Decalogue in *A.J.* 3.90, Josephus remarks that he is not permitted to recount the λόγοι "verbatim."[31] However this ambiguous phrase should be interpreted,[32] Josephus clarifies that he is nevertheless permitted to "reveal their power" (τὰς δὲ δυνάμεις αὐτῶν δηλώσομεν), that is, the force or meaning of the λόγοι. In other words, Josephus offers the reader a paraphrase of the Decalogue that functions to elucidate its essential meaning if not its actual words. With this in mind, his concise restatement of the first two precepts in *A.J.* 3.91, the relevant portion for this analysis, is as follows:

> Διδάσκει μὲν οὖν ἡμᾶς ὁ πρῶτος λόγος, ὅτι θεός ἐστιν εἷς καὶ τοῦτον δεῖ σέβεσθαι μόνον· ὁ δὲ δεύτερος κελεύει μηδενὸς εἰκόνα ζῴου ποιήσαντας προσκυνεῖν·
>
> So then, the first saying teaches us that God is one and he alone should be worshiped. The second commands to make no image of any living being for the purpose of worship.

Several features in this text have been used by interpreters as evidence that Josephus broadens the scope of this commandment to proscribe images in toto. First, Josephus omits completely the opening affirmation of Exod 20:2 ("I am YHWH your God") and further collapses the three prohibitions of 20:3–6 (see the above discussion) into two distinct λόγοι: the first (ὁ πρῶτος λόγος) focuses on the exclusive worship of the Jewish God, summarized within a monotheistic—or perhaps more appropriately, monolatrous—framework (θεός ἐστιν εἷς) that recalls the language of the *Shema*;[33] the second (ὁ δεύτερος) addresses the problem of εἰκόνες. As noted above, this enumeration differs from what would eventually become dominant in the Jewish tradition, although Philo of Alexandria similarly divides the Decalogue (*Decal.* 51). According to Tatum, the effect of Josephus' enumeration of the Decalogue is that, insofar as it distinguishes the prohibition of other gods (ὁ πρῶτος) from the prohibition of images (ὁ δεύτερος), it "possibly opens the way for a more anti-iconic statement."[34] In other words, by separating the issue of εἰκόνες from the issue of cultic allegiance, Josephus reconfigures the source text, at least in Tatum's estimation, to address two seemingly distinct concerns: idolatry on the one hand and images on the other.

Second, with respect to the images prohibited, Tatum draws attention to the fact that Josephus here avoids the language of the LXX, using εἰκών instead of

31. The Greek phrase is as follows: οὓς οὐ θεμιτόν ἐστιν ἡμῖν λέγειν φανερῶς πρὸς λέξιν, which Feldman translates "It is not permitted for us to speak them openly verbatim" (*Judean Antiquities* 1–4, 252–53).

32. See the various proposals listed in ibid., 253 n. 190. It is worth noting that Josephus expresses a similar sentiment with regard to the sacred name of God revealed to Moses, even using the same Greek term (θεμιτόν). On the latter connection, see F. E. Vokes, "The Ten Commandments in the New Testament and in First Century Judaism," *SE* 5 (1968): 149–50.

33. See Deut 6:4, which in the LXX reads κύριος ὁ θεὸς ἡμῶν κύριος εἷς ἐστιν.

34. Tatum, "The LXX Version," 188.

εἴδωλον to translate the Hebrew פסל,[35] even though in other contexts he displays his familiarity with the LXX.[36] On the surface, this lexical choice seems to broaden the scope of this prohibition beyond the category of "idols" in the LXX, assuming εἴδωλον is a term of derision against images of foreign deities,[37] to include images in general. And in fact, the Greek term εἰκών in Josephus does seem to operate broadly as a catchall for various types of figural representations. For example, εἰκών functions as a synonym for sculpture types that are both noncultic—ἀνδριάς and προτομή—and those that are more properly associated with a religious context, such as ἄγαλμα.[38] In contrast, εἴδωλον as a term for statuary appears merely seven times in Josephus, only in the biblical-prophetic portions of *A.J.*, and seems to be a literary remnant from the LXX's prophetic idol polemic.[39] Therefore, by avoiding a term that functions to ridicule the worship of foreign gods, Josephus has seemingly removed, or at the very least minimized, the cultic connotation of the LXX's formulation of Exod 20:4.[40]

Moreover, the three subordinate clauses of Exod 20:4 that originally qualified פסל/εἴδωλον and תמונה/ὁμοίωμα—the cosmological triad mentioned above—are here collapsed into the term ζῷον, defining the forbidden image as a representation of a living being, be it anthropomorphic or theriomorphic. Thus, by avoiding the term εἴδωλον and even ἄγαλμα, the more commonly used Greek term for the statues of gods and goddesses, and instead identifying the prohibited object with the phrase εἰκόνα ζῴου, Josephus seemingly transforms a prohibition against "pagan" idols into an interdiction against figurative art. Tatum concludes: "Jose-

35. Ibid., 188–91. Philo similarly avoids εἴδωλον, although instead of εἰκών he uses the terms ξόανον, ἄγαλμα, and ἀφίδρυμα to denote the forbidden images (see below for a fuller discussion of the second commandment in Philo). For a study of εἴδωλον in the LXX, see Charles A. Kennedy, "The Semantic Field of the Term 'Idolatry'," in *Uncovering Ancient Stones: Essays in Memory of H. Neil Richardson* (ed. Lewis M. Hopfe; Winona Lake, Ind.: Eisenbrauns, 1994), 193–204; and Robert Hayward, "Observations on Idols in Septuagint Pentateuch," in *Idolatry: False Worship in the Bible, Early Judaism, and Christianity* (ed. Stephen C. Barton; London: T&T Clark, 2007), 40–57.

36. Harold W. Attridge, *The Interpretation of Biblical History in the Antiquitates Judaicae of Flavius Josephus* (Missoula, Mont.: Scholars Press, 1976), 31. See also Tatum, "The LXX Version," 188–93.

37. Tatum, "The LXX Version," 184–86. Barclay similarly suggests that εἴδωλον "conveys a sneer, a claim to superior piety or truth" ("Snarling Sweetly," 73). But see also Kennedy, who argues that the pejorative use of εἴδωλον as a term denoting a false god does not appear until Tertullian transliterated this term into the Latin *idolum*, at which point εἴδωλον no longer denoted the more generic meaning "image" ("The Semantic Field of the Term 'Idolatry'," 204).

38. For example, ἀνδριάς: *B.J.* 2.192–194; προτομή: *A.J.* 18.55; ἄγαλμα: *A.J.* 15.279.

39. *A.J.* 9.99, 205, 243, 273; 10.50, 65, 69. On two occasions, Josephus uses εἴδωλον according to the more common usage in Greek literature, namely to denote a phantom-like appearance (*B.J.* 5.513; 7.452).

40. See also the discussion of the LXX and image terminology in Tessa Rajak, *Translation and Survival: The Greek Bible and the Jewish Diaspora* (Oxford: Oxford University Press, 2009), 190.

phus summarizes the Second Commandment not simply in anti-idolic but in anti-iconic terms. The Second Commandment prohibits the making *and/or* adoration of 'an image of any living thing.' "[41]

However, there is more to this text than is typically noted. Indeed, the previous remark by Tatum, and in particular his use of the conjunctions "and/or," is revealing not only for its emphasis on the broad and comprehensive scope of the prohibited object but also in its attempt to downplay an important feature in Josephus' summary of the second commandment. Tatum wants to read the second commandment in *A.J.* 3.91 as a prohibition against *both* the act of making *and* worshiping images, implying two distinct issues. Tatum remarks that, in Josephus' view, the second commandment actually consists of two distinct prohibitions, "one against making 'a sculptured image' . . . and the other against worshipping 'them'. "[42] But this interpretation overlooks the grammatical function of the infinitive προσκυνεῖν. Whereas the Hebrew (and Greek) of Exod 20:4–5 includes two grammatical prohibitions—one addressing the *making* of images (לא תעשׂה) and the other *worship* (לא־תשתחוה להם ולא תעבדם)—Josephus conflates the two into one, with the infinitive προσκυνεῖν functioning as an adverbial qualifier of the participle ποιήσαντας. In other words, προσκυνεῖν in *A.J.* 3.91 is not grammatically independent, as Tatum's interpretation suggests, but is inseparable from the participle, expressing the purpose of ποιήσαντας.

The effect of Josephus' reformulation is not without significance. The proscription in *A.J.* 3.91 addresses not simply craftsmanship, that is, the process of sculpting or making an image of a living being, but craftsmanship *for the purpose of worship*. The second commandment in Josephus' summary of the Decalogue in *A.J.* proscribes not figurative images in general but *cultic* images, notwithstanding the features in the text that seem to indicate otherwise. Taken in isolation, Josephus' interpretation of the second commandment here would thus seem to allow for a possible distinction between εἰκόνες intended for worship and εἰκόνες not intended for worship, with the former being unacceptable and the latter permissible.[43] As will be demonstrated below, this cultic qualification is likewise evident in Josephus' other explicitly exegetical text, *C. Ap.* 2.190–192.

Josephus' *C. Ap.*, the last of his three major compositions, includes in book 2 an extended *apologia* for the Mosaic law or πολιτεία (2.145–286),[44] designated by John Barclay as a "sparkling encomium of the Judean constitution."[45] This material

---

41. Tatum, "The LXX Version," 191 (emphasis mine).

42. Ibid., 188.

43. Lee Levine seems to read this distinction in *A.J.* 3.91 when he likens Josephus' summary of the second commandment to Rabban Gamaliel's prohibition against only those images with cultic significance (*The Ancient Synagogue*, 454, n. 58).

44. On this aspect of *C. Ap.*, see especially Christine Gerber, *Ein Bild des Judentums für Nichtjuden von Flavius Josephus: Untersuchungen zu seiner Schrift Contra Apionem* (Leiden: Brill, 1997), 133–208; and Gunnar Haaland, "Jewish Laws for a Roman Audience: Towards an Understanding of *Contra Apionem*," in *Internationales Josephus-Kolloquium, Brussel 1998* (ed. Folker Siegert and Jürgen U. Kalms; Münster, Germany: Lit, 1999), 282–304.

45. Barclay, *Against Apion*, xvii. See Josephus' objection to the claim that this section of

is an integral part of a larger attempt to refute the slanders of several notorious interlocutors, most notably the Egyptian Apion (*C. Ap.* 2.1–144), but also in the immediate context Apollonius Molon (among other literary antagonists; *C. Ap.* 2.145).[46] Within this larger block of material devoted to the political system of Moses, identified with the neologism θεοκρατία (*C. Ap.* 2.165),[47] Josephus asserts the superiority of the Mosaic constitution and summarizes its central or foundational teachings.[48] Although there is an obvious continuity between *A.J.* and *C. Ap.* in their respective depictions of Jewish law,[49] different emphases are evident, most notably that in *C. Ap.* Josephus conveys his description of Jewish law in more explicitly philosophical terms.[50]

Josephus' opening question in *C. Ap.* 2.190—τίνες οὖν εἰσιν αἱ προρρήσεις καὶ ἀπαγορεύσεις ("What then are the warnings and prohibitions?")—frames this pericope, which extends through 2.219, as a summary of Jewish law. Although the explicit enumeration of the δέκα λόγοι in *A.J.* 3.91–92 is missing here, it is clear from his reference to πρώτη that the Decalogue at the very least stands in the backdrop of the opening lines of his explanation of αἱ προρρήσεις καὶ ἀπαγορεύσεις ("the warnings and prohibitions").[51] And indeed the content of this material, which begins by addressing both the worship of the Jewish God and the question

---

C. Ap. amounts to nothing more than a panegyric for Jewish customs (*C. Ap.* 2.147, 287). On *C. Ap.* as an encomium, see also David L. Balch, "Two Apologetic Encomia: Dionysius on Rome and Josephus on the Jews," *JSJ* 13 (1982): 102–22. Specifically, Balch argues that *C. Ap.* 2.145–295 follows the rhetorical pattern for encomia expressed most clearly in Menander Rhetor's "Praising the city as man."

46. For a structural analysis of *C. Ap.*, see Bilde, *Flavius Josephus*, 113–18, and Barclay, *Against Apion*, xvii–xxii. In discussing the genre of *C. Ap.*, Barclay notes that although from a literary perspective the material is somewhat varied, "it is presented within a unifying structure as a response to slanders against the Judean people" (xxxiii). Thus, even Josephus' summary of the law serves this larger apologetic purpose.

47. Yehoshua Amir, "Θεοκρατία as a Concept of Political Philosophy: Josephus' Presentation of Moses' Politeia," *SCI* 8–9 (1985–88): 83–105.

48. Rajak, "The *Against Apion*," 200–211.

49. On the relationship between *A.J.* and *C. Ap.*, see especially Paul Spilsbury, "*Contra Apionem* and *Antiquitates Judaicae*: Points of Contact," in *Josephus' "Contra Apionem": Studies in Its Character and Context with a Latin Concordance to the Portion Missing in Greek* (ed. Louis H. Feldman and John R. Levison; Leiden: Brill, 1996), 348–68; Silvia Castelli, "Antiquities 3–4 and Against Apion 2.145ff.: Different Approaches to the Law," in *Internationales Josephus-Kolloquium Amsterdam 2000* (ed. Jürgen U. Kalms; Münster, Germany: Lit, 2001), 151–69; Peter Tomson, "Les systèmes de halakha du Contre Apion et des Antiquités," in *Internationales Josephus-Kolloquium Paris 2001* (ed. Folker Siegert and Jürgen U. Kalms; Münster, Germany: Lit, 2002), 189–220.

50. This is apparent in the very term that Josephus invents, θεοκρατία, which obviously subsumes the political under the umbrella of the philosophical; see Barclay, *Against Apion*, xxiii–xxvi. This, however, is only a difference in emphasis, as even *A.J.* places the Mosaic constitution within a philosophical framework (e.g., *A.J.* 1.25–26).

51. Several other scholars likewise see an implicit reference to the Decalogue in *C. Ap.* 190–192; see, for example, Vermès, "Summary of the Law," 293–94; Barclay, *Against Apion*, 276 n. 751; Barclay, "Snarling Sweetly," 82.

of images, confirms that the Decalogue comprises at least part of his explanation of Jewish law.[52] The relevant portion of this text is as follows:

> πρώτη δ' ἡγεῖται ἡ περὶ θεοῦ λέγουσα ὁ θεὸς ἔχει τὰ σύμπαντα, παντελὴς καὶ μακάριος, αὐτὸς αὑτῷ καὶ πᾶσιν αὐτάρκης, ἀρχὴ καὶ μέσα καὶ τέλος οὗτος τῶν πάντων, ἔργοις μὲν καὶ χάρισιν ἐναργὴς καὶ παντὸς οὔτινος φανερώτερος, μορφὴν δὲ καὶ μέγεθος ἡμῖν ἀφανέστατος. πᾶσα μὲν ὕλη πρὸς εἰκόνα τὴν τούτου κἂν ᾖ πολυτελὴς ἄτιμος, πᾶσα δὲ τέχνη πρὸς μιμήσεως ἐπίνοιαν ἄτεχνος· οὐδὲν ὅμοιον οὔτ' εἴδομεν οὔτ' ἐπινοοῦμεν οὔτ' εἰκάζειν ἐστὶν ὅσιον. ἔργα βλέπομεν αὐτοῦ φῶς, οὐρανὸν, γῆν, ἥλιον, ὕδατα, ζῴων γενέσεις, καρπῶν ἀναδόσεις. ταῦτα θεὸς ἐποίησεν οὐ χερσὶν, οὐ πόνοις, οὔ τινων συνεργασομένων ἐπιδεηθείς, ἀλλ' αὐτοῦ θελήσαντος καλῶς ἦν εὐθὺς γεγονότα. τοῦτον θεραπευτέον ἀσκοῦντας ἀρετήν· τρόπος γὰρ θεοῦ θεραπείας οὗτος ὁσιώτατος.

> The first, concerning God, leads the way, affirming that God possesses all things, [being] perfect and blessed, self-sufficient and sufficient for all, he is the beginning and middle and end of all things; he is visible in works and favors, even more manifest than anything else, but concerning his form and greatness he is most invisible to us. Thus every material, however expensive it might be, is inadequate for an image of this [deity], and every work of art is incapable to imagine his likeness. We have neither seen nor imagined anything similar to him, nor is it pious to make an image of him. We can see his works: light, heaven, earth, sun, water, the birth of living creatures, the production of crops. These things God made, not with hands, not with hard labor, not needing any assistants, but when he so desired, they were immediately made in beauty. This one must be worshiped by practicing virtue; for this manner of worshiping God is the most pious. (*C. Ap.* 2.190–192)

The Greek text under discussion includes a philological problem (underlined in the citation above) that, although seemingly minor and inconsequential, affects considerably how the proscription of images is presented in this passage.[53] Niese's *Editio maior*, followed by Thackeray's Loeb edition and John Barclay's recent translation and commentary on *C. Ap.*, reads ἄφατος instead of ἀφανέστατος, a reading that is overwhelmingly supported by the Greek manuscript tradition.[54] By contrast, the reading accepted in this analysis, ἀφανέστατος, is preserved only in Eusebius' *Praeparatio evangelica* 8.8.25.1. Moreover, the earliest Latin translation of *C. Ap.* uses *inenarrabilis* to render the Greek in question, a term that clearly approximates ἄφατος rather than ἀφανέστατος. And ἄφατος does not necessarily render incomprehensible the meaning of the text. Accepting Niese's *Editio maior*, and thus the reading ἄφατος, Thackeray translates the text as follows: "By His

52. However, it is clear that the Decalogue forms only part of the picture here, since Josephus' summary extends through *C. Ap.* 2.219 and includes a broad range of precepts not found in the Decalogue.

53. Heinz Schreckenberg has recently discussed some of the problems in the textual history of *C. Ap.* as well as the need for a more reliable critical edition ("Text, Überlieferung und Textkritik von Contra Apionem," in *Josephus' "Contra Apionem": Studies in Its Character and Context with a Latin Concordance to the Portion Missing in Greek* [ed. Louis H. Feldman and John R. Levison; Leiden: Brill, 1996], 49–82).

54. Niese, *Flavii Josephi Opera*, ad loc; Barclay, *Against Apion*, 277.

works and bounties He is plainly seen, indeed more manifest than ought else; but His form and magnitude surpass our powers of description" (*C. Ap.* 2.190 [Thackeray, LCL]).[55] The function of ἄφατος in this context is thus clear enough: Josephus contrasts the visibility of the deity's works with the ineffability of his form.

Nevertheless there are several reasons to prefer ἀφανέστατος. In the first place, although the manuscript evidence favors the reading ἄφατος, the nature of the textual witnesses, namely that they are, according to Barclay's assessment, "manifestly deficient," lessens the significance of this "majority" reading.[56] Eusebius is the earliest substantial textual witness, and he preserves approximately one-sixth of *C. Ap.*[57] Cassiodorus' sixth-century Latin translation follows, and the first almost complete Greek manuscript (L)—and the first unambiguous witness to the Greek ἄφατος—dates to the eleventh century. Moreover, according to Niese's assessment all subsequent Greek manuscripts are dependent on L,[58] which, if correct,[59] would reduce the number of independent textual witnesses primarily to three: Eusebius, Cassiodorus' Latin translation, and the manuscript tradition originating in L. As such, the minority reading favored in the present analysis constitutes one-third of the independent textual traditions, a minority to be sure, but certainly not insignificant enough to preclude as a possibility. Thus, given the woeful state of manuscript evidence, the material preserved in Eusebius, though by no means perfect, is nevertheless of utmost importance.[60]

Furthermore, comparing the two words in question, there is an obvious potential for haplography, which would then explain the replacement of ἀφανέστατος with ἄφατος in the manuscript tradition. More specifically, one can easily see how a scribe could copy the beginning (ἀφα-) and ending (-τος) of ἀφανέστατος, inadvertently omitting the middle portion of the word and thus resulting in the reading ἄφατος.

Beyond these external considerations, however, several intrinsic factors strongly favor ἀφανέστατος as the original, most notably that this reading fits better the highly sophisticated literary features of the passage. The μὲν . . . δέ construction in which the word in question appears sets up a contrast between two parallel clauses, visibly evident in the following structural layout:

55. Barclay similarly translates: "He is evident through his works and acts of grace, and more apparent than anything else, but in form and greatness beyond our description" (Barclay, *Against Apion*, 277).

56. Ibid., lxi.

57. A convenient list of Eusebius' citations can be found in Schreckenberg, *Die Flavius-Josephus-Tradition*, 82–84.

58. Niese, *Flavii Josephi Opera*, 5:iv–vii.

59. Barclay, following the recently published German critical edition, suggests that manuscripts E (Eliensis; fifteenth century) and S (Schleusingensis; fifteenth–sixteenth century) do preserve some independent value; see Folker Siegert, Heinz Schreckenberg, and Manuel Vogel, eds., *Flavius Josephus: Über das Alter des Judentums (Contra Apionem)* (Tübingen: Mohr Siebeck, 2006), 54–56; Barclay, *Against Apion*, lxiii.

60. According to Niese, Eusebius is the most valuable witness to the original text of *C. Ap.* (Niese, *Flavii Josephi Opera*, 5:xvi–xxi). See also the discussion and notes in Barclay, *Against Apion*, lxii.

A ἔργοις μὲν καὶ χάρισιν ἐναργὴς καὶ παντὸς οὕτινος φανερώτερος
B μορφὴν δὲ καὶ μέγεθος ἡμῖν ἀφανέστατος

The deity's ἔργα and χάριτες, which are unambiguously presented as his *visible* manifestation in clause A, are parallel to and contrasted with this God's μορφή and μέγεθος in clause B, and ἀφανέστατος clearly fits the contrast better than ἄφατος on both semantic and grammatical grounds. Beyond the obvious antithesis between visibility and invisibility expressed in the lexical morpheme ἀ/φαν-, the shift from the comparative φανερώτερος to the superlative ἀφανέστατος establishes a heightened symmetry between clause A and clause B: although the deity is *more* visible than anything else in his works and favors, he is *most* invisible in his form and greatness.

Moreover, with ἀφανέστατος as the original reading, *C. Ap.* 2.190–192 as a whole forms an extended chiasm:

A πρώτη δ᾽ ἡγεῖται ἡ περὶ θεοῦ λέγουσα **ὁ θεὸς** ἔχει τὰ σύμπαντα παντελὴς καὶ μακάριος αὐτὸς αὐτῷ καὶ πᾶσιν αὐτάρκης ἀρχὴ καὶ μέσα καὶ τέλος οὗτος τῶν πάντων
 B **ἔργοις** μὲν καὶ χάρισιν ἐναργὴς καὶ παντὸς οὕτινος **φανερώτερος**
  C μορφὴν δὲ καὶ μέγεθος ἡμῖν **ἀφανέστατος**
  C[1] πᾶσα μὲν ὕλη πρὸς εἰκόνα τὴν τούτου κἂν ᾖ πολυτελὴς ἄτιμος πᾶσα δὲ τέχνη πρὸς μιμήσεως ἐπίνοιαν ἄτεχνος **οὐδὲν ὅμοιον οὔτ᾽ εἴδομεν** οὔτ᾽ ἐπινοοῦμεν οὔτ᾽ εἰκάζειν ἐστὶν ὅσιον
 B[1] **ἔργα βλέπομεν** αὐτοῦ φῶς οὐρανὸν γῆν ἥλιον ὕδατα ζῴων γενέσεις καρπῶν ἀναδόσεις ταῦτα θεὸς ἐποίησεν οὐ χερσὶν οὐ πόνοις οὔ τινων συνεργασομένων ἐπιδεηθείς ἀλλ᾽ αὐτοῦ θελήσαντος καλῶς ἦν εὐθὺς γεγονότα
A[1] τοῦτον θεραπευτέον ἀσκοῦντας ἀρετήν τρόπος γὰρ **θεοῦ** θεραπείας οὗτος ὁσιώτατος

The contents of this chiasm can thus be summarized as follows:

A God is supreme
 B God is manifest in his works and favors
  C God is not manifest in his form
  C[1] God cannot be imaged
 B[1] God is seen in his creation
A[1] Worship God

If the identification of a chiasm is correct here, the text progresses inwardly from God's supremacy (A/A[1]) to his visibility (B/B[1]) to his invisibility (C/C[1]), a stylistic feature that ultimately breaks down with the reading ἄφατος. Therefore, in the light of these intrinsic and extrinsic considerations, especially the congruence of the minority reading with the overall structure of the passage, I argue that ἀφανέστατος is the preferable reading.[61]

61. Although ἄφατος is admittedly the *lectio difficilior*, the cumulative force of these intrinsic and extrinsic considerations is, in my estimation, sufficient in this instance to prefer the reading that best fits the literary context. Beyond the factors detailed above, it should

The impact of this text-critical decision on a proper understanding of Josephus' formulation in *C. Ap.* 2.190–191 is significant. Indeed, the aforementioned structural arrangement that hinges on ἀφανέστατος demonstrates that "*second* commandment" is something of a misnomer in the present context, insofar as the chiastic arrangement inextricably links the proscription of images with the legislation addressing the nature and proper worship of the Jewish God.[62] The pivot of this structure, its point of inversion at C/C¹, underscores the central idea of the passage, namely that the Mosaic rejection of images (C¹) is rooted in the very essence of the divine nature (C). Clauses A and A¹ are concerned with the exalted status of the Jewish God, both in his supremacy and self-sufficiency and in the moral obligation to worship him though virtue and piety. Clauses B and B¹ focus on his *visibility* and both are paralleled quite explicitly in locating the manifestation of this deity primarily in his ἔργα. In contrast, clauses C and C¹ are associated by the deity's *invisibility*, both ontologically (C) and iconographically (C¹): the God's μορφή is not manifest and thus he cannot and must not be imaged in any way.

This structural feature thus frames the "second" commandment as a philosophical critique of images in which the inappropriateness of εἰκόνες flows directly from the nature of the deity.[63] In other words, Josephus' affirmation of aniconic

---

also be noted that the adjective ἀφανής is employed frequently throughout the Josephan corpus, whereas ἄφατος, if accepted, is a *hapax legomenon* occurring only in the passage in question. Of course, lexical distribution is itself ultimately indecisive, and there are indications that Josephus' unique concerns in *C. Ap.* may have led to a higher concentration of distinct vocabulary; see Pieter Willem van der Horst, "The Distinctive Vocabulary of Josephus' *Contra Apionem*," in *Josephus' "Contra Apionem": Studies in Its Character and Context with a Latin Concordance to the Portion Missing in Greek* (ed. Louis H. Feldman and John R. Levison; Leiden: Brill, 1996), 83–93.

62. That the so-called first and second commandments are interrelated in *C. Ap.* is further confirmed by Josephus' enumeration, or lack thereof. Although the opening words of this pericope, and in particular the reference to a "first" (πρώτη) precept addressing cultic allegiance to the one true God, would seem to anticipate a "second" (δεύτερος) focused on the question of images, as with the enumeration of the δέκα λόγοι in A.J. 3.91, Josephus in *C. Ap.* does not actually follow through with this numerical sequence. Instead the issue of image worship is entirely subsumed under the πρώτη.

63. On the whole Josephus' presentation of the Decalogue in *C. Ap.* is much more philosophical than in *A.J.* The concise "God is one" mantra in *A.J.* 3.91 is here expanded into an extended discourse on the nature of the deity: God is perfect (παντελής), entirely self-sufficient (αὐτάρκης), the all-encompassing one who is visible *only* in his works and the benefits he bestows on humanity. Moreover, this account of the divine nature, which of course is not unique to Josephus, recalls the language of *C. Ap.* 2.167, wherein Josephus asserts the superiority of the Mosaic θεοκρατία on the basis of God's perfect nature. The definition of the deity in the 2.167 establishes a contrast between the *knowable* and *unknowable* aspects of the divine: δυνάμει μὲν ἡμῖν γνώριμον ὁποῖος δὲ κατ' οὐσίαν ἐστὶν ἄγνωστον. In 2.190, however, the stress is on the *(in)visibility* of the divine nature, an emphasis that dovetails nicely with the question of images that is raised in 2.191. See the discussion in Barclay, "Snarling Sweetly," 81–83. For similar philosophical conceptions of the deity in Greek and Latin literature, see the list of texts in Barclay, *Against Apion*, nn. 752–53.

worship—the proscription is here formulated more as an affirmation than a restriction—is a logical outcome of God's character. Stated differently, "orthopraxy" (aniconic worship) is for Josephus inextricably linked with "orthodoxy" (a proper conception of the deity).[64] The εἰκών, which by its very nature requires a measure of *similarity* or *semblance* to the object it represents, is inadequate (ἄτιμος) precisely because the essence of the divine nature fundamentally eludes proper representation.[65] Hence, any attempt to image (εἰκάζειν) the divine is impious to the core. As Barclay notes, the rationale here departs considerably from the typical Jewish polemic against those who substitute images for God; the problem here is not *substitution* but the impossibility of *semblance*.[66] Considering again the central question of this chapter—What is the scope of Moses' prohibition against images?—the answer in this context is clear: the second commandment does not proscribe images in general, but *divine* images and, more specifically, iconographical representations of the God of the Jews.

Appearances in Narrative Context

A survey of Josephus' numerous references to the second commandment within a narrative context gives a strikingly different impression than what emerges in *A.J.* 3.91 and *C. Ap.* 2.190–192. Specifically, select passages from Josephus' narratives suggest that the author understood the prohibition of images to include any figurative representation, regardless of context, format, or function.

To take one notable example, according to Josephus the downfall of King Solomon began not with his seven hundred wives and three hundred concubines, as the biblical narrative suggests (1 Kgs 11), but with the installation of theriomorphic images, specifically the bronze oxen that were placed in the temple and the sculpted lions that adorned his throne—items that Josephus explicitly identifies as works of impiety and a violation of the Jewish νόμιμα (*A.J.* 8.195). As is commonly observed, the biblical narrative, although describing in detail the images in question, does not censure Solomon for them.[67] Moreover, the items in question are clearly *not* objects of cultic devotion, but decorative elements adorning temple and royal furniture. Yet in Josephus, these innocuous decorative images, simply because they are images of living creatures (ζῷά), become quintessential marks of Solomon's "apostasy," the initial catalyst for the king's ultimate rejection of the εὐσέβεια and σοφία that characterized the first years of his reign.

In a similar vein, the military trophies that were affixed to the theater in Jerusalem during the reign of Herod the Great were thought to violate the second commandment because they were perceived to be εἰκόνες ἀνθρώπων (*A.J.* 15.276–279). The tension in this narrative revolves not so much around the cultic status of the trophies—indeed, they are not even statues but merely an ornamental display of military accoutrements (e.g., armor, weapons, etc.)—but their apparent ico-

64. As is the requirement for a centralized temple, which in *C. Ap.* 2.193 similarly flows from the nature of the Jewish God.

65. On the meaning of ἄτιμος in this context, see Barclay, *Against Apion*, 277 n. 757.

66. Barclay, "Snarling Sweetly," 83; Barclay, *Against Apion*, 277 n. 757.

67. 1 Kgs 7:23–26 (oxen on the "molten sea"); 1 Kgs 10:18–20 (throne with sculpted lions).

nography, the fact that they *resembled* anthropomorphic (i.e., figurative) statues. Not surprisingly, Gaius Caligula's attempt to erect his own statue (ἀνδριάς) in the temple receives censure (*B.J.* 2.184–203; *A.J.* 18.256–309), but so does the seemingly harmless eagle on the Herodian temple in Jerusalem, identified in *A.J.* as an εἰκών/ζῷον and in *B.J.* as a ζῴου ἔργον (*B.J.* 1.649–650; *A.J.* 17.150–151). The reference to the second commandment in *A.J.*'s account of the temple eagle episode is instructive both in its silence on cultic matters—that is, concerning whether the image in question was worshiped, or even that the image was located in a cultic context—and its focus on iconography: "But the law forbids those who are determined to live by it to think of setting up statues and to make dedications of [statues of] any living creatures" (κωλύει δὲ ὁ νόμος εἰκόνων τε ἀναστάσεις ἐπινοεῖν καί τινων ζῴων ἀναθέσεις ἐπιτηδεύεσθαι τοῖς βιοῦν κατ' αὐτὸν προῃρημένοις; *A.J.* 17.151).

Likewise, the figurative images in Herod the Tetrarch's palace fall under the prohibition of the second commandment, thus resulting in a commission from Jerusalem authorities (indeed, one involving Josephus) to destroy the images (*Vita* 65).[68] Here again, the reference to the proscription places the emphasis on the craftsmanship of figurative images: the mandate for the iconoclastic destruction of the palace art is located in the Jewish laws which prohibit the crafting (κατασκευάζω) of ζῴων μορφαί. The apparently all-encompassing nature of this proscription is perhaps expressed most poignantly in Josephus' account of Pilate's military standards, in which the images (εἰκόνες; προτομαί) affixed to the standards constitute evidence that Pilate was intent "on abolishing the customs of the Jews" (ἐπὶ καταλύσει τῶν νομίμων τῶν Ἰουδαϊκῶν), since "our law forbids the making of images" (εἰκόνων ποίησιν ἀπαγορεύοντος ἡμῖν τοῦ νόμου; *A.J.* 18.55). Josephus here *excludes* the qualification of προσκυνεῖν in his restatement of the second commandment, rendering the injunction as a prohibition of iconic craftsmanship.

The consistent thread in each of the above examples is the emphasis on a disputed image's iconography. The image whose subject matter is either ἄνθρωπος or ζῷον clearly falls within the scope of the Mosaic prohibition. Conversely, concern over the cultic status of an image barely (if at all) registers in the development of the story. It is thus not surprising that the vast majority of scholars conclude that Josephus followed a markedly strict interpretive approach to the injunction in question, one that forbids not simply images of foreign gods or the Jewish God but *figurative art*, that is, any representation of living beings, whether theriomorphic or anthropomorphic. Indeed, as noted earlier, based on this reading of Josephus some have even supposed that all Jews during the Second Temple period, ostensibly held sway by the authority of the pre-destruction rabbis, interpreted the second commandment to preclude all forms of artistic representation, excepting geometric and floral designs.[69]

---

68. Mason, *Life of Josephus*, 58–59.

69. Even Erwin Ramsdell Goodenough, whose massive collection of Jewish iconography from the Greco-Roman period was pivotal in upending the long-held assumption of Jew-

However, a closer analysis of this narrative material suggests a more complicated situation. In the first place, the aforementioned narrative summaries of the second commandment differ significantly from the two occasions where Josephus offers a detailed explanation of this legislation in *A.J.* 3.91 and *C. Ap.* 2.190–192, wherein Josephus explicitly qualifies and restricts the prohibition to cultic images. Second, even the appearance of the second commandment in narrative context is not entirely uniform. For example, observe the differences between the summaries in *B.J.* and *A.J.* with regard to the aforementioned Pilate incident:

οὐδὲν γὰρ ἀξιοῦσιν ἐν τῇ πόλει δείκηλον τίθεσθαι.	εἰκόνων ποίησιν ἀπαγορεύοντος ἡμῖν τοῦ νόμου.
... for it is not lawful to set up an image in the city. (*B.J.* 2.170)	... for our law forbids the making of images. (*A.J.* 18.55)

The dissimilarity between the two summaries in the Pilate episode, evident also in the synoptic accounts of the incident of Herod's eagle and Caligula's statue, raises the possibility that Josephus is reformulating the proscription according to larger rhetorical themes within each of his main compositions, a possibility that I will explore more fully in chapters 4–5 below. For now, it is enough to note the apparent conflict between interpretation (*A.J.* 3.91 and *C. Ap.* 2.190–192) and praxis in the Josephan corpus.

Reading the Second Commandment in Greco-Roman Jewish Literature

Given the preponderance of Jewish (and Christian) texts polemicizing idols during the Greco-Roman period, it is somewhat surprising that very few reflect specifically on the meaning and application of the second commandment.[70] Rather, the classic idol polemic—expressed especially in texts such as the Epistle of Jeremiah, Bel and the Dragon, and the Wisdom of Solomon, to name a few—favors the technique of ridicule, patterned in part after biblical-prophetic texts such as Isaiah and Psalms, as a means of denouncing idolatry and images.[71] Nevertheless,

---

ish aniconism, argued that the rabbis held a relatively "clear and consistent" position with regard to images: "Jews were forbidden to make images of human faces for any purpose whatever, and the strictest rabbis would have destroyed all objects, even of pagan origin." In short, the rabbis "did not like images." Moreover, although Goodenough argues for the marginalization of the rabbis after the destruction of the temple, he nevertheless maintains that they wielded tremendous influence during the Second Temple period (*Jewish Symbols*, 4:19–20). See also the discussion in Konikoff, *The Second Commandment*, 51–64.

70. Cristina Termini notes a general silence on the Decalogue as a whole in a significant number of texts from Greco-Roman antiquity ("Taxonomy of Biblical Laws and φιλοτεχνία in Philo of Alexandria: A Comparison with Josephus and Cicero," *SPhilo* 16 [2004], 13–15).

71. But note also the discussion above in chapter 2, in which I argue that the idol polemic in Jewish-Hellenistic literature is more than simply a recycling of biblical traditions.

the few texts that do explicitly interact with the Decalogue's second commandment articulate an interesting range of exegetical possibilities, from the complete avoidance of the proscription where one would otherwise expect it through the prohibition of cultic images to a seemingly absolute prohibition of all forms of figurative art, cultic or otherwise.

Omitting the Prohibition of Images: Pseudo-Phocylides

This first text, the poem of Pseudo-Phocylides, is noteworthy not so much for what it says but for what it fails (or refuses?) to say, a silence that is potentially pregnant with significance. The poem is a collection of *sententiae* (γνῶμαι), tentatively dated to the first century B.C.E. or first century C.E.,[72] written in an archaic Ionic dialect with traces of Hellenistic forms that betray its pseudepigraphic character.[73] It is generally regarded as a *Jewish* pseudepigraphon from Alexandria,[74] given the author's familiarity with the LXX and the evidence for a distinctly Jewish view of the resurrection of the body.[75]

Following the prologue in lines 1–2, the author mentions or alludes to a cluster of prohibitions and commandments that are found in Exod 20 and Deut 5 (lines 3–8), thus earning the ascription "Summary of the Decalogue" for the material in question.[76] As many as eight precepts seem to correspond to the list of commands found in the Decalogue: the prohibitions against adultery (3), murder (4), theft (6), covetousness (6), and lying (7), and the positive commands to honor God and parents (8). Moreover, although the sequence departs considerably from that of the biblical text, the placement of murder after adultery does reflect the order of the commands in the LXX, suggesting a more explicit connection with the Greek translation of the biblical text.[77]

Nevertheless, there are two additions to the Decalogue laws—prohibitions of "homosexuality" (3) and illicit gains (5)—as well as several striking omissions, most notably the command to keep the Sabbath and, of particular interest here, the prohibition of idolatry/images. The obvious question is: Why would a Jew

72. Pieter Willem van der Horst, *The Sentences of Pseudo-Phocylides* (Leiden: E. J. Brill, 1978), 81–83; Walter T. Wilson, *The Sentences of Pseudo-Phocylides* (Berlin: Walter de Gruyter, 2005), 7.

73. Van der Horst, *The Sentences of Pseudo-Phocylides*, 55–58.

74. Ibid., 82; John J. Collins, *Between Athens and Jerusalem: Jewish Identity in the Hellenistic Diaspora* (Grand Rapids: Eerdmans, 2000), 168–69. Barclay questions the Alexandrian provenance of Ps.-Phoc. (Barclay, *Jews in the Mediterranean Diaspora*, 337).

75. Ps.-Phoc. 103. On the view of the afterlife in this text, see especially F. Christ, "Das Leben nach dem Tode bei Pseudo-Phokylides," *TZ* 31 (1975): 140–49; John J. Collins, "Life after Death in Pseudo-Phocylides," in *Jerusalem, Alexandria, Rome: Studies in Ancient Cultural Interaction in Honour of A. Hillhorst* (ed. Florentino García Martínez and Gerard P. Luttikhuizen; Leiden: Brill, 2003), 75–86; Pieter Willem van der Horst, "Pseudo-Phocylides on the Afterlife: A Rejoinder to John J. Collins," *JSJ* 35 (2004): 70–75.

76. Van der Horst, *The Sentences of Pseudo-Phocylides*, 110; Wilson, *The Sentences of Pseudo-Phocylides*, 73.

77. Van der Horst, *The Sentences of Pseudo-Phocylides*, 112; Wilson, *The Sentences of Pseudo-Phocylides*, 74.

seemingly "conceal his Jewishness" by omitting reference to that which is distinctively Jewish?[78] More to the point, why avoid the Mosaic proscription of images and, even more broadly, the subject of idolatry?

This issue is of course connected to the larger question of the nature and function of the work as a whole. Overall there are at least three proposed solutions to the problem at hand.[79] First, the author was not a Jew at all and should not be expected to incorporate distinctively Jewish practices into his ethical treatise. This was the position of Arthur Ludwich, and he accounts for the clear allusion to the Decalogue by positing a non-Jewish author who was nevertheless familiar with the LXX.[80] Second, the author was Jewish but was in some sense trying to suppress Jewish peculiarities to make his ethical teachings more palatable for a broader gentile audience. For example, Jacob Bernays proposed that the omission of idolatry reflects the rhetorical strategy of Jewish propaganda directed to a non-Jewish audience, an attempt to present a nonoffensive "personal ethic" that excludes "anything pertaining to the exceptional nature of the Jewish nationality."[81] In a similar vein, Gottlieb Klein identified Ps.-Phoc. as "the oldest catechism for the Gentiles" and thus supposed that the prohibition was avoided as part of a larger missionary strategy that intentionally downplayed nationalistic halakah, a strategy not necessarily focused on gaining proselytes per se but on taming "pagans," so to speak, with a form of ethical monotheism.[82] Third, the author was Jewish and writing for a *Jewish* audience in order to "universalize the particular,"[83] to provide for his community a broad collection of ethical teachings that underscored the shared moral values of Jews and non-Jews alike. Although van der Horst expressed ambivalence on the question in his 1978 commentary, he clearly favors this third possibility in a subsequent article published a decade later:

> [T]he characteristics of our poem, such as its pseudonimity, the omission of anything exclusively Jewish . . . , can all be explained on the assumption that the author wrote a kind of compendium of *miṣvot* for daily life which could help Jews in a thoroughly Hellenistic environment to live as Jews without having to abandon their interest in Greek culture.[84]

---

78. Van der Horst, *The Sentences of Pseudo-Phocylides*, 70.

79. For a detailed history of research on Ps.-Phoc. up to 1978, see ibid., 3–54.

80. Arthur Ludwich, "Quaestionum pseudophocylidearum pars altera," in *Programm Königsberg* (Königsberg, Germany: Universität Königsberg, 1904), 29–32.

81. Jacob Bernays, *Gesammelte Abhandlungen* (2 vols.; Berlin: Wilhelm Hertz, 1885), 1:227. Bernays ultimately reproaches the author for failing to address such an important issue as pagan idolatry (1:254).

82. Gottlieb Klein, *Der älteste christliche Katechismus und die jüdische Propagandaliteratur* (Berlin: G. Reimer, 1909), 143.

83. Gregory E. Sterling, "Universalizing the Particular: Natural Law in Second Temple Jewish Ethics," *SPhilo* 15 (2003): 64–80. Sterling explores Ps.-Phoc. as part of a larger tendency to link Mosaic legislation with natural law.

84. Pieter Willem van der Horst, "Pseudo-Phocylides Revisited," *JSP* 3 (1988): 16. On this same question Barclay concludes: "What [the author] provides for his fellow Jews is not circumscribed by the special characteristics of the Jewish community" (*Jews in the Mediter-*

It must be admitted that the precise audience intended in this work, and hence the possible motive for omitting Jewish particulars, is difficult to pin down. It may be, as is suggested by John Collins, that the author intended his work to circulate indiscriminately with the hope that his ethical teachings would "attract students regardless of whether they were Jewish or not."[85] Whether the intended audience was Jewish, non-Jewish, or both, it is nevertheless remarkable that a Jewish author could summarize the core of Mosaic legislation without reference to the prohibition against images. This of course could very well be part of a strategy to universalize the Jewish ethos, but it should be noted that neither Philo nor Josephus, who likewise attempt to emphasize universal aspects of Jewish teachings, shy away from the second commandment.

In the end, it is difficult to know what to make of this omission, and we should be cautious not to read too much into the silence. Did the author intentionally suppress the second commandment, whether to make his teachings palatable for a non-Jewish audience or to assist his fellow Jews in their attempts to live "in a thoroughly Hellenistic environment"? Or did the author simply omit the obvious, thinking it unnecessary to address that which was universally recognized? Unfortunately at this point any attempt to answer such questions enters the realm of speculation.

A Prohibition of Cult Images

The group of texts included in this section, though unique in their various emphases, agree in restricting the scope of proscribed images to *divine* images, or images that are clearly in some sense associated with a cultic context or cultic activities. As such, they more or less comport with Josephus' exegesis in *A.J.* 3.91 and *C. Ap.* 2.190–192. That the majority of texts surveyed in this chapter fall under this category suggests further that Jews in antiquity predominantly read the second commandment as a rejection of idols (i.e., cultic images) and not images in general.

Book of Jubilees. The *Book of Jubilees*, a text originally composed in Hebrew in the middle of the second century B.C.E.,[86] purports to disclose a fuller account of God's revelation given to Moses on Mount Sinai (mediated through the Angel of Presence), a version of divine revelation, culled from the "heavenly tablets," that complements though exceeds that which is found in the Pentateuch.[87] From a lit-

---

ranean Diaspora, 345–46). Wilson likewise suggests that the universalizing impulse was intended in part to bolster the Jewish community, to reinforce "for Jewish readers a sense of their own history and place in the Greek world," though he also leaves open the possibility that this poem could have circulated in non-Jewish circles (*The Sentences of Pseudo-Phocylides*, 7–8).

85. Collins, *Between Athens and Jerusalem*, 174.

86. See the discussion in O. S. Wintermute, "Jubilees: A New Translation and Introduction," in *The Old Testament Pseudepigrapha* (ed. James H. Charlesworth; 2 vols.; New York: Doubleday, 1985), 2:43–44.

87. On the relationship between *Jubilees* and the Mosaic Torah, see Gabriele Boccac-

erary point of view, *Jubilees* forms "an extensive elaboration of Genesis 1–Exodus 12" and can thus be categorized along with other so-called rewritten Bibles,[88] such as, among others, Ps.-Philo's *Liber antiquitatum biblicarum* (see below), the Genesis Apocryphon found among the Dead Sea Scrolls, and, of course, parts of Josephus' *A.J.* The author is expressly concerned with various matters of what came to be known as Jewish halakah, particularly those legal formulations that served to distinguish the Jews from non-Jews. The patriarchal narratives are thus recast and reshaped in *Jubilees* in order to sharply criticize any attempt to imitate a "gentile" way of life.[89]

Although there are repeated warnings against idolatry throughout this text,[90] the second commandment itself appears only once, in *Jubilees* 20:7–8. This version of the prohibition, embedded in a speech by Abraham given to his children just prior to his death, reads as follows:

> I exhort you, my sons, love the God of heaven, and be joined to all of his commands. And do not go after their idols and after their defilement. And do not make gods of molten or carved images for yourselves, because it is vain and they have no spirit. Because they are the work of hands, and all those who trust in them trust in nothing. Do not worship them and do not bow down to them.[91]

The discussion of images in this text clearly recalls the language of the second commandment in Exod 20, particularly in the sequence of the verbs "to make" and "to worship." As noted above, in the Decalogue a prohibition against foreign deities immediately precedes the prohibition against crafting images, leaving ambiguous the precise relationship between the forbidden images and forbidden gods. In *Jubilees*, however, the author clarifies this relationship by conflating the first two prohibitions into one: the interdictions against false gods and sculpted images become a single proscription of "gods of molten or carved images." Furthermore, in Exod 20 the relationship between craftsmanship and cultic activity is ambiguous, given the grammatical incongruity between the singular object of the Hebrew verb for craftsmanship (לא תעשׂה־לך פסל) and the plural objects of the Hebrew verbs for worship (לא־תשתחוה להם ולא תעבדם). *Jubilees* resolves this ambiguity, however, by rendering the forbidden objects in the plural, resulting in a stronger connection between crafting and worshiping images. The grammatical alterations

cini, *Beyond the Essene Hypothesis: The Parting of the Ways between Qumran and Enochic Judaism* (Grand Rapids: Eerdmans, 1998), 88–90. See also the recent publication of the proceedings from the Fourth Enoch Seminar held at Camaldoli (July 8–12, 2007): Gabriele Boccaccini and Giovanni Ibba, eds., *Enoch and the Mosaic Torah: The Evidence of Jubilees* (Grand Rapids: Eerdmans, 2009).

88. George W. E. Nickelsburg, *Jewish Literature between the Bible and the Mishnah* (Minneapolis: Fortress Press, 2005), 69.

89. See for example the repeated censure of intermarriage (20:4; 22:20; 25:1; 27:10; 30:1–15), nudity (3:31), and attempts to conceal circumcision (15:33–34).

90. See for example *Jub.* 11:4, 16; 12:1–8, 12–14; 21:3–5; 22:16–18, 22; 36:5.

91. Trans. Wintermute, *OTP* 2:94.

in this text thus suggest a more limited scope of the prohibition of images, namely images of foreign deities intended for worship.

Temple Scroll. The publication of the Temple Scroll by Yigael Yadin in 1977 underscored the centrality of halakah in the life of the Qumran sectarian community.[92] Although it is difficult to determine a precise date of composition—scholars have proposed dates ranging from the fifth or fourth century B.C.E.[93] to the first century C.E.[94]—sometime during the second or first century B.C.E. is perhaps the most reasonable suggestion.[95] This text, which is preserved mainly in two manuscripts from Cave 11 (11Q19 and 11Q20), presents itself as a supplement to the Mosaic Pentateuch or, in the words of Hartmut Stegemann, a "sixth book of the Torah."[96] Nevertheless, this "new" Torah is more properly identified as a recycling of various laws from the Pentateuch that primarily concern not only the temple and its sacrifices but also the proper observance of festivals and the regulation of purity and impurity. Moreover, the final section of the scroll, columns 51–66, amounts to a rewriting of Deut 12–23, underscoring the essentially midrashic nature of this text.[97]

Although idolatry is a prominent concern in this scroll,[98] the text does not explicitly treat the second commandment proper, that is, the prohibition of images from the Decalogue (whether the version in Exodus or Deuteronomy). Nevertheless, the *Temple Scroll* does engage another Deuteronomic passage, Deut 16:21–22, that can be viewed as an extension of the second commandment. This passage in Deuteronomy proscribes two items, the אשרה (more broadly designated as עץ כל) and the מצבה, both of which are said to be the object of YHWH's hatred (אלהיך אשר שׂנא יהוה).[99] The former likely referred to some kind of cultic object, perhaps a sacred pole, tree, or image associated with the Canaanite goddess Asherah, portrayed as the consort of El in Ugaritic literature. This goddess was apparently asso-

---

92 For the revised English version of the *editio princeps*, which was originally published in Hebrew, see Yigael Yadin, *The Temple Scroll* (4 vols.; Jerusalem: Israel Exploration Society, 1983).

93. Hartmut Stegemann, *The Library of Qumran* (Grand Rapids: Eerdmans, 1998), 96.

94. Barbara Thiering, "The Date of Composition of the Temple Scroll," in *Temple Scroll Studies* (ed. George J. Brooke; Sheffield: JSOT Press, 1989), 99–120.

95. E.-M. Laperrousaz, "Does the Temple Scroll Date from the First or Second Century BCE?" in *Temple Scroll Studies* (ed. George J. Brooke; Sheffield: JSOT Press, 1989), 91–97. For a general discussion of this and other issues surrounding this text, see Florentino García Martínez, "Temple Scroll," in *Encyclopedia of the Dead Sea Scrolls* (ed. Lawrence H. Schiffman and James C. VanderKam; 2 vols.; Oxford: Oxford University Press, 2000), 2:927–33.

96. Stegemann, *The Library of Qumran*, 96.

97. Lawrence H. Schiffman, "Laws Concerning Idolatry in the Temple Scroll," in *Uncovering Ancient Stones: Essays in Memory of H. Neil Richardson* (ed. Lewis M. Hopfe; Winona Lake, Ind.: Eisenbrauns, 1994), 159. See also Martínez, "Temple Scroll," 2:929.

98. Schiffman, "Laws Concerning Idolatry," 159–75.

99. The two prohibitions read as follows: לא תטע לך אשרה כל עץ (16:21); תקים לך מצבה לא (16:22).

ciated with the cult of YHWH for much of Israelite history,[100] and a sculpted image of the goddess (פסל האשרה) was at some point erected in the temple of Jerusalem (2 Kgs 21:7). The second object, the מצבה, designated a sacred stone or pillar that was typically aniconic.[101] Although the latter term is not always condemned in the Hebrew Bible, particularly in the patriarchal narratives where it functions positively as a memorial stone to YHWH,[102] in certain prophetic and legal contexts the מצבה is associated with idolatry and thus censured.[103]

The *Temple Scroll*, however, reformulates and expands on the prohibitions of Deut 16:21–22. Although the relevant material is somewhat fragmentary, enough of the text has been preserved to provide a clear indication of how the author of this text reshapes the passage in Deuteronomy in order to define more explicitly the scope of the original proscription:

19 לוא תעשו בארצכמה כאשר הגואים עושים בכול מקום המה
20 זובחים ונוטעים להמה אשרות ומקימים להמה מצבות
21 ונותנים אבני משכיות להשתחות עליהמה ...
1 [·] אׄכׄלׄ לוא תטע [לכה אשרה כול עץ אצל
2 מזבחי אשר תעשה ל]כׄה ולוא תקים לכה מצבה [אשר שנאתי וא]בׄן
3 [מ]שׂכית [לו]אׄ תעשה לכה בכול ארצכה להשתחׄוׄ[ו]תׄ עליה

19 Do not do in your land as the nations do: in every place they
20 sacrifice and they plant *asherot* and they erect *maṣṣebot* for themselves,
21 and they set up sculpted stones in order to bow down before them . . .
1 [. . .] Do not plant [for yourself an *asherah* or any tree beside
2 the altar which you will make for your]self, and do not erect for yourself a *maṣṣebah* [which I hate, and a s]tone
3 [sc]ulpted you shall [no]t make for yourself in all your land in order to bow dow[n] before it.[104] (11Q19 51.19–52.3)

This passage is broadly concerned to distinguish between insider (Jewish) and outsider (הגואים) worship and divides into two main sections: the first a description of the cultic practices characteristic of non-Jews (51.19–21) and the second an expanded restatement of Deut 16:21–22 that serves to define (albeit negatively)

---

100. The proper identification of אשרה and its relationship to the cult of YHWH is a rather complicated subject that has occupied a significant body of secondary literature. Much of the discussion has centered on the inscriptions from Kuntillet ʿAjrud, which include a reference to YHWH and "his *asherah*." For a helpful overview of the issues and range of interpretations, see Othmar Keel and Christoph Uehlinger, *Gods, Goddesses, and Images of God in Ancient Israel* (Minneapolis: Fortress Press, 1998), 229–48.

101. Mettinger, *No Graven Image*. But for an example of a partially iconic מצבה, see Keel and Uehlinger, *Gods, Goddesses, and Images of God*, 36 fig. 26b.

102. For example, Gen 28:18; 31:45; 35:14.

103. Besides Deut 16:22, see, for example, Exod 23:24; Deut 7:5; 12:3; 2 Kgs 17:10; 18:4; 23:14; Hos 10:1.

104. I am following the reconstructed text in Elisha Qimron, ed., *The Temple Scroll: A Critical Edition with Extensive Reconstructions* (Jerusalem: Ben-Gurion University of the Negev Press and Israel Exploration Society, 1996), 75–76.

the Jewish cult as the inverse of the practice of the "nations" (52.1–3). This contrast between the two groups is also delineated spatially: the territory of the non-Jews, the "every place" (בכול מקום) that is full of forbidden cultic objects, and the territory of the Jews (בכול ארצכה), which ought to be empty of such objects.[105]

That the material in column 52 is not simply a restatement of Deut 16:21–22 is clear enough. In the first place, the *Temple Scroll* changes the source text to include a "sculpted stone" (אבן משכית) in addition to the forbidden אשרה and מצבה. According to Schiffman, the author here expands the original prohibition by conflating Deut 16:21–22 with Lev 26:1, which likewise includes אבן משכית among other forbidden objects.[106] Additionally, again following the Leviticus passage, the prohibition against sculpted stones is qualified with an infinitive of purpose (עליה להשתחוות), further delimiting the nature of the forbidden items to include only those objects with a cultic function. The effect of these changes is not unlike what we observed in Josephus' reformulation of the second commandment in *A.J.* 3.91, where the Greek infinitive προσκυνεῖν likewise qualifies the proscription against images. The author of the *Temple Scroll* thus seems to view the biblical prohibition against images to include only those images that functioned within a cultic context.

Philo of Alexandria. Philo addresses the topic of idolatry, and more specifically the question of figurative art, on numerous occasions, and as Karl-Gustav Sandelin observes, his attitude toward statuary, and images in general, is rather complicated.[107] On the one hand, Philo makes use of the conventional Jewish polemic against idols, as for example when he ridicules those who pray to lifeless gods, images that cannot see, hear, smell, taste, and so on.[108] But on the other hand, he speaks favorably of the art (τέχνη) of the famed sculptor Phidias (Philo, *Ebr.* 89) and even describes the human body, that beautiful form (σώματος εὐμορφίαν) sculpted by God out of the purest clay, as a sacred shrine (ἡ νεὼς ἱερός) of the most godlike of images (ἀγαλμάτων τὸ θεοειδέστατον; *Opif.* 136–137, commenting on Gen 2:7). A detailed analysis of this material is well beyond the scope of the present discussion, so the following focuses on Philo's explanation of the prohibition of images in his *De decalogo* and *De specialibus legibus*.[109]

As noted above, Philo and Josephus both divide the Decalogue along the same

105. For a similar delineation of space, see the discussion of *B.J.* below in chapter 4.

106. Schiffman, "Laws Concerning Idolatry," 162–63. The relevant portion of Lev 26:1 reads as follows:

לא תעשו לכם אלילם ופסל ומצבה לא תקימו לכם ואבן משכית לא תתנו בארצכם להשתחות עליה.

107. Karl-Gustav Sandelin, "Philo's Ambivalence towards Statues," *SPhilo* 13 (2001): 122–38. On Philo's treatment of the topic of idolatry, see Karl-Gustav Sandelin, "The Danger of Idolatry according to Philo of Alexandria," *Temenos* 27 (1991): 109–50.

108. For example, *Decal.* 72–74, though it should be noted that in *Legat.* 290 Philo does seem to recognize a distinction between the gods and their iconographical representation. On this latter point, see Sandelin, "Philo's Ambivalence towards Statues," 133.

109. On Philo's presentation of the Decalogue in general, see Yehoshua Amir, "The Decalogue according to Philo," in *The Ten Commandments in History and Tradition* (ed. Ben-

lines,[110] with the "no other gods" of Exod 20:3 identified as the "first" commandment[111] and the prohibition against images as the "second" commandment.[112] Philo specifically treats the second commandment in two brief summaries (*Decal.* 51 and 156) and two extended discussions (*Decal.* 66–81 and *Spec.* 1.21–31). In each Philo avoids the LXX's εἴδωλον in favor of three common terms for Greek statuary: ξόανον, ἄγαλμα, and ἀφίδρυμα.[113] For instance, the scope of the proscription in *Decal.* 51 is defined to encompass ξόανα, ἀγάλματα, and "generally all erected images made by hand" (συνόλως ἀφιδρυμάτων χειροκμήτων). On the surface, this list of items seems fairly comprehensive, encompassing at the very least all sculpted objects. Elsewhere Philo identifies ξόανον and ἄγαλμα as statues carved of wood and stone respectively (*Contempl.* 7),[114] and, indeed, Philo even places ἀγάλματα and ξόανα (along with ζωγραφήματα) within the broad category of pictorial and plastic art of the Greeks and Barbarians (*Abr.* 267). And the phrase συνόλως ἀφιδρυμάτων χειροκμήτων, which recurs (albeit in a slightly different form) in his summary in *Decal.* 156, would seem to include any man-made statue, regardless of the material used.

However, as noted by both Tatum and Sandelin, Philo frequently employs these three terms together to denote not statues in general but *divine* statuary.[115] For example, Philo derides the human attempt to "make gods" (θεοπλαστέω) by filling the world with ξόανα, ἀγάλματα, "and countless other erected images" (ἀγαλμάτων καὶ ξοάνων καὶ ἄλλων μυρίων ἀφιδρυμάτων . . . κατέπλησε τὴν οἰκουμένην) (*Ebr.* 109).[116] Likewise in his discussion of the biblical injunction against those who curse god,[117] Philo notes that Moses was not speaking of the supreme creator God (τοῦ πρώτου καὶ γεννητοῦ τῶν ὅλων) but of those falsely named (ψευδώνυμοι) gods whose iconographical presence populates the inhabited world: "For the entire inhabited world has become full of ξόανα, ἀγάλματα, and ἀφιδρύματα" (*Mos.* 2.203–205). This triad appears also in Philo's description of the polytheism (πολύθεος) of Tamar's native city. In this context, the language is

---

Zion Segal and Gershon Levi; Jerusalem: Magnes Press, 1990), 121–60. Amir however does not specifically discuss the second commandment.

110. Philo's legal taxonomy is nevertheless much more elaborate than Josephus', particularly in Philo's identification of the Decalogue as the κεφάλαιον of other laws; on this, see especially Termini, "Taxonomy of Biblical Laws," 1–29, esp. 5–10.

111. According to Philo (*Decal.* 65), the "first" is the most sacred of all the commandments.

112. See *Decal.* 82, where the interdiction is designated "the second exhortation" (ἡ δευτέρα παραίνεσις).

113. One exception is the discussion in *Spec.* 1.25–26, in which Philo quotes the injunction against εἴδωλα in Lev 19:4 and then explains that such idols—in this context understood figuratively for wealth and subsequently applied to those wily myth-makers (*Spec.* 1.28)—are like "shadows (σκιαί) and phantoms (φάσματα)."

114. Alice Donohue, however, argues against a perfect typological correspondence between the statues and materials listed, that is, that ξόανα corresponds with ξύλα and ἀγάλματα corresponds with λίθοι (*Xoana and the Origins of Greek Sculpture* [Atlanta: Scholars Press, 1988], 101).

115. Tatum, "The LXX Version," 189; Sandelin, "Philo's Ambivalence towards Statues," 127.

116. See also *Mos.* 1.298; 2.205; *Decal.* 7, 156;

117. Quoting the LXX Lev 24:15: ὃς ἐὰν καταράσηται θεόν.

almost identical to his summary of the second commandment in *Decal.* 51: "[The city] was full of ξόανα, ἀγάλματα, and συνόλως ἀφιδρύματα" (*Virt.* 221). Moreover, in *De specialibus legibus*, Philo explicitly defines the second commandment not in terms of the production of images but the production of divine images, or the fashioning of gods (θεοπλαστέω; *Spec.* 1.21).

When Philo explains the underlying rationale of the Mosaic prohibition, he repeatedly emphasizes that sculpture falls short of an "appropriate conception of the everlasting God" (*Decal.* 67). It is absurd to *deify* perishable material insofar as it is inherently inferior; indeed, it would be better to deify (ἐκθειόω) sculptors and painters rather than their lifeless creations (*Decal.* 69–70). The fundamental problem addressed by these assertions is not the image itself—its iconography and material—but that the ensouled is worshiping the soulless ("Therefore, let no one who has a soul worship something without a soul" [μηδεὶς οὖν τῶν ἐχόντων ψυχὴν ἀψύχῳ τινὶ προσκυνείτω]; *Decal.* 76). From within this conceptual framework, the second commandment is thus not even limited to sculpture per se, or any kind of artistic representation of the divine realm, but can be equally applied to the Egyptian practice of deifying animals and the deification of wealth.[118]

Moreover, Philo's synthesis of the prohibition against images demonstrates that, notwithstanding the numerical distinction between the so-called first and second commandments, the two are inextricably linked:

> ἀνελὼν οὖν ἐκ τῆς ἱερᾶς νομοθεσίας πᾶσαν τὴν τοιαύτην ἐκθέωσιν ἐπὶ τὴν τοῦ πρὸς ἀλήθειαν ὄντος θεοῦ τιμὴν ἐκάλεσεν, ἑαυτοῦ τιμῆς οὐ προσδεόμενος οὐ γὰρ ἑτέρου χρεῖος ἦν ὁ αὐταρκέστατος ἑαυτῷ, βουλόμενος δὲ τὸ γένος τῶν ἀνθρώπων ἀνοδίαις πλαζόμενον εἰς ἀπλανεστάτην ἄγειν ὁδόν, ἵν' ἑπόμενον τῇ φύσει τὸ ἄριστον εὕρηται τέλος, ἐπιστήμην τοῦ ὄντως ὄντος, ὅς ἐστι τὸ πρῶτον ἀγαθὸν καὶ τελεώτατον, ἀφ' οὗ τρόπον πηγῆς ἄρδεται τῷ κόσμῳ καὶ τοῖς ἐν αὐτῷ τὰ ἐπὶ μέρους ἀγαθά.
>
> So then He gave no place in His sacred code of laws to all such setting up of other gods, and called upon men to honour Him that truly is, not because He needed that honour should be paid to Him, for He that is all-sufficient to Himself needs nothing else, but because He wished to lead the human race, wandering in pathless wilds, to the road from which none can stray, so that following nature they might win the best of goals, knowledge of Him that truly is, Who is the primal and most perfect good, from Whom as from a fountain is showered the water of each particular good upon the world and them that dwell therein. (*Decal.* 81 [Colson, LCL])

In sum, although Philo largely avoids the term εἴδωλον in his treatment of the prohibition against images, he nevertheless clearly interprets this proscription "in a polemically anti-idolic and not in an anti-iconic" manner:[119] cult images, and not images in general, fall under the purview of the Mosaic prohibition.

118. On the Egyptians: *Decal.* 76–80; on wealth, *Spec.* 1.25–27.

119. Tatum, "The LXX Version," 189. So also Sandelin, who interprets Philo's reading of the second commandment as "a prohibition of idolatry" ("Philo's Ambivalence towards Statues," 129).

Pseudo-Philo. Ps.-Philo's *Liber antiquitatum biblicarum* (hereafter *L.A.B.*), composed at some point during the first century C.E., perhaps shortly before the destruction of the temple in 70 C.E.,[120] is an expansive retelling of the biblical narrative, encompassing the history of the Israelites from Adam to David. Although *L.A.B.* only survives in Latin translation, it was likely composed in Hebrew and then translated into Greek, on which the Latin translation is based.[121] There are numerous similarities between *L.A.B.* and Josephus' *A.J.*, on both a literary and exegetical level, making this text particularly relevant for the present discussion.[122]

Recent discussion has highlighted the centrality of idolatry in the overarching narrative development,[123] and Ps.-Philo explicitly refers to the second commandment on two separate occasions: *L.A.B.* 11:6 and 44:6–7. The first occurs within his retelling of the Sinai episode and includes an extensive citation of the Sinai legislation interspersed with the author's own elaborations. As is evident in the following comparison, excepting word order the Latin of *L.A.B.* follows closely the Greek and Hebrew of Exod 20:4, with one notable addition, the word *deos*:

MT	לא תעשה לך פסל
LXX	οὐ ποιήσεις σεαυτῷ εἴδωλον
L.A.B.	deos sculptiles non facies tibi

The absence of Exod. 20:3—"You shall not have any other gods besides me"—is noteworthy here, although I am not convinced that the author has "pointedly chosen to leave this out."[124] Rather, as with *Jubilees* the issue of foreign deities is conflated with the issue of images, resulting in a single proscription against sculpted deities (*deos sculptiles*).[125] By conflating the first two commandments, the author has thus emphasized the *cultic* nature of the proscribed images.

The second reference to the prohibition of images occurs in Ps.-Philo's retelling of the Judges narrative, specifically the episode involving the idols that Micah

120. On the date, see the brief discussion in Daniel J. Harrington, "Pseudo-Philo: A New Translation and Introduction," in *The Old Testament Pseudepigrapha* (ed. James H. Charlesworth; 2 vols.; New York: Doubleday, 1985), 2:299.

121. This view was originally proposed in 1898 by Leopold Cohn and has since become generally accepted in scholarship on *L.A.B.* (see "An Apocryphal Work Ascribed to Philo of Alexandria," *JQR* 10 [1898]: 277–332; Daniel J. Harrington, "The Original Language of Pseudo-Philo's *Liber Antiquitatum Biblicarum*," *HTR* 63 [1970]: 503–14).

122. On the relationship between Josephus' *A.J.* and Ps.-Philo's *LAB*, see Louis H. Feldman, "Josephus' *Jewish Antiquities* and Pseudo-Philo's *Biblical Antiquities*," in *Josephus, the Bible, and History* (ed. Louis H. Feldman and Gohei Hata; Detroit: Wayne State University Press, 1989), 59–80.

123. Frederick J. Murphy, "Retelling the Bible: Idolatry in Pseudo-Philo," *JBL* 107 (1988): 275–87; Crispin H. T. Fletcher-Louis, "Humanity and the Idols of the Gods in Pseudo-Philo's *Biblical Antiquities*," in *Idolatry: False Worship in the Bible, Early Judaism, and Christianity* (ed. Stephen C. Barton; London: T&T Clark, 2007), 58–72.

124. Howard Jacobson, *A Commentary on Pseudo-Philo's Liber antiquitatum biblicarum with Latin Text and English Translation* (2 vols.; Leiden: Brill, 1996), 1:460.

125. Jacobson conjectures that the original Hebrew may have read מסכה לא תעשה לך אלהי, a quotation of Exod. 34:17 (ibid).

crafted at the behest of his mother (*L.A.B.* 44:1–5; cf. Judg 17). According to Ps.-Philo, Micah's wicked and impious actions, emblematic of a wider problem of Israelite apostasy, elicits a strong response from the God of Israel, who announces his impending judgment (*L.A.B.* 44:6–10). Embedded within the divine indictment against "the sons of Israel" is a list of nine of the ten commandments given at Sinai, recounted in order to demonstrate, in Frederick Murphy's words, that "[i]dolatry is the root of all evil,"[126] that in violating the prohibition against idols the Israelites had ultimately violated all of God's commandments. The prohibition of images is rephrased twice within this divine speech:

> et dixi ut non facerent idola, et consenserunt ut non sculperent effigies deorum.
>
> I said that they should not make idols, and they agreed not to carve images of gods. (*L.A.B.* 44:6)
>
> <lacuna> ut non facerent idola, nec opera deorum eorum qui nati sunt de corruptela in appellatione sculptilis et eorum per que facta sunt corrupta omnia.
>
> <lacuna> not to make idols nor to perform the service of those gods that have been born from corruption under the name of graven image and of those through which all things have become corrupt.[127] (*L.A.B.* 44:7)

As in the case of *L.A.B.* 11:6, Exod 20:3 is again collapsed into the prohibition against images. Hence the scope of the proscription here is not images per se, but *effigies deorum*, images of the gods. Likewise, in the second instance the act of making an idol is juxtaposed with the act of serving the gods, explicitly forging a clear link between craftsmanship and cultic activity.[128]

A Prohibition of Images In Toto: The Mekilta de R. Yishmael

The *Mekilta de R. Yishmael* (hereafter *Mek. R. Yish.*) is an extended exegetical commentary, consisting of nine tractates (*massekhtot*) devoted primarily (though not exclusively) to the legal material in Exodus, hence its classification among the halakhic midrashim.[129] The date of this material is notoriously slippery, both in its various parts and as a fully redacted composition. Although the halakhic midrashim are generally considered Tannaitic, that is, dating to the so-called period of the Tannaim extending from 70 C.E. through the codification of the Mishnah in the early third century C.E., proposed dates for the final redaction of *Mek. R. Yish.*

---

126. Murphy, "Idolatry in Pseudo-Philo," 279.

127. Trans. Jacobson, *A Commentary on Pseudo-Philo*, 1:166–67.

128. Jacobson suggests that the plural *opera* translates the Hebrew term עבודה, with the implication that the second commandment constitutes a prohibition against making idols for worship (ibid., 2:1011).

129. The sections of Exodus covered in the text are Exod 12:1–23:19; 31:12–17; 35:1–3, or approximately 30 percent of the total book. For an introduction to the various issues surrounding this text, see H. L. Strack and Günter Stemberger, *Introduction to the Talmud and Midrash* (Minneapolis: Fortress Press, 1992), 251–57.

range from the latter half of the third century C.E.[130] to the eighth century C.E.[131] For the present discussion, it is enough to note that this text in its final form is indisputably a postdestruction composition, though it is certainly possible that various exegetical traditions contained therein predate 70 C.E. The relevant portion of *Mek. R. Yish.* for this analysis occurs in the sixth tractate (*Baḥodesh*), which covers Exod 19–20 and includes a lengthy block of material devoted to an explanation of the clause לא תעשה לך פסל in Exod 20:4 (*Mek. R. Yish.*, *Baḥodesh* 6). I include below a structural translation of the full text:[132]

1 "YOU SHALL NOT MAKE FOR YOURSELF A CARVED IMAGE." [Exod 20:4]
2 One should not make for himself one that is engraved (גלופה),
3 but perhaps one can make for himself one that is solid (אטומה)?
4 Scripture says: "NOR ANY LIKENESS." [Exod 20:4]
5 One should not make for himself a solid, but perhaps one can plant for
6 himself a plant?
7 Scripture says: "YOU SHALL NOT PLANT FOR YOURSELF AN
8 *ASHERAH*." [Deut 16:21]
9 One should not plant for himself a plant, but perhaps one can make for
10 himself [an image] from a tree?
11 Scripture says: "ANY TREE." [Deut 16:21]
12 One should not make for himself [an image] from a tree, but perhaps
13 one can make for himself [an image] of stone?
14 Scripture says: "NOR A SCULPTED (משכית) STONE." [Lev 26:1]
15 One should not make for himself [an image] of stone, but perhaps one
16 can make for himself [an image] of silver?
17 Scripture says: "GODS OF SILVER." [Exod 20:20]
18 One should not make for himself [an image] of silver, but perhaps one
19 can make for himself [an image] of gold?
20 Scripture says: "GODS OF GOLD." [Exod 20:20]
21 One should not make for himself [an image] of gold, but perhaps one
22 can make for himself [an image] of copper, tin, or lead?
23 Scripture says: "AND GODS OF MOLTEN METAL (מסכה) YOU SHALL
24 NOT MAKE." [Lev 19:4]
25 One should not make for himself a likeness of any of these
26 [aforementioned items] (דמות כל אלה), but perhaps one can make for
27 himself a likeness of any figure (סמל)?
28 Scripture says: "LEST YOU ACT CORRUPTLY AND MAKE FOR
29 YOURSELVES A CARVED IMAGE (פסל), A LIKENESS OF ANY FIGURE."
[Deut 4:16]
30 One should not make for himself a likeness of any figure, but perhaps
31 one can make for himself a likeness of cattle or a bird?
32 Scripture says: "THE FORM OF ANY CATTLE (תבנית כל בהמה) ON
33 the earth or the form of any winged bird
(תבנית כל צפור כנף)." [Deut 4:17]

---

130. Ibid., 255.

131. Ben-Zion Wacholder, "The Date of the Mekilta de-Rabbi Ishmael," *HUCA* 39 (1968): 117–44.

132. The enumeration of lines and translation are my own.

One should not make for himself a likeness of any of these,
but perhaps one can make for himself a likeness of fish, locusts,
unclean animals, or reptiles?
Scripture says: "THE FORM OF ANY THING THAT CREEPS ON THE
GROUND, THE FORM OF ANY FISH IN THE WATER." [Deut 4:18]
One should not make for himself a likeness of any of these,
but perhaps one can make for himself a likeness of the sun
or the moon, the stars or the planets?
Scripture says: "LEST YOU LIFT UP YOUR EYES TO THE HEAVENS,
ETC." [Deut 4:19]
One should not make for himself a likeness of any of these,
but perhaps one can make for himself a likeness of angels, Cherubim,
Ophannim, or [other] heavenly beings?
Scripture says: "THAT WHICH IS IN THE HEAVENS." [Exod 20:4]
If that which is in the heavens [is prohibited], then perhaps [this only
includes] a likeness of the sun or the moon or the stars or the planets?
Scripture says: "ABOVE" [Exod 20:4], [which means] neither the
likeness of angels, nor the likeness of Cherubim, nor the likeness
of Ophannim.
One should not make for himself a likeness of any of these,
but perhaps one can make for himself a likeness of the abyss or
the darkness or deep darkness?
Scripture says: "AND THAT WHICH IS BENEATH THE EARTH, OR
THAT WHICH IS IN THE WATERS BENEATH THE EARTH" [Exod 20:4].
[This] encompasses a reflected image (הבוביא), according
to the words of R. Aqiva.
But there are others [who say, this] encompasses water
snakes (השבירים).
Scripture so pursued the evil inclination so as not to give it a place to
find for itself a pretext for permitting [idolatry].

This text proceeds through a string of scriptural citations structured around a series of questions and answers whose cumulative effect is to probe the meaning of the initial clause from Exod 20:4—לא תעשה לך פסל. Each subsequent scriptural citation functions both to answer an antecedent question while eliciting another question, which in turn is answered with another scriptural citation, and so on. The rhetorical import of this process of interrogating the biblical text is to establish an all-encompassing definition of the Hebrew term פסל. According to this text, the biblical prohibition against making a פסל thus includes not just an engraved image (גלופה; line 2) but also a solid (אטומה; line 3) image, an image sculpted from wood, stone, silver, gold, or any type of metal (lines 9–24); even a "likeness of any figure" (דמות כל סמל; lines 25–26) is *verboten*, including theriomorphic, astral, and angelic representations (lines 25–52).[133] That the *Mek. R. Yish.* includes in the ban such items as the cherubim, prominent in the numerous literary descriptions of

133. For a discussion of this text in the context of the rabbinic polemic against angel veneration, see Peter Schäfer, *Rivalität zwischen Engeln und Menschen: Untersuchungen zur Rabbinischen Engelvorstellung* (Berlin: Walter de Gruyter, 1975), 67–68.

the iconography of the biblical tabernacle/temple, underscores the unequivocally comprehensive stance of this text: the second commandment forbids all forms of figurative representation.[134] Moreover, there is no hint in this text that the author(s) intended only images with cultic associations.[135]

Why this seemingly "conservative" approach to the second commandment? The final sentence imaginatively depicts scripture as an aggressor in persistent pursuit of the יצר הרע ("evil inclination"), which if left to its own devices will inevitably find a way to permit (אמתלת התר) idolatry. This reference points to the underlying motivation of this text, namely that the frequent repetition of scriptural citations, which collectively expand the scope of the second commandment to all forms of figurative representation, functions as a kind of halakhic border patrol, a protective wall erected to prevent even the potential for committing idolatry.

Although Levine suggests that the *Mek. R. Yish.* is "perhaps more reflective of rabbinic views,"[136] numerous recent studies have drawn attention to a rather lively halakhic debate throughout the rabbinic corpus over the question of images and the second commandment, demonstrating a broad range of legal and exegetical positions—from the so-called stringent to the more lenient—and rendering suspect the notion of a single or even predominant "rabbinic" viewpoint.[137] One fascinating and oft-cited example of an alternative voice is the story of Rabban Gamaliel bathing in front of a statue of Aphrodite in a Roman bathhouse (*m. Avod. Zar.* 3:4–5).[138] Rabban Gamaliel justifies his proximity to the goddess by implicitly appealing to a legal distinction between "permitted" and "forbidden" images. In this particular case, how people treat the goddess on a daily basis in part determines her status as a permitted image:

---

134. Numerous scholars have interpreted this passage as an absolute ban on figurative art; see, for example, Goodenough, *Jewish Symbols*, 4:3–24; Urbach, "Rabbinical Laws on Idolatry," 235; Boaz Cohen, "Art in Jewish Law," *Judaism* 3 (1954): 168; Levine, *The Ancient Synagogue*, 451–53.

135. Contra Gerald Blidstein, "The Tannaim and Plastic Art," *Perspectives in Jewish Learning* 5 (1973): 19–20.

136. Levine, *The Ancient Synagogue*, 451. It should be noted that Levine does discuss other what he calls more lenient stances, particularly the legend of Rabban Gamaliel in the bathhouse (see ibid., 212–13)

137. See especially the following studies by Yaron Eliav: "Viewing the Sculptural Environment," 411–33; "Roman Statues," 99–115; "The Desolating Sacrilege: A Jewish-Christian Discourse on Statuary, Space, and Sanctity," in *The Sculptural Environment of the Roman Near East: Reflections on Culture, Ideology, and Power* (ed. Yaron Z. Eliav, Elise Friedland, and Sharon Herbert; Louvain: Peeters, 2008), 605–27.

138. On this episode, see especially the following studies: Gerald Blidstein, "Nullification of Idolatry in Rabbinic Law," *PAAJR* 41 (1973–74): 4–6; Seth Schwartz, "Gamaliel in Aphrodite's Bath: Palestinian Judaism and Urban Culture in the Third and Fourth Centuries," in *The Talmud Yerushalmi and Graeco-Roman Culture I* (ed. Peter Schäfer; Tübingen: Mohr Siebeck, 1998), 203–17; Eliav, "Viewing the Sculptural Environment," 424–25; Azzan Yadin, "Rabban Gamaliel, Aphrodite's Bath, and the Question of Pagan Monotheism," *JQR* 96 (2006): 149–79.

> Furthermore, [even] if you are given a large sum of money, [would] you enter in to your idolatry naked, [or] polluted from semen, [or would you] urinate in front of her?! And she [Aphrodite] is standing by the drainage and all the people are urinating in front of her. It is said only "their gods," [that is] that which *he treats as a god* is prohibited, but that which *he does not treat as a god* is permitted.[139]

This anecdote involving Rabban Gamaliel suggests that at least for some of the sages represented in the Mishnah iconography alone was insufficient to determine the status of an image. In this example the iconography would on the surface seem especially damning. Surely a three-dimensional anthropomorphic sculpture unambiguously representing the goddess Aphrodite falls within the scope of the פסל in Exod 20:4! Yet for Rabban Gamaliel, that the image in question *looks like* the goddess is immaterial. The central question is: does she *act like* a goddess or, better, is she *treated like* a goddess? From this perspective, function—whether or not an image has some kind of cultic association or ritual status, be it a formally consecrated image or an image treated as such—is critical in determining the status of an image.[140]

This cultic criterion is likewise evident in the wider context of the Gamaliel legend, particularly the opening statement of Mishnah tractate *Avodah Zarah* chapter 3: " 'All statues (כל הצלמים) are forbidden, *since they are worshiped* (נעבדין) once a year,' so the words of R. Meir. But the sages say, 'It [a statue] is not forbidden, except any that have in its hand a rod, or a bird, or a sphere.' Rabban Simeon b. Gamaliel says, 'Any [statue] that has anything in its hand' " (*m. Avod. Zar.* 3:1). The halakhic dispute preserved in this text concerns the scope of forbidden images, and although there is an obvious disagreement over what statues are and are not forbidden—R. Meir on one end of the spectrum and the sages on the other end, with Rabban Simeon taking a mediating position—all parties in the dispute seem to agree that the criterion of worship determines the status of the image. Although R. Meir takes a more comprehensive stance by proscribing all statues, he does so on the assumption, however unlikely, that all statues are worshiped. The sages who then disagree with R. Meir base their argument on the supposition that all statues *are not worshiped*, but only those that bear the iconographic marks of cultic statues: either grasping a staff, bird, or sphere or, in the case of Rabban Simeon, grasping anything.[141]

The traditions preserved in the Mishnah tractate *Avodah Zarah*, in which all agree, at least theoretically, on the categories of "permitted" and "forbidden" images, contrast markedly with halakhic reading of Exod 20:4 in the *Mek. R. Yish.*

139. Trans. Eliav, "Viewing the Sculptural Environment," 424 (emphasis mine).

140. Gerald Blidstein similarly remarks: "Function—and not shape—determines sanctity, and it is sanctity that determines whether an object is or is not idolatrous" ("Nullification of Idolatry," 8). Yaron Eliav likewise points to the centrality of the criterion of worship in such halakhic disputes: "The sages differentiated between statues on the basis of those that were the objects of pagan worship and those that were not" ("Viewing the Sculptural Environment," 421).

141. Yaron Eliav calls this a "plastic language" that was used to determine deified statues ("Viewing the Sculptural Environment," 423).

insofar as the latter seems to preclude even the possibility of "permitted" images. Perhaps the closest parallel to the exegetical stance of the *Mek. R. Yish.* comes from Tertullian in his treatise *De idolatria* (4:1):

> God forbids the making as much as the worship of an idol. If it is forbidden to worship a thing, then, to the extent that making it precedes worshipping it, does the prohibition to make it have priority over the prohibition to worship it. It is for this reason, namely to root out the material occasion for idolatry, that Divine Law proclaims: *you shall make no idol*; and by adding, *nor a likeness of the things which are in the heaven and which are on the earth and which are in the sea*, it has denied the whole world to the servants of God for the practice of these arts.[142]

By divorcing the prohibition of *making* an image from *worshiping* an image, Tertullian is able to read Exod 20:4 as an interdiction against the artistic representation of all observable phenomena, the whole world (*toto mundo*). Indeed, Tertullian eschews any attempt to restrict the forbidden image to that "which has been consecrated in human shape" (*quod humana effigie sit consecratum*; *Idol.* 3:3).[143]

Summary

At least three exegetical approaches to the Mosaic prohibition against images are evident in the above survey of texts. The first possibility is to simply avoid the interdiction. Unfortunately, while the omission of the second commandment in Ps.-Phoc. is tantalizing, it is difficult to know precisely how to interpret this silence. The second, what is clearly the predominant viewpoint evident in a wide range of texts from the pre- and postdestruction periods, is to restrict the prohibition to cultic images. From this perspective, the prohibitions in Exod 20:4–5 against *making* (לא תעשה) and *worshiping* (לא תשתחוה להם and לא תעבדם) images are inextricably linked. By contrast, the third approach, evident most clearly in the postdestruction *Mek. R. Yish.*, but also occasionally in Josephus' narrative summaries, divorces the issue of *making* images from *worshiping* them, effectively transforming the second commandment into a prohibition of *both* figural representation *and* idolatrous worship. This perspective thus precludes even the possibility of "permitted" images.

CONCLUSION

In the prevailing scholarly narrative, based largely on the archaeological record read through the lens of Josephus and the rabbis, the "protagonist" of this chapter—the biblical prohibition of images—plays a clearly defined role. Before 70 C.E., the second commandment is construed as an inflexible proscription of all figurative images, that is, artistic representations of living beings, whether in the flat or round. It matters not what the image happens to represent, how it happens to function, or even where it happens to be located. From this perspective, the

142. Trans. Waszink and Winden, *Tertullianus De Idolatria*, 27 (emphasis mine).

143. Trans. ibid., 27.

only possible exceptions, and the only permissible images, are those consisting of floral or geometric motifs (i.e., anything nonfigurative). But after the destruction of the temple, so the story goes, the situation changes drastically, and Jews began to soften their stance toward images, as even a cursory glance at the synagogue remains demonstrates. Most of the rabbis, the legal scholars responsible for the vast collection of halakhic and haggadic material in the Mishnah, Talmudim, and various midrashic compilations, are evidently persuaded by (or in some reconstructions, responsible for) this more flexible position and even establish the criterion of worship to determine whether an image is "permitted" or "forbidden." Thus, in the postdestruction era, proper interpretation of the second commandment does not primarily revolve around *iconography*, whether an image is figurative or nonfigurative, but *iconolatry*, whether an image is in some sense cultic or noncultic.

Yet a careful reading of a broader range of literary sources complicates this narrative. Indeed, the selection of sources included in this chapter tells a rather different story, one that resists the conventional chronological paradigm outlined above. Although a range of exegetical possibilities does emerge from the texts, the predominant tendency, both *before* and *after* 70 C.E., was to restrict the scope of the second commandment to images that had some kind of cultic association, whether formally consecrated or otherwise deemed an object of worship. Indeed, the only Jewish text that unambiguously asserts otherwise, the *Mek. R. Yish.* (a reading likewise evident in Tertullian's *De idolatria*), dates to the period *after* the destruction of the temple (i.e., during the so-called flexible period), rendering problematic the supposition that Second Temple Jews widely interpreted the second commandment as a proscription against figurative art in general, regardless of context or function.

This is not to say that there were no Jews during the Second Temple period who interpreted Exod 20:4–5 along the lines of the *Mek. R. Yish.*, but only that such an exegetical stance is not unambiguously borne out by the available literary sources from the period in question, with the possible exception of select passages from Josephus. And even Josephus' testimony, as argued above, is not entirely straightforward. While in certain contexts, particularly in narrative retrospective glances at the second commandment, Josephus gives voice to a seemingly strict interpretation of the interdiction, in the two explicitly exegetical contexts (*A.J.* 3.91 and *C. Ap.* 2.190–192) he displays a more nuanced reading of the Decalogue that draws attention to the cultic nature of the proscribed images. The question is: Why this apparent tension between narrative and exegesis? At the very least, this raises the possibility that there is more to Josephus' narrative summaries than meets the eye, that perhaps his reformulation of the second commandment in his various accounts of Jewish "iconoclasm" tells us more about Josephus' *rhetorical* interests than his *exegetical* stance, a possibility that will occupy the focus of the next two chapters.

4

Sculpture and the Politics of Space in *Bellum Judaicum*

People are by nature cartographers. Whether we are speaking of the need to organize newly discovered territories or the impulse to chart beforehand a long journey, mapping space is a fundamental means of understanding one's own place in an otherwise chaotic world.[1] Moreover, the concept of mapping, and more generally the tendency to organize space through conceptual representations (i.e., "mental maps"), is undoubtedly much older than the actual production of maps. As J. Brian Harley notes: "There has probably always been a mapping impulse in human consciousness, and the mapping experience—involving the cognitive mapping of space—undoubtedly existed long before the physical artifacts we now call maps."[2]

This notion of mental mapping, or "cognitive cartography," is particularly relevant for the issues raised in this chapter, mainly because it draws attention not just to the reality of space itself—for example, the precise dimensions of a particular geographical territory, the exact locations of its borders, and so on—but rather to the interplay between person and place, to the way in which people *perceive* and *experience* a particular spatial reality.[3] Of course, an individual's mental map is not drawn from thin air, as it were, but in some sense corresponds, however imperfectly, to the reality it describes. The conceptual and corporeal are inextricably entwined, and people's perceptions cannot be completely isolated from their physical context.[4] Nevertheless, cognitive cartography concerns not only the *organization* of space but also the *creation* of space, and mental constructions of space often

---

1. An abbreviated version of this chapter was published in Jason von Ehrenkrook, "Sculpture, Space, and the Poetics of Idolatry in Josephus' *Bellum Judaicum*," *JSJ* 39 (2008): 170–91.

2. J. Brian Harley, "The Map and the Development of the History of Cartography," in *The History of Cartography: Cartography in Prehistoric, Ancient, and Medieval Europe and the Mediterranean* (ed. J. Brian Harley and David Woodward; Chicago: University of Chicago Press, 1987), 1.

3. David Woodward and G. Malcolm Lewis, "Introduction," *The History of Cartography: Cartography in the Traditional African, American, Arctic, Australian, and Pacific Societies* (ed. David Woodward and G. Malcolm Lewis; Chicago: University of Chicago Press, 1998), 3–4.

4. Indeed, an important assumption of this analysis is that in antiquity, and throughout history, "material reality and human consciousness have been entangled in an endless reciprocal dance" (Yaron Z. Eliav, *God's Mountain: The Temple Mount in Time, Place, and Memory* [Baltimore: Johns Hopkins University Press, 2005], xxviii).

offer a glimpse into "imagined worlds," the territories of the ideal, and the place of the cartographer within such worlds.[5] In other words, such cognitive maps are invaluable not simply to understand *space* itself but the *people* who both inhabit and imagine space, who mediate through cognitive maps a particular understanding of themselves and their place in the world. In short, mapping space becomes a means of mapping culture and identity.

This is particularly true when it comes to the issue of sacred space, a subject that has recently garnered quite a bit of attention in the study of religion.[6] Of course, that many religions (perhaps even most), Judaism included, have distinguished between sacred and profane space is well-known and need hardly be mentioned. However, it is not sufficient simply to identify what is or is not sacred in a particular religious tradition; rather, the fundamental question revolves around the nature of space itself and the people who inhabit such space. *Why* is a particular location sacred? What makes it sacred, and what does this tell us about those for whom it is sacred?

For Mircea Eliade, space becomes sacred through a hierophanic interruption that detaches "a territory from the surrounding cosmic milieu and [makes] it qualitatively different."[7] Eliade calls this phenomenon a "mysterious act," a manifestation of the *ganz andere* (the wholly other), a metaphysical reality that invades the mundane of this world.[8] Although Eliade acknowledges the place of ritual in the creation of holy sites, he nevertheless downplays the humanness of such activities: "We must not suppose that *human* work is in question here, that it is through his own efforts that man can consecrate a space. In reality the ritual by which he constructs a sacred space is efficacious in the measure in which *it reproduces the work of the gods*."[9]

Recent research has called into question Eliade's theoretical framework, shifting the focus instead to the *human activity* of locating the sacred,[10] especially

---

5. Woodward and Lewis, "Introduction," 3. R. J. Zwi Werblowsky makes a similar observation when he remarks that "landscape—whether macro-cosmography or local geography—is shaped, in the very act of our perceiving it, by our mindscape" ("Introduction: Mindscape and Landscape," in *Sacred Space: Shrine, City, Land* [ed. Benjamin Z. Kedar and R. J. Zwi Werblowsky; New York: New York University Press, 1998], 10).

6. See, for example, the collection of essays in Jamie Scott and Paul Simpson-Housley, eds., *Sacred Places and Profane Spaces: Essays in the Geographics of Judaism, Christianity, and Islam* (New York: New York University Press, 1991). More recently, the publication of the proceedings from a conference held at the Hebrew University in Jerusalem encompasses an even broader geographical (and religious) range, including Israel, Japan, Mexico, and India, among other places; see Benjamin Z. Kedar and R. J. Zwi Werblowsky, eds., *Sacred Space: Shrine, City, Land* (New York: New York University Press, 1998).

7. Mircea Eliade, *The Sacred and the Profane: The Nature of Religion* (New York: Harcourt, 1959), 26.

8. Ibid., 11–12.

9. Ibid., 29 (emphasis in original).

10. See the discussion of these issues in Joan R. Branham, "Vicarious Sacrality: Temple Space in Ancient Synagogues," in *Ancient Synagogues: Historical Analysis and Archaeological Discovery* (ed. Dan Urman and Paul V. M. Flesher; 2 vols.; Leiden: Brill, 1995), 2:319–45.

the ritual/liturgical processes involved in transforming space.[11] For example, Jonathan Z. Smith identifies the human as a "world-creating being," one who attempts "to manipulate and negotiate ones [*sic*] 'situation' so as to have 'space' in which to meaningfully dwell."[12] From this perspective, it is not a question of whether a particular place is sacred or profane, since in actuality "there is nothing that is inherently or essentially clean or unclean, sacred or profane. There are situational or relational categories, mobile boundaries which shift according to the map being employed."[13] Therefore, the historian's task is to study the "variety of attempts to map, construct and inhabit . . . positions of power," that is, "power to relate ones [*sic*] domain to the plurality of environmental and social spheres."[14]

Smith's formulation points to two important assumptions that have shaped the discussion in this chapter. First, delineations of space inherently require boundary markers or borderlines, but these are fluid, easily manipulated, and ultimately vary from one "cartographer" to another. Second, sacred maps are more about locating *self* than the *sacred*, about negotiating identity within a particular place and time and in the face of a complex range of socio-politico-cultural forces. With this in mind, I argue in this chapter that embedded in the iconoclastic narratives of *B.J.* is the perception that statuary—and even more broadly all forms of sculptural representation—functions in part as a mapping device, a kind of visual boundary marker of sacred space, tangibly delineating where the divine does and does not reside. Moreover, although this perception is widely attested in Greek and Latin literature, Josephus in this text manipulates such boundaries of Greco-Roman sacrality in a kind of "reversal of norms,"[15] whereby statues become quintessential elements of *profane* space, and, conversely, the absence of statues signals the presence of sanctity. This inversion of Greco-Roman conceptions in turn func-

---

Sarah Hamilton and Andrew Spicer likewise discuss Eliade's "paradigm" in the context of other theoretical models, emphasizing an interdisciplinary focus on "the importance of behaviour in defining sacred space" ("Defining the Holy: The Delineation of Sacred Space," in *Defining the Holy: Sacred Space in Medieval and Early Modern Europe* [ed. Andrew Spicer and Sarah Hamilton; Burlington, Vt.: Ashgate, 2005], 2–5 [quote from p. 4]). See also Eliav, *God's Mountain*, xxviii–xxix.

11. Jonathan Z. Smith, *To Take Place: Toward Theory in Ritual* (Chicago: University of Chicago Press, 1987).

12. Jonathan Z. Smith, *Map Is Not Territory* (Leiden: Brill, 1978), 290–91.

13. Ibid., 291. Smith specifically proposes in this volume that the shifting boundaries within Judaism are manifest in a transformation from a locative to utopian concept of sacred space, that is, from a view that restricts sacrality to the center to a view that moves sacrality to the periphery. For an attempt to examine in more detail the precise nature of this transformation, see Baruch M. Bokser, "Approaching Sacred Space," *HTR* 78 (1985): 279–99.

14. Smith, *Map Is Not Territory*, 291. See also Smith, *To Take Place*, 104–5.

15. Stewart, *Statues in Roman Society*, 276. Although Stewart uses this phrase to explain the practice of *damnatio memoriae*, seeing it as a "negation of the symbolism" of imperial authority (see the discussion below in chapter 6), I believe it aptly applies to Josephus' own inversion of a pervasive norm.

tions in the wider narrative context of *B.J.* as a means of defining identity and charting the boundaries and limits of imperial power within the context of Roman domination.

SCULPTURE AND THE MAPPING OF SPACE IN *BELLUM JUDAICUM*

In the following I will explore the relationship between εἰκόνες (and related terminology) and space in *B.J.*, first considering Josephus' articulation of Judea and Jerusalem as a sacred territory in his narrative excurses, followed by an examination of the role of sculpture as a boundary marker in his so-called iconoclastic narratives. I will then place this narrative material within a wider comparative context, that is, within a broad and diverse selection of Greek and Latin sources, considering Josephus' mapping strategy in the light of a widespread tendency in Greco-Roman sources to link sculpture and sacred space.

Temple–Jerusalem–Judea: Josephus' Concentric Circles of Holiness

The basic spatial layout of Judea is set out in a fairly straightforward manner in *B.J.* 3.51–58: the northern border is marked by the village called Anuathu Borcaeus[16] and the southern by the Arabian village Iardan; on the eastern border runs the Jordan River, and the western limit is marked by the town of Joppa; precisely at the center (μεσαιτάτη) lies the city of Jerusalem, which according to Josephus is identified by some as the "navel of the country" (τινες οὐκ ἀσκόπως ὀμφαλὸν τὸ ἄστυ τῆς χώρας ἐκάλεσαν; *B.J.* 3.52). In this context, Josephus' description of Judea is brief, functioning as the final segment of a narrative excursus on the geographical "stage" of the war against Rome—the two divisions of Galilee (Lower and Upper), Perea, Samaria, and Judea.[17] In each case, Josephus locates the borders and offers a few brief remarks on the general nature and character of the region. Only in his description of Judea, however, does Josephus call attention to both center and periphery. Indeed, by locating Jerusalem at the exact center of Judea, a spatial layout that only approximately reflects the actual geography of Roman Judea, and by linking the city to the Hellenistic notion of ὀμφαλός, which, as exemplified in the famed temple of Apollo at Delphi, represents both the center of the universe and the focal point of sacred activity,[18] this text reflects in skeletal form a sacred cosmography consisting of concentric circles of sanctity

---

16. Michael Avi-Yonah, *The Holy Land from the Persian to the Arab Conquests (536 B.C. to A.D. 640): A Historical Geography* (Grand Rapids: Baker Book House, 1966), 155.

17. Galilee: *B.J.* 3.35–43; Perea: *B.J.* 3.44–47; Samaria: *B.J.* 3.48–50; Judea: *B.J.* 3.51–58. On the narrative use of geography in Josephus and other classical sources, see Yuval Shahar, *Josephus Geographicus: The Classical Context of Geography in Josephus* (Tübingen: Mohr Siebeck, 2004). On the use of narrative digressions in *B.J.*, see Tamar Landau, *Out-Heroding Herod: Josephus, Rhetoric, and the Herod Narratives* (Leiden: Brill, 2006), 245–46.

18. Simon Price, *Religions of the Ancient Greeks* (Cambridge: Cambridge University Press, 1999), 56.

whose very center represents the *axis mundi*, the point at which heaven and earth are joined.[19]

It should be noted that this spatial configuration, with Jerusalem situated at the precise center of a sacred cosmography, is not unique to Josephus. For example, *Jubilees* identifies Mount Zion as the "navel of the earth," one of three holy places created by God (*Jub.* 8:19). The Mishnah tractate *Kelim* (early third century C.E.) identifies ten degrees of space corresponding to increasing degrees of holiness: the land of Israel, Israel's walled cities, the city of Jerusalem, the Temple Mount, the courts enclosed by the *soreg* (balustrade beyond which gentiles were forbidden), the court of women, the court of Israelites, the court of priests, the area surrounding the altar, the sanctuary, and the holy of holies within the sanctuary (*m. Kelim* 1:6–9). Perhaps the most explicit example of this concentric scheme is found in the *Midrash Tanḥuma*:

> Just as the navel is found at the center of a human being, so the land of Israel is found at the center of the world . . . and it is the foundation of the world. Jerusalem is at the center of the land of Israel, the Temple is at the center of Jerusalem, the Holy of Holies is at the center of the Temple, the Ark is at the center of the Holy of Holies and the Foundation Stone is in front of the Ark, which spot is the foundation of the world.[20] (*Tanḥ. Qedoshim* 10)

Josephus' reference to Jerusalem as an ὀμφαλός is admittedly incidental in the aforementioned geographical excursus, functioning mainly to add texture to his account of the revolt against Rome. Moreover, Josephus introduces this concept not as his own but as a common perception of Jerusalem—τινες . . . ἐκάλεσαν—based on its precise location at the center of Judea. Nevertheless, that Josephus shares this perception is evident in his brief assessment of this attribution (οὐκ ἀσκόπως). And indeed, this implicit framework of sacred space in Josephus is made even more explicit in his descriptions of the Herodian temple in *B.J.* 5.184–237, paralleled in *A.J.* 15.391–425.[21] The narrative structure in both descriptions moves from periphery to center, marking out at least four distinct sectors corresponding with an increasing degree of holiness:[22]

---

19. Eliade, *The Sacred and the Profane*, 35, 38; Jonathan Z. Smith, "Gods and Earth," *JR* 49 (1969): 111–14.

20. Cited in Smith, "Gods and Earth," 111.

21. For a discussion of Josephus' view of the Herodian compound in relation to the rabbinic concept of "Temple Mount," see Eliav, *God's Mountain*, 33–45. For a recent discussion of Herod's renovation of the temple and its precinct, see Richardson, *Building Jewish in the Roman East*, 271–98; and Ehud Netzer, *The Architecture of Herod, the Great Builder* (Tübingen: Mohr Siebeck, 2006), 137–78.

22. On the use of concentric descriptions of space in Strabo and Josephus, see Shahar, *Josephus Geographicus*, 232–37. For drawings of the spatial layout of Herod's temple, see Shmuel Safrai, "The Temple," in *The Jewish People in the First Century: Historical Geography, Political History, Social, Cultural, and Religious Life and Institutions* (ed. Shmuel Safrai and Menachem Stern; 2 vols.; Assen, the Netherlands: Van Gorcum, 1974–76), 2:868; and Eliav, *God's Mountain*, 9, map 3. For an extensive discussion of the Herodian temple complex and

1. There is the outer court, the so-called court of the Gentiles, which Josephus designates in *A.J.* as the "first court" (ὁ πρῶτος περίβολος; *A.J.* 15.417). This space was open to both Jews and Gentiles and consisted of a vast courtyard enclosed by a circuit of porticoes, foremost of which was the Royal Stoa at the southern end of the complex (*B.J.* 5.190–192; *A.J.* 15.410–417).[23] In another context, Josephus describes this entire area, inclusive of the temple, with the designation the τέμενος (sacred precinct) of God (*B.J.* 4.388).[24]

2. Proceeding inward, there is a second sacred enclosure (τὸ δεύτερον ἱερόν), which was marked with warnings in Latin and Greek prohibiting foreigners from entering this holy space (μηδένα ἀλλόφυλον ἐντὸς τοῦ ἁγίου παριέναι; *B.J.* 5.193–194).[25] Josephus describes in this area a special section for Jewish women to worship, though this should not be taken to indicate that Jewish men were prohibited within this area (*B.J.* 198–200). Rather, as is indicated explicitly in *A.J.*, this section represented the point beyond which women could not pass (*A.J.* 15.419).[26] In both *B.J.* and *A.J.*, the so-called court of women is considered part of the δεύτερον ἱερόν.

3. Continuing toward the center from the second court is a third court restricted only to priests (*A.J.* 15.419–420). Within this space stood the main temple structure, designated in both *B.J.* and *A.J.* with the Greek terms ναός and ἅγιον ἱερόν, or just ἱερόν (*B.J.* 5.207; *A.J.* 15.421).

4. Finally, there resides within the ναός the sacred center, which was restricted to the High Priest, and that only once a year on the Day of Atonement (*B.J.* 5.236–237). Josephus describes this space as "inaccessible, undefiled, and invisible to all, and it was called the holy of holy" (ἄβατον δὲ καὶ ἄχραντον καὶ ἀθέατον ἦν πᾶσιν ἁγίου δὲ ἅγιον ἐκαλεῖτο; *B.J.* 5.219).

---

its various parts, see Théodore Busink, *Der Tempel von Jerusalem von Salomo bis Herodes: Eine archäologisch-historische Studie unter Berücksichtigung des westsemitischen Tempelbaus* (2 vols.; Leiden: Brill, 1970), 2:1062–251. For a discussion of Josephus' textual representation of the Herodian temple, see Lee I. Levine, "Josephus' Description of the Jerusalem Temple: *War, Antiquities*, and other Sources," in *Josephus and the History of the Greco-Roman Period* (ed. Fausto Parente and Joseph Sievers; Leiden: Brill, 1994), 233–46.

23. On the Royal Stoa, see Busink, *Der Tempel von Jerusalem*, 2:1200–1232; Netzer, *The Architecture of Herod*, 165–71.

24. On the significance of this designation, see Eliav, *God's Mountain*, 39–44.

25. Two extant copies of this inscription have been discovered, one (nearly) complete and the other partial (*CIJ* 2.1400; SEG 8.169).

26. Safrai, "The Temple," 2:867. See also the discussion and bibliography in Busink, *Der Tempel von Jerusalem*, 2:1073–79.

Actually, the four sectors outlined above might better be divided into five, since Josephus regulates the degree of sanctity for a given sector according to the type of people permitted within a given area, moving from the lowest degree of sanctity (ἀλλόφυλοι) to the highest degree (ἀρχιερεύς). Thus, what Josephus identifies as the second court actually consists of two degrees of holiness, the lower corresponding to the border open to Jewish women and the higher corresponding to the border open to Jewish men. In any case, it is important to note again that Josephus views the entire complex, inclusive of the court of the gentiles, as a sacred enclosure, a τέμενος of God, with varying degrees of sanctity therein.[27]

With this spatial configuration in mind, the synoptic descriptions of the porticoes in the outer (first) court, and in particular the language of sculpture included (or excluded), is especially instructive for the present discussion. Both *B.J.* and *A.J.* include an unbridled admiration for this Herodian architectural accomplishment, with emphasis on the magnificent columns of the porticoes, especially the Royal Stoa on the southern end of the temple complex.[28] Speaking of the entire circuit of porticoes surrounding the τέμενος, Josephus in *B.J.* calls them a "noteworthy spectacle" (θεωρίαν ἀξιόλογον), reminiscent of the *periegetic* language of Pausanias' *Periēgēsis Hellados* (*B.J.* 5.191). Similarly, in *A.J.* Josephus says of the Royal Stoa: "It was a work more noteworthy than any under the sun" (ἔργον δ' ἦν ἀξιαφηγητότατον τῶν ὑφ' ἡλίῳ; *A.J.* 15.412). Notwithstanding such superficial similarities between the two accounts, however, Josephus' lavish description in *A.J.* departs markedly from *B.J.* in one important respect, the vivid portrayal of *carvings* (γλυφαί) adorning the Royal Stoa. Specifically, Josephus notes in *A.J.* that the capitals were carved in a Corinthian style (ἑκατὸν κιονοκράνων αὐτοῖς κατὰ τὸν Κορίνθιον τρόπον ἐπεξειργασμένων γλυφαῖς) and, further, that the ceilings within the porticoes "were adorned with wood carvings in all kinds of shapes" (αἱ δ' ὀροφαὶ ξύλοις ἐξήσκηντο γλυφαῖς πολυτρόποις σχημάτων ἰδέαις; *A.J.* 15.414–416).

While the Corinthian γλυφαί on pillar capitals are a fairly straightforward and

27. Contra Meir Ben-Dov, who suggests that the southern end of the complex, the location of the Royal Stoa, was not considered a holy place (*Shadow of the Temple*, 132). This claim completely ignores the fact that Josephus uses the Greek term τέμενος to describe the entire complex, inclusive of the Royal Stoa, and not just the immediate precinct of the temple itself. Moreover, that Josephus calls the area within the *soreg* a δεύτερον ἱερόν implies that what preceded it in his description was the first sacred area.

28. Steven Fine recently suggested that Josephus' admiration of the Herodian temple and, more generally, of monumental Roman architecture, "was typical of attitudes held by Jews in latter Second Temple Palestine" (*Art and Judaism*, 69). While Josephus certainly expressed adulation for the monumentalization of Roman Palestine, it seems methodologically suspect to draw from this meager evidence the sweeping claim that such admiration was *typical* of Jews living in Palestine during the first century. At most, we may suppose that this attitude was typical in Jewish aristocratic circles, and, in any case, it seems more likely that the attitudes expressed in Josephus' writings are more indicative of his Roman context and audience.

well-attested category of sculpture,[29] the γλυφαί adorning the portico ceilings are more ambiguous, and there is no indication of the precise nature of their *schēma* in Josephus' description, apart from the vague reference to πολυτρόποις σχημάτων ἰδέαις. The scant archaeological remains from the temple complex may illuminate the discussion a bit. The discovery of several rock fragments from the vaulted ceilings of a tunnel that ascended from the one of the Hulda Gates (located at the southern end of the Herodian temple complex) to the esplanade includes carvings of geometric and floral motifs.[30] It is thus not unreasonable to suppose that similar geometric and floral γλυφαί likewise adorned the ceilings of the Royal Stoa. If so, then it is probably safe to assume that the description in *A.J.* is the more reliable of the two and that the porticoes of the Herodian temple (as well as other structures perhaps) did include some kind of embossed ornamentation, even if only floral or geometric.[31]

Nevertheless, a completely different impression would emerge if we only had the description in *B.J.* to go by.[32] In fact, Josephus seemingly goes out of his way to emphasize that the porticoes were a "noteworthy spectacle" in part because of the absence of γλυφαί:

> διπλαῖ μὲν γὰρ αἱ στοαὶ πᾶσαι, κίονες δ' αὐταῖς εἰκοσιπέντε πηχῶν τὸ ὕψος ἐφεστήκεσαν, μονόλιθοι λευκοτάτης μαρμάρου, κεδρίνοις δὲ φατνώμασιν ὠρόφωντο. τούτων ἡ μὲν φυσικὴ πολυτέλεια καὶ τὸ εὔξεστον καὶ τὸ ἁρμόνιον παρεῖχε θεωρίαν ἀξιόλογον, οὐδενὶ δὲ ἔξωθεν οὔτε ζωγραφίας οὔτε γλυφίδος ἔργῳ προσηγλάιστο.
>
> All the porticoes were in double rows, and the pillars supporting them were twenty-five cubits high, each made from one stone of pure white marble, *having been covered with a roof of paneled cedar*. The *natural magnificence* of these, and their fine polish and harmonious fit, offered a noteworthy spectacle, *and it had not been adorned externally either with the work of painting or sculpture*. (*B.J.* 5.190–191)

The disparity between the two accounts should be obvious. The wood ceilings in *A.J.* are elaborately adorned with carvings of a variety of shapes; by contrast, the wood ceilings in *B.J.* are described with the Greek term φάτνωμα, which would indicate simple recessed panels.[33] Josephus instead emphasizes the *natural* beauty of the pillars (φυσικὴ πολυτέλεια), seemingly implying that their magnificence was

---

29. The remains of a capital found near the Western Wall of the temple complex contain Corinthian and Ionic features, which would generally accord with the description of the capitals in *A.J.* (Fine, *Art and Judaism*, 78).

30. Ben-Dov, *Shadow of the Temple*, 136–39; Fine, *Art and Judaism*, 78, fig. 23.

31. Meir Ben-Dov's reconstruction of the Royal Stoa favors the description in *A.J.* and assumes a combination of floral and geometric carvings on the ceilings and walls of the structure (*Shadow of the Temple*, 126–27).

32. Although Lee Levine does not mention Josephus' description of the porticoes, he does discuss several other discrepancies between the descriptions of the temple in *B.J.* and *A.J.* ("Josephus' Description of the Jerusalem Temple," 234–35).

33. Whiston translates this term "elaborately engraven," but it seems likely that he is har-

not because of the skill of craftsmen, and he explicitly denies that there were any kind of artistic representations within the porticoes, whether painted (ζωγραφία) or sculpted (γλυφίς).

It seems rather odd that Josephus, a Jew from a priestly family who undoubtedly walked the halls of the Royal Stoa on numerous occasions, would seem confused on this point. To state the matter succinctly: why the discrepancy in Josephus' descriptions if he had firsthand knowledge of the appearance of this structure? This is the crux of the matter, and I submit that Josephus is not confused in this instance but that the description in *B.J.*, however unreliable it may be to the reality it purports to describe, is quite intentional in its removal of sculptural ornamentation from the Herodian complex. Indeed, the discrepancies between the two accounts underscore an important leitmotif in *B.J.*: Judea, Jerusalem, and especially the temple complex represent a place—a sacred territory—*without* sculpture of any type, even seemingly innocuous geometric and floral carvings. Josephus in effect offers the reader of *B.J.* an imagined world, a sculptureless haven in a world full of γλυφαί.

Judea and Jerusalem as a Sculptureless Haven

The above interpretation of Josephus' synoptic descriptions of the temple complex is confirmed by a closer reading of the three iconoclastic narratives in *B.J.* For example, the episode of the notorious Pontius Pilate and his troublesome military standards underscores the extent to which sculpture and space are thematically interwoven in *B.J.* (*B.J.* 2.169–174; cf. *A.J.* 18.55–59).[34] At some point during his tenure as *praefectus* of Judea (26–36 C.E.),[35] Pilate transferred from Caesarea Ma-

---

monizing *B.J.* with *A.J.* in this instance. Thackeray's translation in the LCL is more accurate: "ceiled with panels of cedar."

34. On this episode, see especially the following studies: Carl H. Kraeling, "The Episode of the Golden Standards at Jerusalem," *HTR* 35 (1942): 263–89; Daniel R. Schwartz, "Josephus and Philo on Pontius Pilate," in *The Jerusalem Cathedra: Studies in the History, Archaeology, Geography, and Ethnography of the Land of Israel* (ed. Lee I. Levine; Detroit: Wayne State University Press, 1983), 26–45; Helen K. Bond, *Pontius Pilate in History and Interpretation* (Cambridge: Cambridge University Press, 1998), 52–57; Karl Jaroš, *In Sachen Pontius Pilatus* (Mainz, Germany: Philipp von Zabern, 2002), 53–59; Helen K. Bond, "Standards, Shields, and Coins: Jewish Reactions to Aspects of the Roman Cult in the Time of Pilate," in *Idolatry: False Worship in the Bible, Early Judaism, and Christianity* (ed. Stephen C. Barton; London: T&T Clark, 2007), 88–106; Steve Mason, *Judean War 2* (Flavius Josephus: Translation and Commentary 1b; ed. Steve Mason; Leiden: Brill, 2008), 138–45. Klaus-Stefan Krieger offers a brief synoptic analysis of this episode in order to demonstrate that *A.J.* 18–20 follows and revises the narrative of *B.J.* 2.117–283 ("A Synoptic Approach to B 2:117–283 and A 18–20," in *Internationales Josephus-Kolloquium Paris 2001: Studies on the Antiquities of Josephus* [ed. Folker Siegert and Jürgen U. Kalms; Münster, Germany: Lit Verlag, 2001], 91–93).

35. Kraeling argues that this event occurred in the fall of 26 C.E., during the first year of Pilate's tenure ("Golden Standards," 283). Schwartz, however, rightly notes that there is nothing in Josephus' accounts that requires a date at the beginning of Pilate's term ("Josephus and Philo on Pontius Pilate," 32–33).

ritima to Jerusalem a garrison of troops for the winter.[36] Neither *B.J.* nor *A.J.* states precisely where the troops were stationed, but the fortress Antonia at the northwest corner of the temple complex is a plausible suggestion.[37] What is clear in both accounts is that this action, because it involved not only the presence of troops in Jerusalem but also military standards, created a bit of a stir among certain members of the Jewish populace, who proceeded to petition before Pilate in Caesarea that the standards be removed. Initially Pilate refused, but after much persistence he eventually gave in to their demands, and the standards (but not the troops) were removed and apparently returned to Caesarea.

What type of standards did the troops bring into Jerusalem, and why did this action elicit such a strong opposition? In both accounts, Josephus uses the Greek term σημαία, a variant spelling of σημεία, to designate the offending object.[38] This word is typical in Greek for Roman military standards of all types, corresponding in a general sense with the Latin *signum*.[39] There were at least four main types of Roman standards: (1) the *aquila*, a golden eagle mounted on a pole, which according to Pliny the Elder was the special sign for Roman legions (*Nat.* 10.5);[40]

36. E. Mary Smallwood suggests that this was an act of "conscious provocation" intended to violate Jewish law, a fairly straightforward reading of Josephus' own assessment of Pilate's motives (*The Jews under Roman Rule: From Pompey to Diocletian* [Leiden: Brill, 1976], 161). In contrast, Kraeling suggests that although Pilate may be accused of ignorance, it is likely that his actions were in line with the normal responsibilities of a Roman governor ("Golden Standards," 265–74).

37. Kraeling, "Golden Standards," 279–80; Michael Grant, *The Jews in the Roman World* (London: Weidenfeld and Nicolson, 1973), 100; Smallwood, *Jews under Roman Rule*, 161; John R. Bartlett, *Jews in the Hellenistic World: Josephus, Aristeas, the Sibylline Oracles, Eupolemus* (Cambridge: Cambridge University Press, 1985), 112. Schwartz argues that Philo's account of the idolatrous shields introduced by Pilate in Herod's palace (*Legat.* 299–305) is an alternative and apologetic version of the incident involving the standards in Josephus. Nevertheless, Schwartz suggests that Philo's account, although more biased and thus less reliable, accurately specifies that the incident occurred in Herod's palace ("Josephus and Philo on Pontius Pilate," 33).

38. According to Niese's critical apparatus, the epitome that stands behind the twelfth-century *Chronicon* of Zonaras, dating probably to the tenth or eleventh century, reads τοῖς σημείος instead of ταῖς σημαίαις in *A.J.* 18.55 (*Flavii Josephi Opera*, 4:150).

39. Kraeling identifies two uses of *signum* with reference to military standards: the first as a generic term applying to any or all types of Roman standards; the second as a specific type of standard ("Golden Standards," 269–70).

40. Pliny lists the *aquila* along with four other theriomorphic standards—wolves, minotaurs, horses, and boars—each corresponding with different ranks within a legion. On the *aquila*, see Kraeling, "Golden Standards," 269–70; Michael P. Speidel, "Eagle-Bearer and Trumpeter: The Eagle-Standard and Trumpets of the Roman Legions Illustrated by Three Tombstones Recently Found at Byzantion," *Bonner Jahrbücher* 176 (1976): 123–63; Graham Webster, *The Roman Imperial Army of the First and Second Centuries A.D.* (London: A & C Black, 1985), 135, pl. 7b and pl. 10; Adrian Goldsworthy, *The Complete Roman Army* (London: Thames & Hudson, 2003), 134. In Josephus' account of Vespasian's march into Galilee, he describes the *aquila* standards that followed the cavalry units of the legions in the following terms: "Next the ensigns surrounding the eagle (αἱ σημαῖαι περίσχουσαι τὸν ἀετόν),

(2) the *imago*, which could include either representations of animals (other than the eagle) or of the emperor (*imperatorum imagines*) mounted on the top of a pole;[41] (3) the *signum*, which consisted of a spearhead (or sometimes crowned with a human hand) and pole adorned with *phalerae*, round discs that could be either iconic (embossed with an image of the emperor or a deity) or aniconic, among other accoutrements;[42] and (4) the *vexillum*, a pole with a square cloth flag affixed to a crossbar.[43]

In both accounts Josephus identifies the σημαίαι as εἰκόνες. In *B.J.* 2.169 the standards are identified ambiguously as images of Caesar: τὰς Καίσαρος εἰκόνας αἵ σημαῖαι καλοῦνται ("the images of Caesar, which are called standards"). In *A.J.* 18.55 the nature of the object is seemingly clarified, so that the images of Caesar were not the standards themselves but busts that were attached to the standards (προτομὰς Καίσαρος αἵ ταῖς σημαίαις προσῆσαν). This description would perhaps seem to fit best with the *imperatorum imagines*,[44] although the widely used iconic *signa* could also be in view here.[45] In any case, the critical issue for this discussion is that the standards were iconic, containing anthropomorphic sculptural representations, whether embossed on *phalerae* or three-dimensional imperial busts, and it is the iconic nature of the standards that stands at the center of the dispute in both narratives.

Beyond this superficial agreement, however, the two narratives depart considerably on the purported reasons that the iconic standards were a violation of

---

which in the Roman army precedes every legion, because it is the king and the bravest of all the birds: it is regarded by them as the symbol of empire, and, whoever may be their adversaries, an omen of victory" (*B.J.* 3.123 [Thackeray, LCL]). He subsequently identifies these as sacred objects, τὰ ἱερά (*B.J.* 3.124).

41. Kraeling, "Golden Standards," 269–70; Goldsworthy, *The Complete Roman Army*, 134. See again the reference in Pliny to theriomorphic standards cited in the previous footnote.

42. Kraeling, "Golden Standards," 270. A funerary relief from Mainz shows a *signifer* (a standard-bearer) holding a *signum* with six aniconic *phalerae* (Yann le Bohec, *The Imperial Roman Army* [London: B. T. Batsford, 1994], pl. 5.8). A scene from Trajan's column depicts both *signa* with aniconic *phalerae* and crowned with a human hand and *signa* with iconic *phalerae* (Webster, *The Roman Imperial Army*, pl. 9a).

43. Valerie A. Maxfield, *The Military Decorations of the Roman Army* (London: B. T. Batsford, 1981), 82–84. The base of the column of Antoninus Pius in Rome includes a sequence in relief of a cavalry procession with a *vexillum* (Bohec, *The Imperial Roman Army*, pl. 6.9). For a discussion of a linen flag of a *vexillum* found in Egypt, see M. Rostovtzeff, "Vexillum and Victory," *JRS* 32 (1942): 92–106.

44. Roth, "Ordinance against Images," 170. Thackeray likewise identifies these as *imperatorum imagines* in the notes of his Loeb translation (Thackeray, LCL, 389).

45. Kraeling, "Golden Standards," 273. Kraeling considers it unlikely that a single infantry or cavalry unit would have more than one *imaginifer* (the soldier who carried the *imperatorum imagines*), and Josephus clearly speaks of standards in the plural. He thus argues that iconic *signa* are more likely in view here, given the smaller size of the unit and the fact that this type of standard was much more diffuse throughout the various units of the Roman army.

Jewish law.[46] This becomes clear when the two distinct legal explanations for the prohibition of iconic standards are placed side by side:

> Πεμφθεὶς δὲ εἰς Ἰουδαίαν ἐπίτροπος ὑπὸ Τιβερίου Πιλᾶτος νύκτωρ κεκαλυμμένας εἰς Ἱεροσόλυμα εἰσκομίζει τὰς Καίσαρος εἰκόνας, αἳ σημαῖαι καλοῦνται. τοῦτο μεθ᾿ ἡμέραν μεγίστην ταραχὴν ἤγειρεν Ἰουδαίοις· οἵ τε γὰρ ἐγγὺς πρὸς τὴν ὄψιν ἐξεπλάγησαν ὡς πεπατημένων αὐτοῖς τῶν νόμων, οὐδὲν γὰρ ἀξιοῦσιν ἐν τῇ πόλει δείκηλον τίθεσθαι.
>
> Now Pilate, who was sent by Tiberius into Judea to be procurator, carried into Jerusalem secretly by night the images of Caesar, which are called standards. This act stirred up a great disturbance among the Jews on the following day. For those nearby were panic-struck at the sight, since their laws had been trampled upon; *for it is not lawful to set up an image in the city.* (*B.J.* 2.169–170)

> Πιλᾶτος δὲ ὁ τῆς Ἰουδαίας ἡγεμὼν στρατιὰν ἐκ Καισαρείας ἀγαγὼν καὶ μεθιδρύσας χειμαδιοῦσαν ἐν Ἱεροσολύμοις ἐπὶ καταλύσει τῶν νομίμων τῶν Ἰουδαϊκῶν ἐφρόνησε προτομὰς Καίσαρος, αἳ ταῖς σημαίαις προσῆσαν, εἰσαγόμενος εἰς τὴν πόλιν, εἰκόνων ποίησιν ἀπαγορεύοντος ἡμῖν τοῦ νόμου.
>
> Now Pilate, the procurator of Judea, when he led the army from Caesarea and transferred it to Jerusalem for the winter, was intent on abolishing the customs of the Jews by bringing into the city the busts of Caesar, which were attached to the standards; *for our law forbids the making of images.* (*A.J.* 18.55)

When juxtaposed in this manner, the differences between Josephus' two explanations become fairly obvious. Whereas in *B.J.* Josephus summarizes the second commandment as a prohibition against images *within* a certain spatial delimitation, in this instance, the city of Jerusalem, in *A.J.* the law is more directly a prohibition against the image itself or, rather, against the making (ποίησις) of images. Stated differently, in the former account the problematic nature of the image is directly tied to its location; in the latter, the problem is that an image was made, regardless of its location.

What are we to make of this discrepancy? On the surface, this detail may seem inconsequential, perhaps even pedantic, and one approach is simply to gloss over or harmonize the difference.[47] After all, the two legal explanations are not neces-

---

46. For more on the differences between these two accounts, see Krieger, "A Synoptic Approach," 91–93.

47. Gutmann's discussion of this episode assumes wrongly that the summary of the law in *A.J.* 18.55—a prohibition against making images—is likewise found in *B.J.* 2.170 ("The 'Second Commandment' and the Image," 171). Rajak, in her discussion of the Pilate incident, observes this distinction between the two narratives, though for her the discrepancy merely "suggests a lack of conviction on the author's part." Although she does not explain precisely what is meant by this, I presume it has something to do with Josephus' own views on the second commandment, specifically that he equivocates on the meaning of this law and thus betrays an uncertainty as to how it should be interpreted (*Josephus*, 67). See also

sarily incompatible. Obviously, if the image itself is prohibited, as seems to be the case in *A.J.*, then its intrusion into Judean space would be especially troublesome. Nevertheless, the structural and linguistic links between the standard pericope and the subsequent story of Pilate's construction of the aqueduct with funds from the sacred treasury suggests an alternative explanation, namely that the link between sculpture and space in *B.J.* is intentional, functioning as part of a larger rhetorical strategy.[48]

In the episode of the standards, the offended party petitions before Pilate that the standards be removed from Jerusalem, a confrontation that takes place *in Caesarea* (*B.J.* 2.171–174). The Jews appear before the tribunal of Pilate in the stadium, where he orders his soldiers "to surround the Jews" (κυκλώσασθαι τοὺς Ἰουδαίους), forming a ring of troops three deep (περιστάσης δὲ τριστιχεὶ τῆς φάλαγγος; *B.J.* 2.172–173). The response to Pilate's use of the sacred treasury for the construction of the aqueduct is similar, except in this instance the confrontation with Pilate takes place *in Jerusalem* (*B.J.* 2.175–177). Whereas in the account of this event in *A.J.* it is said only that the Jews assembled (συνέρχομαι) before Pilate in protest (*A.J.* 18.60), in *B.J.* Josephus carries forward the language from the previous pericope, that is, the episode of the standards, only in this case it is the Jews who form a ring around Pilate (περιστάντες τὸ βῆμα). The language here and, in particular, the image of a power shift according to location—the Jews encircled in Caesarea; Pilate encircled in Jerusalem—illustrate the politics of space that stands at the core of this chapter. Caesarea in this narrative represents the territory of the other, in this case Pilate, and Jerusalem the opposite. In other words, there is reflected in the juxtaposition of these two Pilate episodes a subtle mapping of space, a delineation of two realms that corresponds in part with the presence or absence of sculpture.

Two other iconoclastic episodes confirm the hypothesis that sculpture and space are linked in *B.J.* and, further, that Josephus in this text consistently plays up the issue of space in his treatment of the second commandment. In *B.J.* 1.648–655, Josephus recounts an uprising against Herod the Great over an εἰκών within the temple precinct in Jerusalem.[49] At some point during his reign as client king over Judea (37–4 B.C.E.), Herod had erected a statue of a golden eagle on the main gate leading into the sanctuary, called the great gate (ἡ μεγάλη πύλη) by Josephus (*B.J.* 1.650). Although the precise date of the statue's installation is unknown,[50]

Mason, who argues—in part on the basis of *A.J.* 18.121—that Josephus did not intend a spatial qualification of the proscription against images (*Judean War 2*, 142 n. 1064).

48. This is not to imply that the version in *A.J.* is somehow less rhetorical and more historically reliable. Indeed, sculpture plays an equally rhetorical role in *A.J.*, as will become evident in the discussion in chapter 5.

49. For a recent study of this episode, see van Henten, "Ruler or God," 257–86. For an examination of Josephus' Herod narratives within their compositional contexts, see Landau, *Out-Heroding Herod.*

50. It is often assumed that Herod installed the eagle toward the end of his life, and thus the reaction of the zealous iconoclasts was immediate; see, for example, Jones, *The Herods of Judaea*, 147–48. However, Josephus' narratives do not specify when the eagle was erected, only that the uprising occurred near the end of Herod's life. If Michael Grant is correct

Josephus reports that near the end of Herod's life, two Jewish teachers (σοφισταί), Judas and Matthias, used the eagle to incite an uprising amongst a group of zealous youths (νέοι). Identifying the eagle as a violation of their ancestral laws (παρὰ τοὺς πατρίους νόμους), the teachers urged the mob to take action. What follows can only be described as a classic instance of iconoclasm. This army of brash youths entered the temple precinct in the middle of the day, while the daily activities of the cult were well underway, climbed to the top of the temple gate, and proceeded to pull down the eagle and cut it into pieces before a large crowd of worshipers. When word of this uprising reached Herod, he arrested the guilty parties and, accusing them of impious sacrilege, had them burned alive.

In the narrative context of *B.J.*, the episode of the golden eagle is one of a series of misfortunes that plagued Herod in the latter days of his life.[51] What is pertinent for the present analysis is Josephus' description of Herod's offense, that is, the precise reason his actions ostensibly violated Jewish law:

> οἳ τότε τὸν βασιλέα πυνθανόμενοι ταῖς ἀθυμίαις ὑπορρέοντα καὶ τῇ νόσῳ λόγον καθίεσαν εἰς τοὺς γνωρίμους, ὡς ἄρα καιρὸς ἐπιτηδειότατος εἴη τιμωρεῖν ἤδη τῷ θεῷ καὶ τὰ κατασκευασθέντα παρὰ τοὺς πατρίους νόμους ἔργα κατασπᾶν. ἀθέμιτον γὰρ εἶναι κατὰ τὸν ναὸν ἢ εἰκόνας ἢ προτομὰς ἢ ζῴου τινὸς ἐπώνυμον ἔργον εἶναι· κατεσκευάκει δ' ὁ βασιλεὺς ὑπὲρ τὴν μεγάλην πύλην ἀετὸν χρυσοῦν·
>
> When these men [the sophists] learned that the king was slipping away with despondency and disease, they sent word to their friends, that now would be a suitable time to avenge God, and to pull down that which was erected contrary to the laws of their country; for it was unlawful that there should be *in the temple* either images, or busts, or any similar work of a living being. Nevertheless, the king had erected a golden eagle over the great gate [of the temple]. (*B.J.* 1.649–650)

As with the incident of Pilate's standards, Josephus' summary of the second commandment in *B.J.* stresses the role of space in assessing the legitimacy of an εἰκών. Specifically, that which violates ancestral law is the presence of an εἰκών within the area of the temple. This emphasis in *B.J.* is underscored when compared with Josephus' treatment of this incident in *A.J.*, where Herod's actions are deemed παρὰ νόμον τοῦ πατρίου because the law forbids the very making and erecting of such images, regardless of location (*A.J.* 17.150–151).[52] Once again, whereas in *B.J.* an εἰκών within a particular location is problematic, in *A.J.* the εἰκών itself

---

that the most likely date for the erection of this statue was at the completion of the temple structure in 18 B.C.E. (*Herod the Great*, 207), then the statue stood in the temple precinct for approximately fourteen years without controversy, at least as far as our sources indicate.

51. This is reflected in the first line of the pericope (*B.J.* 1.648): Γίνεται δ' ἐν ταῖς συμφοραῖς αὐτῷ καὶ δημοτική τις ἐπανάστασις ("Now there occurred among the misfortunes a certain uprising of the populace against him").

52. Van Henten observes the emphasis on space in *B.J.* but ultimately harmonizes the two accounts, placing this episode among the many indications that some Jews, including Josephus, interpreted the second commandment in its strictest possible sense, that is, as a prohibition against all images of living creatures ("Ruler or God," 276–78).

violates Jewish law, shifting the stress from the *place* to the ποίησις of the offending object.

Josephus' treatment of the infamous incident involving the emperor Gaius Caligula, who in the year 39/40 C.E. threatened to erect statues (ἀνδριάντες) of himself in the temple of Jerusalem, adds an additional layer to this discourse, one that further highlights how statuary in *B.J.* functions as a kind of mapping device, a boundary marker delineating the sacred from the profane (*B.J.* 2.185–203).[53] Although in both *B.J.* and *A.J.* Josephus views Caligula's actions as a potential desecration of sacred territory, only in *B.J.* is there a more pronounced emphasis on the relationship between statuary and Judean space, in particular, on the way in which the former defines the latter. This is especially clear in the confrontation between the Jews and Publius Petronius, the governor of Syria who was ordered to carry out Caligula's demands. Josephus summarizes both Petronius' attempt to convince the Jews to relent to the emperor's edict and the Jewish rebuttal as follows:

> τήν τε Ῥωμαίων διεξῄει δύναμιν καὶ τὰς Καίσαρος ἀπειλάς, ἔτι δὲ τὴν ἀξίωσιν ἀπέφαινεν ἀγνώμονα· πάντων γὰρ τῶν ὑποτεταγμένων ἐθνῶν κατὰ πόλιν συγκαθιδρυκότων τοῖς ἄλλοις θεοῖς καὶ τὰς Καίσαρος εἰκόνας, τὸ μόνους ἐκείνους ἀντιτάσσεσθαι πρὸς τοῦτο σχεδὸν ἀφισταμένων εἶναι καὶ μεθ᾽ ὕβρεως. Τῶν δὲ τὸν νόμον καὶ τὸ πάτριον ἔθος προτεινομένων καὶ ὡς οὐδὲ θεοῦ τι δείκηλον, οὐχ ὅπως ἀνδρός, οὐ κατὰ τὸν ναὸν μόνον ἀλλ᾽ οὐδὲ ἐν εἰκαίῳ τινὶ τόπῳ τῆς χώρας θέσθαι θεμιτὸν εἴη, ὑπολαβὼν ὁ Πετρώνιος ἀλλὰ μὴν καὶ ἐμοὶ φυλακτέος ὁ τοὐμοῦ δεσπότου νόμος.

> He [Petronius] catalogued the power of the Romans and the threats of the emperor, and, additionally, he demonstrated that their demand was senseless, for while all the subjected nations had erected the images of Caesar along with the other gods in their cities, they [the Jews] alone to resist this was not unlike those who revolt, and [it was] injurious. But when they put forward as an objection their law and ancestral custom, how *not only* is it not permitted to place either a representation of God or of man *in the temple but even within any random place of the countryside*, Petronius replied, "I too must observe the law of my master." (*B.J.* 2.193–195)

The statuary language here clearly recalls the Pilate pericope, particularly the phrase τὰς Καίσαρος εἰκόνας and the rather rare term δείκηλον, thus linking these two episodes thematically.[54] Likewise, both the Pilate episode and the Caligula episode in *B.J.* emphasize the problem of statues within a particular location. Indeed, embedded in this exchange between Petronius and the Jews is a configuration of space into two distinct realms governed by two distinct laws—the territory of the Jews, wherein statues of gods and men are forbidden not only within the temple but even "within any random place in the countryside" (ἐν εἰκαίῳ τινὶ τόπῳ τῆς χώρας), and the rest of the Roman world, wherein "all the subjected nations had erected the images of Caesar along with the other gods in their cities" (πάντων

53. For a discussion of this pericope, see most recently Mason, *Judean War 2*, 156–68.

54. Ibid., 162–63 nn. 1226 and 1233.

γὰρ τῶν ὑποτεταγμένων ἐθνῶν κατὰ πόλιν συγκαθιδρυκότων τοῖς ἄλλοις θεοῖς καὶ τὰς Καίσαρος εἰκόνας).

Josephus thus presents in *B.J.* a distinct vision of Jerusalem and Judea as a sculptureless haven in a sculpture-filled world. Indeed, the very sanctity of the temple, city, and even its *chora* is marked by its emptiness, by its lack of sculpted or figurative art. Within this conceptual framework, the second commandment becomes not so much a prohibition against images of other gods, or even the Jewish God, but a prohibition against any kind of sculptural representation *within* Judean territory.

Sculpture and Space in the Ancient Mediterranean World

Josephus' articulation of the relationship between sculpture and space is on the one hand sui generis, a rhetorical maneuver that underscores the uniqueness of Jerusalem vis-à-vis the wider urban context of the Mediterranean basin. Nevertheless, Josephus' sacred map is in another sense fully immersed in the Greco-Roman sculptural environment, insofar as it subverts prevailing perceptions that sculpture functions as a tangible reminder of the *presence* of the sacred and visible markers delimiting holy terrain. This perception is attested in a broad and diverse range of Greek and Latin sources, from philosophical treatises through historiographies and ethnographies to legal documents. For purposes of this analysis, I will discuss a selection of disparate sources reflecting on two major urban centers in the ancient Mediterranean world—Athens and Rome.

Athens: A "Forest of Idols"

Two very different "pilgrims" to Athens—"Saint" Paul and "Pagan" Pausanias—offer a surprisingly similar assessment of the urban landscape of this Greek city.[55] Paul—or more precisely, the literary portrayal of Paul in the Acts of the Apostles—and Pausanias may seem like an odd pairing at first glance.[56] The former was

55. There is much scholarly discussion on whether or not Pausanias should be identified as a devout religious pilgrim, with Jaś Elsner as the most vocal proponent of the pilgrim identity (in contrast with the view of Pausanias as a pedantic antiquarian); see most notably, Jaś Elsner, "Pausanias: A Greek Pilgrim in the Roman World," *PP* 135 (1992): 3–29. For a more recent and broader treatment of icons, pilgrimage, and the politics of cultural identity, see Jaś Elsner, "The Origins of the Icon: Pilgrimage, Religion, and Visual Culture in the Roman East as 'Resistance' to the Centre," in *The Early Roman Empire in the East* (ed. Susan E. Alcock; Oxford: Oxbow Books, 1997), 178–99. On the phenomenon of pilgrimage in the Greco-Roman world, see also the collection of essays in Jaś Elsner and Ian Rutherford, eds., *Pilgrimage in Graeco-Roman and Early Christian Antiquity: Seeing the Gods* (Oxford: Oxford University Press, 2005). In contrast with this view of Pausanias, James Frazer describes Pausanias' intentions as "mainly antiquarian" and the *periēgēsis* as recording "little more than the antiquities of the country and the religious traditions and ritual of the people" (*Pausanias's Description of Greece* [6 vols.; New York: Biblo and Tannen, 1965], 1:xxv). See also the critique of Elsner in Karim W. Arafat, *Pausanias' Greece: Ancient Artists and Roman Rulers* (Cambridge: Cambridge University Press, 1996), 10.

56. I recognize, of course, that in the case of Paul what we actually possess is a narrative *about* Paul and not necessarily Paul's own perception of Athens. As such, the reader

a first-century C.E. Jew devoted to the nascent movement of Jesus followers; the latter, by contrast, was a second-century C.E. devotee to Greek religiosity, most notably as an initiate into the Eleusinian mysteries (Pausanias, *Descr.* 1.38.7), and author of the *Periēgēsis Hellados*, a detailed and colorful description of mainland Greece. Nevertheless, both traveled extensively throughout the Roman Mediterranean and, more importantly for the present discussion, both offer a deeply religious *periēgēsis* of their respective "tours" of Athens, which includes their perceptions of the place of sculpture in this urban landscape.[57]

Assuming that Paul came to Athens by sea, docking at the Piraeus, Athens' main port, his "tour" likely began at the Dipylon, the Double Gate on the north-west side of the city.[58] Entering through the gates and continuing into the agora, Paul is immediately confronted with what is described as a "forest of idols" (κατείδωλος; Acts 17:16).[59] Richard E. Wycherley attempts to clarify more precisely the nature of this κατείδωλος, linking the term with a specific type of Athenian sculpture—the Herms, that is, square pillars, often with an erect phallus at their midpoint, surmounted with the head of Hermes.[60] In a description of fifth-century B.C.E. Ath-

---

should understand any references to Paul throughout this section as references to a *literary* character. Whether the portrayal of Paul's visit to Athens in Acts corresponds, at least in its broader contours, to an actual event or is "purely a literary creation" matters little to the topic at hand. In either case, we have in this narrative not only a description of the urban landscape of Athens but also a record of how this landscape was perceived by some who traversed (or read about) this space. On Acts 17 as a "literary creation," see Pieter Willem van der Horst, "The Altar of the 'Unknown God' in Athens (Acts 17:23) and the Cults of 'Unknown Gods' in the Graeco-Roman World," in *Hellenism–Judaism–Christianity* (Kampen, Germany: Kok Pharos, 1994), 166–67; Hans Conzelmann, "The Address of Paul on the Areopagus," in *Studies in Luke-Acts: Essays Presented in Honor of Paul Schubert* (ed. Leander Keck and J. Louis Martyn; London: SPCK, 1968), 218.

57. Although the Greek term περιήγησις is not used in Acts 17, Dean Zweck applies the term to the narrative's description of Athens ("The *Exordium* of the Areopagus Speech, Acts 17.22, 23," *NTS* 35 [1989]: 102). Van der Horst, who considers the Areopagus speech a Lukan (and not Pauline) composition, suggests in passing, albeit without any concrete evidence, that the author may have had at his disposal a periegetic handbook ("The Altar of the 'Unknown God'," 198).

58. Acts 17:14 seems to imply that Paul traveled to Athens by sea. As such, his approach to Athens mirrors that of Pausanias, who walked from the Piraeus and entered the city from the northwest (Pausanias, *Descr.* 1.2.1–4).

59. This translation of the *hapax legomenon* κατείδωλος was first proposed by Richard E. Wycherley, who, though acknowledging that "full of idols" is perhaps grammatically "more correct," nevertheless contends that the forest metaphor "gives the full flavour of the word, just a little heightened" ("St. Paul at Athens," *JTS* 19 [1968]: 619 [see also Spivey, *Understanding Greek Sculpture*, 13]). The advantage of Wycherley's "forest of idols" is that it captures the ubiquitous and, for some at least, foreboding presence of statues within the Greco-Roman urban landscape. Diodorus Siculus uses a similar construction, κατάδενδρος, to describe a thickly wooded path, which may lend support to Wycherley's metaphorical rendering of this term (Diodorus Siculus, *Bibl. hist.* 17.68.5); see also F. F. Bruce, *The Acts of the Apostles: The Greek Text with Introduction and Commentary* (Grand Rapids: Eerdmans, 1990), 376.

60. Wycherley, "St. Paul at Athens," 620. Pausanias identifies this sculpture type as a

ens, Thucydides notes that a vast number of these statues stood in the doorways of private homes and sanctuaries (*Hist.* 6.27.1). Wycherley remarks that such Herms "were ubiquitous at Athens" and points to a particular concentration of them between the Stoa Poikile (Painted Stoa) and the Stoa Basileios (Royal Stoa), the primary point of entry from the Piraeus.[61] According to Wycherley, this "stoa of the Herms"[62] would have dominated Paul's visual horizon, making "him feel that at Athens idols were like trees in a wood."[63]

It is probably unwise to restrict the meaning of κατείδωλος to this particular sculpture type, though certainly such objects were part of what "invaded" the eyesight of those visiting the city. Instead, we should perhaps try to envision a more comprehensive view of the city of Athens from within the agora, the narrative location of Paul's dispute with the Athenian philosophers.[64] What would a first-century C.E. visitor strolling the streets of Athens see?[65]

As already noted above, the so-called Stoa of the Herms marks the point of entrance into the agora. Passing between the Stoa Poikile and Stoa Basileios on the Street of the Panathenaia, the observer would have been bombarded with a conglomeration of statues, shrines, altars, and other similarly "religious" structures that dominated the cityscape. Just beyond an altar devoted to the twelve (Olym-

---

uniquely Athenian invention (*Descr.* 1.24.3). For a discussion of these Herms and pictures of several examples ranging from the fifth century B.C.E. to the second century C.E., see John M. Camp, *The Athenian Agora: Excavations in the Heart of Classical Athens* (London: Thames and Hudson, 1986), 74–76, figs. 48–50. For other examples from various locations throughout the Greco-Roman Mediterranean, see *LIMC* 5.2: 199–205, esp. nos. 9, 12, 21, 27 (Athens) and 58, 75, 78, 81, 84, 87 (Delos).

61. Wycherley, "St. Paul at Athens," 620. Because Herms were used in Athens to mark entrances, it is not surprising that a concentration of Herms stood at the entrance to the Athenian agora; see Camp, *The Athenian Agora*, 74. In his *Lexicon in decem oratores Atticos* (first to second century C.E.), Harpocration indicates that this area around the Poikile and Basileios was known simply as "the Herms" (οἱ Ἑρμαῖ) because of the number of such statues erected there (*Lex.* s.v. Ἑρμαῖ [ed. Dindorf, 135]).

62. Richard E. Wycherley, *The Stones of Athens* (Princeton, N.J.: Princeton University Press, 1978), 83, fig. 29.

63. Wycherley, "St. Paul at Athens," 620.

64. Based on modern archaeological excavations and ancient literary testimony, we can to some extent reconstruct Athens' visual landscape at the time of Paul. On the archaeology of the Roman Athenian agora, see the survey by Camp, *The Athenian Agora*, 181–214. See also Wycherley, *The Stones of Athens*, 77–90. On the literary evidence, see in general Al. N. Oikonomides, *The Two Agoras in Ancient Athens: A New Commentary on Their History and Development, Topography, and Monuments* (Chicago: Argonaut, 1964).

65. Yaron Eliav imaginatively likens Paul to "a small-town visitor walking into Times Square, stunned by its enormous images and neon signs" ("Roman Statues," 100). I am not entirely convinced by this analogy, however, since Paul grew up in Tarsus, renowned as an important center for Greek culture and philosophy rivaling that of Athens and Alexandria (cf. Strabo, *Geogr.* 14.5.13) and, according to the narrative in Acts, had already frequented several important Mediterranean cities also rich in Greco-Roman sculpture, such as Pisidian Antioch, Lystra, Philippi, and Thessalonica, to name a few.

pian) gods stood the Temple of Ares, which, in addition to housing the cult statue of Ares, included in its immediate vicinity statues of Aphrodite, Athena, Enyo, Heracles, Theseus, and Apollo (Pausanias, *Descr.* 1.8.4). To the west of this temple stood a line of sacred structures: the Stoa of Zeus, in which stood, among other statues, a Zeus Soter (savior) or Eleutherios (freedom);[66] the Temple of Apollo Patroos (paternal), with two statues of Apollo in the *pronaos* (front porch of the temple) on either side of the entrance (Pausanias, *Descr.* 1.3.4);[67] and the Metroon (sanctuary devoted to the mother of the gods), with her requisite cult statue (Pliny the Elder, *Nat.* 36.17; Pausanias, *Descr.* 1.3.5). Behind the Metroon and the Apollo Patroos stood the impressive Hephaisteion, where Hephaistos, the divine craftsman, and Athena, goddess of the city likewise associated with the arts and crafts, were worshiped together.[68] The external sculptures on and around this structure were extensive and varied, a fitting tribute to its gods, and were especially pronounced on its eastern side, making it readily visible from within the agora.[69]

Walking from the Hephaisteion east toward the center of the agora leads the viewer past the monument of the Eponymous Heroes (dating from the fourth century B.C.E. but still standing in Paul's time), a long statue base upon which stood ten bronze heroes bracketed by a tripod at each end (Pausanias, *Descr.* 1.5.2–5),[70] and an altar of Zeus Agoraios.[71] Just south of this altar stood a newer structure (in Paul's day), a small early Roman-period temple likely devoted to the imperial cult,[72] and beyond this temple the Odeon of Agrippa (a small enclosed theater built during Augustus' reign), which included, among other sculptural pieces, an oversized (but not quite colossal) group of heroes in the front.[73] Finally, continuing southeast on the Panathenaia, passing by the Stoa of Attalos, the viewer observes on the horizon the imposing acropolis, replete with statues and altars devoted to various deities and home of the Temple of Athena Nike, the Erechtheion, the tem-

---

66. Isocrates, *Evag.* 57: Διὸς ἄγαλμα τοῦ σωτῆρος; Pausanias, *Descr.* 1.3.2: Ζεὺς ὀνομζόμενος Ἐλευθέριος.

67. Wycherley, *The Stones of Athens*, 67. A large marble statue of a draped Apollo was discovered just south of the temple (Camp, *The Athenian Agora*, 160–61, fig. 33).

68. Camp, *The Athenian Agora*, 82–87, esp. figs. 59–61.

69. Camp remarks that this temple "carries more sculptural decoration than any other Doric temple" (ibid., 84). Pausanias mentions a blue-eyed Athena standing by the temple (*Descr.* 1.14.6).

70. Camp, *The Athenian Agora*, 97–100, figs. 72–74.

71. For the epigraphic and literary testimony for Zeus Agoraios, the local epithet for Zeus Melichios, see Oikonomides, *Two Agoras*, 71–72.

72. Wycherley, *The Stones of Athens*, 85; David W. J. Gill, "Achaia," in *The Book of Acts in Its Graeco-Roman Setting* (ed. David W. J. Gill and Conrad Gempf; Grand Rapids: Eerdmans, 1994), 444.

73. Wycherley, *The Stones of Athens*, 74. For a reconstructed drawing of the Odeon with sculpture pieces, see Camp, *The Athenian Agora*, 185, fig. 54. The entrance to the Odeon originally included six statues of Tritons and Giants. This structure was destroyed by fire in 267 C.E. Four of the six statues were later used for the so-called Palace of the Giants, the gymnasium complex constructed over the ruins of the Odeon.

ple of Roma and Augustus, and the famed Parthenon, renowned for its colossal statue of Athena Parthenos.[74]

This brief and limited depiction of first-century Athens only partially captures the polychromatic contours of a city literally teeming with statues and other such objects of worship (e.g., altars, temples, etc.). As the reader of Pausanias well knows, at every turn the viewer encountered statues of gods, heroes, emperors, and other notable elites—lining the streets, standing between civic and religious buildings, adorning public and private gardens, guarding entrances to homes, and so on—as well as the innumerable votive statuettes crowding in and around the sanctuaries and altars.[75] Of course, in the activities of daily life, not all of these objects had a strictly religious function, at least in the modern sense of the word. For example, the monument of the Eponymous Heroes, beyond representing visually the ten Athenian tribes, seems to have functioned as a kind of public bulletin board, where tribal notices or other general announcements would be affixed beneath the various tribal heroes.[76] Nevertheless, as is evident in the account of Paul's visit to Athens, the cumulative force of this sculptural milieu (κατείδωλος) was to underscore the piety of this city and its inhabitants.

According to the narrator of Acts, this visual experience (θεωρέω/ἀναθεωρέω) elicited a strong emotional response. Paul was "deeply disturbed" or, more literally, "his spirit within himself was provoked" (παρωξύνετο τὸ πνεῦμα αὐτοῦ ἐν αὐτῷ) by what he saw in Athens (Acts 17:16). Presumably, the reader of Acts would interpret these words negatively, understanding Paul's response to Athens' κατείδωλος as one of anger. And indeed, as is evident in Paul's discourse before the Areopagus,[77] the so-called Areopagus speech,[78] Paul does in fact suggest that

74. Wycherley, *The Stones of Athens*, 105–41 (Parthenon); 143–54 (Erechtheion). For a discussion of the Athena Parthenos, with examples of modern and ancient duplicates, see Spivey, *Understanding Greek Sculpture*, 165–69.

75. Ibid., 78–95, esp. fig. 47.

76. Camp, *The Athenian Agora*, 99. Notwithstanding this rather mundane use, Benjamin Isaac maintains that there still remained a vital connection between this monument and the mythology of the Athenian tribes and that the images served "as patrons of Athenian districts" ("Roman Victory Displayed: Symbols, Allegories, Personifications?" in *The Sculptural Environment of the Roman Near East: Reflections on Culture, Ideology, and Power* (ed. Yaron Z. Eliav, Elise Friedland, and Sharon Herbert; Louvain: Peeters, 2008), 583.

77. The term Areopagus, literally referring to the "hill of Ares" (Ἄρειος πάγος) located northwest of the Acropolis, came to be associated with the ancient Athenian council that met on its summit; see, for example, Cicero, *Fam.* 13.1.5. For a recent treatment of this subject, see Robert W. Wallace, *The Areopagos Council, to 307 B.C.* (Baltimore: Johns Hopkins University Press, 1989).

78. It is unnecessary in this chapter to address the provenance of the Areopagus speech—be it Paul's, Luke's, or a combination of the two. Numerous studies have focused on the conventions of Hellenistic rhetoric used in the composition of this oration; see, for example, Zweck, "The *Exordium*," 94–103. Specifically, Zweck identifies three major sections to the speech (97): the *exordium* (vv. 22–23), the *probatio* (vv. 24–29), and the *peroratio* (vv. 30–31). We should also keep in mind the remarks of the Greek historian Thucydides: "As to the speeches that were made by different men, . . . it has been difficult to recall with strict

such man-made symbols of piety are an expression of ignorance,[79] and he subsequently censures the Athenians' attempt to capture the divine nature through the use of art and human imagination (χαράγματι τέχνης καὶ ἐνθυμήσεως ἀνθρώπου; Acts 17:29). This speech ultimately expounds on the highest creator-God who can neither be housed in a man-made temple nor sculpted into an image, but who calls humanity to repentance before the impending judgment to be executed by the resurrected Jesus. Thus, it is not surprising that for many this text is another classic example of the "Jewish-Christian rejection of 'idols'."[80]

However, this focus on a latent antagonism against pagan idolatry can obscure the way in which this text preserves perceptions of the physical context of such "idolatry" that were common throughout the Greco-Roman Mediterranean. This is particularly evident in the opening lines of Paul's speech, the *captatio benevolentiae*:

> Σταθεὶς δὲ [ὁ] Παῦλος ἐν μέσῳ τοῦ Ἀρείου πάγου ἔφη· ἄνδρες Ἀθηναῖοι, κατὰ πάντα ὡς δεισιδαιμονεστέρους ὑμᾶς θεωρῶ. διερχόμενος γὰρ καὶ ἀναθεωρῶν τὰ σεβάσματα ὑμῶν εὗρον καὶ βωμὸν ἐν ᾧ ἐπεγέγραπτο· Ἀγνώστῳ θεῷ.[81]
>
> Then Paul, standing before the Areopagus, said, "Athenian men, *I see* how in all respects you are quite religious. For, as I went throughout [your city] and *carefully observed* your objects of worship, I found also an altar with the inscription, 'To an unknown god'." (Acts 17:22–23a)

The various forms of the Greek verb for seeing (θεωρέω) that appear in the opening lines of the speech are striking, immediately recalling the author's initial description of Paul's first visual encounter with the city of Athens (θεωροῦντος κατείδωλον; Acts 17:16). More significantly, there is an implicit connection in this discourse between seeing and perceiving. Careful observation of the physical context of Athens leads to an assessment of the Athenian people. Paul *sees* an urban landscape full of τὰ σεβάσματα, a Greek term that certainly encompasses the many statues, temples, and altars described above (i.e., the author's κατείδωλος), and Paul *perceives* in this landscape an expression of the Athenians' super-*deisidaimōn*, that is, an expression of devout piety.

It is true that the Greek term δεισιδαίμων (and the related δεισιδαιμονία) is

---

accuracy the words actually spoken.... Therefore the speeches are given in the language in which, as it seemed to me, the several speakers would express, on the subjects under consideration, the sentiments most befitting the occasion" (*Hist.* 1.22.1–2 [Smith, LCL]). This should caution against the naïve assumption that the Pauline speeches in Acts are to be regarded as the *ipsissima verba Pauli*, or even the *proxima verba Pauli*. On this issue, see especially the discussion in Martin Dibelius, *Studies in the Acts of the Apostles* (trans. Mary Ling; London: SCM Press, 1956), 138–85.

79. Acts 17:23: ὃ οὖν ἀγνοοῦντες εὐσεβεῖτε, τοῦτο ἐγὼ καταγγέλλω ὑμῖν ("What then you are worshipping ignorantly, this I proclaim to you").

80. Hans Conzelmann, *Acts of the Apostles* (trans. James Limburg; Philadelphia: Fortress Press, 1987), 138.

81. On the literary and epigraphical evidence for such altars devoted to ἀγνώστῳ θεῷ, see van der Horst, "The Altar of the 'Unknown God'," 168–85.

itself ambiguous and can either denote in a positive (or neutral) sense piety and religious devotion or the more pejorative superstition.[82] Both uses are attested in Jewish-Hellenistic and early Christian sources. For example, Josephus frequently uses the term positively to describe those who carefully observe Jewish law. The Israelite king Manasseh, after repenting of idolatry, pursues δεισιδαιμονία by cleansing Jerusalem and the temple (*A.J.* 10.42). Likewise, δεισιδαιμονία is associated with the practice of keeping the Sabbath (*A.J.* 12.259). Those who resisted Pilate's standards are characterized by their δεισιδαιμονία (*B.J.* 2.174), and those who demanded justice for the desecration of sacred law were motivated by their δεισιδαιμονία (*B.J.* 2.230). On the other hand, Philo consistently uses the term pejoratively. The δεισιδαίμονες are those uninitiated into the sacred mysteries, in contrast with those characterized by true εὐσέβεια (*Cher.* 1.42); likewise, δεισιδαίμων is elsewhere characterized as the antithesis of εὐσέβεια (*Det.* 18, 24), and δεισιδαιμονία is likened to ἀσέβεια (*Sacr.* 15; see also *Deus.* 103, 163–164). The author uses the term on one other occasion in Acts 25:19, where the procurator Festus describes the dispute between Paul and certain Jewish leaders as an in-house squabble concerning their own δεισιδαιμονία. In the context of Paul's Areopagus speech, it seems best to see δεισιδαίμων as a positive assessment of Athenian piety, akin to the usage in Josephus, especially since the term appears in the *captatio benevolentiae*, which functioned in Greek rhetoric as a device to win an audience's favor.[83]

The significance of this assessment should not be overlooked. Although certainly Paul rejected, at least as objects of cultic devotion, the Greek gods of Athens and their various iconographical or monumental displays, he nevertheless expresses what was a widespread perception in the Greco-Roman world: statues were integral components of a *sacred* landscape, marking out visually the dwelling place of the gods (whether believed to be "true" or "false" gods). The sanctity of a *polis* and the piety of its inhabitants were inextricably linked with the presence of the gods or, more precisely, with the presence of the gods' statues. That is to say, it is the *physical* manifestation of the divine realm that defines a particular territory and people as holy.

For the most part, Pausanias, whose descriptions of Athens are found in book 1 of his *Periēgēsis*,[84] would agree with Paul's assessment, although for him these monuments of Athenian piety are not some misguided attempt to grope after the divine but are in fact the highest form of devotion to the gods. Although Pausanias' own stated purpose was to "set out in detail πάντα τὰ Ἑλληνικά" (*Descr.* 1.26.4), a closer reading of this work makes it clear that the scope of πάντα is actually quite limited.[85] Pausanias frequently omits prominent civic structures in the urban

82. Mary Beard, John North, and Simon Price, *Religions of Rome: A History* (Cambridge: Cambridge University Press, 1998), 225.

83. See esp. Zweck, "The *Exordium*," 100.

84. Likely dating to around 160 C.E.; see Ewen Bowie, "Inspiration and Aspiration: Date, Genre, and Readership," in *Pausanias: Travel and Memory in Roman Greece* (ed. Susan E. Alcock, John F. Cherry, and Jaś Elsner; New York: Oxford University Press, 2001), 21.

85. Elsner, *Art and the Roman Viewer*, 141.

landscape, often of Roman origin, in favor of monuments that he deems most important, guiding his reader toward specifically "religious landmarks."[86] Indeed, the wider literary context of his reference to πάντα τὰ Ἑλληνικά is suggestive. This cursory remark is sandwiched between two descriptions of statues: on the one hand a bronze statue of Olympiodorus and a nearby bronze image (ἄγαλμα) of Artemis and, on the other hand, an ἄγαλμα of Athena by the Athenian sculptor Endoeus (*Descr.* 1.26.3–4). It is true that for Pausanias statues provide an important "springboard" for numerous historical and mythological digressions, so that, in one sense, statues are themselves a component of Pausanias' many excurses.[87] But it is equally true that statues comprise an integral feature of Pausanias' *Periēgēsis Attica*, so that to describe πάντα τὰ Ἑλληνικά is to describe the many statues that in his day still marked the landscape of Greece. In other words, statues are in some sense the task at hand, inextricably woven into Pausanias' vision of the Greek landscape.

That Pausanias has a selective eye for statues is confirmed by his use of the phrase θέας ἄξιος, which repeatedly draws the reader's attention toward those locations and monuments deemed most important. This selectivity, moreover, has little to do with *aesthetic* or *artistic* admiration.[88] Indeed, that Pausanias includes among the θέας ἄξιος a decidedly *un*aesthetic "wall of unwrought stones" (τεῖχος ἀργῶν λίθων) in front of a temple of Aphrodite suggests that aesthetics is not a primary criterion of evaluation (*Descr.* 1.37.7). Rather, a survey of θέας ἄξιος in *Periēgēsis Attica* reveals a remarkable interest in—some might even call it an obsession with—sacred landmarks and especially consecrated statues.[89] For example, the statue of Dionysus housed in the Odeum is θέας ἄξιος, likewise the stone Hermae located in the gymnasium, the Aphrodite in the public gardens, and the statues and paintings of Asclepius within his sanctuary.[90] This literary feature thus underscores the extent to which the Athens in *Periēgēsis Attica* is not Athens as it was seen in Pausanias' day but Athens as Pausanias *wanted it to be seen*, the Athens in Pausanias' religious ideology.[91] And sculpture, especially divine statuary,[92] plays a prominent role in the articulation of this "visual theology."[93]

---

86. William Hutton, "The Construction of Religious Space in Pausanias," in *Pilgrimage in Graeco-Roman and Early Christian Antiquity: Seeing the Gods* (ed. Jaś Elsner and Ian Rutherford; Oxford: Oxford University Press, 2005), 301. See also Eliav, "Viewing the Sculptural Environment," 431–32.

87. W. Kendrick Pritchett, *Pausanias Periegetes* (2 vols.; Amsterdam: J. C. Gieben, 1998), 1:67–68.

88. Contra ibid., 2:172.

89. Of the nineteen appearances of θέας ἄξιος in *Attica*, twelve specifically refer to statues. The remaining occurrences, with the possible exception of two, draw the reader's attention to noteworthy temples, sacred groves, or caves and to other similarly cultic locations or structures.

90. Dionysus: Pausanias, *Descr.* 1.14.1; Hermae: Pausanias, *Descr.* 1.17.2; Aphrodite: Pausanias, *Descr.* 1.19.2; Asclepius: Pausanias, *Descr.* 1.21.4.

91. Elsner, *Art and the Roman Viewer*, 132.

92. On Pausanias' tendency to neglect nondivine statuary, see Eliav, "Roman Statues," 111.

93. Spivey, *Understanding Greek Sculpture*, 14.

The centrality of statues in Pausanias' literary world and in particular the perception of statues as visual "signs of orientation,"[94] boundary markers delineating between sacred and profane space, is encapsulated in his description of the famed sanctuary of the Olympian Zeus:

> πρὶν δὲ ἐς τὸ ἱερὸν ἰέναι τοῦ Διὸς τοῦ Ὀλυμπίου—Ἀδριανὸς ὁ Ῥωμαίων βασιλεὺς τόν τε ναὸν ἀνέθηκε καὶ τὸ ἄγαλμα θέας ἄξιον, οὗ μεγέθει μέν, ὅτι μὴ Ῥοδίοις καὶ Ῥωμαίοις εἰσὶν οἱ κολοσσοί, τὰ λοιπὰ ἀγάλματα ὁμοίως ἀπολείπεται, πεποίηται δὲ ἔκ τε ἐλέφαντος καὶ χρυσοῦ καὶ ἔχει τέχνης εὖ πρὸς τὸ μέγεθος ὁρῶσιν—ἐνταῦθα εἰκόνες Ἀδριανοῦ δύο μέν εἰσι Θασίου λίθου, δύο δὲ Αἰγυπτίου· χαλκαῖ δὲ ἑστᾶσι πρὸ τῶν κιόνων ἃς Ἀθηναῖοι καλοῦσιν ἀποίκους πόλεις. ὁ μὲν δὴ πᾶς περίβολος σταδίων μάλιστα τεσσάρων ἐστίν, ἀνδριάντων δὲ πλήρης· ἀπὸ γὰρ πόλεως ἑκάστης εἰκὼν Ἀδριανοῦ βασιλέως ἀνάκειται, καὶ σφᾶς ὑπερεβάλοντο Ἀθηναῖοι τὸν κολοσσὸν ἀναθέντες ὄπισθε τοῦ ναοῦ θέας ἄξιον.
>
> Before the entrance to the sanctuary of Olympian Zeus—Hadrian the Roman emperor dedicated the temple and the statue, *one worth seeing*, which in size exceeds all other statues save the colossi at Rhodes and Rome, and is made of ivory and gold with an artistic skill which is remarkable when the size is taken into account—before the entrance, I say, stand statues of Hadrian, two of Thasian stone, two of Egyptian. Before the pillars stand bronze statues which the Athenians call "colonies." The *whole circumference* of the precinct is about four stades, and they are *full of statues*; for every city has dedicated a likeness of the emperor Hadrian, and the Athenians have surpassed them in dedicating, behind the temple, the *remarkable* colossus. (*Descr.* 1.18.6 [Jones, LCL])

This text is interesting not only for its colorful description of what must have been an impressive population of imperial and divine statuary but also for the strategic placement of this statuary at the entrance to and within a sacred precinct. In so doing, Pausanias provides the reader a map of this particular site that includes both the precise measurements (four stades) and visual boundary markers of the space; the *presence* of statuary signals to the reader (and viewer) the *presence* of sanctity.

Moreover, while this is certainly true for the many temple precincts (like that of the Olympian Zeus described above) in the city, it is also true on a much larger scale. The imposing presence of divine statuary, in addition to the innumerable altars to the various gods situated in nearly every nook and cranny of the Athenian landscape, bespeaks the sanctity of the entire city as well as the piety of its inhabitants—not unlike the impression derived from the narrative about Paul in Acts 17. Pausanias remarks that the citizens of Athens are more pious than others (θεοὺς εὐσεβοῦσιν ἄλλων πλέον) due to the altars placed throughout the *agora* (*Descr.* 1.17.1). Likewise, at the end of a long catalog of divine statuary, Pausanias again reminds his reader of Athenians' exemplary devotion toward the gods, thus forging a clear link between the presence of statues and the piety of the Athenians (*Descr.* 1.24.3). The monuments of Athens, foremost of which are statues of the gods, thus serve to delimit sanctity by their very presence, to mark out the city of Athens as a

94. Eliav, "The Desolating Sacrilege," 625.

locus consecratus and the Athenian citizens as a *populus piissimus*. When these acclamations are read against the backdrop of πάντα τὰ Ἑλληνικά—the interpretive framework for the entire Pausanian project—then it becomes clear that Athenian piety and Ἑλληνικά are in some sense interrelated, that the εὐσέβεια manifest in Athens' sculptural environment is an integral part of Greek identity.

Rome: A City "Full of Gods"

The notion that statues delineate between sacred and profane space is not limited to Paul or Pausanias, or to the city of Athens. Indeed, we can find similar perceptions in the very heart of the Roman Mediterranean, the city of Rome. It should be noted at the outset that both Roman mythology—especially the narratives of the founding of Rome by Romulus—and Roman law define the city of Rome as a sacred place with a sacred boundary, the *pomerium*.[95] The *pomerium*, typically marked out physically with large blocks of stone, approximately one meter square and two meters tall, represented the officially sanctioned borders of the city. In a sense the *pomerium* served to define Rome itself, though ultimately it was not able contain the city's urban sprawl since it would shift from time to time and emperor to emperor. That the *pomerium* was deemed to be a sacred border is clear enough from the literary sources. Livy defines the area within the *pomerium* as a space consecrated through augury (*inaugurato consecrabant*; Livy, *Ab urb.* 1.44.4). Similarly, Lucan's poetic account of the civil wars at the end of the republic, written sometime in the middle of the first century C.E., mentions a particular ritual, intended to reinforce the *pomerium*, that underscores the religious conceptions associated with this border: "The scared citizens march right round the city; and the pontiffs, who have license to perform the ceremony, purify the walls with solemn lustration (*purgantes moenia lustro*) and move round the outer limit of the long *pomerium*" (Lucan, *Bell. civ.* 1.592–595 [Duff, LCL]). The *pomerium* thus served in one sense as an official delineation between sacred and profane space.

However, although the *pomerium* represented an official map of Roman urban (and sacred) space, it is also clear that statues, among other *res sacra*, served as unofficial markers of sanctity. An obscure remark by Varro, preserved in Aulus Gellius' *Noctes atticae* (mid-second century C.E.), underscores the link between statues and the sacrality of space. In discussing the meaning of *favisae Capitolinae*, Varro recalls that after the Capitoline temple was destroyed by fire in 83 B.C.E., Quintus Catulus, proconsul and leader of the *optimates*, was unable to lower the area before and around the temple because of the *favisae*, subterranean chambers used to store ancient statues and other sacred objects (Aulus Gellius, *Noct. att.* 2.10.2–4). It seems that the very presence of consecrated objects within the *favisae*, including statues, "sacralised the land,"[96] rendering it untouchable and circumventing Catulus' ambitious renovation plans.

---

95. On the *pomerium* as a sacred boundary, see Beard, North, and Price, *Religions of Rome*, 177–81.

96. Clifford Ando, "A Religion for the Empire," in *Flavian Rome: Culture, Image, Text* (ed. A. J. Boyle and William J. Dominik; Leiden: Brill, 2003), 336.

This reference in the *Noctes atticae* suggests that in the Roman world there were at least two ways a particular location was deemed sacred: first, through the formal rite of *consecratio*, which served to legally transform space into a *sacrum locum*;[97] second, and of particular relevance to the present discussion, through the presence of *res sacra*, which by proxy infused a particular place with holiness. This twofold concept of sacrilizing space is reflected in Roman legal traditions that distinguish between a *sacrum locum*, a public place officially consecrated, and a *sacrarium*, a repository of sacred objects:

> Sacra loca ea sunt, quae publice sunt dedicate, siue in ciuitate sint siue in agro. Sciendum est locum publicum tunc sacrum fieri posse, cum princeps eum dedicauit vel dedicandi dedit potestatem. Illud notandum est aliud esse sacrum locum, aliud sacrarium. Sacer locus est locus consecratus, sacrarium est locus, in quo sacra reponuntur, quod etiam in aedificio priuato esse potest, et solent, qui liberare eum locum religione uolunt, sacra inde euocare.
>
> Sacred places are those that have been publicly dedicated, whether in the city or in the country. It must be understood that a public place can only become sacred if the emperor has dedicated it or has granted the power of dedicating it. It should also be observed that a sacred place is one thing, a *sacrarium* another. A sacred place is a place that has been consecrated, but a *sacrarium* is a place in which *sacra* have been deposited. This could even be in a private building, and it is customary for those who wish to free such a place from its religious scruple to call forth the *sacra*.[98] (Ulpian, *Digesta* 1.8.9 *praef.*-2)

Although the *sacrarium* and the *sacrum locum* are clearly differentiated in this text, the former is nevertheless still explicitly categorized as a *locus religiosus* by virtue of the presence of *sacra*—to negate its sanctity and thus to render the space profane, one must first remove the *sacra*.

With this in mind, a reference to Rome's sacred status in Livy is particularly instructive. Livy's remark, placed in the mouth of the Roman general Camillus, emphasizes both the *rituals* involved in the sanctification of Rome and the *visual evidence* of the city's sanctity. Camillus, following the sack of Rome by the Gauls in 390 B.C.E., counters a proposal that the Romans should relocate instead of rebuild Rome: "We have a city founded by auspices and inauguration rites; *there is no place in it that is not full of cultic objects and gods*" ("Urbem auspicato inauguratoque conditam habemus; *nullus locus in ea non religionum deorumque est plenus*"; Livy, *Ab urb.* 5.52.2). Camillus' rebuttal depicts Rome as a sacred location from its foundation, comporting with the myth of the *pomerium* in the Romulus narratives. And yet the visual evidence of Rome's sanctity is not the stone blocks of the *pomerium* but the ubiquitous presence of the gods and their cults within the *pomerium*. Rome was a city *religionum deorumque plena*, full of religious objects and gods. *Religionum* here must refer to the various physical manifestations of Rome's cultic activities, such as temples, altars, and other such *res sacra*, and, similarly, *deorum* likely refers

97. See for example the discussion of *consecratio* in Gaius, *Inst.* 2.4–5.

98. Trans. Ando, "A Religion for the Empire," 337.

not simply to the gods and goddesses of Rome but to the iconographical presence of the divine realm. Livy thus identifies statues, among other things, as tangible markers of Rome's sanctity, suggesting that *any* iconographical representation of the divine realm, whether formally consecrated or not, could at least *be perceived* to sacralize a particular location. Thus the legal distinctions between consecrated and profane space are somewhat blurred, opening the possibility that *any* space could be considered sacred, depending on what, or who, was inhabiting its terrain.[99]

In sum, two important observations emerge from the above discussion. First, statues were perceived throughout the Roman world as visual markers of a sacred landscape. That we can detect this perception in a variety of diverse contexts, ranging from Roman legal traditions to Judeo-Christian historiography, suggests that the link between statues—or more broadly any iconographical representations of the divine realm—and sacred space was ubiquitous in the ancient Mediterranean world. This is manifested both formally, in the case of consecrated statues whose very presence imbues a particular location with sanctity, and informally, for example in the conglomeration of Athenian statues and altars that bespeaks the sanctity of the city.[100] Second, implicit in the narrative about Paul and explicit in the writings of Pausanias is the inextricable link among statues, space, and ethno-religious identity. As will be evident in the following section, this aspect likewise appears in Josephus' *B.J.*

Sculpture, Space, and Identity in Greco-Roman Antiquity

In the light of this wider Mediterranean discourse on statues and space, Josephus' mapping of Judea/Jerusalem as a sacred territory represents a remarkable reversal of conceptual norms—it is precisely the very absence of sculpture that defines sanctity, that marks this particular territory as a *locus consecratus*, so much so that even landscape not formally consecrated within the domain of Judea (i.e., the *chora*) is nevertheless deemed sacred by virtue of its statueless status. Moving from the center to periphery, from Jerusalem to Caesarea Maritima, there emerges

99. One possibly extreme example of this appears in a Pompeian lavatory, which contained a fresco of the goddess Fortuna standing next to a squatting man, who is apparently defecating over an altar to the goddess. Above the man is the following graffiti: *cacator cave malum* ("shitter, beware of evil"). Whether or not this is meant to elicit laughter, fear, or perhaps both, it nevertheless indicates that, in the Roman world, the gods (and the sacred) permeated all of reality, extending even to the rankest locations (*CIL* IV 7716, III. V.1). For a colorful, albeit unusual, discussion of this fresco, see Keith Hopkins, *A World Full of Gods: The Strange Triumph of Christianity* (New York: Plume, 1999), 20, pl. 1. See also Eliav, "Roman Statues," 105.

100. Admittedly, the omnipresence of statues in the Greco-Roman urban landscape could also be interpreted as an indication of precisely the opposite point, namely their incidental and, hence, inconsequential role in the process of mapping sacred space; see the brief discussion in James B. Rives, *Religion in the Roman Empire* (Malden, Mass.: Blackwell, 2007), 32–34. However, it is important to distinguish between juridical space—space that is sacralized through formal, official consecration and purification rites—and perceptual space—space that could be perceived as sacred through the presence of certain material objects. Statues in particular play a prominent role in the latter category of space.

an additional layer to this discourse, one that underscores the perception of statuary as a marker of identity. In the Pilate narratives discussed above, Caesarea Maritima and Jerusalem form two distinct realms of power, not of course in any real sense—although the center of Pilate's authority was in fact Caesarea, Jerusalem was obviously within his jurisdiction as governor of Judea—but as ideal realms, the territory of the Ἰουδαῖοι and the territory of the other, in this case Pontius Pilate. This nexus of statues, space, and identity is further crystallized in Josephus' treatment of the social unrest in Caesarea just prior to the outbreak of the revolt against Rome (ca. 59–60 C.E.).

According to Josephus, a conflict erupted in Caesarea between the Jewish and Syrian/Greek inhabitants of the city, setting in motion, at least in Josephus' narrative progression, a series of events that would lead to the Jewish revolt and ultimately the destruction of the temple in Jerusalem (*B.J.* 2.266–270; *A.J.* 20.173–178).[101] Verbal sparring became riotous, and, according to the account in *A.J.*, this civic conflict eventually took on "the shape of war" (ἐν πολέμου τρόπῳ γενομένην; *A.J.* 20.177). Initially, the Jewish contingent appeared to emerge from the fray victorious, although Felix, the procurator of Judea during this time, turned the tide by authorizing his troops to attack and plunder the Jewish residents of Caesarea. The conflict continued until Felix referred the matter to Nero, at which time the Syrian/Greek contingent was awarded preeminence in 66 C.E., immediately prior to the commencement of the revolt against Rome. Josephus then reports that the entire Jewish community in Caesarea—some twenty thousand members strong—was destroyed in the wake of these events (*B.J.* 2.457; 7.362).

Two unique features in *B.J.*'s version of this episode are relevant to the topic at hand. First, after initially identifying the opponents as "Syrians" (Σύροι), Josephus subsequently, and quite consistently, refers to this group as "Greeks" (Ἑλλήνες). This contrasts markedly with the exclusive use of Σύροι in *A.J.* Second, the dispute in *B.J.* concerns not the juridical status of the Jews vis-à-vis their non-Jewish antagonists, the *isopoliteia* question at the center of the dispute in *A.J.*,[102] but rather the very identity of the city itself—whether Jewish or Greek—and ultimately to whom the city belongs. This is apparent in both the claim of the disputing parties and the evidence adduced to support each claim:

> οἱ μὲν γὰρ ἠξίουν σφετέραν εἶναι τὴν πόλιν Ἰουδαῖον γεγονέναι τὸν κτίστην αὐτῆς λέγοντες· ἦν δὲ Ἡρώδης ὁ βασιλεύς· οἱ δὲ ἕτεροι τὸν οἰκιστὴν μὲν προσωμολόγουν Ἰουδαῖον, αὐτὴν μέντοι γε τὴν πόλιν Ἑλλήνων ἔφασαν· οὐ γὰρ ἂν ἀνδριάντας καὶ ναοὺς ἐγκαθιδρῦσαι Ἰουδαίοις αὐτὴν ἀνατιθέντα.

101. On this dispute, see especially the following studies: Lee I. Levine, "The Jewish-Greek Conflict in First Century Caesarea," *JJS* 25 (1974): 381–97; Aryeh Kasher, "The *Isopoliteia* Question in Caesarea Maritima," *JQR* 68 (1977): 16–27; John Kloppenborg, "Ethnic and Political Factors in the Conflict at Caesarea Maritima," in *Religious Rivalries and the Struggle for Success in Caesarea Maritima* (ed. Terence L. Donaldson; Waterloo, Ont.: Canadian Corporation for Studies in Religion, 2000), 227–48.

102. *A.J.* 20.173: Γίνεται δὲ καὶ τῶν Καισάρειαν οἰκούντων Ἰουδαίων στάσις πρὸς τοὺς ἐν αὐτῇ Σύρους περὶ ἰσοπολιτείας ("Now a dispute concerning *isopoliteia* arose among the Jews living in Caesarea against the Syrians in the city").

> For [the Jews] considered the city to be their own, claiming that the city's founder, Herod the king, had been a Jew. Now their opponents admitted that the founder was Jewish, but claimed that the city itself belonged to the Greeks. *For whoever would set up statues and temples in it would not then present the city to the Jews.* (*B.J.* 2.266)

As noted above, what is at stake in this text is not status within the *polis*, as is the case in *A.J.*, but the identity of the *polis*, and the presence or absence of statuary emerges as a primary criterion for defining this identity. I am admittedly skeptical that the account in *B.J.* bears any substantial similarity to the events that actually took place, as if the Jews of Caesarea were really trying, in the words of Lee Levine, "to turn Caesarea into a 'Jewish' city."[103] Rather, this incident filtered through Josephan rhetoric *creates* an opposition between two realms and identities—the territory of the Ἑλλήνες and the Ἰουδαῖοι—and in the process transforms what was likely an incident of social unrest between rival Semitic groups (though certainly one with devastating consequences) into a veritable clash of civilizations, the Jews struggling against the irrepressible Greeks.[104] That the narrative identifies statuary as the quintessence of Caesarea's "Greekness" further implies the inverse: a "Jewish" Caesarea must be a statueless Caesarea.

The use of statuary to map identity is widely attested in Greek literature. As early as Herodotus, statues (along with temples and altars) served to distinguish between the Greeks and the Persians, whose sacred territory was remarkable, at least according to Herodotus' assessment, for its absence of statuary (Herodotus, *Hist.* 1.131–132).[105] The link between statuary and Greek identity is especially noticeable in Pausanias' *Periēgēsis Hellados*. As noted above, statues are inextricably woven into Pausanias' vision of πάντα τὰ Ἑλληνικά, so much so that statuary emerges as the quintessential marker of τὰ Ἑλληνικά. According to Jaś Elsner, the selectivity in Pausanias' description of πάντα τὰ Ἑλληνικά suggests that embedded in his use of Ἑλληνικά is not simply a geographical referent—mainland Greece—but a distinct notion of Greekness, so that by looking at πάντα τὰ Ἑλληνικά Pausanias was in fact "self-consciously exploring Greek identity."[106] In this light, then, statues for Pausanias were important markers of Greekness.[107]

---

103. Levine, "The Jewish-Greek Conflict," 396.

104. On the use of ethnic terminology in Josephus, see Tessa Rajak, "Greeks and Barbarians in Josephus," in *Hellenism in the Land of Israel* (ed. John J. Collins and Gregory E. Sterling; Notre Dame, Ind.: University of Notre Dame Press, 2001), 244–62. For a broader analysis of ethnicity in Josephus, see McClister, "Ethnicity and Jewish Identity in Josephus."

105. Hall, *Hellenicity*, 192.

106. Elsner, *Art and the Roman Viewer*, 128. Elsner's interpretation is thus reflected in his translation of the phrase πάντα τὰ Ἑλληνικά—"all things Greek." By contrast, Jones translates more literally in the LCL: "But my narrative must not loiter, as my task is a general description of all Greece." Similarly, Christian Habicht remarks on this passage: "Pausanias clearly intended to describe Greece in its entirety" (*Pausanias' Guide to Ancient Greece* [Berkeley: University of California Press, 1985], 6). See also Arafat, *Pausanias' Greece*, 8–9.

107. Pausanias likely hailed from western Asia Minor, probably Magnesia ad Sipylum in Lydia, and was thus, strictly speaking, not Greek but was instead, in the words of Christian Jacob, "un *xénos*" traveling in and writing about a foreign land (Christian Jacob, "Paysages

I submit that it is precisely this perception of statuary that has shaped Josephus' own vision of space and identity. The primary *indicia* of Greek space and identity in the Caesarea pericope are statues; conversely, Jewish space and identity are marked by emptiness, by the absence of statues. Whereas Pausanias' notion of Greekness is defined by the numerous statues populating Greece's landscape, Josephus inverts this paradigm in order to map a world and identity without sculpture.[108]

SPACE, POWER, AND CULTURAL POLITICS IN FLAVIAN ROME

I have argued above that sculpture in *B.J.* and, in particular, narratives about Jewish resistance to statues play an important role in defining Judean (sacred) territory and shaping Jewish identity as distinct from Greek space and identity. It is thus appropriate at this point to consider how this literary *topos* functions within its wider narrative context, that is, the role of Josephus' "sacred map" in the development of larger rhetorical themes in *B.J.* Moreover, given the importance of Josephus' compositional context—Rome at the height of the reign of Titus—it is necessary to consider how his configuration of space and identity is both shaped by and contributes to a discourse on culture and power in Flavian Rome. By placing this iconology within its specific historical context, we can begin to see the extent to which Josephus' iconoclastic narratives, beyond describing events that may have occurred *in Judea* before and during the Jewish revolt against Rome, function to navigate the complicated cultural and political terrain *in Rome* following the turbulent rise of a new imperial family. More specifically, a decade after the devastating destruction of the temple, Josephus subtly probes, by means of his "sacred map," the limits of monarchy, defining and distinguishing between tyrannical rule and legitimate expressions of power. In short, the territorial boundaries that emerge in *B.J.* become a kind of measuring stick for imperial (il)legitimacy.

Pausanias again offers an interesting point of comparison. According to Elsner, Pausanias' vision of Ἑλληνικά, his notion of Greekness tangibly evident in the monuments that mark out its sanctity, functions in part "as a resistance to the realities of Roman rule."[109] Embedded in Pausanias' visual map of Greece is thus

---

hantés et jardins merveilleux: La Grèce imaginaire de Pausanias," *L'Ethnographie* 76 [1980–81]: 44). Nevertheless, on a literary level Pausanias speaks not as an outsider to πάντα τὰ Ἑλληνικά but as an intimate insider, as one who has not only traveled but has *experienced* Greece and, by extension, Greekness. This insider's stance both enables Pausanias to guide his reader to the most important sights worth seeing and, conversely, to conceal sights that are prohibited to the uninitiated, such as the Eleusinian sanctuary that Pausanias was forbidden in a dream to describe (Pausanias, *Descr.* 1.38.7). On Pausanias' origins in Asia Minor, see the discussion in Frazer, *Pausanias's Description of Greece*, 1:xix; Arafat, *Pausanias' Greece*, 8.

108. I am not suggesting, of course, that there is some kind of literary relationship between Josephus and Pausanias. Rather, the evidence suggests a common "culture of perception"—they are breathing the same cultural air, so to speak (Leppert, *Art and the Committed Eye*, 11).

109. Elsner, *Art and the Roman Viewer*, 127.

an attempt to chart the proper boundaries of power and authority in a context where such boundaries have seemingly been violated. This is exemplified in his discussion of the bronze Eros erected in Thespiae, wherein Pausanias displays an obvious ambivalence toward Roman hegemony. Gaius Caligula initially stole this unfortunate statue, which Claudius eventually returned to its happy home, only for it to meet a devastating end at the hands of Nero, who brought the statue back to Rome where it perished by fire (Pausanias, *Descr.* 9.27.3–4). This brief account of the travails of Eros conveys an implicit assessment of imperial power, which is measured according to its treatment of sacred (and Greek) space. Power rightly displayed respects the sacred boundaries; conversely, the quintessential mark of abusive and tyrannical power is the violation of such boundaries and the desecration of the sacred. Both Caligula and Nero, by *removing* the statue from its rightful home, desecrated the territory of the Thespians and thus "sinned against the god" (τῶν δὲ ἀσεβησάντων ἐς τὸν θεὸν; Pausanias, *Descr.* 9.27.4). Only Claudius displays a proper use of power by respecting the sacred boundaries of the Greeks.

It is interesting to note that Josephus, too, charts the proper boundaries of power and authority according to his sacred map and even places Gaius Caligula on this map. But in this case it is not the *removal* but the *intrusion* of a statue that points to an abuse of power. Herod, Pilate, and especially Caligula exemplify the dangers of tyranny in their attempts to remap Judea, as it were, to reconfigure Judean space according to the *indicia* of Greek space. We should note, however, that by highlighting the desecrating potential of Greek culture and its links with tyranny, Josephus is not simply expressing a distinctly Jewish concern to preserve cultural "orthodoxy" from the "corrupting" forces of Hellenism. Rather, Josephus here is tapping into a growing "hellenophobia" within certain segments of the Roman elite, expressed most poignantly in Juvenal's lament over a "Greekified Rome" (*Graecam Urbem*).[110]

Plutarch conveys this Roman ambivalence toward Greek culture when he places in the mouth of Marcus Cato the sentiment that "Rome would lose her empire when she had become infected with Greek letters" (*Cat. Maj.* 23.2–3 [Perrin, LCL]).[111] Though recounting the words of an austere defender of the Roman republic from bygone years, Plutarch may very well testify to a simmering angst within his own day.[112] For many in Rome during and even after the Flavian dynasty, the memory

110. The full citation is as follows: "The race that's now most popular with wealthy Romans—the people I want especially to get away from—I'll name them right away, without any embarrassment. My fellow-citizens, I cannot stand a Greekified Rome" (Juvenal, *Sat.* 3.60–61 [Braund, LCL]). On this topic, see especially Nicholas Petrochilos, *Roman Attitudes to the Greeks* (Athens: National and Capodistrian University of Athens, 1974). See also the discussion of this issue in chapter 6.

111. It should be noted that Plutarch is quick to refute this assertion by commenting that Rome at its zenith "made every form of Greek learning and culture her own." For Plutarch, Greekness and Romanness were perfectly compatible, and his own literary project in some sense functioned as a "bridge between Greece and Rome" (see S. C. R. Swain, "Hellenic Culture and the Roman Heroes of Plutarch," *JHS* 110 [1990]: 127).

112. In contrast, Albert Henrichs argues that after the second century B.C.E. the per-

of Nero's philhellenism still lingered; after all, this "tyrant," widely considered to have been enslaved to his Greek passions, was to a large degree—at least according to later historians and biographers whose task it was to condemn the erstwhile emperor—responsible for the demise of the Julio-Claudians and the subsequent civil wars that plagued Rome.[113] From this perspective, Greekness becomes a kind of measuring stick for imperial illegitimacy: the more an emperor displays his proximity to the more excessive elements of Greek culture—for example, sexual license, *luxuria*, and the general inability to govern desires—the more that emperor demonstrates an abusive and tyrannical reign. In short, Greekness run amok leads to power run amok.

Yet for Josephus, as also for other historians in the late first and early second century C.E., Roman rule need not violate the limits of space and power. Indeed, Vespasian and Titus are presented as the antidotes to such excesses, exemplars of moderation and Roman virtue.[114] In the narrative of *B.J.*, Titus especially fulfills the role of ideal *imperator* (and, by extension, *princeps*) in his concern to respect and protect Judean space.[115] His actions contrast markedly with the desecrating impulse of tyranny, which, ironically enough, in *B.J.* finds its fullest expression not in a foreign despot but in the radical Jewish rebels who are ultimately responsible

---

ceived threat of Greek culture had all but dissipated in Rome ("*Graecia Capta*: Roman Views of Greek Culture," *HSCP* 97 [1995]: 243–61).

113. According to Holly Haynes, Tacitus' treatment of Nero reflects the perspective that Nero was a fountainhead of innumerable political crises (*The History of Make-Believe: Tacitus on Imperial Rome* [Berkeley: University of California Press, 2003], 34). On the question of Nero's philhellenism, Tim Whitmarsh remarks: "According to the conventional picture, Nero's celebrated philhellenism inclines more to the seedier side of the Greek heritage, or at least what Roman Hellenophobes represented as such" ("Greek and Roman in Dialogue: The Pseudo-Lucianic Nero," *JHS* 119 [1999]: 145). See also the image of Nero in Suetonius, who repeatedly highlights the emperor's depraved (at least from the perspective of the author) obsession with all things Greek (Suetonius, *Nero* 12.3; 20.1–3; 28.2); Tamsyn Barton, "The *Inventio* of Nero: Suetonius," in *Reflections of Nero: Culture, History, and Representation* (ed. Jaś Elsner and Jamie Masters; London: Duckworth, 1994), 48–63.

114. For example, Suetonius speaks of Vespasian's attempt to restrain an increase in *libido atque luxuria* (*Vesp.* 11; cf. Cassius Dio, *Hist. rom.* 65.10–11), clearly recalling the Neronic era. This tendency in historiography to style the first two Flavians as ideal figures of Roman virtue very likely goes back to the political propaganda of the emperors themselves. A. J. Boyle notes that such posturing is reflected in the semiotics of Flavian portrait busts. Vespasian appears in a "rugged, man-of-the-people style," complete with a "balding head, furrowed brow, lined neck, closely set eyes with crow's feet, hooked nose, creased cheeks and jutting chin," and the "curly-haired, square headed" portraiture of Titus exudes a "kindly beneficence." This portraiture provides a striking contrast with the last of the Flavians, whose "high forehead, protruding upper lip, soft, full cheeks, aquiline nose and stylized hair" is more suggestive of Nero than his Flavian predecessors (A. J. Boyle, "Introduction: Reading Flavian Rome," in *Flavian Rome: Culture, Image, Text* [ed. A. J. Boyle and William J. Dominik; Leiden: Brill, 2003], 34).

115. On the depiction of Titus, see G. M. Paul, "The Presentation of Titus in the 'Jewish War' of Josephus: Two Aspects," *Phoenix* 47 (1993): 56–66.

for the "abomination of desolations," the destruction of the temple. This theme is introduced in the opening pages of the narrative, where the tyranny of the Jewish rebels (οἱ Ἰουδαίων τύραννοι) is juxtaposed with the clemency of Titus, whose compassion for the people of Jerusalem (τὸν δῆμον ἐλεήσας) led him to delay the destruction of the city (*B.J.* 1.10). Even more explicitly, Titus is presented as one who desires "to save the temple and city" (Τίτος σῶσαι τὴν πόλιν καὶ τὸν ναὸν ἐπιθυμῶν); the temple was burnt *against the will of Caesar* (ὁ ναὸς ἄκοντος ἐνεπρήσθη Καίσαρος), who heroically rescues the sacred objects (τὰ ἱερά) from the flames of destruction (*B.J.* 1.27–28).[116]

The depiction of Romans who protect Judean space contrasted with Jews who desecrate space continues throughout the narrative. In *B.J.* 4.181–182 Roman donations to the temple are contrasted with the spoils taken by Jewish rebels. This *topos* receives greater specificity in John of Gischala and his band of zealots, who emerge in *Bellum* as a locus of desecrating tyranny:

> Ἰωάννης δ᾽ ὡς ἐπέλειπον αἱ ἁρπαγαὶ παρὰ τοῦ δήμου πρὸς ἱεροσυλίαν ἐτρέπετο, καὶ πολλὰ μὲν ἐκ τῶν ἀναθημάτων κατεχώνευε τοῦ ναοῦ, πολλὰ δὲ τῶν πρὸς τὰς λειτουργίας ἀναγκαίων σκεύη, κρατῆρας καὶ πίνακας καὶ τραπέζας· ἀπέσχετο δ᾽ οὐδὲ τῶν ὑπὸ τοῦ Σεβαστοῦ καὶ τῆς γυναικὸς αὐτοῦ πεμφθέντων ἀκρατοφόρων. οἱ μέν γε Ῥωμαίων βασιλεῖς ἐτίμησάν τε καὶ προσεκόσμησαν τὸ ἱερὸν ἀεί, τότε δὲ ὁ Ἰουδαῖος καὶ τὰ τῶν ἀλλοφύλων κατέσπα.
>
> But when the plunder from the people dried up, John turned to sacrilege—he melted down many of the temple's votive offerings and numerous vessels required for proper worship, such as the bowls and plates and tables. Nor did he abstain from the vessels for pure wine sent by Augustus and his wife. For indeed Roman emperors continually honored and adorned the temple, in contrast with this Jew, who pulled down even these donations from foreigners. (*B.J.* 5.562–563)

The image of unbridled greed, of an unrestrained pursuit of wealth even at the expense of one's compatriots and God, underscores the leitmotif outlined above: tyranny knows no bounds or limits, only excessive lust manifest in abusive dis-

116. T. D. Barnes discusses an alternative (and, in his opinion, more accurate) version of these events, likely derived from Tacitus, in which Titus fully intended to destroy the Temple ("The Sack of the Temple in Josephus and Tacitus," in *Flavius Josephus and Flavian Rome* [ed. Jonathan Edmondson, Steve Mason, and James Rives; Oxford: Oxford University Press, 2005], 129–44). In a similar vein, James Rives argues that Vespasian's (mis)perception of the Jewish cult led to a policy requiring the destruction of the temple ("Flavian Religious Policy and the Destruction of the Jerusalem Temple," in *Flavius Josephus and Flavian Rome* [ed. Jonathan Edmondson, Steve Mason, and James Rives; Oxford: Oxford University Press, 2005], 145–66). In the light of these considerations, Steve Mason sees in Josephus' portrait of Titus a hint of irony in which the general's clemency reflects not a brilliant military stratagem but an innocent naïveté ("Figured Speech and Irony," 262–67). Mason's subtle reading of these pro-Flavian narratives rightly cautions against the assumption that Josephus simply expresses the blind flattery of a Flavian lackey.

plays of power. That the apex of tyranny resides not in some foreign invader but within the Ἰουδαῖοι is for Josephus a lamentable paradox.[117]

One of the more revealing instances of this paradox of impiety—and one that encapsulates the intersection of sacrilege, tyranny, and Greekness—is found in a rather colorful, if unlikely, depiction of the aforementioned John (identified in the immediate context as a τύραννος) and his rebel followers:

> πόθοι δ᾽ ἦσαν ἁρπαγῆς ἀπλήρωτοι καὶ τῶν πλουσίων οἴκων ἔρευνα, φόνος τε ἀνδρῶν καὶ γυναικῶν ὕβρεις ἐπαίζοντο, μεθ᾽ αἵματός τε τὰ συληθέντα κατέπινον καὶ μετ᾽ ἀδείας ἐνεθηλυπάθουν τῷ κόρῳ, κόμας συνθετιζόμενοι καὶ γυναικείας ἐσθῆτας ἀναλαμβάνοντες, καταντλούμενοι δὲ μύροις καὶ πρὸς εὐπρέπειαν ὑπογράφοντες ὀφθαλμούς. οὐ μόνον δὲ κόσμον, ἀλλὰ καὶ πάθη γυναικῶν ἐμιμοῦντο καὶ δι᾽ ὑπερβολὴν ἀσελγείας ἀθεμίτους ἐπενόησαν ἔρωτας· ἐνηλινδοῦντο δ᾽ ὡς πορνείῳ τῇ πόλει καὶ πᾶσαν ἀκαθάρτοις ἐμίαναν ἔργοις. γυναικιζόμενοι δὲ τὰς ὄψεις ἐφόνων ταῖς δεξιαῖς, θρυπτόμενοί τε τοῖς βαδίσμασιν ἐπιόντες ἐξαπίνης ἐγίνοντο πολεμισταί, τά τε ξίφη προφέροντες ἀπὸ τῶν βεβαμμένων χλανιδίων τὸν προστυχόντα διήλαυνον.

> Now their [i.e., the rebels under John's command] lust for plunder was insatiable, and they ransacked the homes of the rich; they amused themselves in the murder of men and the abuse of women; they drank down their spoils along with blood, and with reckless abandon they played the part of a woman in their insolence, adorning their hair and putting on feminine clothing, bathing themselves in perfume and painting their eyelids for beauty. Moreover, not only did they beautify themselves [like women], but they even imitated the [sexual] passions of women, and through their excessive debauchery they contrived illicit sexual pleasures; and immersing themselves [in sexual decadence] as if in a brothel in the city, *they defiled the entire city* with their impure deeds. But while they womanized their faces, they were murderous with their right hands, and while walking effeminately, they suddenly attacked and became warriors, and drawing their swords from beneath their dyed womanly garments, they lanced everyone they encountered. (*B.J.* 4.560–562)

If nothing else, this image of a blood-drenched sexual rampage indicates in no uncertain terms who the villain is in *B.J.* We should not, of course, naively suppose that Josephus' description bears any resemblance to the historical figures portrayed in this pericope. Rather, the language here echoes Roman stereotypes of Greek decadence, which in turn serve as a point of contrast with Roman ideals of manliness.[118]

That Roman moralists associated excessive displays of *libido* with Greek influ-

---

117. Josephus laments τῆς παραδόξου μεταβολῆς τὴν πόλιν, when foreigners (ἀλλόφυλοι) and enemies (πολέμιοι) must reverse the impiety of Jews (*B.J.* 6.102).

118. On the poetics of gender deviancy in Josephus, including an extended discussion of *B.J.* 4.560–562, see Jason von Ehrenkrook, "Effeminacy in the Shadow of Empire: The Politics of Transgressive Gender in Josephus's *Bellum Judaicum*," *JQR* 101 (2011): 145–63. On masculine identity in ancient Rome, see Maud W. Gleason, *Making Men: Sophists and Self-Presentation in Ancient Rome* (Princeton, N.J.: Princeton University Press, 1995).

ence is well-documented,[119] and certainly the above text comports with the image of Greek licentiousness that we find in authors such as Cicero and Tacitus.[120] But even more explicitly, Josephus' caricature of effeminacy and sexual passivity recalls a long-standing unease with Roman men who behave like women.[121] The second-century B.C.E. Scipio negatively describes P. Sulpicius Gallus as "one who daily perfumes himself and dresses before a mirror, whose eyebrows are trimmed, who walks abroad with beard plucked out and thighs made smooth."[122] Tacitus similarly depicts among the vices of Otho his penchant for cross-dressing: "Was it by his bearing and gait or by his womanish dress (*muliebri ornatu*) that he deserved the throne?" (*Hist.* 1.30 ([Moore, LCL]).[123] Likewise, Roman distaste for male receptivity in the sexual act, expressed in the hierarchical distinction between the penetrator, the embodiment of Roman manliness, and the penetrated (i.e., young boys, slaves, and women) is well-known, exemplified in Martial's repeated censure of male passivity.[124] Such effeminate practices were considered part and parcel of

119. See especially the following studies: Ramsay MacMullen, "Roman Attitudes to Greek Love," *Historia* 31 (1982): 484–502; Judith P. Hallett, "Roman Attitudes toward Sex," in *Civilization of the Ancient Mediterranean: Greece and Rome* (ed. Michael Grant and Rachel Kitzinger; 3 vols.; New York: Charles Scribner's Sons, 1988), 2:1265–78; Craig A. Williams, "Greek Love at Rome," *CQ* 45 (1995): 517–39; Craig A. Williams, *Roman Homosexuality: Ideologies of Masculinity in Classical Antiquity* (Oxford: Oxford University Press, 1999).

120. For example, Cicero, *Tusc.* 4.70; 5.58; Tacitus, *Ann.* 14.20. Tacitus explicitly refers to an "imported licentiousness" whose source is clearly Greece in the broader context (Jackson, LCL).

121. Werner A. Krenkel, "Sex und politische Biographie," *Wissenschaftliche Zeitschrift der Wilhelm- Pieck-Universität Rostock, Gesellschaftliche und sprachwissenschaftliche Reihe* 29 (1980): 65–76; Holt N. Parker, "The Teratogenic Grid," in *Roman Sexualities* (ed. Judith P. Hallett and Marilyn B. Skinner; Princeton, N.J.: Princeton University Press, 1997), 47–65; Jonathan Walters, "Invading the Roman Body: Manliness and Impenetrability in Roman Thought," in *Roman Sexualities* (ed. Judith P. Hallett and Marilyn B. Skinner; Princeton, N.J.: Princeton University Press, 1997), 29–43; Williams, *Roman Homosexuality.*

122. Preserved in Aulus Gellius' second-century C.E. *Noct. att.* 6.12.2; trans. MacMullen, "Roman Attitudes to Greek Love," 484.

123. We could also point to the writings of the poet Phaedrus and satirist Juvenal, who, according to Judith Hallett, "provide negative and feminizing representations of mature men" (Judith P. Hallett, "Female Homoeroticism and the Denial of Roman Reality in Latin Literature," *YJC* 3 [1989]: 223).

124. See the numerous references cited in J. P. Sullivan, "Martial's Sexual Attitudes," *Philologus* 123 (1979): 294 n. 10. Sullivan argues that, notwithstanding Martial's own preference for young boys, his occasional rendezvous with prostitutes, and the frank and uninhibited tone of his epigrams, Martial is on the whole "fairly conventional, if not prudish, in his sexual values" (302). In this light, we should note that it is not male-to-male intercourse per se that is considered immoral, so long as the participants fulfill their proper roles. Moreover, that *some* Roman moralists decry male receptivity should not be taken to mean that *all* Romans rejected homosexual love between two adult males, as if we could even speak of *the* Roman view of sex. For an attempt to uncover other voices in Roman sexuality, see John R. Clarke, *Roman Sex, 100 B.C.–A.D. 250* (New York: Harry N. Abrams, 2003). For an

the more general problem of sexual decadence imported from Greece into the capital.[125]

I propose that the Josephan rhetoric outlined in the above analysis, and in particular the attempt to mediate the nexus of tyranny, sacrilege, and Greek culture through the configuration of sacred space, should be read in the light of this lively discourse on culture and politics in Rome. Josephus here gives voice to certain elite Roman attitudes toward virtue, power, and Roman identity that served both to elicit a sympathetic hearing and to warn against the dangers of imbibing too deeply from the well of Greekness, a danger that had become even more pronounced in the latter decades of the first century C.E. Of course, Josephus is writing in Greek to a literate audience fluent in Greek, so it is not Greek culture per se that is problematic, only an *excessive* infatuation with Greekness. On this point, I submit, such sentiments would certainly have rung true to a moralizing impulse among at least a few members of the literary elite in Flavian Rome.

CONCLUSION

I have argued that Josephus in *B.J.* deploys sculpture as a mapping device, a boundary marker delineating sacred and profane space. The resulting sacred map, however, beyond simply demarcating the limits of sacrality and defining identity, actually functions to chart the proper boundaries of power and authority. Power rightly displayed respects the sacred boundaries; conversely, the quintessential mark of abusive and tyrannical power is the violation of such boundaries and the desecration of the sacred. It is important to note that Josephus' negation of Greco-Roman notions of sacredness vis-à-vis an imagined world without statues does not necessarily express a subversive propaganda for Jewish independence from the "Hellenizing" corruption of Roman power, a clarion call to preserve purity by resisting external profanation. For Josephus, Roman rule need not violate the limits of power and in fact can serve to reinforce the boundaries of authority that ultimately empower Jews *under* Rome—exemplified in Augustus and, even more so, in Vespasian and Titus. So, in one sense, the figures of Herod, Pilate, and Caligula, insofar as their actions violated Judean space, prefigure not the invasion of Vespasian's army into Judea nor the destruction of the temple under the command of Titus but the unrestrained tyranny of the radical Jewish rebels whose lust for power forced the hand of Rome.

Moreover, the stark polarization between Judean and Greek landscapes and, by extension, Jewish and Greek identities, when read against this backdrop, points to a nexus between Greekness and desecrating tyranny, underscored especially in the caricature of an excessively depraved John of Gischala. It is a mistake, however, to draw from this rhetorical antithesis the conclusion that Judaism and Hellenism

---

alternative view on the question of Greek influence in sexuality, see Williams, "Greek Love at Rome," 517–39.

125. MacMullen, "Roman Attitudes to Greek Love," 493–94; Hallett, "Female Homoeroticism," 209–12.

were fundamentally and irreconcilably opposed in antiquity, an interpretation that fails to appreciate both the complexity of Greco-Roman culture and the subtlety of Josephus' rhetoric. In fact, the polarization that emerges in *B.J.* is actually not a *Jewish* opposition to *Greekness* but a *Roman* or, perhaps better, *Romano-Jewish* resistance to elements of Greek culture. Josephus thus reconfigures the uneasy relationship between Jews and sculpture for a distinctly Roman audience, conveying through the aniconic rhetoric of *B.J.* not simply a radically strict interpretation of the second commandment but the strategy of a cartographer whose "sacred map" serves to navigate the complex cultural and political terrain of Flavian Rome.

5

Idealizing an Aniconic Past in *Antiquitates Judaicae*

Figurative art and religious devotion are seemingly inseparable. From the cache of divine sculpture found at the Sumerian Tel Asmar (the temple of the god Abu, ca. 2700–2600 B.C.E.) through the proliferation of icons and images in Christianity to the iconic representation of the Hindu gods Visnu, Siva, and the Goddess and images of the Buddha,[1] there is an abundance of material and literary evidence attesting to the near ubiquitous human impulse to image the gods, to mediate cultic devotion through artistic representation. Nevertheless, the fact that, in Volkhard Krech's words, "art has constantly inspired popular piety" ought not overshadow an opposing *conceptual* tendency to link aniconism, the absence of figurative cult images, and spirituality.[2] As David Freedberg observes, this notion—the idea that aniconism is "an index of the degree of 'spirituality' of a culture"—sporadically surfaces in a variety of contexts across the wide spectrum of human history.[3] That is to say, for some in antiquity, as also in the present, a culture or religion whose thought is "more spiritualized" will "tend more or less rigorously to aniconism."[4]

Judaism, insofar as it is typically, if inaccurately, identified as an aural, nonvisual "book" religion, is often put forward as exemplary of this aniconic spirituality. For example, a quick perusal of Helen Gardner's widely used and repeatedly revised historical survey of art is quite telling. Although the volume covers a broad range of cultures (including, in addition to the well-known "Western" cultures, Islamic, Chinese, Japanese, Native American, and South Pacific art, among others) and

1. On image finds at Tel Asmar, see H. Frankfort, *Sculpture of the Third Millennium from Tell Asmar and Khafaje* (Chicago: University of Chicago Press, 1939). For a survey of Christian art through the centuries, see Helen de Brochgrave, *A Journey into Christian Art* (Minneapolis: Fortress Press, 2000). On Hindu and Buddhist images, see Richard H. Davis, "Indian Image-Worship and Its Discontents," in *Representation in Religion: Studies in Honor of Moshe Barasch* (ed. Jan Assmann and Albert I. Baumgarten; Leiden: Brill, 2001), 107–32; and Koichi Shinohara, "The 'Iconic' and 'Aniconic' Buddha Visualization in Medieval Chinese Buddhism," in *Representation in Religion: Studies in Honor of Moshe Barasch* (ed. Jan Assmann and Albert I. Baumgarten; Leiden: Brill, 2001), 133–48.

2. Volkhard Krech, "Art and Religion," in *Religion Past and Present: Encyclopedia of Theology and Religion* (ed. Hans Dieter Betz et al.; 4th ed.; 13 vols.; Leiden: Brill, 2007), 1:400.

3. Freedberg, *The Power of Images*, 54. According to Freedberg, although this notion of a spiritual aniconism is expressed in both antiquity and the present, it is fundamentally a myth that belies a near universal impulse to create images.

4. R. Assunto, "Images and Iconoclasm," in *Encyclopedia of World Art* (New York: McGraw-Hill, 1959–87), 7:801.

time periods (paleolithic to the present), Judaism, or Jewish religious art, at least as a separate category of discussion, is conspicuously absent, except for a brief notation that the sacred *book* of Judaism, the "legacy of Israel . . . contributed so much to the formation of the Western spirit."[5] Likewise, Heinrich Graetz's well-known essay, "The Structure of Jewish History," contrasts the "Pagan" belief that a deity is revealed visually to the Jewish notion that "God reveals Himself . . . through the medium of the ear. . . . Paganism sees its god, Judaism hears Him," rendering the representation of the divine as something fundamentally "alien to Judaism."[6]

As Freedberg and many others have correctly noted, however, this image of Judaism is more myth than reality, the product of a persistent ethnic stereotype that masks an abundance of material evidence attesting to a vibrant production of Jewish art.[7] Moreover, the tendency to restrict aniconism to the so-called monotheistic book religions often mutes aniconic voices from cultures otherwise saturated with the iconic. This is evident particularly in the study of Greco-Roman antiquity, where the notion of the ancient Jew as the aniconic "other" tends to obscure the fact that Greeks and Romans could also, notwithstanding the ubiquitous diffusion of figurative sculpture and painting throughout their respective landscapes, affirm the piety of aniconic religion, albeit locating such cultic practices in the distant past, a long-lost primitive age of pious religiosity. Indeed, as will be discussed below, some Greek and Roman authors identify the rise of iconic worship as symptomatic of the gradual corruption of the piety and virtue of ancestral customs.

The central hypothesis of this chapter is that Josephus' discussion of εἰκών in *A.J.* fits within this broader Greco-Roman discourse on aniconism. Specifically, I will argue the following theses. First, Josephus constructs an image of an aniconic ideal, originating in the deep past and rooted in the legislation of a lawgiver whose πολιτεία represents the perfect repository of virtue (ἀρετή; *virtus*) and piety (εὐσέβεια; *pietas*). Moreover, this image of a primitive age of pious aniconism, rather than functioning to *distinguish* Jews from their iconic Roman counterparts, actually represents a facet of religio-cultural *confluence*, serving as a cohesive element that links Jews with Romans, at least with the *ancient* (from a first-century perspective) Romans who functioned as *exempla* of true Romanness. By constructing an image of a pristine aniconic age, Josephus thus taps into a trajectory of Roman cultural discourse that similarly idealized an aniconic past, albeit one that had long since dissipated. Finally, the supposition of a pious aniconic πολιτεία also functions in *A.J.* to explain Jewish resistance to images in the present. In other words, Josephus counters the belief that the sporadic moments of iconoclastic activity during the Herodian and early Roman periods were fundamentally *anti*-Roman by positing the opposite: Jews resisted images precisely because they *shared with* Romans a love for and loyalty to the ancient laws and customs, the *mos*

5. Horst de la Croix, Richard G. Tansey, and Diane Kirkpatrick, eds., *Gardner's Art through the Ages* (9th ed.; Orlando: Harcourt Brace College, 1991), 24.

6. Heinrich Graetz, *The Structure of Jewish History and Other Essays* (trans. Ismar Schorsch; New York: Jewish Theological Seminary of America, 1975), 68.

7. Freedberg, *The Power of Images*, 55–59; Fine, *Art and Judaism*. See additionally the discussion of the "aniconic Jew" in chapter 2.

maiorum, stemming from the deep past. Jewish iconoclasm is thus framed as an attempt to preserve that which the Romans had long since lost.

Ἀρχαιολογία and a Golden Age of Primitive Piety

The preface in *A.J.* sets out in explicit terms Josephus' main literary agenda: to convey for a Greek-speaking audience the complete ἀρχαιολογία and the διάταξις τοῦ πολιτεύματος of the Jews (*A.J.* 1.5). Josephus' use of the term ἀρχαιολογία situates his work within a stream of "antiquarian rhetorical historiography."[8] Indeed many have suggested that Dionysius of Halicarnassus, the Greek historian (during the reign of Augustus) whose literary oeuvre included the twenty-volume *Antiquitates Romanae*, or at least the historiographical tradition that he represented, served as an explicit model for Josephus' *magnum opus*,[9] due mainly to a number of striking similarities between the two in structure and content.[10] Whether Dionysius was actually a blueprint for *A.J.*, or whether both texts independently employ similar rhetorical strategies and forms,[11] by identifying his project with the Greek term ἀρχαιολογία, Josephus imbues this work with the spirit of Greco-Roman antiquarianism, aiming his "archaeology" of the Jews to an audience and culture that "placed an almost absolute value on antiquity."[12]

While in modern usage antiquarianism typically denotes an interest in *preserv-*

---

8. Gregory E. Sterling, *Historiography and Self-Definition: Josephos, Luke-Acts, and Apologetic Historiography* (Leiden: Brill, 1992), 285. But see the objections raised in Tessa Rajak, "Josephus and the 'Archaeology' of the Jews," in *The Jewish Dialogue with Greece and Rome: Studies in Cultural and Social Interaction* (ed. Tessa Rajak; Leiden: Brill, 2001), 241–55. Specifically, Rajak argues that despite a few superficial similarities, Josephus' treatment of the primitive past is substantially different from other ancient historiographical texts, indicating that *A.J.* really has "no parallel . . . in the Graeco-Roman world" (254). Rajak may be correct that the differences far outweigh the similarities, but this does not mitigate the possibility that Josephus has at least superficially located his work within this historiographical tradition, that is, that although Josephus may differ with Dionysius of Halicarnassus and other Greek historians on a number of substantive details, particularly in the method of using sources, he has nevertheless attempted to situate his work within this broad stream of antiquarian historiography. At the very least, Rajak overstates the differences when she places Josephus "in a class apart from the Greek and Roman antiquarians" (253).

9. For example, Thackeray, *Josephus*, 56–58; Jackson, *Josephus and the Jews*, 247–48; Robert James H. Shutt, *Studies in Josephus* (London: SPCK, 1961), 92–101; Attridge, *Interpretation of Biblical History*, 43–60; Sterling, *Historiography and Self-Definition*, 284–90.

10. Most notably, both works consist of twenty books and both include nearly identical titles, Ῥωμαϊκὴ Ἀρχαιολογία and Ἰουδαϊκὴ Ἀρχαιολογία respectively.

11. Balch, "Two Apologetic Encomia," 102–22. Balch argues that Josephus' *C. Ap.* and Dionysius' *Ant. rom.* use an identical form of encomium, preserved in Menander's third-century C.E. rhetorical handbook (Περὶ ἐπιδεικτικῶν), suggesting that Josephus literary oeuvre fits "into the international atmosphere of the Roman Empire" (122).

12. Boccaccini, *Middle Judaism*, 245. Boccaccini stresses the role of memory of the past in Josephus as a means of asserting the "national and religious identity of the Jewish people" (243). He subsequently remarks that Josephus' main task is "to place side by side, if not op-

ing the past through the collection of old, rare artifacts,[13] in Roman antiquarianism past and present are inseparably wedded, with the former serving the cultural and political needs of the latter. In other words, Roman antiquarianism, not unlike what Jonathan Z. Smith identifies as the "complex and deceptive" nature of memory, only "appears to be preeminently a matter of the past, yet it is as much an affair of the present."[14] In this sense, antiquarian historiography should not be read, strictly speaking, as a record of events and human exploits from bygone eras, though indeed such "brute facts" *may* be preserved in these narratives. Rather, "past" in these texts becomes a conduit for "present" values and ideals. The way it *was* may or may not actually be the way it *was* but, from the vantage point of the Roman antiquarian, the way it *was* is certainly the way it *should be*.[15]

This ideological function of Roman antiquarianism has long been noted in scholarship. According to Arnaldo Momigliano, "Emperors like Augustus and Claudius were quick to grasp the advantages inherent in a well-exploited antiquarianism."[16] Mary Beard, John North, and Simon Price similarly note that the marked attempt to revive "native" practices and "old, half-forgotten rituals" functioned even in Republican Rome, especially during the imperial period, as a means of explaining Rome's present power and potential expansion, that is, as an integral component in the ideology of imperialism.[17] One important facet of this antiquarian interest was a "cultural nostalgia" that forged an explicit link between the deep past and Roman *virtus* and *pietas*.[18] Stories about ancestral laws, deeds, and *mores*, collectively embodied in the politically and culturally charged concept of the *mos maiorum*, fostered an image of a glorious era of pristine piety and morality, when men were men, social hierarchies were properly aligned, and the worship of the gods was at its purest. Early imperial philosophical trends, particularly among the Stoics and middle Platonists, similarly constructed a vision of the primitive past

---

posite one another, the memory of the Greek and Roman peoples and the memory of the Jewish people—Jewish antiquities against Greek and Roman antiquities" (248).

13. For example, the American Antiquarian Society was established in 1812 to, in the words of its founder Isaiah Thomas, "encourage the collection and preservation of the Antiquities of our country"; cited in "A Brief History of the American Antiquarian Society," n.p. (accessed 22 May 2011). Online: http://www.americanantiquarian.org/briefhistory.htm.

14. Smith, *To Take Place*, 25.

15. Freedberg identifies this idealization of the primitive as "a deep and persistent myth," noting that such "historigraphical inventions" arise "from the need to claim for a particular culture a superior spirituality" (Freedberg, *The Power of Images*, 54, 60).

16. Arnaldo Momigliano, *The Classical Foundations of Modern Historiography* (Berkeley: University of California Press, 1990), 68.

17. Beard, North, and Price, *Religions of Rome*, 113.

18. Rebecca Langlands, *Sexual Morality in Ancient Rome* (Cambridge: Cambridge University Press, 2006), 13. See also the discussion of historiographical *exempla* in Christina S. Kraus, "From *Exempla* to *Exemplar*? Writing History around the Emperor in Imperial Rome," in *Flavius Josephus and Flavian Rome* (ed. Jonathan Edmondson, Steve Mason, and James Rives; Oxford: Oxford University Press, 2005), 186–88.

as a repository of pristine wisdom.[19] Likewise, as is demonstrated in Paul Zanker's study of Augustan period art and architecture, Augustus' penchant for archaizing and classicizing fits into this antiquarian context, functioning as a vehicle for the emperor's "new mythology," that is, Augustus' attempt to initiate a "program of religious revival" by injecting a measure of ancestral *pietas* into the physical landscape of Rome.[20]

This idealized Roman past, moreover, functioned as a critical index for the present health of the Roman state. On the one hand, as in the case of Emperor Augustus' program of cultural renewal discussed in Zanker, the golden era of the distant past could function as the prototype for the present, a pattern for the dawning of a new age of virtue and piety. On the other hand, the *virtus* and *pietas* of "Old Rome," particularly in narratives of decline, often served as a point of contrast to perceived departures in the present. Such is the case in Juvenal's eleventh satire (*Sat.* 11.77–129; cf. *Sat.* 3.314), which includes "an extended contrast between the virtuous simplicity of countrified old Rome and modern, urbanized luxury."[21] According to Steve Mason, this obsession with a "long-lost golden age" was an important tenet within certain conservative circles among Rome's literary elite, who had encountered what they perceived to be "a rise in corruption, social dislocation, violence, and political upheaval."[22]

This notion of moral decline, reaching a fever pitch in the late Republican period, is succinctly formulated in Sallust's *Bellum Catilinae* (ca. 42/41 B.C.E.), which laments that through avarice the *virtus* upon which Rome was founded devolved into *malus*:

> Since the occasion has arisen to speak of the morals of our country (*moribus civitatis*), the nature of my theme seems to suggest that I go farther back and give a brief account of the institutions of our forefathers in peace and in war, how they governed the commonwealth, how great it was when they bequeathed it to us, and how by gradual changes it has ceased to be the noblest and best, and has become the worst and most vicious. (*Bell. Cat.* 5.9 [Rolfe, LCL])

Following this summary statement, Sallust then spells out in greater detail Rome's putative decline, honing in especially on the vice of avarice (*Bell. Cat.* 6.1–13.5).

In a similar vein, and again highlighting the role of *avaritia luxuriaque* in the decay of Roman *mores*, the Roman historian Livy, whose literary career spanned the principate of Augustus, sets out in the preface of his *Ab urbe condita* his main purpose in telling the story of Rome:

> Here are the questions to which I would have every reader give his close attention—what life and morals were like (*quae vita qui mores fuerint*); through what men and by what policies, in peace and in war, empire (*imperium*) was estab-

19. Gregory R. Boys-Stones, *Post-Hellenistic Philosophy* (Oxford: Oxford University Press, 2001), 111–12.

20. Zanker, *The Power of Images*, 239–63.

21. Donohue, *Xoana and the Origins of Greek Sculpture*, 136.

22. Mason, "Introduction to the *Judean Antiquities*," xxiii.

> lished and enlarged; then let him note how, with the gradual relaxation of discipline (*paulatim disciplina velut desidentis*), morals first gave way (*primo mores sequatur animo*), as it were, then sank lower and lower (*deinde ut magis magisque lapsi sint*), and finally began the downward plunge (*praecipito*) which has brought us to the present time, when we can endure neither our vices nor their cure. (*Ab urb.* 1.*praef.*9 [Foster, LCL])

Livy's point, vividly captured with the language of the gradual sinking of morality ultimately giving way to a dangerous free fall toward destruction, is unmistakably clear: present corruption contrasts sharply with past glory. He thus envisions his narrative of Rome's past as a beacon that shines into the darkness of the present, preserving an exemplum, a *monumentum* for all to see and follow (Livy, *Ab urb.* 1.*praef.*10).[23] As Rebecca Langlands puts it, the idealization of Rome's past vis-à-vis perceived corruption in the present was not simply "an expression of regret at the loss of innocence" but instead functioned as "a powerful weapon in the armoury of Roman ethical teaching."[24] At the core of this ideology is the remark by the Roman poet Quintus Ennius (239–169 B.C.E.) in his *Annales*: "The Roman state and its strength depend upon its ancient customs" (*Moribus antiquis res stat Romana viresque*; Ennius, *Ann.* 5.156 [500]).[25]

Although the narrative arc of *A.J.* does not necessarily follow a scheme of decline, I submit that Josephus' treatment of ἀρχαιολογία/*antiquitates* must be read against the backdrop of a culture that idealized the deep past as a golden age, that perceived in bygone eras a moral compass for the present. Returning to *A.J.* 1.5, it becomes immediately clear when read in the context of the entire prologue that Josephus' story of the ἀρχαιολογία τῶν Ἰουδαίων pivots around the antiquity and consequent superiority of the Jewish "constitution."[26] In justifying the need to present for a Greek-speaking audience an account of the διάταξις τῆς πολιτείας (*A.J.* 1.10),[27] Josephus underscores the superiority of the Jewish πολιτεία by appealing

23. Cicero similarly justifies the composition of his *De divinatione* as an educational tool for those in the present who had been led astray by moral laxity (*Div.* 2.2.4).

24. Langlands, *Sexual Morality in Ancient Rome*, 78. See also her discussion of *exempla* in Valerius Maximus' *Facta et Dicta Memorabilia* (123–91).

25. Text from Otto Skutsch, *The Annals of Q. Ennius* (Oxford: Clarendon Press, 1985), 84.

26. Josephus in fact remarks in *C. Ap.* 2.287 that his main purpose in writing *A.J.* was to provide "an accurate account of our laws (νόμοι) and constitution (πολιτεία)." Steve Mason is thus correct in noting that *A.J./Vita* is "from start to finish about the Judean constitution" ("Aim and Audience," 81). Elizabeth Asmis notes that Cicero's *De republica* is similarly an extended treatise on the superiority of the Roman constitution ("A New Kind of Model: Cicero's Roman Constitution in *De republica*," *AJP* 126 [2005]: 377–416).

27. The Greek term πολιτεία is here juxtaposed with ἡμέτερος νόμος, establishing an explicit link between political order of a state and divine legislation. Note also Cicero's discussion of law in his *De legibus*, which argues in part for the nexus of divine laws and the laws that govern human affairs (*Leg.* 2.4–9). On the use of πολιτεία in Greco-Roman Jewish sources, see Lucio Troiani, "The πολιτεία of Israel in the Graeco-Roman Age," in *Josephus and the History of the Greco-Roman Period: Essays in Memory of Morton Smith* (ed. Fausto Parente and Joseph Sievers; Leiden: Brill, 1994), 11–22.

specifically to the lawgiver's (νομοθέτης) antiquity and his worthy conception of the deity's nature, noting that Moses "was born two thousand years ago, of such a span of time their poets did not even dare ascribe the origins of the gods, let alone the deeds or the laws of men" (*A.J.* 1.15–16).[28] By juxtaposing here the antiquity of Moses vis-à-vis the Greek poets with Moses' ability to keep his discourse pure of mythology (καθαρὸς ... ἀσχήμονος μυθολογίας), Josephus implicitly sets up a contrast between on the one hand the lawgiver and the πολιτεία of the Jews—a repository of pure religiosity—and on the other hand that of the Greeks, with the latter having accrued corruptions not found in the former. Indeed, this antithesis becomes even more explicit just a few sentences later, where Josephus again contrasts "other legislators" (ἄλλοι νομοθέται), whose law codes are inherently flawed insofar as they follow fables (τοῖς μύθοις ἐξακολουθήσαντες) and thus foolishly attribute to the gods the wickedness of humanity (τῶν ἀνθρωπίνων ἁμαρτημάτων), with "our legislator" (ἡμέτερος νομοθέτης), whose legal code mirrors God's perfect ἀρετή (*A.J.* 1.22–23).[29]

The image of Moses as a very ancient νομοθέτης thus underscores the excellence of the Mosaic law code.[30] He, and by extension the πολιτεία he founded, was a fountain through which the Jews "were instructed in piety (εὐσέβεια) and the practice of virtue (ἄσκησις ἀρετῆς)" (*A.J.* 1.6).[31] Given that the primary audience for *A.J.* was Greek-speaking Romans,[32] the use of νομοθέτης undoubtedly would recall, in addition to legendary Greeks such as the Spartan Lycurgus and the Athenian Solon, the famed Roman lawgiver Numa Pompilius, whose law code was widely considered to have embodied virtue and piety—the two qualities emphasized in Josephus' portrayal of Moses.[33] Indeed, Plutarch's biography of Numa,

28. On Josephus' portrait of Moses, see especially Louis Feldman's three-part series: "Josephus' Portrait of Moses," *JQR* 82 (1992): 285–328; "Josephus' Portrait of Moses: Part Two," *JQR* 83 (1992): 7–50; "Josephus' Portrait of Moses: Part Three," *JQR* 83 (1993): 301–30.

29. This point is developed even more explicitly in *C. Ap.*, where Moses is said to be the "most ancient of legislators" (νομοθετῶν ἀρχαιότητης), compared to which Greek legislators such as Lycurgus, Solon, and Zaleucus "appear to have been born but yesterday" (*C. Ap.* 2.154).

30. Cicero likewise connects the purity and authority of the ideal law code with its antiquity (*Leg.* 2.7).

31. Cf. *A.J.* 1.14, where Josephus identifies the primary value of his narrative as its capacity to morally instruct its readers. On the link between Moses and ἀρετή, Feldman remarks: "Josephus' treatment of Moses is a veritable *aretalogy*, such as would be appreciated especially by a Roman society which admired the portrait of the ideal Stoic sage" ("Portrait of Moses," 292).

32. See especially the discussion in Mason, "Aim and Audience," 64–103. As noted in chapter 1, the idea of a *Roman* audience for *A.J.* is contested by some scholars, who instead suppose that Josephus wrote *A.J.* in part as an attempt to regain favor with his Jewish compatriots.

33. Feldman, "Portrait of Moses: Part Two," 9. Feldman goes on to note the link between piety and justice in Josephus and compares this to Dionysius' characterization of Numa's civic legislation in *Ant. rom.* 2.62.5 (44). See also Louis H. Feldman, "Parallel Lives of Two Lawgivers: Josephus' Moses and Plutarch's Lycurgus," in *Flavius Josephus and Flavian Rome*

written perhaps only a decade or so after *A.J.*,[34] highlights the centrality of εὐσέβεια and ἀρετή in the image of the ideal lawgiver. Numa is said to have possessed a renowned virtue (γνώριμον ... ἀρετήν) and to be naturally (φύσις) accustomed to the practice of πᾶσα ἀρετή (Plutarch, *Numa* 3.3, 5). Conversely, Numa kept himself removed from πᾶσα κακία, further establishing the Roman lawgiver as a radiant model of virtue (τὴν ἀρετὴν ἐν εὐδήλῳ παραδείγματι καὶ λαμπρῷ; *Numa* 20.6, 8). Likewise, Numa was believed to have excelled in εὐσέβεια, being renowned as the "most pious and divinely loved" (εὐσεβέστατος καὶ θεοφιλέστατος) among men (*Numa* 7.3). Indeed, these two attributes intersect in Plutarch's narrative when the Romans plead with Numa to accept the nomination as king on the basis of his exemplary ἀρετή and εὐσέβεια (*Numa* 6.2).

While there is no indication that Josephus was acquainted either with Plutarch or his writings, particularly since most of the latter postdate *A.J.*,[35] it is certainly reasonable to suppose that the Numa traditions standing behind Plutarch's biography were well-known in literary circles of Flavian Rome and had even left traces on Josephus' image of Moses as νομοθέτης. As will be discussed in the following section, this possibility becomes even stronger in light of the fact that both lawgivers are associated with legislation prohibiting images.

Idealizing an Aniconic Past in Greco-Roman Antiquity

Insofar as *A.J.* functions in part to explain the Judean πολιτεία, Josephus incorporates an account of the origins of the Mosaic law code and an extended, though not exhaustive, summary of its contents.[36] Included in his summary is legislation dealing with the question of cult images: "The second commands to make no image of any living being for the purpose of worship" (ὁ δὲ δεύτερος κελεύει μηδενὸς εἰκόνα ζῴου ποιήσαντας προσκυνεῖν; *A.J.* 3.91).

As discussed at length in chapter 3, although Josephus' restatement of the second commandment restricts its scope to cult images, more often than not this qualifi-

(ed. Jonathan Edmondson, Steve Mason, and James Rives; Oxford: Oxford University Press, 2005), 209–42. On the comparison between Moses and Numa, see the discussion in Jürgen C. H. Lebram, "Der Idealstaat der Juden," in *Josephus-Studien: Untersuchungen zu Josephus, dem antiken Judentum und dem Neuen Testament* (ed. Otto Betz, Klaus Haacker, and Martin Hengel; Göttingen: Vandenhoeck & Ruprecht, 1974), 237–44.

34. On the date of Plutarch's writings, see especially Christopher P. Jones, "Towards a Chronology of Plutarch's Works," *JRS* 56 (1966): 61–74.

35. Given that Plutarch spent considerable time in the capital city during the Flavian period, it is tempting to wonder whether their paths ever crossed, though of course no concrete evidence exists to establish (or preclude) a direct relationship between the two Greek authors. For a discussion of this possibility in the context of similarities between Plutarch's Lycurgus and Josephus' Moses, see Feldman, "Parallel Lives," 234–37. In the end, Feldman considers it more likely that a common source explains the similarities between the two (237–41).

36. Josephus repeatedly announces his intention to produce a more exhaustive treatment of the subject, though apparently this text was never completed (or even begun?) before his death (*A.J.* 1.25, 29, 192, 214; 3.94, 143, 205, 230, 257, 259, 264; 4.198; 20.268).

cation disappears in the numerous narrative retrospective glances at the prohibition, creating the distinct impression of a more expansive aniconism, that is, that the Mosaic πολιτεία prohibited figurative (anthropomorphic or theriomorphic) images in toto. As will be argued below, Josephus' portrayal of the distant past, the so-called rewritten Bible of *A.J.* 1–11, comports with this tendency, particularly in his repeated effort to purge or suppress details that might otherwise undermine the image of primitive aniconism. Insofar as this account of Judean ἀρχαιολογία conflicts with both the biblical narrative and archaeological remains from the Bronze and Iron Age Levant,[37] Josephus' treatment of ancestral aniconism can be rightly classified as "historiographic myth."[38] Nevertheless, as will be evident in the ensuing discussion, this mythic past bespeaks the religio-cultural concerns of the present, tapping into a broader impulse in Greco-Roman antiquity to imagine, and even idealize, a primitive age of aniconic worship.

Aniconizing the Biblical Narrative in A.J. *1–11*

Notwithstanding Josephus' claim in the preface of *A.J.* to have followed the biblical narrative with great care and accuracy (ἀκριβής), setting forth the details of the narrative according to its correct order (κατὰ τὴν οἰκείαν τάξιν) without adding to or subtracting from the record (οὐδὲν προσθεὶς οὐδ' αὖ παραλιπών; *A.J.* 1.17), even a superficial reading of *A.J.* 1–11 belies this declaration.[39] This is noticeably evident in his treatment of εἰκών and related terminology, where there is a marked tendency to proffer an image of strict aniconism either by omitting or altering certain details in the biblical text.

There have been numerous attempts to explain the obvious dissonance between the ideals of accuracy set out in the preface of *A.J.* and the realities of the narrative itself, ranging from the carelessness of Josephus as a "translator" of scripture[40] to the formulaic and somewhat meaningless nature of claims to accuracy in ancient Greek historiography.[41] It is true that departures from the biblical text need not indicate rhetorical significance. The massive scope of diverse material Josephus

37. Keel and Uehlinger, *Gods, Goddesses, and Images of God.*

38. Freedberg, *The Power of Images*, 54.

39. See the discussion in Louis H. Feldman, *Studies in Josephus' Rewritten Bible* (Leiden: Brill, 1998), 539–43, and idem, *Judean Antiquities 1–4*, 7–8. Josephus similarly remarks in *C. Ap.* 1.42 that no one would have the temerity to add to, subtract from, or change in any fashion these writings (οὔτε προσθεῖναί τις οὐδὲν οὔτε ἀφελεῖν αὐτῶν οὔτε μεταθεῖναι). In *A.J.* 4.196–197, Josephus again reiterates his commitment not to add to (προστίθημι) the Mosaic record, yet here he does confess the need to rearrange material into a more orderly fashion (τάσσω), since the laws of Moses were transmitted in a scattered manner (σποράδην).

40. On Josephus' claim that *A.J.* 1–11 is a translation (μεθερμηνεύω) of the Hebrew scriptures, see *A.J.* 1.5 and *C. Ap.* 1.54 and the discussion in Sterling, *Historiography and Self-Definition*, 252–56.

41. See Feldman's discussion of the various proposals in scholarship in Feldman, *Judean Antiquities 1–4*, 7–8. See also the discussion in Willem Cornelis van Unnik, *Flavius Josephus als historischer Schriftsteller* (Heidelberg: Lambert Schneider, 1978), 26–40, and Sterling, *Historiography and Self-Definition*, 253–55.

attempts to recount surely required judicious selectivity, that is, expedient omissions. Moreover, the "Bible" itself had by the first century C.E. accrued a host of interpretive traditions, so much so that retelling the biblical narrative often involved the unconscious inclusion of additional material, popular interpretations that had become inseparable from the biblical text itself.[42] While the modern critical scholar through careful comparison may deem this or that detail an addition or omission, it is not always clear that ancient authors were equally aware that they were adding to or altering the source text.

That being said, given the central role accorded to the Mosaic legislation on images as an integral, even essential, component of the Jewish πολιτεία in Josephus' account of "postbiblical" events (see the discussion below), it is much more likely that Josephus' treatment of the biblical narrative would comport with this leitmotif, that is, that the omission or extrabiblical censure of potentially incriminating episodes involving sculpted images is quite intentional. In other words, in the departures from the biblical narrative detailed below, I argue that Josephus *consciously suppresses* an iconic past, constructing an image of a pristine era when the Jewish state was devoid of figurative images.

The first indication of this aniconic tendency is evident in Josephus' summary of the creation narrative. Whereas the biblical narrative (Gen 1:27) reports that the first human was created on the sixth day *in the image of God* (בצלם אלהים ברא אתו; LXX κατ' εἰκόνα θεοῦ ἐποίησεν αὐτόν), Josephus rather tersely remarks: "Now on this day he also formed humanity" (ἐν ταύτῃ δὲ καὶ τὸν ἄνθρωπον ἔπλασε; *A.J.* 1.32). This is a curious departure from the biblical text, and, as Jacob Jervell observes, reference to the εἰκὼν θεοῦ is consistently omitted throughout *A.J.* 1–11:

> Josephus has suppressed the language of the divine likeness of humans in other places: With regard to Gen 5:1–3 he mentions the birth of Seth, but not the divine likeness of Adam (Gen 5:1) and the inferred likeness of Seth (Ant 1.83). In the account of Gen 9:6, the prohibition of murder is not grounded in the divine likeness of humanity, as it is in the biblical text (Ant 1.101). Likewise in his treatment of Gen 3:5, 22, the *eritis sicut dii* is reinterpreted as the promise of a "blessed life, which is in no respect inferior to (the life of) God" (Ant 1.42).[43]

Such remarkable consistency suggests intentionality, that is, that for whatever reason Josephus systematically *suppresses* (*unterdrückt*, to borrow Jervell's terminology) εἰκὼν θεοῦ and related concepts from his narrative. According to Jervell's analysis, this omission must be understood within the context of Josephus' understanding of the nature of God and the second commandment in *C. Ap.* 2.167, 190ff.: "For Josephus there is no *imago Dei*, because God himself, his essence, his form, cannot be represented.... Thus he combined creation history with the first

42. James L. Kugel, *Traditions of the Bible: A Guide to the Bible as It Was at the Start of the Common Era* (Cambridge: Harvard University Press, 1998), 23.

43. Jacob Jervell, "Imagines und Imago Dei: Aus der Genesis-Exodus des Josephus," in *Josephus-Studien: Untersuchungen zu Josephus, dem antiken Judentum und dem Neuen Testament* (ed. Otto Betz, Klaus Haacker, and Martin Hengel; Göttingen: Vandenhoeck & Ruprecht, 1974), 198.

and second commandments (prohibition of images). For him this renders impossible the notion of the image of God."[44] While it is perhaps an overstatement to suggest that Josephus is plagued with an acute case of iconophobia, possessing what Jervell describes as an "allergic" (*allergisch*) reaction to images,[45] he is nevertheless correct in linking the omission of εἰκὼν θεοῦ with Josephus' broader treatment of the topic of images and the second commandment.

In a provocative essay on cult statues devoted to YHWH during the first-temple period, Herbert Niehr raises the possibility that צלם and דמות in Gen 1:26–27 are used synonymously for "statue" and further suggests that humans in this text are "thus created to be the living statues of the deity."[46] Whether or not Niehr's analysis of the original text is correct, there are indications that later Jews and Christians interpreted the *imago Dei* of Gen 1 in this sense, that is, that צלם אלהים/εἰκὼν θεοῦ was in some fashion viewed through the lens of the numerous statues that populated the Mediterranean landscape.[47] For example, the pseudepigraphical *Vita Adae et Evae* repeatedly invokes the language of cult images in its description of Adam and even claims that God required all the angels to bow down and worship (*adora*) this *imago Dei* (*Vita Adae et Evae* 13.3; 14.1–2; 15.2). Likewise, Philo of Alexandria, commenting on Gen 2:7, describes the human body as the most godlike of images (ἀγαλμάτων τὸ θεοειδέστατον; *Opif.* 136–137), an interpretation that is perpetuated in both Origen and Clement of Alexandria, who juxtapose ἄγαλμα, the conventional term for a cult statue, along with εἰκών in their interaction with the *imago Dei* of Gen 1 (Origen, *Cels.* 8.17–18; Clement of Alexandria, *Protr.* 10.98.3; 12.121.1). Pseudo-Justin Martyr also seems to share this perspective when he claims that the Greeks learned to fashion images of the gods from Moses' words "let us make man in our image" (*Cohort. ad gent.* 34).

Moreover, the link between humanity and cult statues is not unique to Jews and Christians but can be found in other Greek and Latin texts from antiquity. For example, on two occasions Plutarch uses ἄγαλμα for humans, once by noting that humans through virtue become an ἄγαλμα (*Princ. Iner.* 780F1) and, in another context, identifying a human father as an ἄγαλμα of Zeus that deserves respect (*Frag.* 46.17–19).[48] Josephus' omission of εἰκὼν θεοῦ should thus be understood within this broader context. In other words, given the potentially cultic implica-

---

44. Ibid., 202–3. See also Jervell's discussion of other scholarly proposals on pp. 199–200.

45. Ibid., 204.

46. Herbert Niehr, "In Search for YHWH's Cult Statue in the First Temple," in *The Image and the Book: Iconic Cults, Aniconism, and the Rise of Book Religion in Israel and the Ancient Near East* (ed. Karel van der Toorn; Louvain: Peeters, 1997), 93–94.

47. Morton Smith, "The Image of God: Notes on the Hellenization of Judaism, with Especial Reference to Goodenough's Work on Jewish Symbols," *BJRL* 40 (1958): 473–512; Morton Smith, "On the Shape of God and the Humanity of Gentiles," in *Religions in Antiquity: Essays in Memory of Erwin Ramsdell Goodenough* (ed. Jacob Neusner; Leiden: Brill, 1968), 315–26; Fletcher-Louis, "The Worship of Divine Humanity," 120–28.

48. For a general discussion of humans as statues, see Stewart, *Statues in Roman Society*, 112–16.

tions associated with this phrase, Josephus alters his narrative accordingly, removing anything that might possibly stand in tension with his portrayal of a primitive aniconic past.

Several other conspicuous omissions in *A.J.* 1–11 confirm the present hypothesis, most notably the famed golden statue of a calf, fashioned by none other than Aaron, Moses' brother and priest of YHWH (Exod 32). The absence of the golden-calf episode—the story of Moses' prolonged encounter with YHWH on Mount Sinai; the subsequent cultic festival to YHWH (חג ליהוה), which included sacrifices and worship offered to a golden statue of a calf (עגל מסכה); and finally the indelible image of Moses casting down and shattering the covenant tablets, which included the "writing of God engraved upon [them]"—is particularly striking, given its importance in both the biblical narrative and other Second Temple retellings of the Israelite story, such as Philo and Ps.-Philo (Philo, *Mos.* 2.161–162; *Ebr.* 95–96; Ps.-Philo, *L.A.B.* 12.2). Why avoid this episode?

According to Feldman, the image of an angry Moses breaking the tablets of God and destroying the calf would have conflicted with Josephus' otherwise self-controlled, Stoic Moses, the ideal lawgiver.[49] Additionally, the episode obviously reflects poorly on Moses' brother Aaron, the progenitor of a priestly lineage from which Josephus proudly hails, a detail that may have supplied further motivation to avoid the story.[50] While Feldman's interpretation may be correct, it seems likely that, given Josephus' overarching interests discussed in the present chapter, this episode also proved too damaging both to his portrait of a pristine aniconic past as well as the superior legal constitution on which it was based. In his account of Moses' leadership over the Israelites, Josephus points to the "fact" that the Hebrews had always observed the precepts of this constitution to the fullest extent, not having transgressed any of its laws, as evidence for the superiority of the Mosaic πολιτεία (*A.J.* 3.223). Although Josephus does acknowledge that a few in the distant past did violate the law against images, most notably the Israelite king Solomon (see below), it seems that the proximity of Aaron's egregious violation to the very origins of the law would have been especially troublesome.

In a similar vein, Josephus' omission of Moses' bronze statue of a serpent on a staff should be understood as an attempt to sanitize, so to speak, the biblical narrative, to remove any element that may undermine his portrait of an aniconic πολιτεία. According to Num 21, God commanded Moses to make a bronze serpent and to set it onto a pole:

> Then the LORD sent poisonous serpents among the people, and they bit the people, so that many Israelites died. The people came to Moses and said, "We have sinned by speaking against the LORD and against you; pray to the LORD to take away the serpents from us." So Moses prayed for the people. And the LORD said to Moses, "Make a poisonous serpent, and set it on a pole; and everyone who is bitten shall look at it and live." So Moses made a serpent of bronze (נחש נחשת; LXX ὄφις χαλκοῦς), and put it upon a pole (נס; LXX σημεῖον); and whenever a

49. Feldman, *Judean Antiquities 1–4*, 256.
50. Ibid., 255.

serpent bit someone, that person would look at the serpent of bronze and live. (Num 21:6–9 [nrsv])

Several features in this text could have been potentially problematic for Josephus. In the first place, a theriomorphic sculpture placed upon a standard (σημεῖον) recalls the Roman iconic *imago* that was usually crowned either with theriomorphic or anthropomorphic sculptures.[51] Obviously the image of Moses carrying an iconic standard would have stood in some tension with the Jews later in the narrative who resisted Pilate's iconic standards in defense of the Mosaic legislation against εἰκὼν ζῷου. That the very same νομοθέτης responsible for this aniconic legislation would, in response to a divine directive, craft (עשה/ποιέω) this figurative object adds an additional layer of difficulty to the episode—it is precisely the ποίησις of such images that Moses forbids in *A.J.*'s reformulation of the second commandment (*A.J.* 18.55).

Moreover, this particular sculpted image could plausibly be thought to have cultic associations, insofar as it contained healing properties and clearly mediated in some fashion the divine realm,[52] not unlike many of the Greco-Roman statues whose medicinal capacity could be awakened though sacrifices, rituals of consecration, or *formulae magicae*.[53] Indeed, given the popularity of the cult of Asclepius in the Greek and Roman periods,[54] a Roman reader would have undoubtedly associated the iconography of Moses' healing rod with the staff of the medicinal god Asclepius, which included a serpent entwined around a rod.[55] It is thus not at all surprising that Josephus would want to avoid the tale of Moses' bronze healing serpent.

In addition to the omissions detailed above, Josephus likewise felt free to alter certain apparently uncomfortable details in the biblical narrative in order to comport with his image of pristine aniconism. For example, the biblical account of Jacob's covert departure from his father-in-law Laban's house in Genesis includes a seemingly offhand remark that as they departed his wife Rachel "stole the figurines (תרפים; lxx εἴδωλα) of her father" (Gen 31:19). The biblical text never censures

51. See the discussion and literature cited in chapter 4

52. Indeed, cultic activity—incense offerings—is explicitly associated with the bronze serpent in the first temple (2 Kgs 18:4).

53. Although composed in the late fourth century c.e., Libanius' attempt to "desacralize" (rhetorically) the statue of Asclepius at Beroea in his *Pro Templis* oration attests to the widespread perceived healing potency of the god's image (see Ellen Perry, "Divine Statues in the Works of Libanius of Antioch: The Actual and Rhetorical Desacralization of Pagan Cult Furniture in the Late Fourth Century c.e.," in *The Sculptural Environment of the Roman Near East: Reflections on Culture, Ideology, and Power* [ed. Yaron Z. Eliav, Elise A. Friedland, and Sharon Herbert; Louvain: Peeters, 2008], 437–48).

54. Alice Walton, *The Cult of Asklepios* (Boston: Ginn, 1894); Emma J. Edelstein and Ludwig Edelstein, *Asclepius: Collection and Interpretation of the Testimonies* (Baltimore: Johns Hopkins University Press, 1998); Rives, *Religion in the Roman Empire*, 96.

55. A survey of extant representations of Asclepius (e.g., statues, relief portraits, coins, etc.) demonstrates the extent to which the image of a healing serpent staff was diffused throughout the Greco-Roman Mediterranean; see *LIMC* II.2, s.v. "Asklepios."

this act, and in any case it is not clear that the תרפים originally held any explicitly cultic association; nor does the narrator explain precisely why she stole the images. In the course of the narrative, Laban tries unsuccessfully to retrieve the images, after which the תרפים no longer play a role in the story.

Several features in Josephus' treatment of this episode, however, suggest a slight discomfort with the narrative as it stands.[56] In the first place, whereas the biblical text offers no motive for the theft, Josephus fills in this vacancy in a manner that exonerates Rachel from any potential charge of idolatry:[57]

> τοὺς δὲ τύπους ἐπεφέρετο τῶν θεῶν ἡ Ῥαχήλα καταφρονεῖν μὲν τῆς τοιαύτης τιμῆς τῶν θεῶν διδάξαντος αὐτὴν Ἰακώβου, ἵνα δ' εἰ καταληφθεῖεν ὑπὸ τοῦ πατρὸς αὐτῆς διωχθέντες ἔχοι τούτοις προσφυγοῦσα συγγνώμης τυγχάνειν.

> Now Rachel was carrying the images of the gods. Although Jacob taught her to despise this form of honoring the gods, [she took them] in order that, should they be pursued and overtaken by her father, she could find refuge in them to secure pardon. (*A.J.* 1.311)

As Feldman notes in his commentary on this passage, Josephus is not the only ancient Jewish interpreter to supply the missing motive.[58] Several later Jewish texts suggest that Rachel stole the תרפים precisely because she considered them efficacious. More specifically, because the תרפים were thought to possess powers of speaking,[59] Rachel was trying to keep them from disclosing to Laban their precise whereabouts (e.g., *Tg. Ps.-J.* Gen 31:19). According to Josephus, however, the תרפים (τύποι τῶν θεῶν) were stolen not to harness their divine powers, nor even for Rachel's personal cultic use, but as bargaining chips that, should the need arise, could be used to appease Laban's anger.[60]

Moreover, by noting that Jacob *had already* taught Rachel to despise idol worship, Josephus further mitigates the potential that Rachel was motivated by cultic allegiance. Josephus in this instance conflates Gen 31:19 with Gen 35:2, which does indeed present Jacob teaching his household to "put away the foreign gods among you" (הסרו את־אלהי הנכר אשר בתככם). However, in the biblical narrative, this instruction occurs *well after* the incident involving Laban's תרפים. Josephus shifts the chronology of Jacob's instruction to *precede* Rachel's actions and thus intimates that the theft had no connection to cultic activity. At the time of the theft, Rachel knew quite well Jacob's warning against idolatry. Finally, that Josephus sees fit in the wider context to highlight that Rachel alone was not honored with a distinguished burial at Hebron, an issue that is not accorded dishonor in the biblical narrative, may reflect a subtle criticism of the incident. In other words, regardless

56. See in general the discussion in Feldman, *Judean Antiquities 1–4*, 117.
57. Spilsbury, *The Image of the Jew*, 79–80.
58. Feldman, *Judean Antiquities 1–4*, 117.
59. For example, the תרפים of Zech 10:2 are said to speak: התרפים דברו־און.
60. Spilsbury, *The Image of the Jew*, 80.

of her motives, Rachel suffered the just consequences of her actions (*A.J.* 1.343; cf. Gen 35:19–20).[61]

Josephus' treatment of the תרפים in the story of David may show a similar aniconizing tendency. As the tension between David, anointed to be the next king of Israel, and Saul, his monarch father-in-law stricken with a fit of jealous rage, escalates, David enlists his wife Michal to cover for him while he flees the palace for safety. According to the account in 1 Samuel, Michal places תרפים under a garment on David's bed, with a quilt of goat's hair to resemble David's head, crafting a "mannequin" that would hopefully leave the impression that her husband was merely sick in bed (1 Sam 19:13–14). But notice how Josephus, in his retelling of this episode, explicitly removes the reference to the תרפים:

> ἔπειτα σκευάσασα τὴν κλίνην ὡς ἐπὶ νοσοῦντι καὶ ὑποθεῖσα τοῖς ἐπιβολαίοις ἧπαρ αἰγός, ἅμ' ἡμέρᾳ τοῦ πατρὸς ὡς αὐτὴν πέμψαντος ἐπὶ τὸν Δαυίδην ὠχλῆσθαι διὰ τῆς νυκτὸς εἶπε τοῖς παροῦσιν, ἐπιδείξασα τὴν κλίνην κατακεκαλυμμένην καὶ τῷ πηδήματι τοῦ ἥπατος σαλεύοντι τὴν ἐπιβολὴν πιστωσαμένη τὸ κατακείμενον τὸν Δαυίδην ἀσθμαίνειν.
>
> Then she prepared the bed as for one who was sick, and she placed in the covers a goat's liver. At daybreak, when her father sent for David, she informed those who had come that he had had a restless night, showing them the bed that had been covered over. And by shaking the covering and thus moving the liver, she persuaded them that David was sick in bed, breathing heavily. (*A.J.* 6.217)

The textual tradition for the original passage in 1 Samuel is actually somewhat garbled, so there is some question as to whether or not Josephus here intentionally removes the reference to the תרפים. The Latin Vulgate translates תרפים with both *statua* and *simulacrum*, and the Targum Jonathan and the Peshitta similarly translate the object in question with צלמניא and צלמא respectively. By contrast, the LXX substitutes κενοτάφια ("sarcophagi") for תרפים and further translates עזים ("goat's hair") with ἧπαρ τῶν αἰγῶν ("liver of goats"). If Josephus was working from or was familiar with the LXX (or a related) version of this text, which is certainly plausible given the shared reference to a goat's liver,[62] then the omission of תרפים may simply reflect a particular textual tradition and not a rhetorical maneuver. Nevertheless, in light of Josephus' obvious penchant elsewhere to omit or change the narrative to fit his overall aniconic scheme, we should not rule out the possibility of another aniconizing alteration in this instance.

Finally, Josephus' account of Solomon's "apostasy" perhaps best captures this tendency to sanitize or, in this case, to inject censure of, any potentially incriminating εἰκόνες in the biblical text. That Josephus devotes significantly more space to Solomon than the biblical text itself indicates the importance of this character

---

61. This point was raised by both Spilsbury and Feldman (Spilsbury, *The Image of the Jew*, 80; Feldman, *Judean Antiquities 1–4*, 124).

62. Although in Josephus the liver has, quite literally, a much more animated role in the narrative.

in *A.J.*[63] The narrative is on the whole positive, portraying Solomon as a paragon of virtue (ἀρετή), one who is characterized by courage, moderation, justice, and especially wisdom (σοφία) and piety (εὐσέβεια).[64] In particular, Solomon's exemplary εὐσέβεια is on display in his magnificent temple, which he constructed "for the honor of God" (εἰς τὴν τοῦ θεοῦ τιμήν; *A.J.* 8.95), a deed that ultimately established Solomon, at least in Josephus' estimation, as "the most glorious among all the kings (πάντων βασιλέων ἐνδοξότατος), and the most loved by God (θεοφιλέστατος)" (*A.J.* 8.190).[65] Nevertheless, when Josephus finally turns to the unavoidable topic of Solomon's downfall, his "departure from the observation of ancestral customs" (καταλιπὼν τὴν τῶν πατρίων ἐθισμῶν φυλακήν), it is this very testament of the king's εὐσέβεια—that is, his architectural achievements—that contains the first elements of his ἀσέβεια: theriomorphic images housed in the temple of God, as well as in the palace of the king (*A.J.* 8.190).[66]

The biblical text—more precisely, the Deuteronomic version of Solomon's reign—likewise follows a similar narrative trajectory, moving from Solomon's glorious beginning to his ultimate demise, although the emphasis here is on Solomon's insatiable desire for foreign women—(in)famously taking seven hundred wives and three hundred concubines from among the Egyptians, Moabites, Ammonites, Edomites, Sidonians, and Hittites—as a catalyst for his pursuit of foreign worship: "His women turned away his heart toward other gods (אלהים אחרים)" (1 Kgs 11:1–4). Josephus similarly mentions Solomon's trouble with women and the concomitant idolatry and even "heightens the erotic element,"[67] portraying Solomon as "insane" (ἐκμαίνω) for women, possessing an inability to control his passion for sexual pleasure (ἀφροδίσιος) and succumbing to the worship of other gods (θρησκεύειν θεούς) because of his consuming desire (ἔρως) for foreign women (*A.J.* 8.191–192). Nevertheless, in contrast with the biblical narrative, which unambiguously deploys the foreign women as the fountain of apostasy,

63. 1 Kgs 1:11–11:43; 1 Chr 22:2–23:1; 28:1–29:30; Josephus, *A.J.* 7.335–342, 348–362, 370–388; 8.2–211; Louis H. Feldman, "Josephus' Portrait of Solomon," *HUCA* 66 (1995): 109–10. See also Feldman's earlier treatment of the subject in "Josephus as an Apologist to the Greco-Roman World: His Portrait of Solomon," in *Aspects of Religious Propaganda in Judaism and Early Christianity* (ed. Elizabeth S. Fiorenza; Notre Dame, Ind.: University of Notre Dame Press, 1976), 69–98.

64. Feldman, "Portrait of Solomon," 165. According to Feldman, Josephus' portrayal of Solomon is rich with "Hellenizations," that is, material drawn from Greek authors such as Homer and Thucydides, among others (157–62).

65. Josephus uses the Greek term θεοφιλής earlier when he summarizes his purpose in relating the story of Solomon: "that all might know the magnificence of his nature, and that he was loved by God (τὸ θεοφιλές), and that the extraordinary quality of the king in every kind of virtue (πᾶν εἶδος ἀρετῆς) might not escape the notice of any under the sun" (*A.J.* 8.49).

66. On Solomon's apostasy in Josephus, see Christopher T. Begg, "Solomon's Apostasy (1 Kgs 11,1–13) according to Josephus," *JSJ* 28 (1997): 294–313; Spilsbury, *The Image of the Jew*, 184–87.

67. Christopher T. Begg and Paul Spilsbury, *Judean Antiquities 8–10* (Flavius Josephus: Translation and Commentary 5; ed. Steve Mason; Leiden: Brill, 2005), 50 n. 622.

Josephus identifies an earlier episode that marked the beginning of the end of the king's εὐσέβεια:

> καὶ πρὸ τούτων δὲ ἁμαρτεῖν αὐτὸν ἔτυχε καὶ σφαλῆναι περὶ τὴν φυλακὴν τῶν νομίμων, ὅτε τὰ τῶν χαλκῶν βοῶν ὁμοιώματα κατεσκεύασε τῶν ὑπὸ τῇ θαλάττῃ τῷ ἀναθήματι καὶ τῶν λεόντων τῶν περὶ τὸν θρόνον τὸν ἴδιον· οὐδὲ γὰρ ταῦτα ποιεῖν ὅσιον εἰργάσατο.
>
> But even *before* these [problems associated with foreign women], it so happened that he sinned and stumbled in the observance of the laws, when he made the representations of the bronze oxen beneath the "sea" as a votive offering, and the representations of lions which surrounded his own throne; for by making these things he produced that which was unholy.[68] (*A.J.* 8.195)

The forbidden objects in Josephus are described in detail in the biblical narrative, although, rather than censuring the images, the narrator describes them, along with other features adorning the Solomonic temple and palace, with language that approaches fawning admiration. The molten sea (הים מוצק), a large water basin supported by twelve oxen, is among a litany of temple vessels and architectural features devoted to and unambiguously accepted by YHWH, who consecrated (קדש) Solomon's temple (and by implication everything contained therein) and established his name there forever (1 Kgs 7:23–26; 9:3). Nevertheless, in Josephus' version of the Solomonic story, these very items—the theriomorphic images on the water basin, as well as those adorning the king's throne—function as the initial catalyst for Solomon's departure from the εὐσέβεια and σοφία of his youth.

In sum, Josephus' treatment of the biblical narrative in *A.J.* 1–11 betrays an interest in fostering an image of pristine aniconism, of an era in the primitive history of the Jews marked by the almost complete absence of figurative images. In other words, in the narrative world that Josephus constructs, the pious aniconic cult first instituted by Moses the lawgiver remains relatively intact, with only a few exceptional (and duly censured) moments of divergence from this ideal (most notably Solomon). As will be evident in the following, this idealization of primitive aniconism is not unique to Josephus but is in fact well attested in a wide range of non-Jewish Greek and Latin sources.

Aniconic Alterity and the "Evolution" of Mimesis

There is abundant archaeological evidence for the widespread use of aniconic cult objects—unworked stones, pillars, empty thrones, and other nonfigurative artifacts—in the Greco-Roman Mediterranean East.[69] Ethnographic literature, or ethnography embedded in other literary genres, would seem to confirm this general picture, frequently identifying aniconism, either the absence of cult images altogether or the use of nonfigurative cult objects, as a peculiar trait of alterity, a

68. Josephus mentions both of these sculpted items earlier without censure: bronze calves (μόσχοι instead of βόες) in *A.J.* 8.80 and lions in *A.J.* 8.140.

69. George F. Moore, "Baetylia," *AJA* 7 (1903): 198–208; Mettinger, *No Graven Image*; Stewart, "Baetyls as Statues," 297–314.

cultural symbol that in some sense functioned as an *indicium* of ethnic and, from a Greek or Roman perspective, foreign (usually Eastern) identity. Strabo, composing his *Geographica* either in the late first century B.C.E. or early first century C.E., is exemplary in this regard, noting with very little commentary that the Persians were distinct in their refusal to erect cult statues (ἀγάλματα) and altars (βωμοί; *Geogr.* 15.3.13), that the Nabateans similarly tended to avoid sculpted images (*Geogr.* 16.4.26), and that the Judeans were conspicuous for refusing the practice of image-carving (ξοανοποιέω), the shaping of gods in human form (ἀνθρωπομόρφους τυποῦντες), instead insisting on an empty sanctuary, a cult without an image (ἕδους χωρίς; *Geogr.* 16.2.35). Strabo likewise describes Egyptian temples that had no cult statue (ξόανον) in human form (ἀνθρωπόμορφον), though they did contain theriomorphic images (*Geogr.* 17.1.28). Robert Parker's observation on the inextricable link in Greek society between ethnicity and deity—"between who you are and who you worship"—is thus in some sense equally true with respect to the perception of cult objects: you are *what* you worship, with the implication that the aniconic worship of Eastern *ethnē* marked these cultures as "others," as the antithesis of the Greeks and Romans.[70]

Nevertheless, notwithstanding the frequent link between aniconism and ethnic alterity, numerous sources from antiquity additionally characterize *primitive* Greek and Roman worship as aniconic, underscoring a *chronological* dimension of aniconic alterity. For example, the *Diegesis* to *Aetia*, a summary (ca. 100 C.E.) of a Greek poem by Callimachus (a third-century B.C.E. Greek poet from Cyrene), mentions that in the distant past (πάλαι) the ξόανον of Hera was "unworked, seeing that the art of carving *agalmata* was not yet advanced" (*Diegesis* to Callimachus, *Aetia* IV fr. 100).[71] Likewise, the second-century C.E. Pausanias, in commenting on the square stones (τετράγωνοι λίθοι) worshiped by the people of Pharae, remarks: "Even among all the Greeks, *in a more remote age* (παλαιότερα), unworked stones (ἀργοὶ λίθοι) received divine honors instead of cult statues (ἀγάλματα)" (*Descr.* 7.22.4).[72] Although Pausanias' occasional reference to similar unworked aniconic objects in Greece presumes their presence in his day,[73] when juxtaposed with his descriptions of a Greek landscape saturated with innumerable anthropomorphic statues, the reader is left with the unmistakable impression that such aniconic artifacts are merely fossilized remnants of a distant past.[74]

As a literary trope, the nexus of aniconism and archaic alterity can be traced back as far as Herodotus (fifth century B.C.E.), and it is here that we can first observe both the ethnic and chronological dimensions of aniconic identity that will become a staple in literary portrayals of aniconism in subsequent centuries. On at least two occasions Herodotus forges an explicit link between aniconism and

70. Robert Parker, *Cleomenes on the Acropolis* (Oxford: Clarendon Press, 1998), 12.

71. Trans. Donohue, *Xoana and the Origins of Greek Sculpture*, 265.

72. On Greek aniconism, see especially Marinus Willem de Visser, *Die nicht menschengestaltigen Götter der Griechen* (Leiden: Brill, 1903); Dieter Metzler, "Anikonische Darstellungen," *Visible Religion* 5 (1986): 96–113; Gaifman, "Beyond Mimesis."

73. Stewart, *Statues in Roman Society*, 68.

74. Gaifman, "Beyond Mimesis," 14.

foreign cults, although, in both cases, the emphasis in the broader context is not on the cult objects per se but on the ritual activities, especially sacrificial practices, associated with a particular ethnic group.[75] In his description of the Persians, the historian remarks:

> Πέρσας δὲ οἶδα νόμοισι τοιοισίδε χρεωμένους, ἀγάλματα μὲν καὶ νηοὺς καὶ βωμοὺς οὐκ ἐν νόμῳ ποιευμένους ἱδρύεσθαι, ἀλλὰ τοῖσι ποιεῦσι μωρίην ἐπιφέρουσι, ὡς μὲν ἐμοὶ δοκέειν, ὅτι οὐκ ἀνθρωποφυέας ἐνόμισαν τοὺς θεοὺς κατά περ οἱ Ἕλληνες εἶναι.
>
> As to the usages of the Persians, I know them to be these. It is not their custom to make and set up statues and temples and altars, but those who make such they deem foolish, as I suppose, because they never believed the gods, as do the Greeks, to be in the likeness of men. (*Hist.* 1.131 [Godley, LCL])

This passage, by excluding from the domain of Persia what François Hartog has identified as the quintessential "signs of Greekness" (i.e., the triad of statues, temples, and altars), portrays the Persians as the antithesis of the Greeks.[76] Herodotus proffers a theological explanation for this practice, whereby the presence or absence of figurative cult images is directly linked to conflicting perceptions of the divine—that is, whether or not the gods are perceived to embody a human likeness (ἀνθρωποφυής).

Herodotus' description of the Scythians likewise employs the absence of this same cultic triad—statues, temples, and altars—as a defining feature of this *ethnos*, noting only the exception of the cult of Ares, whose ἄγαλμα among the Scythians is nevertheless non-anthropomorphic, an ancient iron scimitar (ἀκινάκης ἀρχαῖος; *Hist.* 4.59–62).[77] Leaving aside the accuracy of Herodotus' claims or whether the author is sympathetic toward such aniconic practices,[78] that Herodotus elsewhere identifies this cultic triad as an invention of the Egyptians, which was then passed on to the Greeks (*Hist.* 2.4), suggests that the absence of the triad bespeaks the persistence of a primitive cult, that the Persians and Scythians are still "living in a bygone age."[79] This interpretation is further confirmed by Herodotus' reference to the antiquity (ἀρχαῖος) of the Scythian non-anthropomorphic ἄγαλμα. Moreover, that primitive Greeks acquired the cultic triad at some point in history implies that they too were once marked by the aniconism of the Persians and Scythians, at least until coming under the influence of the Egyptians. In other words, Greek figurative cult objects were the result of a diachronic development.

In the light of evidence, both archaeological and literary, attesting to an archaic Greek aniconism, art historians have tended to view the use of aniconic cult ob-

75. Ibid., 105–13.

76. François Hartog, *The Mirror of Herodotus: The Representation of the Other in the Writing of History* (Berkeley: University of California Press, 1988), 176.

77. On the Scythian worship of the scimitar, see also Clement of Alexandria, *Protr.* 4.40.

78. But see the discussion and literature cited in Gaifman, "Beyond Mimesis," 111–12.

79. Hartog, *The Mirror of Herodotus*, 176.

jects as merely a early phase in the evolution of *mimesis*, a primitive era of crude artistic skill that gradually progresses through semi-iconic artifacts (such as the herm, a pillar typically adorned with a phallus and crowned with a fully figural bust) until it blossoms into the anthropomorphic sophistication of classical Greek sculpture.[80] Whereas later Greeks and Romans thus represent the apex of artistic sophistication (*mimesis*), masters of the art of naturalism, Eastern cultures and "prehistoric" Greeks represent the antithesis of "good art," a crude, rustic, unrefined, inferior mode of representation.

Recent scholarship has rightly called into question this evolutionary model as well as many of the assumptions on which it is based, particularly that aniconism was *merely* a primitive phase of artistic expression and that aniconism and iconism were mutually exclusive modes of representation.[81] Nevertheless, as Alice Donohue notes, it is precisely because numerous ancient sources preserve the notion of aniconism as a vestige of primitive alterity that modern scholars "have seized upon this testimony" to posit the idea of evolutionary *mimesis*.[82] While this literary testimony may in fact distort the situation "on the ground," it nevertheless attests to a pervasive *perception* that aniconic worship bespeaks "otherness," not only the alterity of ethnicities, but also of bygone eras.

The Piety of Primitive Aniconism

In a historical context that valued the distant past, that found in the characters, deeds, and customs of remote ages exempla for the present, it is not surprising that the link between aniconism and archaism discussed above would engender a notion of aniconic piety, that ancestral aniconic worship, because of its antiquity and simplicity, was somehow thought to be purer than the present manifestation and multiplication of anthropomorphic gods.[83] For example, Porphyry, the third-century C.E. pupil of the famed Neoplatonic philosopher Plotinus, remarks:

> διὰ τοῦτο καὶ τοῖς κεραμεοῖς ἀγγείοις καὶ τοῖς ξυλίνοις καὶ πλεκτοῖς ἐχρῶντο καὶ μᾶλλον πρὸς τὰς δημοτελεῖς ἱεροποιίας, τοιούτοις χαίρειν πεπεισμένοι τὸ θεῖον. ὅθεν καὶ τὰ παλαιότατα ἔδη κεραμεᾶ καὶ ξύλινα ὑπάρχοντα μᾶλλον θεῖα νενόμισται διά τε τὴν ὕλην καὶ τὴν ἀφέλειαν τῆς τέχνης. τὸν γοῦν Αἰσχύλον φασί, τῶν Δελφῶν ἀξιούντων εἰς τὸν θεὸν γράψαι παιᾶνα, εἰπεῖν ὅτι βέλτιστα Τυννίχῳ πεποίηται· παραβαλλόμενον δὲ τὸν αὑτοῦ πρὸς τὸν ἐκείνου ταὐτὸν πείσεσθαι τοῖς ἀγάλμασιν τοῖς καινοῖς πρὸς τὰ ἀρχαῖα· ταῦτα γὰρ καίπερ ἀφελῶς

---

80. See the discussion of this trend in scholarship in Gaifman, "Beyond Mimesis," 29–57.

81. Gaifman notes, for example, that the archaeological evidence from fifth-century B.C.E. Greece indicates that archaic, unworked aniconic cult objects were often placed side-by-side with iconic images (ibid., 11–12). See also Alice Donohue's study of ξόανον, which among other things documents the coexistence of iconic with aniconic in the Roman Imperial period (*Xoana and the Origins of Greek Sculpture*).

82. Ibid., 219.

83. Dieter Metzler observes that, at least with some Greeks and Romans, aniconism was perceived as especially sublime (*sublim*) and unspoiled (*unverdorben*) ("Anikonische Darstellungen," 100).

> πεποιημένα, θεῖα νομίζεσθαι, τὰ δὲ καινὰ περιέργως εἰργασμένα θαυμάζεσθαι μέν, θείου δὲ δόξαν ἧττον ἔχειν.
>
> On account of this they use vessels of clay and wood and wicker, and especially for public sacrifices, believing that divinity takes pleasure in such things. For this reason, too, the oldest enthroned gods that are of clay and wood are considered to be more divine on account of both the material and the simplicity of their craft. It is said too that Aeschylus, when the Delphians had asked him to write a *paean* in honor of Apollo, said that the best had been done by Tynnichus; if his own work were compared with that man's, the same thing would happen as when new statues are compared with old ones; for these, although made simply, are considered divine, while the new ones that are elaborately worked, although they are marveled at, have an inferior notion of god.[84] (*Abst.* 2.18)

Porphyry's comment points to the iconographic and materialistic simplicity of ancient statues as an indication of a heightened divine presence, contrasting the more divine though rustic ἀρχαῖα with the newer but spiritually inferior ἀγάλματα. While Porphyry's ἀρχαῖα are not explicitly identified as nonfigurative per se, that elaborate craftsmanship functions as an index of an "inferior notion of god" implies the inverse. The less intricate the craftsmanship, and unworked aniconic objects would certainly represent the pinnacle of simplicity, the higher the notion of god. Moreover, by locating the simplicity of craftsmanship within the distant past, the historiographic implication is clear: figuring images, or *mimesis*, was an indication of a *decline* in cultic piety.[85] Peter Stewart's recent comments on this perception of archaic images are worth noting in this regard: "In general, archaism in Greco-Roman art can be seen as a means to endow particular iconic cult images with a certain sort of aura: it is the stylistic antidote to iconography, the antidote to anthropomorphism and naturalism."[86]

The historiographical schema that posits a correlation between the rise of *mimesis* and decline of piety is particularly evident in traditions of Rome's mythical aniconic past.[87] That some Roman traditionalists longed for the artistic and ar-

84. Trans. adapted from Donohue, *Xoana and the Origins of Greek Sculpture*, 430.

85. In addition to archaic simplicity discussed in this chapter, another explanation for the heightened spirituality attached to aniconic objects, particularly the various meteoric rocks that were worshiped in antiquity, was the belief that these heaven-sent objects, precisely because of their origins in the heavenly realms, were somehow imbued with divine powers. For example, Philo of Byblos remarks in his Phoenician history that "the God Ouranos invented *baetyli*, devising animated stones (λίθοι ἔμψυχοι)" (*apud* Eusebius, *Praep. ev.* 1.10.23). Likewise, Pliny describes *baetulos* as *sacra* with special powers (*Nat.* 37.46). As Freedberg correctly observes, "It is . . . not surprising that black meteoric stones falling from the sky should have come to be worshiped. Their divine origins were self-evident; they seemed to be sent by specific gods and to be animated by the gods of whom they were a token" (*The Power of Images*, 66).

86. Stewart, "Baetyls as Statues," 302.

87. See in general Lily Ross Taylor, "Aniconic Worship among the Early Romans," in *Classical Studies in Honor of John C. Rolfe* (ed. George Depue Hadzsits; Philadelphia: University of Pennsylvania Press, 1931), 305–14.

chitectural simplicity of Old Rome is apparent in Cato's lament, cited in Livy, that foreign *signa* (from Syracuse) and *ornamenta* (Corinthian and Athenian) were indicative of a lurking "danger" (*infesta*) in the Rome of his day (Livy, *Ab urb.* 34.4.4). In speaking to the ancestral (and archaic) *Lares*, which consisted of rustic old logs, the Roman poet Albius Tibullus (ca. 55–19 B.C.E.) recalls with nostalgia a day long ago when Romans "kept better faith" (*melius tenuere fidem*).[88] It seems that in certain segments of elite Roman society the notion of *Romana simplicitas* became a powerful tool for decrying perceived present-day corruptions.

The idea that Rome once worshiped the gods without images needs to be understood within the context of this moralizing impulse and nostalgia for the pious simplicity of bygone years. The most explicit representative of this perspective is the Roman antiquarian Varro (first century B.C.E.), whose various comments on Rome's aniconic origins in his now lost *Antiquitates rerum divinarum*, fragments of which are preserved in Augustine's *De civitate Dei*,[89] encapsulate this perception of primitive *pietas* eventually giving way to inferior forms of iconic worship.[90] Augustine first summarizes Varro's view of images as follows:

> Hunc Varro credit etiam ab his coli, qui unum Deum solum sine simulacro colunt, sed alio nomine nuncupari. Quod si ita est, cur tam male tractatus est Romae (sicut quidem et in caeteris gentibus), ut ei fieret simulacrum? Quod ipsi etiam Varroni ita displicet, ut cum tantae civitatis perversa consuetudine premeretur, nequaquam tamen dicere et scribere dubitaret quod hi qui populis instituerunt simulacra, et metum dempserunt, et errorem addiderunt.

> Varro believes that [Jupiter] is worshipped even by those who worship one God only, without an image, though he is called by another name. If this is true, why was he so badly treated in Rome, and also by other peoples, that an image was made for him? This fact displeased even Varro so much that, although bound by the perverse custom of his great city, he still never scrupled to say and write that those who had set up images for their peoples had both subtracted reverence and added error. (*Civ.* 4.9 [Green, LCL])

This excerpt underscores the link between aniconism and pious worship, with the presence of *simulacra* in Rome functioning for Varro, at least according to Augustine's assessment, as a critical index for Rome's departure from "reverent" worship.

---

88. Text and translation from Stewart, *Statues in Roman Society*, 73.

89. Burkhart Cardauns, *M. Terentius Varro Antiquitates rerum divinarum* (2 vols.; Wiesbaden, Germany: Franz Steiner, 1976).

90. For Varro's views on cult images, see especially the following studies: Taylor, "Aniconic Worship," 305–14; Hubert Cancik and Hildegard Cancik-Lindemaier, "The Truth of Images: Cicero and Varro on Image Worship," in *Representation in Religion: Studies in Honor of Moshe Barasch* (ed. Jan Assmann and Albert I. Baumgarten; Leiden: Brill, 2001), 43–49; George H. van Kooten, "Pagan and Jewish Monotheism according to Varro, Plutarch, and St Paul: The Aniconic, Monotheistic Beginnings of Rome's Pagan Cult—Romans 1:19–25 in a Roman Context," in *Flores Florentino: Dead Sea Scrolls and Other Early Jewish Studies in Honour of Florentino García Martínez* (ed. Anthony Hilhorst, Émile Puech, and Eibert Tigchelaar; Leiden: Brill, 2007), 637–42.

There is thus an explicit correlation between *simulacra* and *error*, with the former bearing responsibility for introducing the latter.

This framework of diachronic decline is given a more precise historical context in a second excerpt, which preserves several explicit citations of Varro:

> Dicit etiam antiquos Romanos plus annos centum et septuaginta deos sine simulacro coulisse. "Quod si adhuc," inquit, "mansisset, castius dii observarentur." Cui sententiae suae testem adhibet inter caetera etiam gentem Judaeam: nec dubitat eum locum ita concludere, ut dicat, qui primi simulacra deorum populis posuerunt, eos civitatibus suis et metum dempsisse, et errorem addidisse; prudenter existimans deos facile posse in simulacrorum stoliditate contemni. Quod vero non ait, Errorem tradiderunt; sed, addiderunt; jam utique fuisse etiam sine simulacris intelligi vult errorem. Quapropter cum solos dicit animadvertisse quid esset Deus, qui eum crederent animam mundum gubernantem, castiusque existimat sine simulacris observari religionem, quis non videat quantum propinquaverit veritati? Si enim aliquid contra vetustatem tanti posset erroris, profecto et unum Deum, a quo mundum crederet gubernari, et sine simulacro colendum esse censeret.
>
> He also says that for more than one hundred and seventy years the ancient Romans worshipped the gods without an image. "If this usage had continued to our own day," he says, "our worship of the gods would be more devout." And in support of his opinion he adduces, among other things, the testimony of the Jewish race. And he ends with the forthright statement that those who first set up images of the gods for the people diminished reverence in their cities as they added to error, for he wisely judged that gods in the shape of senseless images might easily inspire contempt. And when he says, not "handed down error," but "added to error," he certainly wants it understood that there had been error even without the images. Hence when he says that only those who believe God to be the soul which governs the world have discovered that he really is, and when he thinks that worship is more devout without images, who can fail to see how near he comes to the truth? If only he had had the strength to resist so ancient an error, assuredly he would have held that one God should be worshipped without an image. (*Civ.* 4.31 [Green, LCL])

Obviously Augustine here is exploiting Varro's remarks for his own polemical purposes, as evidenced in his attempt to seize on the verb *addo* to claim the presence of *error* even among Rome's aniconic ancestors.[91] Nevertheless, the explicit citations embedded within Augustine's polemics and, in particular, Varro's use of the comparative adjective *castius* are sufficient to establish that, for Varro, the aniconic worship of Rome's ancestors was in some sense *better* or *more pure* than present forms of iconic worship and, hence, "the development from an aniconic to an iconic religion is seen as a decline of Rome's religious golden age."[92] More-

91. Tertullian similarly assesses Roman religion, noting that "idolatry" was present even before the actual "idol" had been invented (*Idol.* 3.1).

92. Van Kooten, "Pagan and Jewish Monotheism," 638. Van Kooten thus rightly places Varro's comments within the context of what he terms the "historiography of decline," the notion that a golden age of pristine piety has gradually devolved into religious error.

over, according to Augustine, Varro supported his claim of aniconic superiority by pointing favorably to the example of the Jews. Although the reference to the *gens Iudaea* is Augustine's, that several other non-Jewish authors mention Jewish aniconism positively strengthens the likelihood that Augustine is accurately relaying the views of Varro.[93]

Nowhere do the surviving fragments of *Antiquitates rerum divinarum* identify the precise origins of Roman aniconism, though, presumably, given the framework of decline from a pristine golden age, Varro's putative aniconic era began with the foundation of Rome in 753 B.C.E. If so, then iconic worship was introduced, according to the implicit calculation in Varro's reference to 170 years, in 583 B.C.E., during the reign of Rome's fifth king, Tarquinius Priscus (616–579 B.C.E.). Lily Ross Taylor posits a legislative proscription of images very early in Rome's history, issued in an ultimately unsuccessful "effort to keep the native religion free from foreign ideas."[94] Taylor is perhaps too optimistic on the historical value of the collection of traditions attesting to this aniconic era, all of which postdate the founding of Rome by at least seven centuries. Roman aniconic legislation is probably best understood as an example of Freeberg's "historiographic myth."[95] Nevertheless, although Taylor's historical interpretation is dubious, and although Varro does not mention any specific *lex contra simulacra*,[96] several surviving traditions on Numa Pompilius, Rome's legendary second king and famed lawgiver, attest that at least by the first century C.E. the memory of an ancient Roman legal proscription against images was in circulation.

The most explicit and detailed discussion of Numa's aniconic legislation is preserved in Plutarch's biography of the king. Plutarch, like Varro, mentions an aniconic era consisting of 170 years,[97] though he adds (or at least preserves what may now be lost from Varro) an explicit link between this era and Rome's famed lawgiver Numa and further frames Numa's legislation against images within a philosophical context, specifically the teachings of Pythagorus:

---

93. In addition to Varro, the following non-Jewish sources refer, either substantively or in passing, to Jewish aniconism: Hecataeus of Abdera, *Aegyptiaca* (*apud* Diodorus Siculus, *Bibl. hist.* 40.3.3–4); Strabo of Amaseia, *Geogr.* 16.2.35; Livy, *Ab urb.* (*apud Scholia in Lucanum* 2.593 [see Stern, *Greek and Latin Authors*, 1:130]); Tacitus, *Hist.* 5.5.4; 5.9.1; Cassius Dio, *Hist. rom.* 37.17.2. With the possible exception of Tacitus, whose disdain for the *Iudaeus* is fairly transparent throughout his narrative, these authors describe Jewish aniconism in positive or, at the very least, neutral terms. For example, Cassius Dio remarks that Jews, insofar as they have no statue of their deity and instead believe the deity to be invisible (ἀειδῆ), "worship in a most remarkable fashion among men" (περισσότατα εἰκόνες θρησκεύουσι).

94. Taylor, "Aniconic Worship," 310.

95. Freedberg, *The Power of Images*, 54.

96. That we know of, although given the fragmentary state of this text and the possibility that Plutarch's reference to Numa's legislation is dependent upon Varro, it is reasonable to suppose that Varro did in fact discuss a specific prohibition against images.

97. The shared 170-year time frame raises the likelihood that Plutarch is dependent upon Varro (van Kooten, "Pagan and Jewish Monotheism," 645).

Ἔστι δὲ καὶ τὰ περὶ τῶν ἀφιδρυμάτων νομοθετήματα παντάπασιν ἀδελφὰ τῶν Πυθαγόρου δογμάτων. οὔτε γὰρ ἐκεῖνος αἰσθητὸν ἢ παθητόν, ἀόρατον δὲ καὶ ἄκτιστον καὶ νοητὸν ὑπελάμβανεν εἶναι τὸ πρῶτον, οὗτός τε διεκώλυσεν ἀνθρωποειδῆ καὶ ζῳόμορφον εἰκόνα θεοῦ Ῥωμαίους νομίζειν. οὐδ' ἦν παρ' αὐτοῖς οὔτε γραπτὸν οὔτε πλαστὸν εἶδος θεοῦ πρότερον, ἀλλ' ἐν ἑκατὸν ἑβδομήκοντα τοῖς πρώτοις ἔτεσι ναοὺς μὲν οἰκοδομούμενοι καὶ καλιάδας ἱερὰς ἱστῶντες, ἄγαλμα δὲ οὐδὲν ἔμμορφον ποιούμενοι διετέλουν, ὡς οὔτε ὅσιον ἀφομοιοῦν τὰ βελτίονα τοῖς χείροσιν οὔτε ἐφάπτεσθαι θεοῦ δυνατὸν ἄλλως ἢ νοήσει.

Now the laws [of Numa] concerning images are wholly consistent with the doctrines of Pythagoras. For he held that the first principle of being was neither perceptible nor capable of feeling, but was invisible, uncreated, and accessible only through the mind. In this vein Numa prohibited the Romans to worship an image of god in the form of a human or an animal. Neither was there any painted nor sculpted image of god among them during this time. Although they were building temples and setting up sacred shrines during the first hundred and seventy years, they did not make for themselves any figurative statue, since they did not believe it pious to liken that which is superior to that which is inferior, nor did they think it possible to apprehend god other than through the mind.[98] (*Numa* 8.7–8)

Earlier in this chapter I discussed Numa's reputation in Plutarch as a pious νομοθέτης, and the reference to this particular legislation should be viewed within that context. Numa functions as a hero of true piety, a legislator whose laws and constitution, including this particular proscription against images, reflect the purest expression of religiosity. Although Varro's chronological framework of decline is missing here, Plutarch nevertheless implies, by linking this legislation to sophisticated Pythagorean theology, its inherent superiority to the more iconic forms of cultic devotion.

Moreover, and herein lies the central relevance of this material for present discussion, Plutarch's description of Numa's aniconic legislation is strikingly reminiscent of Josephus' portrayal of the second commandment in *A.J.* As discussed in chapter 3, *A.J.* repeatedly places the stress on the craftsmanship (ποίησις) and iconography (εἰκών ζῴου/ἀνθρώπου) of the proscribed objects, in contrast with *B.J.*, which instead highlights the placement or location of an εἰκών. Plutarch likewise defines the scope of Numa's legislation with similar language, mentioning the same two iconographic categories—ἀνθρωποειδῆ καὶ ζῳόμορφον εἰκόνα—and stressing that the law prohibited *making* (ποιέω) statues in bodily form (ἔμμορφος). Additionally, the philosophical framework undergirding Plutarch's summary of Numa's legislation, although less conspicuous in *A.J.*, does recall Josephus' summary of the second commandment in another treatise composed shortly after *A.J.*, namely *C. Ap.* 2.190–192. In both Plutarch and Josephus the act of making bodily

98. See also Tertullian, *Apol.* 25.12–13, and Clement of Alexandria, *Strom.* 1.15.17.

statues is considered impious (οὔτε ὅσιον); both likewise stress the impossibility of a μορφή to capture that which can only be apprehended through νόησις.[99]

To be clear, I am not suggesting that Josephus' portrayal of the Mosaic legislation against images is dependent upon Plutarch's Numa, or vice versa. Rather, Plutarch's testimony attests to the fact that some Romans (and also Greeks) admired aniconic forms of cultic devotion and recalled a primitive age in Rome's history when a pious lawgiver, Numa, proscribed images in an effort to preserve the purity of Roman religiosity. In other words, Plutarch's legend of Numa attests to a sentimental nostalgia, likely circulating while Josephus was living in Rome and composing *A.J.*, for a time when "Old Rome was pure, manly, and aniconic [before] it was corrupted by the introduction of foreign art and foreign practices."[100] That Josephus' portrayal of Moses the νομοθέτης and his aniconic legislation recalls the language of Numa and Rome's aniconic golden age suggests not literary dependence but participation in a common cultural discourse. Josephus is sculpting, so to speak, Jewish aniconism into the image of Roman aniconism.

In sum, Josephus constructs in *A.J.* an image of Jewish ἀρχαιολογία centered on a lawgiver and his πολιτεία, the perfect embodiment of the moral ingredients—ἀρετή and εὐσέβεια—needed for a society to survive and even thrive. Integral to his portrayal of the primitive past is legislation establishing aniconic worship as an essential component of this ideal state and constitution; in other words, the absence of figural images bespeaks the health and piety of society. Moreover, Josephus' depiction of an aniconic ideal rooted in the legislation of a pious lawgiver is steeped in a Roman antiquarian tradition that idealized Rome's golden age, including the period of aniconic devotion, when her lawgivers exuded *virtus* and *pietas*, nurturing the state in peace and stability.

But as in the case of Rome's *antiquitates*, Josephus was well aware of the potential threat to this stability when the constitution and its laws were ignored. For example, Korah's resistance to Moses' leadership and legislation, though not involving a violation of the proscription of images, stirred up a rebellion (στάσις) that threatened to destroy the order of their constitution (ὁ κόσμος τῆς καταστάσεως; *A.J.* 4.36).[101] Indeed, the Korah pericope encapsulates a pervasive theme in *A.J.*, namely "the degree to which στάσις is the mortal enemy of political states."[102] And

99. For a fuller treatment of *C. Ap.* 2.190–192, see chapter 3 and Barclay, "Snarling Sweetly," 73–87.

100. Freedberg, *The Power of Images*, 63.

101. The use of κατάστασις here is synonymous with πολιτεία. The two terms are found together in *A.J.* 6.35, where Samuel's sons, unlike their father, pursue opulence and luxury (τρυφή) instead of justice and in the process wreak havoc "on their former ordinance and constitution" (ἐξυβριζόντων [εἰς] τὴν προτέραν κατάστασιν καὶ πολιτείαν). This usage continues in *C. Ap.*, where Josephus argues that the Judean κατάστασις is very ancient (*C. Ap.* 1.58) and then sets out to summarize the "whole constitution" of the Judean *politeuma* (περὶ τῆς ὅλης ἡμῶν καταστάσεως τοῦ πολιτεύματος; *C. Ap.* 2.145, and similar language in *C. Ap.* 2.184).

102. Feldman, "Portrait of Moses," 316–17. Feldman underscores the roots of this *topos* in Thucydides.

as the exemplum of Solomon demonstrates, the installation of figurative εἰκόνες, insofar as it represents a breach of the Judean πολιτεία, signals a decline from the ἀρετή and εὐσέβεια first envisioned by Moses. But even more significantly, as the tumultuous civil wars in Solomon's wake illustrate, departure from this aniconic ideal underscores the threat an εἰκών poses to the stability of the state. As I will argue in the following section, it is precisely this danger of στάσις—the anxiety over the potential destruction (ἀφανισμός) or dissolution (κατάλυσις) of the Mosaic πολιτεία and hence the stability and order of the entire Jewish state—that stands at the core of Josephus' treatment of the iconoclastic activity during the Herodian and early Roman periods.

ICONOCLASM AND CRISES OF πολιτεία

As noted above, the Korah rebellion introduces a major *topos* in *A.J.*: the Judean state has repeatedly faced down threats to constitutional stability imposed by civic strife. Actually, Josephus stresses that στάσις is a perennial danger shared by *both* Romans and Jews. His account of Gnaeus Sentius Saturninus' speech before the Senate, in response to the soldiers' attempt to elect Claudius emperor upon the death of Gaius Caligula, includes a rehearsal of Roman history that underscores the threat of στάσις to the Roman πολιτεία, focusing especially on the στάσις induced by Julius Caesar, who was disposed to "destroy the democracy" (ἐπὶ καταλύσει τῆς δημοκρατίας) when "he disrupted the constitution by wreaking havoc on the order of [Roman] laws" (διαβιασάμενος τὸν κόσμον τῶν νόμων τὴν πολιτείαν συνετάραξεν; *A.J.* 19.173). And following this pattern, Saturninus notes that Julius Caesar's successors likewise set out to "abolish the way of the ancestors" (ἐπ᾽ ἀφανισμῷ τοῦ πατρίου), leaving Rome and its constitution in a fragile state (*A.J.* 19.174).

The constellation of key terms that emerges in Saturninus' speech—στάσις; κατάλυσις; πολιτεία; νόμος; πάτριος—reappears with regular frequency in Josephus' treatment of εἰκών (and related terminology) in *A.J.*, suggesting that the major concern in *A.J.* is not simply a statue's violation of sacred space, as is the case in *B.J.*, but the capacity of an εἰκών to devastate the order and stability of Judean civilization. This is not to suggest that the issue of sacred space disappears altogether in *A.J.*, although in a few episodes of iconoclasm space does not enter the discussion, but that the constitutional threat consistently takes center stage, underscoring the danger an εἰκών poses for the survival of the Jewish πολιτεία. Indeed, the very preservation of the latter depends in part on the persistent refusal of the former.

For example, Josephus recounts an episode, absent from *B.J.*, involving a group of unidentified "young men" (νεανίσκοι) who attempt to erect a statue of the emperor (Καίσαρος ἀνδριάς) in the synagogue of Dora, a Phoenician coastal city just a few miles to the north of Caesarea Maritima (*A.J.* 19.300–311).[103] The letter of

---

103. The precise identification of the νεανίσκοι is unclear. Josephus relates that Publius Petronius responded to the crisis by sending a letter to the ἀποστᾶσι τῶν Δωριτῶν (*A.J.* 19.302), perhaps implying that the perpetrators were in some sense Ἰουδαῖοι who had de-

Publius Petronius, the governor of Syria at the time, in response to the crisis does indeed identify the location of the statue as a problem, since by placing the statue "in it" (ἐν αὐτῇ; i.e., the synagogue) the perpetrators prevented the Jews from gathering together (συναγωγὴν Ἰουδαίων κωλύοντας). Presumably (though not explicitly) this was because the Jews considered the statue a desecration, although from Petronius' perspective the act violated an imperial decree granting the Jews power over their own space (τῶν ἰδίων τόπων κυριεύειν; *A.J.* 19.305). What is clear, however, is that Josephus frames this act not simply as a potential desecration of sacred space but as an act of sedition or rebellion (στάσις and ταραχή; *A.J.* 19.311). The perpetrators in the narrative are portrayed as an irrational and impious mob, on the cusp of unleashing civic chaos. They prized rash audacity (τόλμα) and "were recklessly arrogant by nature" (πεφυκότες εἶναι παραβόλως θρασεῖς), acting "by the impulse of a mob" (τῇ τοῦ πλήθους ὁρμῇ; *A.J.* 19.300, 307). Their attempt to erect the statue of Caesar was thus tantamount to an attempt to "dissolve his [i.e., Agrippa's] ancestral laws" (κατάλυσιν γὰρ τῶν πατρίων αὐτοῦ νόμων ἐδύνατο; *A.J.* 19.301). Petronius' response likewise focuses on the right of the Jews "to observe their ancestral ways" (φυλάσσειν τὰ πάτρια) and "to act according to their own customs" (τοῖς ἰδίοις ἔθεσι χρῆσθαι; *A.J.* 19.304). Indeed, it is precisely the preservation of these ancestral customs that will ensure civic order in Dora, enabling both the Jews and the Greeks to coexist as fellow citizens (συμπολιτεύεσθαι; *A.J.* 19.306).

The elements of civic strife detailed in the Dora pericope—portrayals of reckless youths and demagogues stirring up discord among the rabble, undermining ancestral ways and in the process wreaking havoc on the ancient constitution—recur with regular frequency in Roman literature as well, especially in the late Republican and early Imperial periods.[104] Plutarch's account of the turbulent years under Gaius Marius' multiple consulships is rife with such language, particularly in treating Marius' alliance with the tribune Lucius Saturninus, who along with Glaucia "had rash men and an unruly and tumultuous crowd at their disposal" (ἀνθρώπους θρασυτάτους καὶ πλῆθος ἄπορον καὶ θορυβοποιὸν ὑφ' αὑτοῖς ἔχοντας; *Mar.* 28.7). According to Plutarch, Saturninus' τόλμα led to "tyranny and the overthrow of the constitution" (τυραννίς καὶ πολιτείας ἀνατροπή; *Mar.* 30.1). The στάσις in the wake of Saturninus' demagoguery never fully subsided and again reached a boiling point in the conflict between Sulla and Marius, which inflicted on the city of Rome a "disease" (νοσέω) and incited Marius to pursue another "tool for the destruction of the state" (ὄργανον πρὸς τὸν κοινὸν ὄλεθρον) in the rash (θράσος) Sulpicius

fected from the ways of their ancestors. However, the actual letter included in the narrative is addressed to the city magistrates (Δωριέων τοῖς πρώτοις in *A.J.* 19.303; τοῖς πρώτοις ἄρχουσι in *A.J.* 19.308). It may be that while the official correspondence was indeed addressed to city officials, Josephus mistakenly narrates that the letter was addressed to the perpetrators. If this is the case, then it still perhaps suggests that at least in Josephus' view the νεανίσκοι were ἀποστάντες.

104. See for example the useful material collected in Paul J. J. Vanderbroeck, *Popular Leadership and Collective Behavior in the Late Roman Republic (ca. 80–50 B.C.)* (Amsterdam: Gieben, 1987).

(*Mar.* 32.5; 35.1). This conflict then climaxed with a Marius-Cinna alliance in an effort to continue this "war against the established constitution" (πολεμοῦντα τῇ καθεστώσῃ πολιτείᾳ; *Mar.* 41.5).

Whatever the truth that lies behind Plutarch's obvious bias in relating these events, it is abundantly clear in this and other similar texts that the preservation of ancestral ways to ensure the stability of political constitutions was very much a live issue in first-century c.e. Roman society, particularly in the wake of the political crises and civil wars following the death of Nero. In depicting the tension over the Καίσαρος ἀνδριάς in Dora, Josephus thus echoes this larger civic discourse, framing the Jews' resistance to statues as an effort to preserve the stability and order of the commonwealth.[105]

A closer look at the other accounts of first-century Jewish iconoclasm in *A.J.* confirms the centrality of the theme of constitutional stability through the preservation of ancestral ways. The account of Caligula's statue, which in *B.J.*'s much shorter version restricts the focus to the impiety (ἀσεβής) of an emperor who would dare desecrate the temple in Jerusalem (*B.J.* 2.184–203), opens in *A.J.* not with the potential desecration of Jerusalem but with a στάσις that had erupted in Alexandria between the Ἰουδαῖοι and the Ἕλληνες (*A.J.* 18.257–260). Delegates from the various factions, which included Philo and Apion, were sent to Rome to appear before the emperor Gaius, with Apion blaming the στάσις in part on the Jews' refusal to honor the emperor with statues (ἀνδριάντες). The irony as the narrative progresses, however, is that only by insisting on the statues, insofar as Gaius' demand necessitated a departure from the code of the νομοθέτης and προπάτορες by transgressing ancestral law (παραβάσει τοῦ πατρίου νόμου; *A.J.* 18.263–264), would the threat of στάσις be exacerbated, resulting in war, the chaos of banditry, and the slaughter of thousands, among other potential calamities (*A.J.* 18.274–278). Petronius' response to the Jews' refusal thus focuses on their legitimate right to insist on fidelity "to the virtue of the law" (τῇ ἀρετῇ τοῦ νόμου), contrasting adherence to τὰ πάτρια with the "hubris of imperial authority" (ὕβρει . . . τῆς τῶν ἡγεμονευόντων ἐξουσίας; *A.J.* 18.280). Likewise, Agrippa I's intervention before Gaius on behalf of the Ἰουδαῖοι, details of which are not recounted in *B.J.*, stresses the tranquillity of the commonwealth (τοῦ κοινοῦ ἡ εὐθυμία) by paying special honor in part to Jewish νόμοι (*A.J.* 18.300).

The episode involving Pilate's military standards similarly underscores this leitmotif. As noted in chapter 4, whereas Josephus in *B.J.* concentrates on the *placement* of the iconic standards as the locus of conflict,[106] in *A.J.* the standards violate a law that forbids the very making of images (εἰκόνων ποίησις). An additional difference between the two, however, resides in the characterization of Pilate and the purported effect of his actions.[107] While in both what is at stake is a violation

105. Mason discusses briefly the need to read Josephus' treatment of constitutional themes in the context of Roman political discourse (Mason, "Aim and Audience," 80–87).

106. *B.J.* 2.170, where the law forbids placing an image in the city (ἐν τῇ πόλει δείκηλον τίθεσθαι).

107. Contra Seth Schwartz, who suggests that the two portrayals of Pilate "scarcely differ" (Schwartz, *Josephus and Judaean Politics*, 197).

of Jewish law, only in *A.J.* are the military standards introduced as an act of intentional provocation, contributing to a more insidious and malevolent caricature of Pilate:

> Πιλᾶτος δὲ ὁ τῆς Ἰουδαίας ἡγεμὼν στρατιὰν ἐκ Καισαρείας ἀγαγὼν καὶ μεθιδρύσας χειμαδιοῦσαν ἐν Ἱεροσολύμοις ἐπὶ καταλύσει τῶν νομίμων τῶν Ἰουδαϊκῶν ἐφρόνησε.
>
> Now when Pilate, the procurator of Judea, led the army from Caesarea and transferred it to Jerusalem for winter quarters, he was intent on the subversion of Jewish laws. (*A.J.* 18.55)

The version of this episode in *B.J.* includes no such ascription of motive, but in *A.J.* Pilate's attempt to introduce "busts of Caesar affixed to standards" (προτομὰς Καίσαρος αἳ ταῖς σημαίαις προσῆσαν) is quite explicitly an act of political subversion, an audacious attempt to transgress the ancestral ways of the Jews. Josephus further underscores this flaw in Pilate's character by contrasting Pilate with the previous procurators who used "standards with no such adornments" (ταῖς μὴ μετὰ τοιῶνδε κόσμων σημαίαις; *A.J.* 18.56). Pilate in *A.J.* is also implicitly contrasted in this regard with Vitellius, the governor of Syria, who upheld the πάτριον of the Jews both by not bringing military standards into Judea and by partaking in the celebration of a Jewish ancestral festival (ἑορτὴ πατρίου; *A.J.* 18.120–122). Whereas in the episode of the εἰκών in Dora it is a youthful mob that threatens to wreak havoc on the health of the commonwealth through its blatant disregard of ancestral customs, in the pericope involving Pilate, as also that of Gaius Caligula, the emphasis shifts to a careless authority figure who similarly destabilizes civic tranquillity by subverting τὰ πάτρια. This feature, as we will now see, is likewise apparent in *A.J.*'s treatment of iconoclasm under Herod the Great's rule.

It has long been noted that the character of Herod becomes significantly darker in *A.J.* vis-à-vis *B.J.*[108] Some have explained the seemingly contradictory portraits of Herod as an indication of Josephus' careless and indiscriminate use of disparate sources.[109] Others have suggested a change in Josephus' own religious attitude, seeing in *A.J.* a more pronounced nationalism and "religious-Pharisaic bias" that leads to a more hostile treatment of Herod.[110] But the evidence for a "Pharisaic bias" or advocacy of an emerging rabbinic movement in *A.J.* is dubious,[111] and it seems more likely that the different portrayals of Herod should be attributed to rhetorical or compositional strategies. Specifically, while both texts feature the

108. See, for example, Laqueur, *Der jüdische Historiker Flavius Josephus*, 127–34; Cohen, *Josephus in Galilee and Rome*, 56–57; Fuks, "Josephus on Herod's Attitude," 238–45; Tessa Rajak, "The Herodian Narratives of Josephus," in *The World of the Herods* (vol. 1 of *The International Conference: The World of the Herods and the Nabataeans* (ed. Nikos Kokkinos; Stuttgart: Franz Steiner Verlag, 2007), 23–34.

109. See, for example, Solomon Zeitlin, "Herod a Malevolent Maniac," *JQR* 54 (1963): 1–27; and Moses Aberbach, "Josephus: Patriot or Traitor?" *Jewish Heritage* 10 (1967): 13–19.

110. Cohen, *Josephus in Galilee and Rome*, 148–49.

111. See especially Mason, *Flavius Josephus on the Pharisees.*

problem of στάσις as a threat to civic order, in *A.J.* Josephus highlights in a more pronounced fashion the culpability of rogue authority figures, whereas *B.J.* is more interested in placing responsibility on Jewish revolutionary groups, particularly as an explanation for the revolt against Rome in 66 C.E.

The problem of the εἰκών during Herod the Great's rule is likewise more enhanced in *A.J.* than in *B.J.* While both narratives describe the incident involving the eagle erected over the temple gate, Josephus adds in *A.J.* a second episode—the trophies adorning the theater in Jerusalem—that heightens the threat posed by an εἰκών and underscores the role of a reckless tyrant in precipitating a constitutional crisis through the blatant disregard of ancestral customs (*A.J.* 15.267–291).

The literary structure of the pericope involving the trophy crisis is framed by two central concerns: an endangered constitution on the one end (*A.J.* 15.267) and the threat of open rebellion (ἀπόστασις) on the other end (*A.J.* 15.291).[112] The opening sentence explicitly underscores the first of these two interrelated problems: "For this reason also [Herod] utterly departed from the ancestral customs, and he corrupted with foreign practices the ancient constitution" (διὰ τοῦτο καὶ μᾶλλον ἐξέβαινεν τῶν πατρίων ἐθῶν καὶ ξενικοῖς ἐπιτηδεύμασιν ὑποδιέφθειρεν τὴν πάλαι κατάστασιν; *A.J.* 15.267). The immediate antecedent of διὰ τοῦτο is a depiction of Herod's unbridled lust for power. After successfully besieging and overtaking a Jerusalem under the control of the Hasmonean Antigonus, Herod orders the brutal execution of the family of Hyrcanus, effectively consolidating the Judean kingdom under his own power and removing any potential "obstacle to block his lawless behavior" (παρανομέω; *A.J.* 15.266). In this light, διὰ τοῦτο then initiates a catalog of impious deeds, including the erection of τρόπαια in the theater of Jerusalem, that serve to demonstrate the various ways the Judean king displays tyranny by wreaking havoc on τὰ πάτρια ἔθη and ἡ πάλαι κατάστασις.

On the surface the crisis of this narrative revolves around Herod's theater in Jerusalem, both as the primary stage—literally and literarily—on which the events transpire and as the focal point of the controversy. Indeed, the very first charge leveled against Herod was that "he instituted the quinquennial athletic contests in honor of Caesar and erected a theater in Jerusalem, and following this a very large amphitheater in the plain."[113] Josephus notes that these remarkably extravagant (περίοπτα τῇ πολυτελείᾳ) structures were "foreign to Jewish custom" (κατὰ

112. On this passage in general, see Jan Willem van Henten, "The Panegyris in Jerusalem: Responses to Herod's Initiative (Josephus, *Antiquities* 15.268-291)," in *Empsychoi Logoi—Religious Innovations in Antiquity: Studies in Honour of Pieter Willem van der Horst* (ed. Alberdina Houtman, Albert de Jong, and Magda Misset-van de Weg; Leiden: Brill, 2008), 151–73.

113. On possible traces of the theater and amphitheater in the archaeological record, see C. Schick, "Herod's Amphitheatre," *PEQ* 19 (1887): 161–66; R. Reich and Y. Billig, "A Group of Theater Seats Discovered Near the South-western Corner of the Temple Mount," *IEJ* 50 (2000): 175–84. For the argument that Herod's theater was a temporary wooden structure, see Patrich, "Herod's Theatre in Jerusalem," 231–39; Achim Lichtenberger, "Jesus and the Theater in Jerusalem," in *Jesus and Archaeology* (ed. James H. Charlesworth; Grand Rapids: Eerdmans, 2006), 283–99.

τοὺς Ἰουδαίους ἔθους ἀλλότρια) insofar as they housed "spectacles" (θεάματα) unknown to Jewish tradition (*A.J.* 15.268).[114] He further underscores the problem of "the spectacle of dangers" (ἡ θέα κινδύνων), contrasting the reactions of the ξένοι, who are both amazed and entertained, and the ἐπιχώριοι, who viewed the spectacle as a "blatant disregard for the customs which were esteemed by them" (φανερὰ κατάλυσις τῶν τιμωμένων παρ' αὐτοῖς ἐθῶν; *A.J.* 15.274).

Yet as the narrative continues to unfold, the reader soon discovers, perhaps with an element of surprise, that while "throwing men to beasts to thrill spectators was impious (ἀσεβής)," as was "exchanging [Jewish] customs with foreign practices," what exceeded all of these immoral deeds (πάντων μᾶλλον), and what constituted the greatest danger to the πάλαι κατάστασις, were the τρόπαια τῶν ἐθνῶν adorning the theater (*A.J.* 15.275–276). The use of μᾶλλον here thus heightens the extent of the impiety introduced by Herod, locating the apex of ἀσεβής and κατάλυσις ἐθῶν not primarily in the bloody spectacles transpiring in the theater but in the τρόπαια adorning the structure.

Why such vexation over these seemingly innocuous objects? The ensuing γάρ clause explains: the problem was actually not the trophies themselves, but what the Jewish protagonists perceived (δοκέω) the trophies to be—εἰκόνες "encased within the weaponry." Josephus again heightens the impious nature of the τρόπαια (as εἰκόνες) vis-à-vis the institution of the games, making the rather striking claim that, if given a choice, the Jews would much prefer the bloody spectacles to the εἰκόνες:

> οὐ μὴν ἔπειθεν, ἀλλ' ὑπὸ δυσχερείας ὧν ἐδόκουν ἐκεῖνον πλημμελεῖν ὁμοθυμαδὸν ἐξεβόων, εἰ καὶ πάντα δοκοῖεν οἰστά, μὴ φέρειν εἰκόνας ἀνθρώπων ἐν τῇ πόλει, τὰ τρόπαια λέγοντες οὐ γὰρ εἶναι πάτριον αὐτοῖς.
>
> However, he did not persuade them, but, because of their disgust at that deed of which they supposed he had erred, they cried out together that although everything else could be endured, they could not tolerate the images of men—by which they meant the trophies—in the city, since this was not consistent with ancestral law. (*A.J.* 15.277)

The phrase εἰκόνες ἀνθρώπων, recalling the language εἰκὼν ζῴου in *A.J.* 3.91, further clarifies the nature of the problem. The trophies, insofar as they were perceived to be anthropomorphic statues and objects of cultic devotion,[115] were viewed as a

114. These monumental entertainment structures and the θεάματα are further identified as evidence for Herod's φιλοτιμία (*A.J.* 15.271). On θέαμα in Josephus' *B.J.*, see especially Honora H. Chapman, "Spectacle and Theater in Josephus's *Bellum Judaicum*" (Ph.D. diss., Stanford University, 1998), and idem, "Spectacle in Josephus' *Jewish War*," in *Flavius Josephus and Flavian Rome* (ed. Jonathan Edmondson, Steve Mason, and James Rives; Oxford: Oxford University Press, 2005), 289–313.

115. Josephus explicitly links the trophies with the perception of cultic activity, describing them as "ornaments for cult statues" (κατασκευαὶ τῶν ἀγαλμάτων; *A.J.* 15.279) and noting that it was prohibited "to worship such things" (τὰ τοιαῦτα σέβειν; *A.J.* 15.276). On the cultic function of τρόπαια, see Gilbert Charles Picard, *Les trophées romains: Contribution à l'histoire de la religion et de l'art triomphal de Rome* (Paris: E. de Boccard, 1957), 95–97;

blatant violation of ancestral law (πάτριον). Only after Herod dismantles the trophies to reveal the true nature of the τρόπαια—"naked wood" (γυμνὰ τὰ ξύλα) beneath the military armor—is the crowd finally pacified (*A.J.* 15. 278–279).[116]

Although Roman military trophies are never described with the language of anthropomorphic statuary (apart from the pericope under discussion),[117] the extant "iconography"—mainly literary descriptions and representations in sculptural relief and on coins and seals—does illustrate the potential for such mistaken identity, confirming the plausibility of the scenario envisioned in Josephus' narrative.[118] As Valerie Hope notes, following Gilbert Charles Picard's analysis, the earliest type of trophy consisted of "a lopped tree adorned with captured weapons and to which prisoners were chained."[119] This is illustrated, for example, in the triumphal frieze from the Temple of Apollo Sosianus in Rome, which portrays Roman slaves preparing to lift a platform holding two prisoners chained beneath an armored trophy, clearly a wooden pole adorned with military accoutrements.[120] Yet the image conveyed in this scene is not simply the display of captured war booty, but of an armored conqueror—the τρόπαιον—holding captive vanquished soldiers. Likewise, while a close inspection of the military trophies from the Dacian wars represented on Trajan's column clearly indicates the true nature of this object, a wooden pole adorned with armor, shields, weapons, and crowned with a helmet, the trophies nevertheless could certainly conjure, at least from a distance, the specter of an εἰκὼν ἀνθρώπου.[121]

In one sense, then, the present disturbance can be boiled down to a case of mistaken identity. The reaction of the inhabitants of Jerusalem is the result of trompe l'oeil, so to speak, the capacity of τρόπαια to deceive the viewer. Nevertheless, in

---

Valerie M. Hope, "Trophies and Tombstones: Commemorating the Roman Soldier," *World Archaeology* 35 (2003): 81; van Henten, "The Panegyris in Jerusalem," 161–64.

116. With the exception of ten conspirators, who were plotting Herod's assassination (*A.J.* 15.280–291).

117. There is some evidence, however, that marble trophies could be used as a supporting structure for a freestanding statue, as in the case of the marble trophy from late Hellenistic Marathon discussed in Eugene Vanderpool, "The Marble Trophy from Marathon in the British Museum," *Hesperia* 36 (1967): 109.

118. See especially the following detailed studies of trophies in antiquity, both published in the same year: Andreas Jozef Janssen, *Het antieke Tropaion* (Brussels: Paleis der Academiën, 1957); Picard, *Les trophées romains*.

119. Hope, "Trophies and Tombstones," 80. See especially Picard's discussion of early Greek trophies (*Les trophées romains*, 16–64). Archaeological remains from the Roman Republic indicate that in later periods more permanent military trophies were also erected, consisting either of stone or bronze; see, for example, John M. Camp et al., "A Trophy from the Battle of Chaironeia of 86 B.C.," *AJA* 96 (1992): 448–49, esp. fig. 6.

120. Zanker, *The Power of Images*, 70, fig. 55. For a similar example, see also Mary Beard, *The Roman Triumph* (Cambridge and London: Belknap Press of Harvard University Press, 2007), 146, fig. 26. A relief from Spalato, the commercial port of Dalmatia, likewise portrays two prisoners sitting beneath a trophy; see Picard, *Les trophées romains*, pl. XII.

121. Maamoun Abdulkarim et al., eds., *Apollodorus of Damascus and Trajan's Column: From Tradition to Project* (Rome: L'Erma di Bretschneider, 2003), 50–51 nn. 8–9.

the narrative world Josephus constructs, this episode underscores again, even if Herod is ultimately exonerated (in this instance), the potentially calamitous effect the despotic imposition of an εἰκών can have on civic order and stability. Insofar as the τρόπαια were thought to be εἰκόνες, an intentional subversion of Judean πάτριον, Jerusalem was in danger of ἀπόστασις. Only when the *aniconic* nature of the trophies is established does this threat of rebellion subside.

As the narrative on Herod's reign unfolds, however, the trophy incident merely presages the controversy surrounding the erection of an unambiguous εἰκὼν ζῴου, the statue of an eagle in the temple precincts (*A.J.* 17.149–167). Here again, as in the trophy pericope, Herod's despotic demeanor is emphasized from the start, with the king and the population of Jerusalem trapped in a vicious cycle of erratic behavior and violent rebellion respectively. As the monarch becomes increasingly "wild, treating everyone with excessive anger (ἀκράτῳ τῇ ὀργῇ) and bitterness," albeit in part because of a mysterious illness, "popular figures" (δημοτικωτέρων ἀνθρώπων) emerge from the woodwork fomenting uprisings (ἐπανίστημι; *A.J.* 17.148). Josephus thus locates the outbreak over the eagle within these tense and unstable circumstances:

> οἵ τε πυνθανόμενοι τοῦ βασιλέως τὴν νόσον θεραπεύειν ἄπορον οὖσαν, ἐξῆραν τὸ νεώτερον, ὥστε ὁπόσα παρὰ νόμον τοῦ πατρίου κατεσκεύαστο ἔργα ὑπὸ τοῦ βασιλέως, ταῦτα καθελόντες εὐσεβείας ἀγωνίσματα παρὰ τῶν νόμων φέρεσθαι· καὶ γὰρ δὴ διὰ τὴν τόλμαν αὐτῶν παρ᾽ ὃ διηγόρευεν ὁ νόμος τῆς ποιήσεως τά τε ἄλλα αὐτῷ συντυχεῖν,... ἦν γὰρ τῷ Ἡρώδῃ τινὰ πραγματευθέντα παρὰ τὸν νόμον, ἃ δὴ ἐπεκάλουν οἱ περὶ τὸν Ἰούδαν καὶ Ματθίαν. κατεσκευάκει δὲ ὁ βασιλεὺς ὑπὲρ τοῦ μεγάλου πυλῶνος τοῦ ναοῦ ἀνάθημα καὶ λίαν πολυτελές, ἀετὸν χρύσεον μέγαν· κωλύει δὲ ὁ νόμος εἰκόνων τε ἀναστάσεις ἐπινοεῖν καί τινων ζῴων ἀναθέσεις ἐπιτηδεύεσθαι τοῖς βιοῦν κατ᾽ αὐτὸν προῃρημένοις.
>
> And when they learned that the king's disease was incurable, they stirred up the youth so that they might tear down all of the works that the king had set up *contrary to ancestral law* and, in so doing, to gain the prizes of piety from the law. For it was indeed because of his *reckless abandon* in making that which was contrary to what the law declares that these things came upon him. . . . For certain tasks undertaken by Herod were contrary to the law, which things indeed Judas, Matthias, and their colleagues brought an accusation against him. For the king had erected over the great gate of the temple an exceedingly costly votive offering, a great golden eagle. But the law forbids those who are determined to live by it to think of setting up *statues* and to make dedications of [statues of] any *living creatures*. (*A.J.* 17.150–151)

Here again, both *B.J.* and *A.J.* frame Herod's actions, the erection of an εἰκών, as a violation of ancestral law, although only in *B.J.* is the specific legislation defined according to spatial limitations (κατὰ τὸν ναόν; *B.J.* 1.650). By contrast, the emphasis shifts in *A.J.* to Herod's "savage temper" (ὠμότης) and the resulting civic chaos (*A.J.* 17.164). Indeed, Josephus' account of the eagle episode in *A.J.* consolidates in one place many of the key terms and elements of civic unrest evident in Plutarch's account of Gaius Marius, most notably a recklessly arrogant (τόλμα) autocrat hell-bent on destroying ancestral law and the consequent outbreak of rebellion (στάσις) at the hands of an angry mob (ὄχλος) of "young men" (νέοι) portrayed in a state of chaotic disorder (ἀσύντακτος; *A.J.* 17.155–156). In so doing, Josephus recalls for his Roman readers a very familiar *topos*, a constitutional crisis at the hands of despotism run amok, with one significant difference. In Plutarch, the mob represents the antithesis of Roman virtue (i.e., Romanness), a destabilizing force under the spell of the autocrat, complicit in Gaius Marius' devious plot (from Plutarch's perspective at least) to undermine the *mos maiorum* and ultimately undo the order and stability of Rome itself. For Josephus, however, the iconoclastic mob, by attempting to preserve the νόμος τοῦ πατρίου, embodies the very ideals of Roman virtue, described in strikingly Roman language. Their actions are portrayed as "a virtue most becoming of men" (μετ' ἀρετῆς ἀνδράσι πρεπωδεστάτης), clearly tapping into Roman notions of manly virtue as a quintessential element of Romanness (*A.J.* 17.158).[122] Indeed, this portrayal of the iconoclastic mob underscores the major thesis of this chapter, namely that although Jewish iconoclasm may seem like a fundamentally *anti*-Roman act, Josephus attempts in *A.J.* to portray it as an expression of Roman virtue.

To summarize, a comparison of the three episodes of iconoclasm recounted in both *B.J.* and *A.J.* demonstrates distinct emphases within each composition. Whereas in *B.J.* Josephus stresses the *location* of an εἰκών, highlighting its capacity to desecrate sacred space, in *A.J.* emphasis shifts to the devastating effect of an εἰκών on civic tranquillity, its role in fomenting chaos and rebellion. The two episodes of iconoclasm unique to *A.J.*, the imperial statue brought into the synagogue of Dora and the trophies adorning the theater in Jerusalem, likewise contribute to this theme of εἰκών as an agent of στάσις. This is not to suggest that στάσις and other similar civic problems are absent in *B.J.*; indeed, στάσις plays a central role in Josephus' account of the Judean revolt.[123] Nevertheless, only in *A.J.* is the problem of στάσις consistently linked to the episodes of iconoclasm.

Conclusion

I have argued in this chapter that the Josephan discourse on εἰκών in *A.J.* is steeped in Roman antiquarian traditions that idealized primitive aniconic piety. Josephus' portrayal of the Jewish ἀρχαιολογία thus echoes extant traditions of Rome's aniconic golden age, in particular Varro's correlation between the decline of *pietas* and the rise of iconic forms of cultic activity and Plutarch's link between Rome's aniconic era and the exemplary legislation of one of her heroes of virtue and piety, the legendary νομοθέτης Numa, a Roman par excellence. As with Numa,

122. On the importance of masculine virtue in Roman society, see Gleason, *Making Men*; Walters, "Invading the Roman Body," 29–43; Williams, *Roman Homosexuality*, esp. 125–59. On Josephus' use of "manly virtue" in *B.J.*, see Mason, "Greeks and the Distant Past," 104.

123. See for example the discussion of similar "*polis* themes" in Mason, "Greeks and the Distant Past," 93–130. See also the discussion of στάσις in Rajak, *Josephus*, 91–96.

Moses' legislation against images in *A.J.* is embedded within a superior πολιτεία originating in the distant past, a legal repository of ancestral laws, customs, and deeds—corresponding with the Roman notion of *mos maiorum* and embodying the Roman qualities of εὐσέβεια and ἀρετή—which collectively serve to maintain societal order, stability, and harmony. Moreover, by "sanitizing" the biblical narrative in *A.J.* 1–11, Josephus, too, imagines a golden age of aniconic piety, an era in primitive history that was mostly devoid of figurative images. Indeed, it is precisely this idealized golden age and ancient legislation that become a critical reference point for his treatment of the period of Herodian-Roman rule, framing recent Jewish iconoclastic activity as a noble attempt both to preserve civic stability and to stem the tide of moral decline by faithful adherence to ancestral custom.

6

The Poetics of Idolatry and the Politics of Identity

A rather stark polarity between εἰκών and Ἰουδαῖος does indeed emerge in the writings of the Jewish historian Flavius Josephus, particularly noticeable in his portrayal of an increasingly volatile iconoclastic behavior—that is, Jews resisting and, in at least one instance, even destroying statues—during the decades leading up to the Judean revolt and the destruction of the temple in Jerusalem. This narrative material, combined with a striking absence of figurative remains (especially statues) in the archaeological record of Second Temple Jerusalem has understandably contributed to the near ubiquitous assumption in modern scholarship of a monolithic antagonism toward all forms of figurative art during the Second Temple period. In particular, many scholars have characterized the relationship between Jews and images in antiquity according to a model of diachronic exegetical transmutation. In the wake of the Hasmonean war against the Seleucids, Jewish authorities, in order to stem the threat of pagan idolatry, imposed a prohibition of images in toto, rooted in an expansion of the scope of the biblical פסל and תמונה to include not just cult images but all theriomorphic and anthropomorphic representation. Following the destruction of the temple, Jewish authorities—typically identified as the rabbis of the Mishnah and Talmudim—began to soften their exegetical stance in response to idolatry's (perceived) waning threat, resulting in the flourishing of figurative art in the synagogue remains of late antiquity.

I have tried in the present investigation to complicate this interpretive model. In the first place, while a selection of Jewish sources and archaeological remains from the Second Temple period may attest to an uneasy, perhaps even antagonistic attitude toward figurative art in general (and not just cult images) on the part of *some* Jews, there is no warrant for the supposition of uniformity *either* before *or* after the destruction of the temple in 70 c.e. Rather, scattered hints in the archaeological record viewed through more nuanced models of cultural interaction in the ancient Mediterranean world, combined with the overwhelming tendency in the literary sources to restrict the scope of the second commandment to cultic images, suggest the possibility that synchronic regional variation offers a better explanatory model than diachronic exegetical transmutation. In other words, the restrictive approach to figurative art seemingly attested in a variety of sources may be indicative of a Second Temple *Judean* phenomenon and not a Second Temple *Jewish* phenomenon.

Moreover, a close examination of the evidence from Josephus—the primary focus of the present study—likewise exposes more complexity than is typically allowed. Rather than a straightforward account of events on the ground, Josephus is crafting or sculpting distinct portraits of aniconism that contribute to larger rhetorical interests. In the case of *B.J.*, Josephus deploys sculpture and, more specifically, the Jewish resistance to sculpture, as a mapping device, articulating a conception of Judea, and especially Jerusalem, as sacred territories *without sculpture*. Moreover, this cartographic strategy, which includes a rather stark polarization between Judean and Greek landscapes, contributes to a broader discourse on the nature of imperial power and the dangerous link between tyranny and excessive displays of Greekness. When viewed from within this framework, Jewish resistance to sculpture represents an effort to stem the tide of philhellenic tyrants, a concern likewise attested in coeval Roman sources. In *A.J.*, by contrast, Josephus shifts focus away from the issue of sacred space to the ancient aniconic origins of the Jewish πολιτεία, tapping into the moralizing memory of a pristine age of *Roman* aniconism. In so doing, Josephus presents the Jewish resistance to images as the preservation of an ancestral system of values, akin to the Roman notion of the *mos maiorum*, thus framing iconoclastic behavior not as an expression of cultural otherness, a peculiarity of strange foreigners from the East, but as an expression of cultural sameness, an element that binds Jewish and Roman identities.

The importance of Josephus' compositional context in the above analysis should be fairly evident. Josephus' historiographical enterprise surfaces within the turbulent cultural and political currents of Flavian Rome, and the author's attempt to Romanize Jewish aniconism, to tap into the values of *Romanitas* as a means of accounting for Jewish behavior and articulating an image of Jewish identity, sheds light on the difficult circumstances surrounding Jewish life in Rome following the destruction of Jerusalem as well as the strategies by which some Jews attempted to navigate this difficult terrain. At this point in the discussion it is perhaps worth reflecting a bit more on these complex dynamics, stepping back from the minutiae of the present argument in order to better synthesize and contextualize Josephus' rhetoric and to further underscore the broader significance of this study.

The occasional disturbance over images, often imperial statues, in the first centuries B.C.E./C.E. was likely viewed by many in antiquity, particularly in Rome, as an act of political subversion, a manifestation of a "Jewish hatred of Rome's oppressive rule."[1] For the present discussion, it matters not whether this was *actually* the case; it is enough to note that this was a likely *perception* of Jewish anti-iconic behavior. The practice of iconoclasm, especially as a form of *damnatio memoriae*, was quite familiar in the Roman world, whether we are speaking of the official, state-sponsored destruction of the statues of "bad" emperors or "those occasions on which angry crowds, acting spontaneously, and not according to any official decree, inflicted violence upon the emperor's images," whether a "good" or "bad" emperor.[2]

Moreover, if the (re)production and dissemination of an emperor's images functioned as an integral component of imperial propaganda, as Paul Zanker has

1. Gutmann, "The 'Second Commandment' and the Image," 170.

2. Stewart, *Statues in Roman Society*, 269.

convincingly demonstrated,[3] then the official enactment of *damnatio* on a particular emperor's statues functioned as a propagandistic response to a shift of power, signaling a "reversal of fortunes" that simultaneously delegitimized one locus of authority while reinforcing a new locus of authority.[4] This official "language" of iconoclasm, however, suggests a corollary: the spontaneous and unofficial destruction of imperial statues, particularly of still living, still legitimate emperors, likely denoted for many an anticipation of, or desire for, a shift of power, a signal of a coup d'état in the making.[5]

Jewish resistance to images, especially statues with an explicit or implicit association with the Roman state (e.g., Herod's eagle, Pilate's standards, and, most obviously, Caligula's statue), were likely viewed by Romans within this light, particularly *after* the revolt of 66–73 C.E. That is to say, in the wake of the war against Rome, accounts of Jewish iconoclastic activity were probably interpreted from a Roman perspective as politically subversive acts against the state, attempts at a kind of *damnatio memoriae* directed not at a particular emperor but the empire at large. Such behavior thus could be thought to ultimately portend the Jews' brazen and catastrophic attempt to reverse their own fortunes, to replace Roman hegemony with an independent Judean state. Tacitus hints at this perception when he seemingly casts aspersions on the Jews for refusing to honor emperors with statues (*Hist.* 5.5.4). John Pollini's remarks about an incident in Jamnia when a group of Jews destroyed an altar of Caligula—an episode recounted in Philo (*Legat.* 202)—is equally applicable to the present discussion of images: "To the Romans, the Jews' destruction of the altar was regarded as not only sacrilegious but also seditious, since an attack on an altar to the divinity of the *princeps* of Rome was tantamount to an attack on the Roman state itself."[6]

There is some indication that Josephus was sensitive to problems arising from the potentially subversive implications of distinct Jewish beliefs and customs, that is, behavior that seemed out of step with, and at times antagonistic toward, Roman customs. For example, Josephus unequivocally asserts in *C. Ap.* that while Jews were required to observe their own πάτριον, they were also expressly forbidden to criticize (κατηγορέω) the πάτριον of foreigners. To support this assertion, Josephus appeals to Exod 22:27, which in the LXX translation forbids ridiculing the gods of foreigners (θεοὺς οὐ κακολογήσεις), claiming that "our lawgiver openly denounced the mocking (χλευάζω) or blaspheming (βλασφημέω) of the gods esteemed by others" (*C. Ap.* 2.237). In a similar vein, Josephus remarks in *A.J.*: "Let

3. Zanker, *The Power of Images*.

4. Stewart, *Statues in Roman Society*, 277.

5. For example, according to Cassius Dio soldiers destroyed Nero's statues to signal their desire that Nero's general receive the title Caesar and Augustus, an acclamation that the general immediately refused (*Rom. hist.* 63.25.1–2); see the discussion in Stewart, *Statues in Roman Society*, 271–72.

6. John Pollini, "Gods and Emperors in the East: Images of Power and the Power of Intolerance," in *The Sculptural Environment of the Roman Near East: Reflections on Culture, Ideology, and Power* (ed. Yaron Z. Eliav, Elise A. Friedland, and Sharon Herbert; Louvain: Peeters, 2008), 192.

no one blaspheme the gods esteemed in other cities, nor steal from foreign temples, nor seize a treasure devoted to any god" (*A.J.* 4.207).[7] Presumably, this could be thought to include the gods' (and emperors') images as well. Even more relevant to the present discussion, Josephus in *C. Ap.* attributes to Moses a preemptive qualification to the prohibition of images, claiming that the lawgiver proscribed images "*not* as a prophecy that Roman authority ought not be honored" (*C. Ap.* 2.75). This protest, I would argue, is pregnant with significance, speaking to a very real perception in Josephus' own context.

There is little doubt that anti-Jewish resentment in Rome was significantly exacerbated in the aftermath of the revolt, and stories of Jewish iconoclasm would certainly have added more fuel to the fire. For Jews living in the capital city, and indeed throughout the Roman Mediterranean, the final decades of the first century C.E., the period of Flavian hegemony, must have been especially challenging. If the decisive defeat of the Judean rebels and the destruction of Jerusalem were not enough, the punitive *fiscus Iudaicus*, a two-*denarii* tax imposed on all Jews throughout the Roman empire in order to fund the temple of Jupiter Optimus Maximus Capitolinus in Rome, bore public witness to an ever deepening fissure between Jews and Romans.[8] This rift was perhaps most palpably felt by Jews residing in Rome, who were surrounded by a world literally saturated with lavish displays of their own subjugation: first the parade of Titus the *triumphator* down the Via Sacra, accompanied by the exhibition of Judean spoils and captives;[9] the massive construction of Vespasian's Templum Pacis, funded with Judean war booty and housing an impressive display of art and artifacts from around the world, including objects from the Jerusalem temple;[10] the completion of the Colosseum in 80 C.E., financed in part with spoils from the Judean war,[11] and a year later the Arch of Titus with its now familiar display of captured spoils from the Jewish temple;[12] and finally the circulation of *Iudea capta* coins trumpeting Rome's masculine dominance of an effeminized Judea.[13] In short, following the revolt "[t]he

7. Philo similarly follows the LXX's interpretation of Exod 22.27 in *Mos.* 2.205 and *Spec.* 1.53.

8. See especially Martin Goodman, "The *Fiscus Iudaicus* and Gentile Attitudes to Judaism in Flavian Rome," in *Flavius Josephus and Flavian Rome* (ed. Jonathan Edmondson, Steve Mason, and James Rives; Oxford: Oxford University Press, 2005), 166–77.

9. See especially Josephus' eyewitness account of the Flavian triumphal procession in *B.J.* 7.123–157 and the discussion in Fergus Millar, "Last Year in Jerusalem: Monuments of the Jewish War in Rome," in *Flavius Josephus and Flavian Rome* (ed. Jonathan Edmondson, Steve Mason, and James Rives; Oxford: Oxford University Press, 2005), 101–28.

10. On the Templum Pacis as a museum of artifacts, see Pliny, *Hist.* 34.84; Josephus, *B.J.* 7.158–162; Pausanias, *Descr.* 2.9.3.

11. The link between the Colosseum and Judean spoils was first uncovered in 1995, when Géza Alföldy deciphered a dedicatory inscription identifying Vespasian as the one to initiate the construction with funds "from the spoils of war" (*ex manubi[i]s*); see *CIL* 6.40454a. See also the discussions in Barbara Levick, *Vespasian* (London: Routledge, 1999), 127–28; Boyle, "Reading Flavian Rome," 61; Millar, "Last Year in Jerusalem," 117–19.

12. Millar, "Last Year in Jerusalem," 119–27.

13. As Davina Lopez notes, much of the visual language of Rome's dominance is thor-

centre of Rome was remodeled under the Flavians to reflect the glory of the war . . . [and] victory in Judea became part of the historical consciousness of ordinary Romans."[14] As Goodman aptly notes, although prior to the war Jews were likely quite comfortable with their dual identity as Jewish Romans (or Roman Jews), "the change in their status in Rome after the failure of the Jewish Revolt must have come as an awful shock."[15]

I submit that Josephus' iconology, and in particular his effort to Romanize Jewish iconoclastic behavior, must be viewed against this postwar backdrop. By placing "Jewish aniconic peculiarity on the map of Greek and Roman culture,"[16] Josephus attempts to bridge the ever widening gulf between Roman and Jew by portraying Jewish iconoclasm not as a *resistance to* but an *expression of* Romanness, a shining exemplum of the values of *Romanitas*. This Romanization of Jewish particularity, however, does not reflect a betrayal of Jewishness in favor of Romanness, the abandonment of a cultural heritage by a quisling looking to manipulate circumstances for his own advantage.[17] For Josephus, Jewishness and Romanness are not mutually exclusive, and his *entire* literary enterprise—including both *B.J.* and *A.J.*—represents a sustained attempt to articulate in the aforementioned contentious circumstances an image of Jewish identity that could potentially enable his compatriots to navigate this difficult terrain.

It is thus not at all surprising that Josephus gravitates toward those elements in Roman cultural discourse that were particularly central to a resurgent moralizing impulse in the wake of Nero's demise and the subsequent civil wars and imperial regime change. From the start the Flavian propaganda machine was especially diligent in fostering the impression of a revival of traditional *Romanitas*. Moral values typically associated with the Roman republic—for example, *moderatio*, *integritas*, *virtus*, *abstinentia*, *prudentia*, and so on—were quickly attached to the new imperial family, while an equally potent constellation of vices—for example, *luxuria*, *mollitia*, *libido*, *avaritia*, *tyrannis*, and so on—were inextricably linked with that

---

oughly gendered, with Rome's masculinity visibly and quite explicitly (and occasionally with phallic overtones) juxtaposed with the femininity of the conquered *ethnē* ("Before Your Very Eyes: Roman Imperial Ideology, Gender Constructs, and Paul's Inter-Nationalism," in *Mapping Gender in Ancient Religious Discourses* (ed. Todd Penner and Caroline Vander Stichele; Leiden: Brill, 2007), esp. 117–23. See also the discussion in von Ehrenkrook, "Effeminacy in the Shadow of Empire," 156–63.

14. Goodman, *Rome and Jerusalem*, 554.

15. Goodman, "Josephus as Roman Citizen," 331.

16. Barclay, "Snarling Sweetly," 74.

17. As noted in the introduction, one unfortunate consequence of the Laqueur interpretive trajectory is the tendency to bifurcate "Roman" and "Jewish" elements in the Josephan corpus and to view the presence of the former as an index of a deficiency in the latter. Thus Josephus' lavish praise of Titus and Vespasian in *B.J.* bespeaks the sentiments of a Flavian lackey who had betrayed his Jewish identity; conversely, his detailed treatment of Jewish ἀρχαιολογία in *A.J.* reflects a "chastened" traitor attempting to regain an identity he formerly betrayed.

notorious "villain" of the Julio-Claudians, Nero.[18] Whether Nero actually deserved this reputation,[19] he soon became the emblem of all that could undermine and potentially destroy Roman culture and the stability of the empire. This framework through which to view Nero was particularly evident in his historiographical legacy. Holly Haynes notes, for example, that, for Tacitus, Nero represents "the floodgate for all the problems of empire that the shadow of Augustus previously kept in check."[20] According to Joan-Pau Rubiés' assessment, Nero's portrait becomes increasingly depraved in successive accounts, from Tacitus to Suetonius to Cassius Dio.[21]

As noted already in chapter 4, one prominent facet of Nero's image that became a favorite target of invective was his putative philhellenism, which was conventionally framed as a heightened inclination "to the seedier side of the Greek heritage."[22] Given that an increasing number of Roman traditionalists viewed the Greeks as "excessively self-indulgent and inordinately fond of a life of luxury,"[23] it is not entirely surprising that Vespasian would seek to distance himself from this perceived infatuation with all things Greek, revoking Nero's grant of freedom to Greece and reducing Achaea to provincial status (Suetonius, *Vesp.* 8), advertising Flavian architecture as an example of "public munificence" and not "private luxury,"[24] disseminating official portraiture that departed from "Hellenic ideals" in favor of a return to "traditional republican realism,"[25] and in general fostering an image of a "neo-veristic, rugged, man-of-the-people" emperor,[26] striving to restrain a rampant *libido atque luxuria* (Suetonius, *Vesp.* 11). As Miriam Griffin notes in her study of early Flavian posturing, Vespasian's carefully crafted image was intended to recall "the glory and patriotism of the Roman heroes."[27]

Josephus' voice emerges in the midst of, and is directly shaped by, this lively

---

18. On the politically charged nature of this discourse, see Catharine Edwards, *The Politics of Immorality in Ancient Rome* (Cambridge: Cambridge University Press, 1993).

19. See especially the collection of essays in Jaś Elsner and Jaime Masters, eds., *Reflections of Nero: History, Culture, and Representation* (London: Duckworth, 1994).

20. Haynes, *The History of Make-Believe*, 34.

21. Joan-Pau Rubiés, "Nero in Tacitus and Nero in Tacitism: The Historian's Craft," in *Reflections of Nero: Culture, History, and Representation* (ed. Jaś Elsner and Jamie Masters; London: Duckworth, 1994), 40. See also in that same volume, Barton, "The *Inventio* of Nero," 48–63.

22. Whitmarsh, "Greek and Roman in Dialogue," 145. See also the discussion in T. E. J. Wiedemann, "Tiberius to Nero," in *The Cambridge Ancient History Volume X: The Augustan Empire, 43 B.C.–A.D. 69* (ed. Alan K. Bowman, Edward Champlin, and Andrew Lintott; Cambridge: Cambridge University Press, 1996), 241–55.

23. Williams, *Roman Homosexuality*, 68.

24. Miriam T. Griffin, "The Flavians," in *The Cambridge Ancient History Volume XI: The High Empire, A.D. 70–192* (ed. Alan K. Bowman, Peter Garnsey, and Dominic Rathbone; Cambridge: Cambridge University Press, 2000), 20.

25. Ronald Mellor, "The New Aristocracy of Power," in *Flavian Rome: Culture, Image, Text* (ed. A. J. Boyle and W. J. Dominik; Leiden: Brill, 2003), 83.

26. Boyle, "Reading Flavian Rome," 34.

27. Griffin, "The Flavians," 25.

discourse on *Romanitas*. The polarization of Greek and Judean landscapes, and by extension Greek and Jewish identities, in *B.J.* should thus not be viewed as a manifestation of the struggle between Judaism and Hellenism as such, with Hellenism representative of anything foreign, whether Greek or Roman. Rather, Josephus taps into a distinctly *Roman* angst over Greek influences, constructing an antithesis that would have resonated with the prevailing cultural winds of Flavian Rome in the decades of Vespasian's and Titus' reigns. Likewise the emphasis in *A.J.* on the antiquity and consequent superiority of the Jewish πολιτεία vis-à-vis Greek constitutions, in which Josephus' aniconic rhetoric plays a central role, serves to narrow the breach between Romans and Jews at the expense of Greeks, often with language quite familiar to that employed by those in Rome who were inclined to protect the *mos maiorum* ostensibly jeopardized by the philhellenic Nero.[28]

Josephus, however, exploits Roman cultural discourse not as a Roman lackey groveling for attention and acceptance at the feet of his Flavian superiors but as a faithful Jew hoping to gain "maximal advantage for himself *and for his people*, within the constraints of his social and political environment."[29] Josephus' rhetorical strategies should thus be viewed not simply through the lens of cultural assimilation, wherein the colonized quietly absorbs the culture of the hegemonic group, but through what Barclay identifies as a model of "resistant adaptation," wherein the colonized "can employ the dominant culture *for their own ends*."[30]

Furthermore, implicit in this concept of "resistant adaptation" is an element of subversion, akin to Homi Bhabha's notion of mimicry, that is, the discursive strategy of approaching the limits of cultural resemblance or sameness in order to expose differences that can potentially (if subtly) undermine the authority of the dominant culture.[31] This subversive dimension of mimicry is particularly noticeable in the treatment of aniconism in *A.J.* Although Josephus skillfully portrays the Jewish resistance to images in language that is steeped in Roman antiquarian traditions, likening Jewish aniconism to Rome's pious aniconic past, this appropriation of sameness simultaneously conveys an implicit critique: the Jews were able to accomplish what the Romans quite obviously failed to do—to preserve the pious worship of their own *mos maiorum*. While Rome's golden age had long since passed, at least according to the historiographical tradition preserved in Varro and Plutarch, the Jews had successfully persisted in the aniconic ways of their an-

---

28. As Martin Goodman notes, "The qualities in Judaism which [Josephus] picked out to make his point were strikingly similar to those aspects of Roman *mos* that Latin authors trumpeted when they too wanted to compare themselves favourably to the Greeks" ("Josephus as Roman Citizen," 334–35). Goodman similarly likens Josephus' *C. Ap.* to the *Collatio Legum Mosaicarum et Romanarum* (fourth or fifth century C.E.), which stresses that "Roman *mores*, as enshrined in Roman law, were not only compatible with Judaism but actually derived from the Law of Moses" ("The Roman Identity of Roman Jews," 96–97).

29. Barclay, "The Empire Writes Back," 315 (emphasis mine).

30. Ibid., 318 (emphasis mine).

31. Homi K. Bhabha, *The Location of Culture* (London: Routledge, 1994), 85–92. Bhabha refers to this as the "ambivalence of mimicry," the almost-but-not-quite appropriation of culture that functions as a menacing disturbance to the colonizer.

cestors. The relationship between Roman and Jewish cultures in Josephus is thus much more complex than binary models of assimilation/antagonism or acceptance/resistance allow, pointing instead to the distinct possibility "that in a melody apparently composed of complicity and cultural subservience, there can be sound soft notes of self-assertion and resistance, at least for some ears."[32]

Was Josephus' rhetorical enterprise successful? While a definitive answer to this question is in the end elusive, there are some hints in the surviving data that suggest his efforts on behalf of his compatriots were ultimately in vain, at least in the short term. If Cotton and Eck are correct that Josephus throughout his literary career remained a lonely and isolated figure, marginalized from the elite social and political circles in Rome, the very people from whom Josephus had hoped to gain a hearing, then the reach of Josephus' *apologia* on behalf of his compatriots was likely quite limited. Moreover, that anti-Jewish vitriol increases dramatically in the Latin sources of this period suggests that for many of these preachers of *Romanitas* the Ἰουδαῖοι remained among the litany of foreign pollutants that, at least according to Juvenal's pungent assessment, were infecting the Tiber (Juvenal, *Sat.* 3.60–61). Indeed, that Juvenal can treat with bitter disdain even the most pro-Roman of Jews, Agrippa II and his sister Berenice, as well as Philo's nephew Tiberius Julius Alexander, equestrian governor of Judea (46–48 C.E.) and Egypt (68–69 C.E.), underscores the extent to which the Jews living in Rome after the Judean war had an uphill battle, carrying the stigma of a humiliated *ethnos* on the margins of society.[33]

In the end, however, that Josephus' literary project may not have ultimately achieved its desired effect ought not detract from his efforts to navigate a clear path through the thick and tangled forest of Jewish life in Rome after the war. While it remains a distinct possibility that the flurry of iconoclastic activity during the decades preceding the revolt did indeed emerge from a deep-seated hatred of Roman hegemony on the part of some Jews in Judea, Josephus skillfully reshapes this seemingly anti-Roman behavior in language that would surely have resonated with even the most ardent advocate of *Romanitas*. Josephus' attempt to mitigate the increasingly tense relationship between Roman and Jew thus marks him as one who remained deeply loyal to his people throughout his literary career in Rome. Perhaps, then, the dark and traitorous shadow of Jotapata did not reach as far as is often supposed.

---

32. Barclay, "The Empire Writes Back," 332. Steve Mason argues for a similar subversive dimension in Josephus' representation of the Flavian emperors, especially Titus, reading this rhetoric as a form of "safe criticism," an ironic ploy or kind of double-speak whose surface praise masks a subtle critique of the emperors ("Figured Speech and Irony," 262–67). On the use of irony in *B.J.*, see also Brighton, *The Sicarii*, 25–29.

33. Agrippa II and Berenice: Juvenal, *Sat.* 6.156–160; Tiberius Julius Alexander: Juvenal, *Sat.* 1.130–146.

APPENDIX 1

Statuary Lexicon in the Josephan Corpus

ἄγαλμα
B.J. 7.136, 151; *A.J.* 15. 279, 329, 339; 18.79; 19.11; *C. Ap.* 1.199

ἀνδριάς
B.J. 2.185, 192, 266; *A.J.* 6.10, 15; 10.206–207, 213-214; 18.1, 258, 261, 264, 269, 271, 272, 274, 297, 301; 19.7, 300, 305, 357; 20.212

ἀφίδρυμα
A.J. 18.344

γλυφή/γλυφίς
B.J. 5.191 (γλυφίς); *A.J.* 8.136; 15.414, 416; 19.7, 185

δείκηλον
B.J. 2.170, 195

εἴδωλον
B.J. 5.513; 7.452; *A.J.* 9.99, 205, 243, 273; 10.50, 65, 69

εἰκών
B.J. 1.439, 650; 2.169, 173, 194, 197; 5.212; *A.J.* 3.91; 6.333; 8.26, 44; 14.153; 15.26–27, 276, 277, 279; 16.158; 17.151; 18.55, 56, 57, 59, 121; 19.185; 20.212; *C. Ap.* 2.191

ἱέρωμα
A.J. 1.119, 322

κολοσσός
B.J. 1.413, 414

μορφή
B.J. 2.101, 104; *A.J.* 2.61, 84, 98, 102, 232; 3.113, 126, 137; 5.125, 213; 6.45, 162, 333; 7.190; 15.51; 16.7; 17.324, 329; *C. Ap.* 2.128, 190, 248, 252

ξόανον
B.J. 5.384; *C. Ap.* 1.244, 249

προτομή
B.J. 1.650; 3.214; *A.J.* 8.140; 18.1, 55

σημαία
B.J. 2.169, 171, 174; 3.123; 5.48 (2x); 6.225, 226, 316, 403; 7.14; *A.J.* 18.55, 56, 121

τρόπαιον
A.J. 13.251; 15.272, 276, 277, 278; 18.287

APPENDIX 2

The Second Commandment in Josephus

Source	Prohibited Objects	Legal Nomenclature	Summary of Prohibition
B.J. 1.649–650	εἰκών; προτομή; ζῴου ἔργον	πάτριος νόμος	Statues, busts or works of living beings not permitted in the temple.
B.J. 2.170	δείκηλον; εἰκών (169)	νόμος; τὰ πάτρια (171)	Representation/image (on standard) not permitted in the city of Jerusalem.
B.J. 2.195	θεοῦ δείκηλον; ἀνδρός δείκηλον; εἰκών (194); ἀνδριάς (185)	νόμος; τὸ πάτριον ἔθος	Representations of God or man not permitted in temple or even Judea.
A.J. 3.91	εἰκών ζῴου	ὁ δεύτερος λόγος	Images of living beings for worship not permitted.
A.J. 8.195	χαλκῶν βοῶν ὁμοίωμα; τῶν λεόντων (ὁμοίωμα)	νόμιμος	Images of cattle and lions not permitted; Solomon's erection of said images not pious (ὅσιος).
A.J. 9.99	εἴδωλά	πάτριος νόμιμος	Jehoram violates ancestral laws by worshipping idols (σέβειν).
A.J. 9.205	εἴδωλά	νόμος (παράνομος)	Jeroboam violates ancestral laws by worshipping idols (σέβειν).

Source	Prohibited Objects	Legal Nomenclature	Summary of Prohibition
A.J. 9.243	εἴδωλά	πάτριος νόμος	Jotham violates ancestral laws by offering sacrifices to idols (θύειν).
A.J. 10.213–214	ἀνδριάς	πάτριος νόμος	Worshiping Nebuchadnezzar statue would transgress ancestral laws.
A.J. 15.276–279	ἄγαλμα; εἰκών; εἰκόνες	πάτριος	Not permitted to worship (σέβειν) images or erect images of men in Jerusalem
A.J. 15.328–329	ἄγαλμα; τύπους μεμορφωμένους τιμᾶν	ἔθος; νόμιμος	Not permitted to honor cult statues and other types of images
A.J. 16.158	εἰκών	νόμος	Jewish law does not permit honorary statues for kings
A.J. 17.150–151	εἰκών; ζῷον	νόμος τοῦ πατρίου; νόμος	Images and representations of living beings not permitted
A.J. 18.55	εἰκών; προτομή	νόμιμος τῶν Ἰουδαϊκῶν; νόμος	Making (ποίησις) images is not permitted
A.J. 18.121	εἰκών	πάτριος	Images on standards not permitted
A.J. 18.261–268	ἀνδριάς	πάτριος νόμος; ἀξίωμα τοῦ νομοθέτου καὶ προπατόρων τῶν ἡμετέρων; νόμος; πάτριος	Ancestral law does not permit the erection of a statue
Vita 65	ζῴου μορφή	νόμος	Making (κατασκευάζειν) images of living beings not permitted
C.Ap. 2.190–192	εἰκών; μορφή	αἱ προρρήσεις καὶ ἀπαγορεύσεις	God's invisible nature precludes iconic representation of the deity

Bibliography

Abdulkarim, Maamoun, et al., eds. *Apollodorus of Damascus and Trajan's Column: From Tradition to Project*. Roma: L'Erma di Bretschneider, 2003.

Aberbach, Moses. "Josephus: Patriot or Traitor?" *Jewish Heritage* 10 (1967): 13–19.

Alcock, Susan, and Robin Osborne, eds. *Placing the Gods: Sanctuaries and Sacred Space in Ancient Greece*. Oxford: Clarendon, 1994.

Alexander, Paul. "Hypatius of Ephesus: A Note on Image Worship in the Sixth Century." *Harvard Theological Review* 45 (1952): 177–84.

Amir, Yehoshua. "The Decalogue according to Philo." Pages 121–60 in *The Ten Commandments in History and Tradition*. Edited by Ben-Zion Segal and Gershon Levi. Jerusalem: Magnes Press, 1990.

———. "Θεοκρατία as a Concept of Political Philosophy: Josephus' Presentation of Moses' Politeia." *Scripta Classica Israelica* 8–9 (1985–88): 83–105.

Ando, Clifford. "A Religion for the Empire." Pages 323–44 in *Flavian Rome: Culture, Image, Text*. Edited by A. J. Boyle and William J. Dominik. Leiden: Brill, 2003.

Arafat, Karim W. *Pausanias' Greece: Ancient Artists and Roman Rulers*. Cambridge: Cambridge University Press, 1996.

Ararat, Nisan. "The Second Commandment: 'Thou Shalt Not Bow Down unto Them, nor Serve Them, for I the Lord Thy God Am a Jealous God'." *Shofar* 13 (1995): 44–57.

Asmis, Elisabeth. "A New Kind of Model: Cicero's Roman Constitution in *De republica*." *The American Journal of Philology* 126 (2005): 377–416.

Assunto, R. "Images and Iconoclasm." Pages 798–822 in vol. 7 of *Encyclopedia of World Art*. Edited by Bernard Samuel Myers. 17 vols. New York: McGraw-Hill, 1959–87.

Attridge, Harold W. *The Interpretation of Biblical History in the Antiquitates Judaicae of Flavius Josephus*. Missoula, Mont.: Scholars Press, 1976.

Avigad, Nahman. *Beth She'arim*. 3 vols. New Brunswick, N.J.: Rutgers University Press, 1976.

———. *The Herodian Quarter in Jerusalem: Wohl Archaeological Museum*. Jerusalem: Keter, 1989.

Avi-Yonah, Michael. "The Caesarea Porphyry Statue." *Israel Exploration Journal* 20 (1970): 203–8.

———. *The Holy Land from the Persian to the Arab Conquests (536 B.C. to A.D. 640): A Historical Geography*. Grand Rapids: Baker Book House, 1966.

Balch, David L. "Two Apologetic Encomia: Dionysius on Rome and Josephus on the Jews." *Journal for the Study of Judaism in the Persian, Hellenistic, and Roman Period* 13 (1982): 102–22.

Barasch, Moshe. *Icon: Studies in the History of an Idea*. New York: New York University Press, 1992.

Barclay, John M. G. *Against Apion*. Flavius Josephus: Translation and Commentary 10. Edited by Steve Mason. Leiden: Brill, 2007.

———. "The Empire Writes Back: Josephan Rhetoric in Flavian Rome." Pages 315–32 in

Flavius Josephus and Flavian Rome. Edited by Jonathan Edmondson, Steve Mason, and James Rives. Oxford: Oxford University Press, 2005.

———. *Jews in the Mediterranean Diaspora: From Alexander to Trajan (323 BCE–117 CE)*. Berkeley: University of California Press, 1996.

———. "Judean Historiography in Rome: Josephus and History in *Contra Apionem* Book 1." Pages 29–43 in *Josephus and Jewish History in Flavian Rome and Beyond*. Edited by Joseph Sievers and Gaia Lembi. Leiden: Brill, 2005.

———. "Snarling Sweetly: Josephus on Images and Idolatry." Pages 73–87 in *Idolatry: False Worship in the Bible, Early Judaism and Christianity*. Edited by Stephen C. Barton. London: T&T Clark, 2007.

Barish, D. A. "The 'Autobiography' of Josephus and the Hypothesis of a Second Edition of His 'Antiquities'." *Harvard Theological Review* 71 (1978): 61–75.

Barnard, Leslie W. *The Graeco-Roman and Oriental Background of the Iconoclastic Controversy*. Leiden: Brill, 1974.

Barnes, T. D. "The Sack of the Temple in Josephus and Tacitus." Pages 129–44 in *Flavius Josephus and Flavian Rome*. Edited by Jonathan Edmondson, Steve Mason, and James Rives. Oxford: Oxford University Press, 2005.

Bartlett, John R. *Jews in the Hellenistic World: Josephus, Aristeas, the Sibylline Oracles, Eupolemus*. Cambridge: Cambridge University Press, 1985.

Barton, John. " 'The Work of Human Hands' (Psalm 115:4): Idolatry in the Old Testament." Pages 194–203 in *The Ten Commandments: The Reciprocity of Faithfulness*. Edited by William P. Brown. Louisville: Westminster John Knox Press, 2004.

Barton, Tamsyn. "The *Inventio* of Nero: Suetonius." Pages 48–63 in *Reflections of Nero: Culture, History, and Representation*. Edited by Jaś Elsner and Jamie Masters. London: Duckworth, 1994.

Baynes, Norman H. "The Icons before Iconoclasm." *Harvard Theological Review* 44 (1951): 93–106.

Beard, Mary. *The Roman Triumph*. Cambridge and London: Belknap Press of Harvard University Press, 2007.

———. "The Triumph of Flavius Josephus." Pages 543–89 in *Flavian Rome: Culture, Image, Text*. Edited by A. J. Boyle and W. J. Dominik. Leiden: Brill, 2003.

Beard, Mary, John North, and Simon Price, eds. *Religions of Rome: A History*. Cambridge: Cambridge University Press, 1998.

Becker, Adam H., and Annette Yoshiko Reed, eds. *The Ways That Never Parted: Jews and Christians in Late Antiquity and the Early Middle Ages*. Minneapolis: Fortress Press, 2007.

Beentjes, P. C. "Satirical Polemics against Idols and Idolatry in the Letter of Jeremiah (Baruch ch. 6)." Pages 121–45 in *Aspects of Religious Contact and Conflict in the Ancient World*. Edited by Pieter Willem van der Horst. Utrecht: Faculteit der Godgeleerdheid, Universiteit Utrecht, 1995.

Begg, Christopher T. *Judean Antiquities 5-7*. Flavius Josephus: Translation and Commentary 4. Edited by Steve Mason. Leiden: Brill, 2005.

———. "Solomon's Apostasy (1 Kgs 11,1–13) according to Josephus." *Journal for the Study of Judaism in the Persian, Hellenistic, and Roman Period* 28 (1997): 294–313.

Begg, Christopher T., and Paul Spilsbury. *Judean Antiquities 8–10*. Flavius Josephus: Translation and Commentary 5. Edited by Steve Mason. Leiden: Brill, 2005.

Ben-Dov, Meir. *In the Shadow of the Temple: The Discovery of Ancient Jerusalem*. Translated by Ina Friedman. Jerusalem: Keter, 1985.

Bentwich, Norman. *Josephus*. Philadelphia: Jewish Publication Society of America, 1914.

Benzinger, Immanuel. "Art among the Ancient Hebrews." Pages 138–41 in vol. 2 of *The Jewish Encyclopedia*. Edited by Isodore Singer. 12 vols. New York: Funk and Wagnalls, 1901.

Berlin, Andrea M. "Jewish Life before the Revolt: The Archaeological Evidence." *Journal for the Study of Judaism in the Persian, Hellenistic, and Roman Period* 36 (2005): 417–70.

———. "Power and Its Afterlife: Tombs in Hellenistic Palestine." *Near Eastern Archaeology* 65 (2002): 138–48.

Bernays, Jacob. *Gesammelte Abhandlungen*. 2 vols. Berlin: Wilhelm Hertz, 1885.

Besançon, Alain. *The Forbidden Image: An Intellectual History of Iconoclasm*. Translated by Jane Marie Todd. Chicago: University of Chicago Press, 2000.

Bevan, Edwyn. *Holy Images: An Inquiry into Idolatry and Image-Worship in Ancient Paganism and in Christianity*. London: George Allen & Unwin, 1940.

Bhabha, Homi K. *The Location of Culture*. London: Routledge, 1994.

Bilde, Per. *Flavius Josephus between Jerusalem and Rome*. Sheffield: Sheffield Academic Press, 1988.

Bland, Kalman P. *The Artless Jew: Medieval and Modern Affirmations and Denials of the Visual*. Princeton, N.J.: Princeton University Press, 2000.

Blidstein, Gerald. "Nullification of Idolatry in Rabbinic Law." *Proceedings of the American Academy for Jewish Research* 41 (1973–74): 1–44.

———. "The Tannaim and Plastic Art." *Perspectives in Jewish Learning* 5 (1973): 13–27.

Bloch, René S. *Antike Vorstellungen vom Judentum: Der Judenexkurs des Tacitus im Rahmen der griechisch-römischen Ethnographie*. Stuttgart: Franz Steiner Verlag, 2002.

Boccaccini, Gabriele. *Beyond the Essene Hypothesis: The Parting of the Ways between Qumran and Enochic Judaism*. Grand Rapids: Eerdmans, 1998.

———. "Hellenistic Judaism: Myth or Reality?" Pages 55–76 in *Jewish Literatures and Cultures: Context and Intertext*. Edited by Anita Norich and Yaron Z. Eliav. Providence, R.I.: Brown Judaic Studies, 2008.

———. *Middle Judaism: Jewish Thought, 300 B.C.E. to 200 C.E.* Minneapolis: Fortress Press, 1991.

———. *Portraits of Middle Judaism in Scholarship and Arts: A Multimedia Catalog from Flavius Josephus to 1991*. Turin, Italy: S. Zamorani, 1992.

———. "Il Tema della Memoria in Giuseppe Flavio." *Henoch* 6 (1984): 147–63.

Boccaccini, Gabriele, and Giovanni Ibba, eds. *Enoch and the Mosaic Torah: The Evidence of Jubilees*. Grand Rapids: Eerdmans, 2009.

Bohec, Yann le. *The Imperial Roman Army*. London: B. T. Batsford, 1994.

Bokser, Baruch M. "Approaching Sacred Space." *Harvard Theological Review* 78 (1985): 279–99.

Bond, Helen K. *Pontius Pilate in History and Interpretation*. Cambridge: Cambridge University Press, 1998.

———. "Standards, Shields, and Coins: Jewish Reactions to Aspects of the Roman Cult in the Time of Pilate." Pages 88–106 in *Idolatry: False Worship in the Bible, Early Judaism, and Christianity*. Edited by Stephen C. Barton. London: T&T Clark, 2007.

Bowersock, Glen W. "Foreign Elites at Rome." Pages 53–62 in *Flavius Josephus and Flavian Rome*. Edited by Jonathan Edmondson, Steve Mason, and James Rives. Oxford: Oxford University Press, 2005.

Bowie, Ewen. "Inspiration and Aspiration: Date, Genre, and Readership." Pages 21–32 in *Pausanias: Travel and Memory in Roman Greece*. Edited by Susan E. Alcock, John F. Cherry, and Jaś Elsner. New York: Oxford University Press, 2001.

Bowley, James E. "Josephus' Use of Greek Sources for Biblical History." Pages 202–15 in *Pur-*

suing the Text: Studies in Honour of Ben Zion Wacholder on the Occasion of His Seventieth Birthday. Sheffield: Sheffield Academic Press, 1994.

Boyarin, Daniel. *Border Lines: The Partition of Judaeo-Christianity*. Philadelphia: University of Pennsylvania, 2004.

———. "Semantic Differences; or, 'Judaism'/'Christianity'." Pages 65–85 in *The Ways That Never Parted: Jews and Christians in Late Antiquity and the Early Middle Ages*. Edited by Adam H. Becker and Annette Yoshiko Reed. Minneapolis: Fortress Press, 2007.

Boyle, A. J. "Introduction: Reading Flavian Rome." Pages 1–67 in *Flavian Rome: Culture, Image, Text*. Edited by A. J. Boyle and William J. Dominik. Leiden: Brill, 2003.

Boyle, A. J., and W. J. Dominik, eds. *Flavian Rome: Culture, Image, Text*. Leiden: Brill, 2003.

Boys-Stones, Gregory R. *Post-Hellenistic Philosophy*. Oxford: Oxford University Press, 2001.

Branham, Joan R. "Vicarious Sacrality: Temple Space in Ancient Synagogues." Pages 319–45 in vol. 2 of *Ancient Synagogues: Historical Analysis and Archaeological Discovery*. Edited by Dan Urman and Paul V. M. Flesher. Leiden: Brill, 1995.

Brighton, Mark. *The Sicarii in Josephus's Judean War: Rhetorical Analysis and Historical Observations*. Atlanta: Society of Biblical Literature, 2009.

Brochgrave, Helen de. *A Journey into Christian Art*. Minneapolis: Fortress Press, 2000.

Broshi, Magen. "Estimating the Population of Ancient Jerusalem." *Biblical Archaeology Review* 4, no. 2 (1978): 10–15.

Brown, Peter. *Society and the Holy in Late Antiquity*. Berkeley: University of California Press, 1982.

Bruce, F. F. *The Acts of the Apostles: The Greek Text with Introduction and Commentary*. Grand Rapids: Eerdmans, 1990.

Busink, Théodore. *Der Tempel von Jerusalem von Salomo bis Herodes: eine archäologisch-historische Studie unter Berücksichtigung des westsemitischen Tempelbaus*. 2 vols. Leiden: Brill, 1970.

Camp, John M. *The Athenian Agora: Excavations in the Heart of Classical Athens*. London: Thames & Hudson, 1986.

Camp, John M., et al. "A Trophy from the Battle of Chaironeia of 86 B.C." *American Journal of Archaeology* 96 (1992): 443–55.

Campbell, Brian, ed. *The Roman Army, 31 BC–AD 337: A Sourcebook*. London and New York: Routledge, 1994.

Cancik, Hubert, and Hildegard Cancik-Lindemaier. "The Truth of Images: Cicero and Varro on Image Worship." Pages 43–61 in *Representation in Religion: Studies in Honor of Moshe Barasch*. Edited by Jan Assmann and Albert I. Baumgarten. Leiden: Brill, 2001.

Cardauns, Burkhart. *M. Terentius Varro Antiquitates rerum divinarum*. 2 vols. Wiesbaden, Germany: Franz Steiner, 1976.

Carroll, Robert P. "The Aniconic God and the Cult of Images." *Studia Theologica* 31 (1977): 51–64.

Castelli, Silvia. "Antiquities 3–4 and Against Apion 2.145ff.: Different Approaches to the Law." Pages 151–69 in *Internationales Josephus-Kolloquium Amsterdam 2000*. Edited by Jürgen U. Kalms. Münster, Germany: Lit, 2001.

Chancey, Mark A. *Greco-Roman Culture and the Galilee of Jesus*. Cambridge: Cambridge University Press, 2005.

Chapman, Honora H. "Spectacle and Theater in Josephus's *Bellum Judaicum*." Ph.D. diss., Stanford University, 1998.

———. "Spectacle in Josephus' *Jewish War*." Pages 289–313 in *Flavius Josephus and Flavian*

Rome. Edited by Jonathan Edmondson, Steve Mason, and James Rives. Oxford: Oxford University Press, 2005.

Christ, F. "Das Leben nach dem Tode bei Pseudo-Phokylides." *Theologische Zeitschrift* 31 (1975): 140–49.

Clarke, John R. *Art in the Lives of Ordinary Romans: Visual Representation and Non-elite Viewers in Italy, 100 B.C.–A.D. 315*. Berkeley: University of California Press, 2003.

———. *Roman Sex, 100 B.C.–A.D. 250*. New York: Harry N. Abrams, 2003.

Clerc, Charly. *Les théories relatives au culte des images chez les auteurs grecs du IIme siècle aprés J.-C.* Paris: Fontemoing, 1915.

Cohen, Boaz. "Art in Jewish Law." *Judaism* 3 (1954): 165–76.

Cohen, Shaye. *Josephus in Galilee and Rome: His Vita and Development as a Historian*. Leiden: Brill, 1979. Repr., Leiden: Brill, 2002.

———. *The Beginnings of Jewishness: Boundaries, Varieties, Uncertainties*. Berkeley: University of California Press, 1999.

Cohn, Leopold. "An Apocryphal Work Ascribed to Philo of Alexandria." *Jewish Quarterly Review* 10 (1898): 277–332.

Collins, John J. *Between Athens and Jerusalem: Jewish Identity in the Hellenistic Diaspora*. Grand Rapids: Eerdmans, 2000.

———. "Life after Death in Pseudo-Phocylides." Pages 75–86 in *Jerusalem, Alexandria, Rome: Studies in Ancient Cultural Interaction in Honour of A. Hillhorst*. Edited by Florentino García Martínez and Gerard P. Luttikhuizen. Leiden: Brill, 2003.

Collins, John J., and Gregory E. Sterling, eds. *Hellenism in the Land of Israel*. Notre Dame, Ind.: University of Notre Dame Press, 2001.

Conzelmann, Hans. *Acts of the Apostles*. Translated by James Limburg. Philadelphia: Fortress Press, 1987.

———. "The Address of Paul on the Areopagus." Pages 217–30 in *Studies in Luke-Acts: Essays Presented in Honor of Paul Schubert*. Edited by Leander Keck and J. Louis Martyn. London: SPCK, 1968.

Cotton, Hannah M., and Werner Eck. "Josephus' Roman Audience: Josephus and the Roman Elites." Pages 37–52 in *Flavius Josephus and Flavian Rome*. Edited by Jonathan Edmondson, Steve Mason, and James Rives. Oxford: Oxford University Press, 2005.

Croix, Horst de la, Richard G. Tansey, and Diane Kirkpatrick, eds. *Gardner's Art through the Ages*. 9th ed. Orlando, Fla.: Harcourt Brace College, 1991.

Davis, Richard H. "Indian Image-Worship and Its Discontents." Pages 107–32 in *Representation in Religion: Studies in Honor of Moshe Barasch*. Edited by Jan Assmann and Albert I. Baumgarten. Leiden: Brill, 2001.

Dibelius, Martin. *Studies in the Acts of the Apostles*. Translated by Mary Ling. London: SCM Press, 1956.

Dilke, Oswald A. W. *Greek and Roman Maps*. London: Thames & Hudson, 1985.

Dohmen, Cristoph. *Das Bilderverbot: Seine Entstehung und Entwicklung im Alten Testament*. Bonn: Hanstein, 1985.

Donohue, Alice A. *Xoana and the Origins of Greek Sculpture*. Atlanta: Scholars Press, 1988.

Dougherty, Carol, and Leslie Kurke. "Introduction: The Cultures within Greek Culture." Pages 1–19 in *The Cultures within Ancient Greek Culture: Contact, Conflict, Collaboration*. Edited by Carol Dougherty and Leslie Kurke. Cambridge: Cambridge University Press, 2003.

Droge, Arthur J. "Josephus between Greeks and Barbarians." Pages 115–42 in *Josephus' Contra Apionem: Studies in Its Character and Context with a Latin Concordance to the Portion Missing in Greek*. Leiden: Brill, 1996.

Droysen, J. G. *Geschichte des Hellenismus*. Tübingen: Mohr, 1952.

Edelstein, Emma J., and Ludwig Edelstein. *Asclepius: Collection and Interpretation of the Testimonies*. Baltimore: Johns Hopkins University Press, 1998.

Edmondson, Jonathan, Steve Mason, and James Rives, eds. *Flavius Josephus and Flavian Rome*. Oxford: Oxford University Press, 2005.

Edwards, Catharine. *The Politics of Immorality in Ancient Rome*. Cambridge: Cambridge University Press, 1993.

Ehrenkrook, Jason von. "Effeminacy in the Shadow of Empire: The Politics of Transgressive Gender in Josephus's *Bellum Judaicum*." *Jewish Quarterly Review* 101 (2011): 145–63.

———. "Image and Desire in the Wisdom of Solomon." *Zutot* 7 (2011): 41–50.

———. "Sculpture, Space, and the Poetics of Idolatry in Josephus' *Bellum Judaicum*." *Journal for the Study of Judaism in the Persian, Hellenistic, and Roman Period* 39 (2008): 170–91.

Ehrlich, Carl S. "Du sollst dir kein Gottesbildnis machen: Das zweite Gebot im Judentum." Pages 71–86 in *Bibel und Judentum: Beiträge aus dem christlich-jüdischen Gespräch*. Edited by Carl S. Ehrlich. Zürich: Pano, 2004.

Eliade, Mircea. *The Sacred and the Profane: The Nature of Religion*. New York: Harcourt, 1959.

Eliav, Yaron Z. "The Desolating Sacrilege: A Jewish-Christian Discourse on Statuary, Space, and Sanctity." Pages 605–27 in *The Sculptural Environment of the Roman Near East: Reflections on Culture, Ideology, and Power*. Edited by Yaron Z. Eliav, Elise Friedland, and Sharon Herbert. Louvain: Peeters, 2008.

———. *God's Mountain: The Temple Mount in Time, Place, and Memory*. Baltimore: Johns Hopkins University Press, 2005.

———. "Roman Statues, Rabbis, and Greco-Roman Culture." Pages 99–115 in *Jewish Literatures and Cultures: Context and Intertext*. Edited by Anita Norich and Yaron Z. Eliav. Providence, R.I.: Brown Judaic Studies, 2008.

———. "Viewing the Sculptural Environment: Shaping the Second Commandment." Pages 411–33 in *Talmud Yerushalmi and Graeco-Roman Culture*. Edited by Peter Schäfer. Tübingen: Mohr Siebeck, 2003.

Eliav, Yaron Z., Elise A. Friedland, and Sharon Herbert, eds. *The Sculptural Environment of the Roman Near East: Reflections on Culture, Ideology, and Power*. Louvain: Peeters, 2008.

Elsner, Jaś. "Archaeologies and Agendas: Reflections on Late Ancient Jewish Art and Early Christian Art." *Journal of Roman Studies* 93 (2003): 114–28.

———. *Art and the Roman Viewer: The Transformation of Art from the Pagan World to Christianity*. Cambridge: Cambridge University Press, 1995.

———. "The Origins of the Icon: Pilgrimage, Religion, and Visual Culture in the Roman East as 'Resistance' to the Centre." Pages 178–99 in *The Early Roman Empire in the East*. Edited by Susan E. Alcock. Oxford: Oxbow Books, 1997.

———. "Pausanias: A Greek Pilgrim in the Roman World." *Past and Present* 135 (1992): 3–29.

———. "Structuring 'Greece': Pausanias's *Periegesis* as a Literary Construct." Pages 3–20 in *Pausanias: Travel and Memory in Roman Greece*. Edited by Susan E. Alcock, John F. Cherry, and Jaś Elsner. Oxford: Oxford University Press, 2000.

———. "Visual Mimesis and the Myth of the Real: Ovid's Pygmalion as Viewer." *Ramus* 20 (1991): 154–68.

Elsner, Jaś, and Jaime Masters, eds. *Reflections of Nero: History, Culture, and Representation*. London: Duckworth, 1994.

Elsner, Jaś, and Ian Rutherford, eds. *Pilgrimage in Graeco-Roman and Early Christian Antiquity: Seeing the Gods*. Oxford: Oxford University Press, 2005.

Enns, Peter. *Exodus Retold: Ancient Exegesis of the Departure from Egypt in Wis 10:15–21 and 19:1–9*. Atlanta: Scholars Press, 1997.

Faur, José. "The Biblical Idea of Idolatry." *Jewish Quarterly Review* 69 (1978): 1–15.

Feldman, Louis H. "Flavius Josephus Revisited: The Man, His Writings, and His Significance." *Aufsteig und Niedergang der römischen Welt: Geschichte und Kultur Roms im Spiegel der neueren Forschung* II.21.2 (1984): 763–862.

———. *Josephus and Modern Scholarship (1937–1980)*. Berlin and New York: De Gruyter, 1984.

———. "Josephus as an Apologist to the Greco-Roman World: His Portrait of Solomon." Pages 69–98 in *Aspects of Religious Propaganda in Judaism and Early Christianity*. Edited by Elizabeth S. Fiorenza. Notre Dame, Ind.: University of Notre Dame Press, 1976.

———. *Josephus: A Supplementary Bibliography*. New York: Garland, 1986.

———. "Josephus' *Jewish Antiquities* and Pseudo-Philo's *Biblical Antiquities*." Pages 59–80 in *Josephus, the Bible, and History*. Edited by Louis H. Feldman and Gohei Hata. Detroit: Wayne State University Press, 1989.

———. "Josephus' Portrait of Moses." *Jewish Quarterly Review* 82 (1992): 285–328.

———. "Josephus' Portrait of Moses: Part Two." *Jewish Quarterly Review* 83 (1992): 7–50.

———. "Josephus' Portrait of Moses: Part Three." *Jewish Quarterly Review* 83 (1993): 301–30.

———. "Josephus' Portrait of Solomon." *Hebrew Union College Annual* 66 (1995): 103–67.

———. *Josephus's Interpretation of the Bible*. Berkeley: University of California Press, 1998.

———. *Judean Antiquities 1–4*. Flavius Josephus: Translation and Commentary 3. Edited by Steve Mason. Leiden: Brill, 2000.

———. "Parallel Lives of Two Lawgivers: Josephus' Moses and Plutarch's Lycurgus." Pages 209–42 in *Flavius Josephus and Flavian Rome*. Edited by Jonathan Edmondson, Steve Mason, and James Rives. Oxford: Oxford University Press, 2005.

———. *Studies in Josephus' Rewritten Bible*. Leiden: Brill, 1998.

Feldman, Louis H., and Meyer Reinhold, eds. *Jewish Life and Thought among Greeks and Romans: Primary Readings*. Minneapolis: Fortress Press, 1996.

Fine, Steven. *Art and Judaism in the Greco-Roman World: Toward a New Jewish Archaeology*. Cambridge: Cambridge University Press, 2005.

Finkbeiner, Douglas P. "The Essenes according to Josephus: Exploring the Contribution of Josephus' Portrait of the Essenes to his Larger Literary Agenda." Ph.D. diss., University of Pennsylvania, 2010.

Finney, Paul Corby. *The Invisible God: The Earliest Christians on Art*. New York: Oxford University Press, 1994.

———. "The Rabbi and the Coin Portrait (Mark 12:15b, 16): Rigorism Manqué." *Journal of Biblical Literature* 112 (1993): 629–44.

Fischer, Moshe L. *Marble Studies: Roman Palestine and Marble Trade*. Konstanz, Germany: UVK, 1998.

———. "Sculpture in Roman Palestine and Its Architectural and Social Milieu: Adaptability, Imitation, Originality? The Ascalon Basilica as an Example." Pages 483–508 in *The Sculptural Environment of the Roman Near East: Reflections on Culture, Ideology, and Power*. Edited by Yaron Z. Eliav, Elise Friedland, and Sharon Herbert. Louvain: Peeters, 2008.

Fletcher-Louis, Crispin H. T. "Humanity and the Idols of the Gods in Pseudo-Philo's *Biblical Antiquities*." Pages 58–72 in *Idolatry: False Worship in the Bible, Early Judaism, and Christianity*. Edited by Stephen C. Barton. London: T&T Clark, 2007.

———. "The Worship of Divine Humanity as God's Image and the Worship of Jesus." Pages 112–28 in *The Jewish Roots of Christological Monotheism*. Edited by Carey C. Newman, James R. Davila, and Gladys S. Lewis. Leiden: Brill, 1999.

Foerster, Gideon. "Art and Architecture in Palestine." Pages 971–1006 in *The Jewish People in the First Century: Historical Geography, Political History, Social, Cultural, and Religious Life and Institutions*. Edited by Shmuel Safrai et al. Philadelphia: Fortress Press, 1987.

Formstecher, Solomon. *Die Religion des Geistes: Eine wissenschaftliche Darstellung des Judenthums nach seinem Charakter, Entwicklungsgange und Berufe in der Menschheit*. Frankfurt am Main: J. C. Hermann, 1841.

Frankfort, H. *Sculpture of the Third Millennium from Tell Asmar and Khafaje*. Chicago: University of Chicago Press, 1939.

Frankfurter, David. "The Vitality of Egyptian Images in Late Antiquity: Christian Memory and Response." Pages 659–78 in *The Sculptural Environment of the Roman Near East: Reflections on Culture, Ideology, and Power*. Edited by Yaron Z. Eliav, Elise Friedland, and Sharon Herbert. Louvain: Peeters, 2008.

Frantsouzoff, Serguei A. "A Parallel to the Second Commandment in the Inscriptions of Raybūn." *Proceedings of the Seminar for Arabian Studies* 28 (1998): 61–67.

Frazer, James G. *Pausanias's Description of Greece*. 6 vols. New York: Biblo and Tannen, 1965.

Freedberg, David. *The Power of Images: Studies in the History and Theory of Response*. Chicago: University of Chicago Press, 1989.

Freedman, H., and Maurice Simon, eds. *Midrash Rabbah*. London: Soncino Press, 1939.

Frischer, B. *The Sculpted Word: Epicureanism and Philosophical Recruitment in Ancient Greece*. Berkeley: University of California Press, 1982.

Fuks, Gideon. "Josephus on Herod's Attitude towards Jewish Religion: The Darker Side." *Journal of Jewish Studies* 53 (2002): 238–45.

Gabba, Emilio. "The *Collegia* of Numa: Problems of Method and Political Ideas." *Journal of Roman Studies* 74 (1984): 81–86.

Gaifman, Milette. "Beyond Mimesis in Greek Religious Art: Aniconism in the Archaic and Classical Periods." Ph.D. diss., Princeton University, 2005.

Garnsey, Peter, and C. R. Whittaker, eds. *Imperialism in the Ancient World: The Cambridge University Research Seminar in Ancient History*. Cambridge: Cambridge University Press, 1978.

Geertz, Clifford. "Religion as a Cultural System." Pages 87–125 in *The Interpretation of Cultures: Selected Essays*. Edited by Clifford Geertz. London: Fontana Press, 1993.

Geffcken, Johannes. "Der Bilderstreit des heidnischen Altertums." *Archiv für Religionswissenschaft* 19 (1919): 286–315.

Gerber, Christine. *Ein Bild des Judentums für Nichtjuden von Flavius Josephus: Untersuchungen zu seiner Schrift Contra Apionem*. Leiden: Brill, 1997.

Gersht, Rivka. "Caesarean Sculpture in Context." Pages 509–38 in *The Sculptural Environment of the Roman Near East: Reflections on Culture, Ideology, and Power*. Edited by Yaron Z. Eliav, Elise Friedland, and Sharon Herbert. Louvain: Peeters, 2008.

———. "The Sculpture of Caesarea Maritima." Ph.D. diss., Tel Aviv University, 1987.

Geva, Hillel, ed. *Jewish Quarter Excavations in the Old City of Jerusalem: The Finds from Areas A, W, and X-2 Final Report*. 3 vols. Jerusalem: Israel Exploration Society, Institute of Archaeology, Hebrew University of Jerusalem, 2003.

Gilbert, Maurice. *La critique des dieux dans le Livre de la Sagesse*. Rome: Biblical Institute Press, 1973.

Gill, David W. J. "Achaia." Pages 433–53 in *The Book of Acts in Its Graeco-Roman Setting*. Edited by David W. J. Gill and Conrad Gempf. Grand Rapids: Eerdmans, 1994.

Gleason, Maud W. *Making Men: Sophists and Self-Presentation in Ancient Rome*. Princeton, N.J.: Princeton University Press, 1995.

Goldhill, Simon. "The Erotic Eye: Visual Stimulation and Cultural Conflict." Pages 154–94 in *Being Greek under Rome: Cultural Identity, the Second Sophistic, and the Development of Empire*. Edited by Simon Goldhill. Cambridge: Cambridge University Press, 2001.

Goldstein, Jonathan. "Jewish Acceptance and Rejection of Hellenism." Pages 64–87, 318–26 in *Aspects of Judaism in the Graeco-Roman Period*. Vol. 2 of *Jewish and Christian Self-Definition*. Edited by E. P. Sanders, A. L. Baumgarten, and Alan Mendelson. Philadelphia: SCM Press, 1981.

Goldsworthy, Adrian. *The Complete Roman Army*. London: Thames & Hudson, 2003.

Goodenough, Erwin Ramsdell. *Jewish Symbols in the Greco-Roman Period*. 13 vols. New York: Pantheon Books, 1953.

———. *Jewish Symbols in the Greco-Roman Period: Abridged Edition*. Edited by Jacob Neusner. Princeton, N.J.: Princeton University Press, 1988.

Goodman, Martin. "Coinage and Identity: The Jewish Evidence." Pages 163–66 in *Coinage and Identity in the Roman Provinces*. Edited by Christopher Howgego, Volker Heuchert, and Andrew Burnett. Oxford: Oxford University Press, 2005.

———. "The *Fiscus Iudaicus* and Gentile Attitudes to Judaism in Flavian Rome." Pages 167–77 in *Flavius Josephus and Flavian Rome*. Edited by Jonathan Edmondson, Steve Mason, and James Rives. Oxford: Oxford University Press, 2005.

———."A Note on Josephus, the Pharisees, and Ancestral Tradition." *Journal of Jewish Studies* 50 (1999): 17–20.

———. "Jews, Greeks, and Romans." *Jews in a Graeco-Roman World*. Edited by Martin Goodman. Oxford: Clarendon Press, 1998.

———. "Josephus as Roman Citizen." Pages 329–38 in *Josephus and the History of the Greco-Roman Period: Essays in Memory of Morton Smith*. Edited by Fausto Parente and Joseph Sievers. Leiden: Brill, 1994.

———. *Rome and Jerusalem: The Clash of Ancient Civilizations*. New York: Alfred A. Knopf, 2007.

———. "The Pilgrimage Economy of Jerusalem in the Second Temple Period." Pages 69–76 in *Jerusalem: Its Sanctity and Centrality to Judaism, Christianity, and Islam*. Edited by Lee I. Levine. New York: Continuum, 1999.

———. "The Roman Identity of Roman Jews." Pages 85–99 in *The Jews in the Hellenistic-Roman World: Studies in Memory of Menahem Stern*. Edited by Isaiah M. Gafni, Aharon Oppenheimer, and Daniel R. Schwartz. Jerusalem: Zalman Shazar Center for Jewish History, 1996.

Graetz, Heinrich. *The Structure of Jewish History and Other Essays*. Translated by Ismar Schorsch. New York: Jewish Theological Seminary of America, 1975.

Grant, Michael. *Herod the Great*. New York: American Heritage Press, 1971.

———. *The Jews in the Roman World*. London: Weidenfeld and Nicolson, 1973.

———. *Nero*. London: Weidenfeld and Nicolson, 1970.

Gregory, A. P. " 'Powerful Images': Responses to Portraits and the Political Uses of Images in Rome." *Journal of Roman Studies* 7 (1994): 80–99.

Griffin, Miriam T. "The Flavians." Pages 1–83 in *The Cambridge Ancient History Volume XI: The High Empire, A.D. 70–192*. Edited by Alan K. Bowman, Peter Garnsey, and Dominic Rathbone. Cambridge: Cambridge University Press, 2000.

———. *Nero: The End of a Dynasty*. London: B. T. Batsford, 1984.

Groag, Edmund. "Zur Kritik von Tacitus' Quellen in den Historien." *Jahrbücher für classische Philologie* Suppl. 23 (1897): 709–99.

Gruen, Erich S. "Greeks and Jews: Mutual Misperceptions in Josephus' *Contra Apionem*." Pages 31–51 in *Ancient Judaism in Its Hellenistic Context*. Leiden: Brill, 2005.

———. *Heritage and Hellenism: The Reinvention of Jewish Tradition*. Berkeley: University of California Press, 1998.

Gutmann, Joseph. "The 'Second Commandment' and the Image in Judaism." *Hebrew Union College Annual* 32 (1961): 161–74.

Haaland, Gunnar. "Jewish Laws for a Roman Audience: Towards an Understanding of *Contra Apionem*." Pages 282–304 in *Internationales Josephus-Kolloquium, Brussel 1998*. Edited by Folker Siegert and Jürgen U. Kalms. Münster, Germany: Lit, 1999.

———. "What Difference Does Philosophy Make? The Three Schools as a Rhetorical Device in Josephus." Pages 262–88 in *Making History: Josephus and Historical Method*. Edited by Zuleika Rodgers. Leiden: Brill, 2007.

Habicht, Christian. *Pausanias' Guide to Ancient Greece*. Berkeley: University of California Press, 1985.

Hachlili, Rachel. *Ancient Jewish Art and Archaeology in the Diaspora*. Leiden: Brill, 1998.

———. *Ancient Jewish Art and Archaeology in the Land of Israel*. Leiden: Brill, 1988.

———. *Jewish Ornamented Ossuaries of the Late Second Temple Period*. Haifa, Israel: Reuben and Edith Hecht Museum, University of Haifa, 1988.

Hadas-Lebel, Mireille. "Flavius Josephus, Historian of Rome." Pages 99–106 in *Josephus and the History of the Greco-Roman Period*. Leiden: Brill, 1994.

Halbertal, Moshe, and Avishai Margalit. *Idolatry*. Cambridge: Harvard University Press, 1992.

Hall, Jonathan M. *Ethnic Identity in Greek Antiquity*. Cambridge: Cambridge University Press, 1997.

———. *Hellenicity: Between Ethnicity and Culture*. Chicago: University of Chicago Press, 2002.

Hallett, Judith P. "Female Homoeroticism and the Denial of Roman Reality in Latin Literature." *Yale Journal of Criticism* 3 (1989): 209–27.

———. "Roman Attitudes toward Sex." Pages 1265–78 in vol. 2 of *Civilization of the Ancient Mediterranean: Greece and Rome*. Edited by Michael Grant and Rachel Kitzinger. 3 vols. New York: Charles Scribner's Sons, 1988.

Hamilton, Sarah, and Andrew Spicer. "Defining the Holy: The Delineation of Sacred Space." Pages 1–23 in *Defining the Holy: Sacred Space in Medieval and Early Modern Europe*. Edited by Andrew Spicer and Sarah Hamilton. Burlington, Vt.: Ashgate, 2005.

Harley, J. Brian. "The Map and the Development of the History of Cartography." Pages 1–42 in *The History of Cartography: Cartography in Prehistoric, Ancient, and Medieval Europe and the Mediterranean*. Edited by J. Brian Harley and David Woodward. Chicago: University of Chicago Press, 1987.

Harlow, Daniel C. "Idolatry and Alterity: Israel and the Nations in the *Apocalypse of Abraham*." Pages 302–30 in *The "Other" in Second Temple Judaism: Essays in Honor of John J. Collins*. Edited by Daniel C. Harlow et al. Grand Rapids: Eerdmans, 2011.

Harrington, Daniel J. "The Original Language of Pseudo-Philo's *Liber Antiquitatum Biblicarum*." *Harvard Theological Review* 63 (1970): 503–14.

———. "Pseudo-Philo: A New Translation and Introduction." Pages 297–377 in vol. 2 of *The Old Testament Pseudepigrapha*. Edited by James H. Charlesworth. 2 vols. New York: Doubleday, 1985.

Hartog, François. *The Mirror of Herodotus: The Representation of the Other in the Writing of History*. Berkeley: University of California Press, 1988.

Haynes, Holly. *The History of Make-Believe: Tacitus on Imperial Rome*. Berkeley: University of California Press, 2003.

Hayward, Robert. "Observations on Idols in Septuagint Pentateuch." Pages 40–57 in *Idolatry: False Worship in the Bible, Early Judaism, and Christianity*. Edited by Stephen C. Barton. London: T&T Clark, 2007.

Hegel, Georg W. F. "Der Geist des Christentums und sein Schicksal." Pages 241–342 in *Hegels theologische jugendschriften nach den handschriften der Kgl. Bibliothek in Berlin*. Edited by Herman Nohl. Tübingen: Mohr Siebeck, 1907.

———. *On Art, Religion, Philosophy: Introductory Lectures to the Realm of Absolute Spirit*. New York and Evanston, Ill.: Harper & Row, 1970.

Hendel, Ronald S. "The Social Origins of the Aniconic Tradition in Early Israel." *Catholic Biblical Quarterly* 50 (1988): 365–82.

Hengel, Martin. *The "Hellenization" of Judaea in the First Century after Christ*. Eugene, Oreg.: Wipf and Stock, 1989.

———. *Jews, Greeks, and Barbarians*. Philadelphia: Fortress Press, 1980.

———. *Judaism and Hellenism*. Translated by John Bowden. London: SCM Press, 1974. Translation of *Judentum und Hellenismus*. Tübingen: Max Niemeyer Verlag, 1969.

Henrichs, Albert. "Graecia Capta: Roman Views of Greek Culture." *Harvard Studies in Classical Philology* 97 (1995): 243–61.

Hershkovitz, Malka. "Gemstones." Pages 296–301 in vol. 2 of *Jewish Quarter Excavations in the Old City of Jerusalem: The Finds from Areas A, W, and X-2 Final Report*. Edited by Hillel Geva. 3 vols. Jerusalem: Israel Exploration Society, Institute of Archaeology, Hebrew University of Jerusalem, 2003.

Holter, Knut. *Deuteronomy 4 and the Second Commandment*. New York: Peter Lang, 2003.

Hope, Valerie M. "Trophies and Tombstones: Commemorating the Roman Soldier." *World Archaeology* 35 (2003): 79–97.

Hopkins, Keith. *A World Full of Gods: The Strange Triumph of Christianity*. New York: Plume, 1999.

Horbury, William, and David Noy, eds. *Jewish Inscriptions of Greco-Roman Egypt*. Cambridge: Cambridge University Press, 1992.

Horst, Pieter Willem van der. "The Altar of the 'Unknown God' in Athens (Acts 17:23) and the Cults of 'Unknown Gods' in the Graeco-Roman World." Pages 165–202 in *Hellenism–Judaism–Christianity*. Kampen, Germany: Kok Pharos, 1994.

———. "The Distinctive Vocabulary of Josephus' *Contra Apionem*." Pages 83–93 in *Josephus' Contra Apionem: Studies in Its Character and Context with a Latin Concordance to the Portion Missing in Greek*. Edited by Louis H. Feldman and John R. Levison. Leiden: Brill, 1996.

———. "Pseudo-Phocylides on the Afterlife: A Rejoinder to John J. Collins." *Journal for the Study of Judaism in the Persian, Hellenistic, and Roman Period* 35 (2004): 70–75.

———. "Pseudo-Phocylides Revisited." *Journal for the Study of the Pseudepigrapha* 3 (1988): 3–30.

———. *The Sentences of Pseudo-Phocylides*. Leiden: E. J. Brill, 1978.

Houtman, Cornelis. *Exodus*. 3 vols. Kampen, Germany: Kok, 1993.

Hutton, William. "The Construction of Religious Space in Pausanias." Pages 291–317 in *Pilgrimage in Graeco-Roman and Early Christian Antiquity: Seeing the Gods*. Edited by Jaś Elsner and Ian Rutherford. Oxford: Oxford University Press, 2005.

Isaac, Benjamin. "Roman Victory Displayed: Symbols, Allegories, Personifications?" Pages 575–604 in *The Sculptural Environment of the Roman Near East: Reflections on Culture,*

Ideology, and Power. Edited by Yaron Z. Eliav, Elise Friedland, and Sharon Herbert. Louvain: Peeters, 2008.

Jackson, F. J. Foakes. *Josephus and the Jews: The Religion and History of the Jews as Explained by Flavius Josephus*. London: SPCK, 1930.

Jacob, Benno. "The Decalogue." *Jewish Quarterly Review* 14 (1923): 141–87.

———. "The First and Second Commandments." *Judaism* 13 (1964): 3–18.

Jacob, Christian. "Paysages hantés et jardins merveilleux: La Grèce imaginaire de Pausanias." *L'Ethnographie* 76 (1980–81): 35–67.

Jacobson, Howard. *A Commentary on Pseudo-Philo's Liber antiquitatum biblicarum with Latin Text and English Translation*. Leiden: Brill, 1996.

Janssen, Andreas Jozef. *Het antieke Tropaion*. Brussels: Paleis der Academiën, 1957.

Japp, Sarah. *Die Baupolitik Herodes' des Großen: Die Bedeutung der Architektur für die Herrschaftslegitimation eines römischen Klientelkönigs*. Leidorf, Germany: Rahden/Westf., 2000.

Jaroš, Karl. *In Sachen Pontius Pilatus*. Mainz, Germany: Philipp von Zabern, 2002.

Jeremias, Joachim. *Jerusalem in the Time of Jesus: An Investigation into Economic and Social Conditions during the New Testament*. London: SCM, 1969.

Jervell, Jacob. "Imagines und Imago Dei: Aus der Genesis-Exodus des Josephus." Pages 197–204 in *Josephus-Studien: Untersuchungen zu Josephus, dem antiken Judentum und dem Neuen Testament*. Edited by Otto Betz, Klaus Haacker, and Martin Hengel. Göttingen: Vandenhoeck & Ruprecht, 1974.

Jones, A. H. M. *The Herods of Judaea*. Oxford: Clarendon Press, 1967.

Jones, Brian W. *The Emperor Domitian*. London and New York: Routledge, 1992.

———. *The Emperor Titus*. New York: St. Martin's Press, 1984.

Jones, Brian W., and Robert Milns. *Seutonius: The Flavian Emperors. A Historical Commentary*. London: Bristol Classical Press, 2002.

Jones, Christopher P. "Josephus and Greek Literature in Flavian Rome." Pages 201–8 in *Flavius Josephus and Flavian Rome*. Edited by Jonathan Edmondson, Steve Mason, and James Rives. Oxford: Oxford University Press, 2005.

———. "Towards a Chronology of Plutarch's Works." *Journal of Roman Studies* 56 (1966): 61–74.

Kalmin, Richard. "Idolatry in Late Antique Babylonia: The Evidence of the Babylonian Talmud." Pages 629–57 in *The Sculptural Environment of the Roman Near East: Reflections on Culture, Ideology, and Power*. Edited by Yaron Z. Eliav, Elise Friedland, and Sharon Herbert. Louvain: Peeters, 2008.

Kasher, Aryeh. "The *Isopoliteia* Question in Caesarea Maritima." *Jewish Quarterly Review* 68 (1977): 16–27.

———. "Polemic and Apologetic Methods of Writing in *Contra Apionem*." Pages 143–86 in *Josephus' Contra Apionem*. Edited by John R. Levison and Louis H. Feldman. Leiden: Brill, 1996.

———. "The Target Audience of '*Against Apion*' by Flavius Josephus." Pages 81–91 in *Hellenic and Jewish Arts: Interaction, Tradition, and Renewal*. Tel Aviv: Ramot, 1998.

Kedar, Benjamin Z., and R. J. Zwi Werblowsky, eds. *Sacred Space: Shrine, City, Land*. New York: New York University Press, 1998.

Keel, Othmar, and Christoph Uehlinger. *Gods, Goddesses, and Images of God in Ancient Israel*. Minneapolis: Fortress Press, 1998.

Kennedy, Charles A. "The Semantic Field of the Term 'Idolatry'." Pages 193–204 in *Uncovering Ancient Stones: Essays in Memory of H. Neil Richardson*. Edited by Lewis M. Hopfe. Winona Lake, Ind.: Eisenbrauns, 1994.

Kessler, Herbert L. "'Thou Shalt Paint the Likeness of Christ Himself': The Mosaic Prohibition as Provocation for Christian Images." Pages 124–39 in *The Real and Ideal Jerusalem in Jewish, Christian, and Islamic Art*. Edited by Bianca Kühnel. Jerusalem: Hebrew University, 1998.

Klein, Gottlieb. *Der älteste christliche Katechismus und die jüdische Propagandaliteratur*. Berlin: G. Reimer, 1909.

Kloppenborg, John. "Ethnic and Political Factors in the Conflict at Caesarea Maritima." Pages 227–48 in *Religious Rivalries and the Struggle for Success in Caesarea Maritima*. Edited by Terence L. Donaldson. Waterloo, Ont.: Canadian Corporation for Studies in Religion, 2000.

Kohler, Kaufman. "Art, Attitudes of Judaism Toward." Pages 138–41 in vol. 2 of *The Jewish Encyclopedia*. Edited by Isodore Singer. 12 vols. New York: Funk and Wagnalls, 1901.

Konikoff, Carmel. *The Second Commandment and Its Interpretation in the Art of Ancient Israel*. Geneva: Imprimerie du Journal de Genève, 1973.

Kooten, George H. van. "Pagan and Jewish Monotheism according to Varro, Plutarch, and St Paul: The Aniconic, Monotheistic Beginnings of Rome's Pagan Cult—Romans 1:19–25 in a Roman Context." Pages 633–51 in *Flores Florentino: Dead Sea Scrolls and Other Early Jewish Studies in Honour of Florentino García Martínez*. Edited by Anthony Hilhorst, Émile Puech, and Eibert Tigchelaar. Leiden: Brill, 2007.

Kraeling, Carl H. "The Episode of the Golden Standards at Jerusalem." *Harvard Theological Review* 35 (1942): 263–89.

Kraus, Christina S. "From Exempla to Exemplar? Writing History around the Emperor in Imperial Rome." Pages 181–200 in *Flavius Josephus and Flavian Rome*. Edited by Jonathan Edmondson, Steve Mason, and James Rives. Oxford: Oxford University Press, 2005.

Krech, Volkhard. "Art and Religion." Pages 398–418 in *Religion Past and Present: Encyclopedia of Theology and Religion*. Edited by Hans Dieter Betz et al. 4th ed. 13 vols. Leiden: Brill, 2007.

Krenkel, Werner A. "Sex und politische Biographie." *Wissenschaftliche Zeitschrift der Wilhelm- Pieck-Universität Rostock, Gesellschaftliche und sprachwissenschaftliche Reihe* 29 (1980): 65–76.

Krieger, Klaus-Stefan. "A Synoptic Approach to B 2:117–283 and A 18–20." Pages 90–100 in *Internationales Josephus-Kolloquium Paris 2001: Studies on the Antiquities of Josephus*. Edited by Folker Siegert and Jürgen U. Kalms. Münster, Germany: Lit Verlag, 2001.

Kugel, James L. *Traditions of the Bible: A Guide to the Bible as It Was at the Start of the Common Era*. Cambridge: Harvard University Press, 1998.

Kuntz, Paul Grimley. "Philo Judaeus: A Decalogue in Balance." Pages 11–26 in *The Ten Commandments in History: Mosaic Paradigms for a Well-Ordered Society*. Grand Rapids: Eerdmans, 2004.

Kutsch, Ernst. "'Du sollst dir kein Gottesbild machen': Zu Weisheit Salomos 14,15." Pages 279–86 in *Alttestamentlicher Glaube und Biblische Theologie*. Edited by Horst Dietrich Preuß. Stuttgart: Verlag W. Kohlhammer, 1992.

Landau, Tamar. *Out-Heroding Herod: Josephus, Rhetoric, and the Herod Narratives*. Leiden: Brill, 2006.

Lange, N. R. M. de. "Jewish Attitudes to the Roman Empire." Pages 255–81 in *Imperialism in the Ancient World: The Cambridge University Research Seminar in Ancient History*. Edited by Peter Garnsey and C. R. Whittaker. Cambridge: Cambridge University Press, 1978.

Langlands, Rebecca. *Sexual Morality in Ancient Rome*. Cambridge: Cambridge University Press, 2006.

Laperrousaz, E.-M. "Does the Temple Scroll Date from the First or Second Century BCE?" Pages 91–97 in *Temple Scroll Studies*. Edited by George J. Brooke. Sheffield: JSOT Press, 1989.

Laqueur, Richard. *Der jüdische Historiker Flavius Josephus: Ein biographischer Versuch auf neuer quellenkritischer Grundlage*. Gießen, Germany: Münchow, 1920.

Lebram, Jürgen C. H. "Der Idealstaat der Juden." Pages 233–53 in *Josephus-Studien: Untersuchungen zu Josephus, dem antiken Judentum und dem Neuen Testament*. Edited by Otto Betz, Klaus Haacker, and Martin Hengel. Göttingen: Vandenhoeck & Ruprecht, 1974.

Leppert, Richard D. *Art and the Committed Eye: The Cultural Functions of Imagery*. Boulder, Colo.: Westview Press, 1996.

Levick, Barbara. *Vespasian*. London: Routledge, 1999.

Levine, Lee I. *The Ancient Synagogue: The First Thousand Years*. New Haven: Yale University Press, 2000.

———. "Figural Art in Ancient Judaism." *Ars Judaica* 1 (2005): 9–26.

———. *Jerusalem: Portrait of the City in the Second Temple Period (538 B.C.E.–70 C.E.)*. Philadelphia: Jewish Publication Society, 2002.

———. "The Jewish-Greek Conflict in First Century Caesarea." *Journal of Jewish Studies* 25 (1974): 381–97.

———. "Josephus' Description of the Jerusalem Temple: *War*, *Antiquities*, and Other Sources." Pages 233–46 in *Josephus and the History of the Greco-Roman Period*. Edited by Fausto Parente and Joseph Sievers. Leiden: Brill, 1994.

———. *Judaism and Hellenism in Antiquity: Conflict or Confluence?* Peabody, Mass.: Hendrickson, 1999.

———. "Second Temple Jerusalem: A Jewish City in the Greco-Roman Orbit." Pages 53–76 in *Jerusalem: Its Sanctity and Centrality to Judaism, Christianity, and Islam*. Edited by Lee I. Levine. New York: Continuum, 1999.

Lewis, T. J. "Divine Image: Aniconism in Ancient Israel." *Journal of the American Oriental Society* 118 (1998): 36–53.

Lichtenberger, Achim. *Die Baupolitik des Herodes des Großen*. Wiesbaden, Germany: Harrassowitz Verlag, 1999.

———. "Jesus and the Theater in Jerusalem." Pages 283–99 in *Jesus and Archaeology*. Edited by James H. Charlesworth. Grand Rapids: Eerdmans, 2006.

Lieberman, Saul. *Hellenism in Jewish Palestine*. New York: Jewish Theological Seminary, 1950.

Lieu, Judith. "Not Hellenes but Philistines? The Maccabees and Josephus Defining the 'Other'." *Journal of Jewish Studies* 53 (2002): 246–63.

Lightfoot, Jane L. *Lucian: On the Syrian Goddess*. Oxford: Oxford University Press, 2003.

Lilla, Mark. *The Stillborn God: Religion, Politics, and the Modern West*. New York: Alfred A. Knopf, 2007.

Lindner, Helgo. *Die Geschichtsauffassung des Flavius Josephus im Bellum Judaicum*. Leiden: Brill, 1972.

Lopez, Davina C. "Before Your Very Eyes: Roman Imperial Ideology, Gender Constructs, and Paul's Inter-nationalism." Pages 115–62 in *Mapping Gender in Ancient Religious Discourses*. Edited by Todd Penner and Caroline Vander Stichele. Leiden: Brill, 2007.

Lüderitz, Gert, ed. *Corpus jüdischer Zeugnisse aus der Cyrenaika*. Wiesbaden, Germany: Ludwig Reichert, 1983.

Ludwich, Arthur. "Quaestionum pseudophocylidearum pars altera." Pages 27–32 in *Programm Königsberg*. Königsberg, Germany: Universität Königsberg, 1904.

Lunt, H. G. "Ladder of Jacob: A New Translation and Introduction." Pages 401–11 in vol. 2 of *The Old Testament Pseudepigrapha*. Edited by James H. Charlesworth. 2 vols. New York: Doubleday, 1985.

MacMullen, Ramsay. "Roman Attitudes to Greek Love." *Historia* 31 (1982): 484–502.

Mader, Gottfried. *Josephus and the Politics of Historiography: Apologetic and Impression Management in the Bellum Judaicum*. Leiden: Brill, 2000.

Malkin, Irad, ed. *Ancient Perceptions of Greek Ethnicity*. Cambridge: Harvard University Press, 2001.

Mango, Cyril. "Antique Statuary and the Byzantine Beholder." *Dumbarton Oaks Papers* 17 (1963): 55–75.

Martínez, Florentino García. "Temple Scroll." Pages 927–33 in vol. 2 of *Encyclopedia of the Dead Sea Scrolls*. Edited by Lawrence H. Schiffman and James C. VanderKam. 2 vols. Oxford: Oxford University Press, 2000.

Mason, Steve. "The *Contra Apionem* in Social and Literary Context: An Invitation to Judean Philosophy." Pages 187–228 in *Josephus' "Contra Apionem": Studies in Its Character and Context with a Latin Concordance to the Portion Missing in Greek*. Edited by Louis H. Feldman and John R. Levison. Leiden: Brill, 1996.

———. "Figured Speech and Irony in T. Flavius Josephus." Pages 243–88 in *Flavius Josephus and Flavian Rome*. Edited by Jonathan Edmondson, Steve Mason, and James Rives. Oxford: Oxford University Press, 2005.

———. "Flavius Josephus in Flavian Rome: Reading on and between the Lines." Pages 559–89 in *Flavian Rome: Culture, Image, Text*. Edited by A. J. Boyle and W. J. Dominik. Leiden: Brill, 2003.

———. *Flavius Josephus on the Pharisees: A Compositional-Critical Study*. Leiden: Brill, 2001.

———. "The Greeks and the Distant Past in Josephus's *Judaean War*." Pages 93–130 in *Antiquity in Antiquity: Jewish and Christian Pasts in the Greco-Roman World*. Edited by Gregg Gardner and Kevin L. Osterloh. Tübingen: Mohr Siebeck, 2008.

———. "Introduction to the Judean Antiquities." Pages ix–xxxvi in *Judean Antiquities 1–4*. Flavius Josephus: Translation and Commentary 3. Edited by Steve Mason. Leiden: Brill, 2000.

———. "Jews, Judaeans, Judaizing, Judaism: Problems of Categorization in Ancient History." *Journal for the Study of Judaism in the Persian, Hellenistic, and Roman Period* 38 (2007): 457–512.

———. "Josephus, Daniel, and the Flavian House." Pages 161–91 in *Josephus and the History of the Greco-Roman Period*. Edited by Fausto Parente and Joseph Sievers. Leiden: Brill, 1994.

———. *Judean War 2*. Flavius Josephus: Translation and Commentary 1b. Edited by Steve Mason. Leiden: Brill, 2008.

———. *Life of Josephus*. Flavius Josephus: Translation and Commentary 9. Edited by Steve Mason. Leiden: Brill, 2001.

———. "Of Audience and Meaning: Reading Josephus' *Bellum Judaicum* in the Context of a Flavian Audience." Pages 71–100 in *Josephus and Jewish History in Flavian Rome and Beyond*. Edited by Joseph Sievers and Gaia Lembi. Leiden: Brill, 2005.

———. " 'Should Any Wish to Enquire Further' (Ant. 1.25): The Aim and Audience of Josephus's *Judean Antiquities/Life*." Pages 64–103 in *Understanding Josephus: Seven Perspectives*. Edited by Steve Mason. Sheffield: Sheffield Academic Press, 1998.

Maxfield, Valerie A. *The Military Decorations of the Roman Army*. London: B. T. Batsford, 1981.

McClister, David. "Ethnicity and Jewish Identity in Josephus." Ph.D. diss., University of Florida, 2008.

McCracken, George E. *Arnobius of Sicca: The Case against the Pagans*. Westminster, Md.: Newman Press, 1949.

Mellor, Ronald. "The New Aristocracy of Power." Pages 69–101 in *Flavian Rome: Culture, Image, Text*. Edited by A. J. Boyle and W. J. Dominik. Leiden: Brill, 2003.

Meshorer, Ya'akov. *A Treasury of Jewish Coins from the Persian Period to Bar Kokhba*. Jerusalem: Yad Ben-Zvi Press, 2001.

Mettinger, Tryggve. *No Graven Image? Israelite Aniconism in Its Ancient Near Eastern Context*. Stockholm: Almqvist & Wiksell, 1995.

Metzler, Dieter. "Anikonische Darstellungen." *Visible Religion* 5 (1986): 96–113.

Millar, Fergus. "Last Year in Jerusalem: Monuments of the Jewish War in Rome." Pages 101–28 in *Flavius Josephus and Flavian Rome*. Edited by Jonathan Edmondson, Steve Mason, and James Rives. Oxford: Oxford University Press, 2005.

———. *The Roman Near East: 31 BC–AD 337*. Cambridge: Harvard University Press, 1993.

Mitchell, W. J. T. *Iconology: Image, Text, Ideology*. Chicago: University of Chicago Press, 1986.

———. *Picture Theory: Essays on Verbal and Visual Interpretation*. Chicago: University of Chicago Press, 1994.

Moehring, Horst R. "Joseph ben Matthia and Flavius Josephus: The Jewish Prophet and Roman Historian." *Aufsteig und Niedergang der römischen Welt: Geschichte und Kultur Roms im Spiegel der neueren Forschung* II.21.2 (1984): 864–944.

Momigliano, Arnaldo. *The Classical Foundations of Modern Historiography*. Berkeley: University of California Press, 1990.

Moore, Carey A. *Daniel, Esther, and Jeremiah: The Additions*. Garden City, N.Y.: Doubleday, 1977.

Moore, George F. "Baetylia." *American Journal of Archaeology* 7 (1903): 198–208.

Mossman, Judith. "Plutarch's Use of Statues." *Georgica: Greek Studies in Honour of George Cawkwell*. Edited by Michael A. Flower and Mark Toher. London: Institute of Classical Studies, 1991.

Murphy, Frederick J. "Retelling the Bible: Idolatry in Pseudo-Philo." *Journal of Biblical Literature* 107 (1988): 275–87.

Nat, P. G. Van Der. "Observations on Tertullian's Treatise on Idolatry." *Vigiliae Christianae* 17 (1963): 71–84.

Netzer, Ehud. *The Architecture of Herod, the Great Builder*. Tübingen: Mohr Siebeck, 2006.

Newell, Raymond. "The Forms and Historical Value of Josephus' Suicide Accounts." Pages 278–294 in *Josephus, the Bible, and History*. Edited by Louis H. Feldman and Gohei Hata. Detroit: Wayne State University Press, 1989.

Nickelsburg, George W. E. *Jewish Literature between the Bible and the Mishnah*. Minneapolis: Fortress Press, 2005.

Nicolet, Claude. *Space, Geography, and Politics in the Early Roman Empire*. Ann Arbor: University of Michigan, 1991.

Niehr, Herbert. "In Search for YHWH's Cult Statue in the First Temple." Pages 73–95 in *The Image and the Book: Iconic Cults, Aniconism, and the Rise of Book Religion in Israel and the Ancient Near East*. Edited by Karel van der Toorn. Louvain: Peeters, 1997.

Niese, Benedict, ed. *Flavii Josephi Opera*. 7 vols. Berlin: Weidmann, 1885.

Nodet, Étienne. "Josephus' Attempt to Reorganize Judaism from Rome." Pages 103–22 in *Making History: Josephus and Historical Method*. Edited by Zuleika Rodgers. Leiden: Brill, 2007.

Nodet, Étienne, ed. *Flavius Josèphe, Les Antiquitiés Juives*. 2 vols. Paris: Les Éditions du Cerf, 1990.
Noy, David, ed. *Jewish Inscriptions of Western Europe: The City of Rome*. Cambridge: Cambridge University Press, 2005.
Oikonomides, Al. N. *The Two Agoras in Ancient Athens: A New Commentary on Their History and Development, Topography, and Monuments*. Chicago: Argonaut, 1964.
Olin, Margaret. *The Nation without Art: Examining Modern Discourses on Jewish Art*. Lincoln: University of Nebraska Press, 2001.
Ornan, Tallay. "Idols and Symbols: Divine Representation in First Millennium Mesopotamian Art and Its Bearing on the Second Commandment." *Tel Aviv* 31 (2004): 90–121.
Ouellette, Jean. "Le deuxième commandement et le role de l'image dans la symbolique religieuse de l'Ancien Testament: Essai d'interprétation." *Revue Biblique* 74 (1967): 504–16.
Ovadiah, Asher. *Hellenic and Jewish Arts: Interaction, Tradition, and Renewal*. Tel Aviv: Ramot, Tel Aviv University, 1998.
Parker, Holt N. "The Teratogenic Grid." Pages 47–65 in *Roman Sexualities*. Edited by Judith P. Hallett and Marilyn B. Skinner. Princeton, N.J.: Princeton University Press, 1997.
Parker, Robert. *Cleomenes on the Acropolis*. Oxford: Clarendon Press, 1998.
———. *Miasma: Pollution and Purification in Early Greek Religion*. Oxford: Oxford University Press, 1983.
Patrich, Joseph. *The Formation of Nabatean Art: Prohibition of a Graven Image among the Nabateans*. Jerusalem: Magnes Press, 1990.
———. "Herod's Theatre in Jerusalem: A New Proposal." *Israel Exploration Journal* 52 (2002): 231–39.
———. "Nabataean Art between East and West: A Methodological Assessment." Pages 79–101 in *The World of the Nabataeans*. Vol. 2 of *The International Conference: The World of the Herods and the Nabataeans*. Edited by Konstantinos D. Politis. Stuttgart: Franz Steiner Verlag, 2007.
Paul, G. M. "The Presentation of Titus in the 'Jewish War' of Josephus: Two Aspects." *Phoenix* 47 (1993): 56–66.
Penwill, John L. "Expelling the Mind: Politics and Philosophy in Flavian Rome." Pages 345–68 in *Flavian Rome: Culture, Image, Text*. Edited by A. J. Boyle and W. J. Dominik. Leiden: Brill, 2003.
Perry, Ellen. "Divine Statues in the Works of Libanius of Antioch: The Actual and Rhetorical Desacralization of Pagan Cult Furniture in the Late Fourth Century C.E." Pages 437–48 in *The Sculptural Environment of the Roman Near East: Reflections on Culture, Ideology, and Power*. Edited by Yaron Z. Eliav, Elise A. Friedland, and Sharon Herbert. Louvain: Peeters, 2008.
Petrochilos, Nicholas. *Roman Attitudes to the Greeks*. Athens: National and Capodistrian University of Athens, 1974.
Pfeiffer, R. H. "The Polemic against Idolatry in the Old Testament." *Journal of Biblical Literature* 43 (1924): 229–40.
Picard, Gilbert Charles. *Les trophées romains: Contribution à l'histoire de la religion et de l'art triomphal de Rome*. Paris: E. de Boccard, 1957.
Pollini, John. "Gods and Emperors in the East: Images of Power and the Power of Intolerance." Pages 165–94 in *The Sculptural Environment of the Roman Near East: Reflections on Culture, Ideology, and Power*. Edited by Yaron Z. Eliav, Elise A. Friedland, and Sharon Herbert. Louvain: Peeters, 2008.
Porter, James I. "Ideals and Ruins: Pausanias, Longinus, and the Second Sophistic." Pages

63–92 in *Pausanias: Travel and Memory in Roman Greece*. Edited by Susan E. Alcock, John F. Cherry, and Jaś Elsner. Oxford: Oxford University Press, 2000.

Poulsen, F. "Talking, Weeping, and Bleeding Statues." *Acta Archaeologica* 16 (1945): 178–95.

Préaux, Claire. *Le monde hellénistique: La Grèce et l'Orient de la mort d'Alexandre à la conquête romaine de la Grèce*. Paris: Presses universitaires de France, 1978.

Price, Jonathan J. "The Provincial Historian in Rome." Pages 101–18 in *Josephus and Jewish History in Flavian Rome and Beyond*. Edited by Joseph Sievers and Gaia Lembi. Leiden: Brill, 2005.

Price, Simon. *Religions of the Ancient Greeks*. Cambridge: Cambridge University Press, 1999.

Pritchett, W. Kendrick. *Pausanias Periegetes*. 2 vols. Amsterdam: J. C. Gieben, 1998.

Prudký, Martin. " 'You Shall Not Make Yourself an Image': The Intention and Implications of the Second Commandment." Pages 37–51 in *The Old Testament as Inspiration in Culture*. Edited by Hana Hlaváčková. Třebenice: Mlýn, 2001.

Qimron, Elisha, ed. *The Temple Scroll: A Critical Edition with Extensive Reconstructions*. Jerusalem: Ben-Gurion University of the Negev Press and Israel Exploration Society, 1996.

Rahmani, L. Y. "Jason's Tomb." *Israel Exploration Journal* 17 (1967): 61–100.

Rajak, Tessa. "The *Against Apion* and the Continuities in Josephus' Political Thought." Pages 195–217 in *The Jewish Dialogue with Greece and Rome: Studies in Cultural and Social Interaction*. Edited by Tessa Rajak. Leiden: Brill, 2001.

———. "Benefactors in the Greco-Jewish Diaspora." Pages 373–91 in *The Jewish Dialogue with Greece and Rome: Studies in Cultural and Social Interaction*. Edited by Tessa Rajak. Leiden: Brill, 2001.

———. "Ethnic Identities in Josephus." Pages 137–46 in *The Jewish Dialogue with Greece and Rome: Studies in Cultural and Social Interaction*. Edited by Tessa Rajak. Leiden: Brill, 2001.

———. "Greeks and Barbarians in Josephus." Pages 244–62 in *Hellenism in the Land of Israel*. Edited by John J. Collins and Gregory E. Sterling. Notre Dame, Ind.: University of Notre Dame Press, 2001.

———. "The Hasmoneans and the Uses of Hellenism." Pages 261–80 in *A Tribute to Geza Vermes: Essays on Jewish and Christian Literature and History*. Edited by Philip R. Davies and Richard T. White. Sheffield: JSOT Press, 1990.

———. "The Herodian Narratives of Josephus." Pages 23–34 in *The World of the Herods*. Vol. 1 of *The International Conference: The World of the Herods and the Nabataeans*. Edited by Nikos Kokkinos. Stuttgart: Franz Steiner Verlag, 2007.

———. "Josephus and the 'Archaeology' of the Jews." Pages 241–55 in *The Jewish Dialogue with Greece and Rome: Studies in Cultural and Social Interaction*. Edited by Tessa Rajak. Leiden: Brill, 2001.

———. *Josephus: The Historian and His Society*. Philadelphia: Fortress Press, 1984.

———. *Translation and Survival: The Greek Bible and the Jewish Diaspora*. Oxford: Oxford University Press, 2009.

Rasp, Hans. "Flavius Josephus und die jüdischen Religionsparteien." *Zeitschrift für die neutestamentliche Wissenschaft und die Kunde der älteren Kirche* 23 (1924): 27–47.

Reich, R., and Y. Billig. "A Group of Theater Seats Discovered Near the South-Western Corner of the Temple Mount." *Israel Exploration Journal* 50 (2000): 175–84.

Reventlow, Henning. *Gebot und Predigt im Dekalog*. Gütersloh, Germany: G. Mohn, 1962.

Reynolds, J., and R. Tannenbaum. *Jews and Godfearers at Aphrodisias*. Cambridge: Cambridge Philological Society, 1987.

Rhodes, P. J. "In Defense of the Greek Historians." *Greece and Rome* 41 (1994): 156–71.

Richardson, Peter. *Building Jewish in the Roman Near East*. Waco, Tex.: Baylor University Press, 2004.

Ricken, Friedo. "Gab es eine hellenistische Vorlage für Weish 13–15?" *Biblica* 49 (1968): 54–86.

Rives, James B. "Flavian Religious Policy and the Destruction of the Jerusalem Temple." Pages 145–66 in *Flavius Josephus and Flavian Rome*. Edited by Jonathan Edmondson, Steve Mason, and James Rives. Oxford: Oxford University Press, 2005.

———. *Religion in the Roman Empire*. Malden, Mass.: Blackwell, 2007.

Robert, Louis, ed. *Nouvelles inscriptions de Sardes*. Paris: Librairie d'Amérique et d'Orient, 1964.

Roberts, Alexander, and James Donaldson, eds. *Ante-Nicene Fathers: The Writings of the Fathers Down to A.D. 325*. 24 vols. Edinburgh: T&T Clark, 1867.

Roller, Duane W. *The Building Program of Herod the Great*. Berkeley: University of California Press, 1998.

Rosenfeld, Ben-Zion. "Flavius Josephus and His Portrayal of the Coast (*Paralia*) of Contemporary Roman Palestine: Geography and Ideology." *Jewish Quarterly Review* 91 (2000): 143–83.

Rostovtzeff, M. "Vexillum and Victory." *Journal of Roman Studies* 32 (1942): 92–106.

Roth, Cecil. "An Ordinance against Images in Jerusalem, A.D. 66." *Harvard Theological Review* 49 (1956): 169–77.

Roth, Wolfgang M. W. "For Life, He Appeals to Death (Wis 13:18): A Study of Old Testament Idol Parodies." *Catholic Biblical Quarterly* 37 (1975): 21–47.

Roux, G., and J. Roux. "Un décret des Juifs de Bérénike." *Revue des études grecques* 62 (1949): 281–96.

Rubiés, Joan-Pau. "Nero in Tacitus and Nero in Tacitism: The Historian's Craft." Pages 29–47 in *Reflections of Nero: Culture, History, and Representation*. Edited by Jaś Elsner and Jamie Masters. London: Duckworth, 1994.

Safrai, Shmuel. "The Temple." Pages 865–907 in vol. 2 of *The Jewish People in the First Century: Historical Geography, Political History, Social, Cultural, and Religious Life and Institutions*. Edited by Shmuel Safrai and Menachem Stern. 2 vols. Assen, the Netherlands: Van Gorcum, 1976.

Sandelin, Karl-Gustav. "The Danger of Idolatry according to Philo of Alexandria." *Temenos* 27 (1991): 109–50.

———. "Philo's Ambivalence towards Statues." *The Studia Philonica Annual* 13 (2001): 122–38.

Sartre, Maurice. "The Nature of Syrian Hellenism in the Late Roman and Early Byzantine Periods." Pages 25–49 in *The Sculptural Environment of the Roman Near East: Reflections on Culture, Ideology, and Power*. Edited by Yaron Z. Eliav, Elise Friedland, and Sharon Herbert. Louvain: Peeters, 2008.

Satlow, Michael L. "Beyond Influence: Explaining Similarity and Difference among Jews in Antiquity." Pages 37–53 in *Jewish Literatures and Cultures: Context and Intertext*. Edited by Anita Norich and Yaron Z. Eliav. Providence, R.I.: Brown Judaic Studies, 2008.

Schäfer, Peter. *Rivalität zwischen Engeln und Menschen: Untersuchungen zur Rabbinischen Engelvorstellung*. Berlin: Walter de Gruyter, 1975.

Schalit, Abraham. "Josephus und Justus: Studien zur Vita des Josephus." *Klio* 26 (1933): 67–95.

———. *König Herodes: Der Mann und Sein Work*. Berlin: De Gruyter, 2001.

Schechter, Solomon. "The Dogmas of Judaism." *Jewish Quarterly Review* 1 (1888): 48–61.

Scherberich, Klaus. "Sueton und Josephus über die Ermordung des Caligula." *Rheinisches Museum für Philologie* 142 (1999): 74–83.

Schick, C. "Herod's Amphitheatre." *Palestine Exploration Quarterly* 19 (1887): 161–66.

Schiffman, Lawrence H. "Laws Concerning Idolatry in the Temple Scroll." Pages 159–75 in *Uncovering Ancient Stones: Essays in Memory of H. Neil Richardson*. Edited by Lewis M. Hopfe. Winona Lake, Ind.: Eisenbrauns, 1994.

Schmidt, Brian. "The Aniconic Tradition: On Reading Images and Viewing Texts." Pages 75–105 in *The Triumph of Elohim: From Yahwisms to Judaisms*. Edited by Diana Vikander-Edelman. Grand Rapids: Eerdmans, 1996.

———. "The Iron Age Pithoi Drawings from Horvat Teman or Kuntillet 'Ajrud: Some New Proposals." *Journal of Ancient Near Eastern Religions* 2 (2002): 91–125.

Schmidt, Gilga G., ed. *The First Buber: Youthful Zionist Writings of Martin Buber*. Syracuse, N.Y.: Syracuse University Press, 1999.

Schreckenberg, Heinz. *Bibliographie zu Flavius Josephus*. Leiden: Brill, 1968.

———. *Bibliographie zu Flavius Josephus: Supplementband mit Gesamtregister*. Leiden: Brill, 1979.

———. *Die Flavius-Josephus-Tradition in Antike und Mittelalter*. Leiden: Brill, 1972.

———. "Text, Überlieferung und Textkritik von Contra Apionem." Pages 49–82 in *Josephus' Contra Apionem: Studies in Its Character and Context with a Latin Concordance to the Portion Missing in Greek*. Edited by Louis H. Feldman and John R. Levison. Leiden: Brill, 1996.

Schröder, Bernd. *Die "väterlichen Gesetze": Flavius Josephus als Vermittler von Halachah an Griechen und Römer*. Tübingen: Mohr Siebeck, 1996.

Schürer, Emil. *The History of the Jewish People in the Age of Jesus Christ*. Edited by Fergus Millar, Geza Vermes, and Matthew Black. Edinburgh: T&T Clark, 1973.

Schwartz, Daniel R. "Herodians and *Ioudaioi* in Flavian Rome." Pages 63–78 in *Flavius Josephus and Flavian Rome*. Edited by Jonathan Edmondson, Steve Mason, and James Rives. Oxford: Oxford University Press, 2005.

———. "Josephus and Philo on Pontius Pilate." Pages 26–45 in *The Jerusalem Cathedra: Studies in the History, Archaeology, Geography, and Ethnography of the Land of Israel*. Edited by Lee I. Levine. Detroit: Wayne State University Press, 1983.

———. "On Abraham Schalit, Herod, Josephus, the Holocaust, Horst R. Moehring, and the Study of Ancient Jewish History." *Jewish History* 2 (1987): 9–28.

Schwartz, Seth. "The Composition and Publication of Josephus' *Bellum Judaicum* Book 7." *Harvard Theological Review* 79 (1986): 373–86.

———. "Gamaliel in Aphrodite's Bath: Palestinian Judaism and Urban Culture in the Third and Fourth Centuries." Pages 203–17 in *The Talmud Yerushalmi and Graeco-Roman Culture I*. Edited by Peter Schäfer. Tübingen: Mohr Siebeck, 1998.

———. *Josephus and Judaean Politics*. Leiden: Brill, 1990.

Scott, Jamie, and Paul Simpson-Housley, eds. *Sacred Places and Profane Spaces: Essays in the Geographics of Judaism, Christianity, and Islam*. New York: New York University Press, 1991.

Shahar, Yuval. *Josephus Geographicus: The Classical Context of Geography in Josephus*. Tübingen: Mohr Siebeck, 2004.

Shavit, Yaacov. *Athens in Jerusalem: Classical Antiquity and Hellenism in the Making of the Modern Secular Jew*. London: Vallentine Mitchell, 1997.

Shinohara, Koichi. "The 'Iconic' and 'Aniconic' Buddha Visualization in Medieval Chinese Buddhism." Pages 133–48 in *Representation in Religion: Studies in Honor of Moshe Barasch*. Edited by Jan Assmann and Albert I. Baumgarten. Leiden: Brill, 2001.

Shutt, Robert James H. *Studies in Josephus*. London: SPCK, 1961.

Siegert, Folker, Heinz Schreckenberg, and Manuel Vogel, eds. *Flavius Josephus: Über das Alter des Judentums (Contra Apionem)*. Tübingen: Mohr Siebeck, 2006.

Sievers, Joseph, and Gaia Lembi, eds. *Josephus and Jewish History in Flavian Rome and Beyond*. Leiden: Brill, 2005.

Skutsch, Otto. *The Annals of Q. Ennius*. Oxford: Clarendon Press, 1985.

Smallwood, E. Mary. *The Jews under Roman Rule: From Pompey to Diocletian*. Leiden: Brill, 1976.

Smith, Jonathan Z. "Gods and Earth." *Journal of Religion* 49 (1969): 103–27.

———. *Map Is Not Territory*. Leiden: Brill, 1978.

———. *To Take Place: Toward Theory in Ritual*. Chicago: University of Chicago Press, 1987.

Smith, Morton. "The Image of God: Notes on the Hellenization of Judaism, with Especial Reference to Goodenough's Work on Jewish Symbols." *Bulletin of the John Rylands Library* 40 (1958): 473–512.

———. "On the Shape of God and the Humanity of Gentiles." Pages 315–26 in *Religions in Antiquity: Essays in Memory of Erwin Ramsdell Goodenough*. Edited by Jacob Neusner. Leiden: Brill, 1968.

Speidel, Michael P. "Eagle-Bearer and Trumpeter: The Eagle-Standard and Trumpets of the Roman Legions Illustrated by Three Tombstones Recently Found at Byzantion." *Bonner Jahrbücher* 176 (1976): 123–63.

Spilsbury, Paul. "*Contra Apionem* and *Antiquitates Judaicae*: Points of Contact." Pages 348–68 in *Josephus' Contra Apionem: Studies in Its Character and Context with a Latin Concordance to the Portion Missing in Greek*. Edited by Louis H. Feldman and John R. Levison. Leiden: Brill, 1996.

———. *The Image of the Jew in Flavius Josephus' Paraphrase of the Bible*. Tübingen: Mohr Siebeck, 1998.

———. "Reading the Bible in Rome: Josephus and the Constraints of Empire." Pages 209–27 in *Josephus and Jewish History in Flavian Rome and Beyond*. Edited by Joseph Sievers and Gaia Lembi. Leiden: Brill, 2005.

Spivey, Nigel J. "Bionic Statues." Pages 442–59 in *The Greek World*. Edited by Anton Powell. London and New York: Routledge, 1995.

———. *Understanding Greek Sculpture: Ancient Meanings, Modern Readings*. London: Thames & Hudson, 1996.

Stamm, J. J. *The Ten Commandments in Recent Research*. Translated by M. E. Andrew. Naperville, Ill.: Alec R. Allenson, 1967.

Starr, Raymond J. "The Circulation of Literary Texts in the Roman World." *The Classical Quarterly* 37 (1987): 213–23.

Stegemann, Hartmut. *The Library of Qumran*. Grand Rapids: Eerdmans, 1998.

Steiner, Deborah Tarn. *Images in Mind: Statues in Archaic and Classical Greek Literature and Thought*. Princeton, N.J.: Princeton University Press, 2001.

Sterling, Gregory E. *Historiography and Self-Definition: Josephos, Luke-Acts, and Apologetic Historiography*. Leiden: Brill, 1992.

———. "Universalizing the Particular: Natural Law in Second Temple Jewish Ethics." *The Studia Philonica Annual* 15 (2003): 64–80.

Stern, David. "Introduction." *Poetics Today* 19 (1998): 1–17.

Stern, Menahem, ed. *Greek and Latin Authors on Jews and Judaism*. 2 vols. Jerusalem: Israel Academy of Sciences and Humanities, 1974.

Stewart, Peter. "Baetyls as Statues? Cult Images in the Roman Near East." Pages 297–314 in

The Sculptural Environment of the Roman Near East: Reflections on Culture, Ideology, and Power. Edited by Yaron Z. Eliav, Elise Friedland, and Sharon Herbert. Louvain: Peeters, 2008.

———. *Statues in Roman Society: Representation and Response*. Oxford: Oxford University Press, 2003.

Strack, H. L., and Günter Stemberger. *Introduction to the Talmud and Midrash*. Minneapolis: Fortress Press, 1992.

Strange, John. "Herod and Jerusalem: The Hellenization of an Oriental City." Pages 97–113 in *Jerusalem in Ancient History and Tradition*. Edited by Thomas L. Thompson. London and New York: T&T Clark International, 2003.

Sullivan, J. P. "Martial's Sexual Attitudes." *Philologus* 123 (1979): 288–302.

Swain, S. C. R. "Hellenic Culture and the Roman Heroes of Plutarch." *Journal of Hellenic Studies* 110 (1990): 126–45.

Szkolut, Pawel. "The Eagle as a Symbol of Divine Presence and Protection in Ancient Jewish Art." *Studia Judaica* 5 (2002): 1–11.

Tatum, W. Barnes. "The LXX Version of the Second Commandment (Ex 20:3-6 = Deut 5:7–10): A Polemic against Idols, Not Images." *Journal for the Study of Judaism in the Persian, Hellenistic, and Roman Period* 17 (1986): 177–95.

Taylor, Lily Ross. "Aniconic Worship among the Early Romans." Pages 305–14 in *Classical Studies in Honor of John C. Rolfe*. Edited by George Depue Hadzsits. Philadelphia: University of Pennsylvania Press, 1931.

Tcherikover, Victor A., and Alexander Fuks, eds. *Corpus Papyrorum Judaicarum*. 3 vols. Cambridge: Harvard University Press, 1957.

Termini, Cristina. "Taxonomy of Biblical Laws and φιλοτεχνία in Philo of Alexandria: A Comparison with Josephus and Cicero." *The Studia Philonica Annual* 16 (2004): 1–29.

Thackeray, Henry S. J. *Josephus: The Man and the Historian*. New York: Ktav, 1929.

Thiering, Barbara. "The Date of Composition of the Temple Scroll." Pages 99–120 in *Temple Scroll Studies*. Edited by George J. Brooke. Sheffield: JSOT Press, 1989.

Tomson, Peter. "Les systèmes de halakha du Contre Apion et des Antiquités." Pages 189–220 in *Internationales Josephus-Kolloquium Paris 2001*. Edited by Folker Siegert and Jürgen U. Kalms. Münster, Germany: Lit, 2002.

Trebilco, Paul R. *Jewish Communities in Asia Minor*. Cambridge: Cambridge University Press, 1991.

Troiani, Lucio. "The πολιτεία of Israel in the Graeco-Roman Age." Pages 11–22 in *Josephus and the History of the Greco-Roman Period: Essays in Memory of Morton Smith*. Edited by Fausto Parente and Joseph Sievers. Leiden: Brill, 1994.

Tromp, Johannes. "The Critique of Idolatry in the Context of Jewish Monotheism." Pages 105–20 in *Aspects of Religious Contact and Conflict in the Ancient World*. Edited by Pieter Willem van der Horst. Utrecht: Faculteit der Godgeleerdheid, Universiteit Utrecht, 1995.

Unnik, Willem Cornelis van. *Flavius Josephus als historischer Schriftsteller*. Heidelberg: Lambert Schneider, 1978.

Urbach, E. E. "The Rabbinical Laws on Idolatry in the Second and Third Centuries in the Light of Archaeological and Historical Facts." *Israel Exploration Journal* 9 (1959): 149–65, 229–45.

Vanderbroeck, Paul J. J. *Popular Leadership and Collective Behavior in the Late Roman Republic (ca. 80–50 B.C.)*. Amsterdam: Gieben, 1987.

Vanderpool, Eugene. "The Marble Trophy from Marathon in the British Museum." *Hesperia* 36 (1967): 108–10.

van Henten, Jan Willem. "Ruler or God? The Demolition of Herod's Eagle." Pages 257–86 in *The New Testament and Early Christian Literature in Greco-Roman Context: Studies in Honor of David E. Aune*. Edited by John Fotopoulos. Leiden: Brill, 2006.

———. "The Panegyris in Jerusalem: Responses to Herod's Initiative (Josephus, *Antiquities* 15.268–291)." Pages 151–73 in *Empsychoi Logoi—Religious Innovations in Antiquity: Studies in Honour of Pieter Willem van der Horst*. Edited by Alberdina Houtman, Albert de Jong, and Magda Misset-van de Weg. Leiden: Brill, 2008.

Vasunia, Phiroze. "Plutarch and the Return of the Archaic." Pages 369–89 in *Flavian Rome: Culture, Image, Text*. Edited by A. J. Boyle and W. J. Dominik. Leiden: Brill, 2003.

Vermès, Géza. *Scripture and Tradition in Judaism*. Leiden: Brill, 1973.

———. "A Summary of the Law by Flavius Josephus." *Novum Testamentum* 24 (1982): 289–303.

Vermeule, Cornelius, and Kristin Anderson. "Greek and Roman Sculpture in the Holy Land." *The Burlington Magazine* 123 (1981): 7–8, 10–19.

Visser, Marinus Willem de. *Die nicht menschengestaltigen Götter der Griechen*. Leiden: Brill, 1903.

Vokes, F. E. "The Ten Commandments in the New Testament and in First Century Judaism." *Studia Evangelica* 5 (1968): 146–54.

Wacholder, Ben-Zion. "The Date of the Mekilta de-Rabbi Ishmael." *Hebrew Union College Annual* 39 (1968): 117–44.

Wallace, Robert W. *The Areopagos Council, to 307 B.C.* Baltimore: Johns Hopkins University Press, 1989.

Wallach, Luitpold. "A Palestinian Polemic against Idolatry." *Hebrew Union College Annual* 19 (1946): 389–404.

Walters, Jonathan. "Invading the Roman Body: Manliness and Impenetrability in Roman Thought." Pages 29–43 in *Roman Sexualities*. Edited by Judith P. Hallett and Marilyn B. Skinner. Princeton, N.J.: Princeton University Press, 1997.

Walton, Alice. *The Cult of Asklepios*. Boston: Ginn & Co., 1894.

Waszink, J. H., and J. C. M. Van Winden. *Tertullianus De Idolatria: Critical Text, Translation, and Commentary*. Leiden: Brill, 1987.

Webster, Graham. *The Roman Imperial Army of the First and Second Centuries A.D.* London: A & C Black, 1985.

Weitzman, Steven. "Unbinding Isaac: Martyrdom and Its Exegetical Alternatives." Pages 79–89 in *Contesting Texts: Jews and Christians in Conversation about the Bible*. Edited by Melody D. Knowles et al. Minneapolis: Fortress Press, 2007.

Wenning, Robert. "Die Stadtgöttin von Caesarea Maritima." *Boreas* 9 (1986): 113–29.

Wensinck, A. J. "The Second Commandment." *Mededeelingen der Koninklijke Akademie van Wetenschappen* 59 (1925): 159–65.

Werblowsky, R. J. Zwi. "Introduction: Mindscape and Landscape." Pages 9–17 in *Sacred Space: Shrine, City, Land*. Edited by Benjamin Z. Kedar and R. J. Zwi Werblowsky. New York: New York University Press, 1998.

Wharton, Annabel Jane. "Jewish Art." *Images* 1 (2007): 1–7.

White, L. Michael. "The Delos Synagogue Revisited: Recent Fieldwork in the Graeco-Roman Diaspora." *Harvard Theological Review* 80 (1987): 133–60.

Whitmarsh, Tim. "Greek and Roman in Dialogue: The Pseudo-Lucianic Nero." *Journal of Hellenic Studies* 119 (1999): 142–60.

Wiedemann, T. E. J. "Tiberius to Nero." Pages 198–255 in *The Cambridge Ancient History Volume X: The Augustan Empire, 43 B.C.–A.D. 69*. Edited by Alan K. Bowman, Edward Champlin, and Andrew Lintott. Cambridge: Cambridge University Press, 1996.

Williams, Craig A. "Greek Love at Rome." *The Classical Quarterly* 45 (1995): 517–39.

———. *Roman Homosexuality: Ideologies of Masculinity in Classical Antiquity*. Oxford: Oxford University Press, 1999.

Wilson, Marcus. "After the Silence: Tacitus, Suetonius, Juvenal." Pages 523–42 in *Flavian Rome: Culture, Image, Text*. Edited by A. J. Boyle and W. J. Dominik. Leiden: Brill, 2003.

Wilson, Walter T. *The Sentences of Pseudo-Phocylides*. Berlin: Walter de Gruyter, 2005.

Wintermute, O. S. "Jubilees: A New Translation and Introduction." Pages 35–142 in vol. 2 of *The Old Testament Pseudepigrapha*. Edited by James H. Charlesworth. 2 vols. New York: Doubleday, 1985.

Woodward, David, and G. Malcolm Lewis. "Introduction." Pages 1–10 in *The History of Cartography: Cartography in the Traditional African, American, Arctic, Australian, and Pacific Societies*. Edited by David Woodward and G. Malcolm Lewis. Chicago: University of Chicago Press, 1998.

Wycherley, Richard E. "St. Paul at Athens." *The Journal of Theological Studies* 19 (1968): 619–21.

———. *The Stones of Athens*. Princeton, N.J.: Princeton University Press, 1978.

Yadin, Azzan. "Rabban Gamaliel, Aphrodite's Bath, and the Question of Pagan Monotheism." *Jewish Quarterly Review* 96 (2006): 149–79.

Yadin, Yigael. *The Finds from the Bar Kokhba Period in the Cave of Letters*. 2 vols. Jerusalem: Israel Exploration Society, 1963.

———. *The Temple Scroll*. Jerusalem: Israel Exploration Society, 1983.

Yavetz, Z. "Reflections on Titus and Josephus." *Greek, Roman, and Byzantine Studies* 16 (1975): 411–32.

Yeivin, Shmuel. "Excavations at Caesarea Maritima." *Archaeology* 8 (1955): 122–29.

Zanker, Paul. *The Power of Images in the Age of Augustus*. Ann Arbor: University of Michigan Press, 1988.

Zeitlin, Solomon. "Herod a Malevolent Maniac." *Jewish Quarterly Review* 54 (1963): 1–27.

———. "Josephus—Patriot or Traitor?" *Jewish Chronicle* 94 (1934): 26–30.

Zimmerli, Walther. "Das Zweite Gebot." Pages 550–63 in *Festschrift für Alfred Bertholet zum 80*. Edited by Walter Baumgartner et al. Tübingen: Mohr Siebeck, 1950.

Zweck, Dean. "The *Exordium* of the Areopagus Speech, Acts 17.22, 23." *New Testament Studies* 35 (1989): 94–103.

Index of Ancient Sources

Hebrew Bible

PHILO

Greco-Roman Literature

Index of Modern Authors

Subject Index

www.ingramcontent.com/pod-product-compliance
Lightning Source LLC
LaVergne TN
LVHW091047080826
845145LV00002B/658
* 9 7 8 1 5 8 9 8 3 6 2 2 8 *